P9-CEH-968

Islands of Australia's Great Barrier Reef

Hugh Finlay
Mark Armstrong
Tony Wheeler

Islands of Australia's Great Barrier Reef

3rd edition

Published by
Lonely Planet Publications
Head Office: PO Box 617, Hawthorn, Vic 3122, Australia
Branches: 150 Linden Street, Oakland, CA 94607, USA
                10a Spring Place, London NW5 3BH, UK
                71 bis rue du Cardinal Lemoine, 75005 Paris, France

Printed by
Colorcraft Ltd, Hong Kong

Photographs by
Michael Aw   Robert Charlton   Great Barrier Reef Marine Park Authority (GBRMPA)
Simon Foale   Hugh Finlay   Queensland Tourist & Travel Corporation
Holger Leue   Mark Norman   Nick Tapp
Tony Wheeler

Front cover: Aerial shot of a section of the Great Barrier Reef (Richard I'Anson)

First Published
July 1990

This Edition
September 1998

Although the authors and publisher have tried to make the information as accurate as possible, they accept no responsibility for any loss, injury or inconvenience sustained by any person using this book.

National Library of Australia Cataloguing in Publication Data

Finlay, Hugh.
  Islands of Australia's Great Barrier Reef.

  3rd ed.
  Includes index.
  ISBN 0 86442 563 5.

  1. Great Barrier Reef (Qld.) – Guidebooks. I. Title.
  (Series: Lonely Planet Australia guide).

919.43

Hugh Finlay

Deciding there must be more to life than civil engineering, Hugh took off around Australia in the mid-70s, working at everything from spray painting to diamond prospecting before hitting the overland trail. He joined Lonely Planet in 1985 and has written *Jordan & Syria* and *Northern Territory*, co-authored *Kenya* and *Morocco, Algeria & Tunisia*, and updated *Nepal* and the Queensland chapter of *Australia*. He lives in central Victoria with his partner, Linda, and daughters Ella and Vera.

Mark Armstrong

Mark was born in Melbourne and completed his tertiary studies at Melbourne University. He lived in Barcelona for a couple of years and has travelled in South-East Asia, Europe and North America. Being robbed overseas three times has in no way diminished his passion for foreign lands (or, unfortunately, honed his instincts), but as a precaution he now travels with the words 'I already gave' stencilled on his money belt. Mark has written Lonely Planet's *Melbourne*, *Victoria* and *Queensland* guides, co-authored *Spain*, and worked on updates of *Australia*, *Mediterranean Europe* and *Western Europe*.

Tony Wheeler

Tony was born in England but spent most of his youth overseas. He returned to England to do a university degree in engineering, worked as an automotive engineer, returned to university to complete an MBA then dropped out on the Asian overland trail with his wife, Maureen. They've been travelling, writing and publishing guidebooks ever since, having set up Lonely Planet Publishing in the mid-70s.

This Book

The 1st edition of this book was written by Tony Wheeler. The 2nd edition was updated by Mark Armstrong and, now, the 3rd edition has been thoroughly updated by Hugh Finlay.

From the Publisher

This is the fourth and final (for now, anyway) production of Lonely Planet's dynamic duo: Louise Klep and Darren Elder. Louise was assisted with mapping by Jenny Jones and Ann Jeffree, and with the illustrations by Tass Wilson and Trudi Canavan. Editorially, Darren was assisted by Ada Cheung and Liz Filleul, and Mary Neighbour helped compile and edit the Reef Life section. The cover was designed by Simon Bracken and the climate charts were compiled by Anthony Phelan. Peter Gesner, Maritime Coordinator of the Queensland Museum, helped write several asides and also checked the book for historical inaccuracies. Thanks also to the seniors for their guidance and assistance: Marcel Gaston, Jane Fitzpatrick and Tass and Mary (again).

Thanks

Many thanks to the travellers who used the last edition and wrote to us with helpful hints, interesting anecdotes and other useful advice: Steve Boniface, John Harding, Alain Jost, Simone Mendes, J Schuttevaer, David Hounsome, Margaret Levin, Paul Lewis and Frank Vergona.

Warning & Request

Things change – prices go up, schedules change, good places go bad and bad places go bankrupt – nothing stays the same. So, if you find things better or worse, recently opened or long since closed, please tell us and help make the next edition even more accurate and useful.

We value all of the feedback we receive from travellers. Julie Young coordinates a small team who read and acknowledge every letter, postcard and email, and ensure that every morsel of information finds its way to the appropriate authors, editors and publishers.

Everyone who writes to us will find their name in the next edition of the appropriate guide and will also receive a free subscription to our quarterly newsletter, *Planet Talk*. The very best contributions will be rewarded with a free Lonely Planet guide.

Excerpts from your correspondence may appear in new editions of this guide; in our newsletter, *Planet Talk*; or in updates on our Web site – so let us know if you don't want your name or letter published.

Contents

Boxed Text

Map Legend

ROUTES

	.... Major Road
	.... Secondary Road
	...... Secondary Road - Unsealed
	.... Minor Road
	.... Minor Road - Unsealed
	................................City Road
	.... City Street
	...........Train Route, with Station
	..............................Ferry Route
	.... Walking Track

AREA FEATURES

	.... Built-Up Area
	.... Building
	.... Market
	.... National Park
	.... Beach or Desert
	.... Reef

BOUNDARIES

	.... International Boundary
	.... Marine Park Boundary

HYDROGRAPHIC FEATURES

	...................................Coastline
	.... River
	.... Creek
	.... Intermittent Creek
	.... Waterfall
	.... Lake
	.... Mangroves

OTHER

	.................................Equator
	.... Tropics
	.... Latitudes & Longitudes

SYMBOLS

◉ CAPITAL	...... Provincial Capital	Ā	.... Camping Area	🏛	...................Museum
● CITY	.................................City	🛉	....................Church	P	.... Parking
● Town	.... Town	◣	.... Dive Site	★	.... Police Station
● Village	......................Village	↾	.... Golf Course	✉	.... Post Office
■	............Place to Stay	✪	.... Hospital	⚓	.... Shipwreck
▼	.... Place to Eat	❶	...............Information	▣	.... Snorkelling
⛾	.... Pub or Bar	🜊	.... Lighthouse	◎	.... Spring
✝	.... Airfield	※	...................Lookout	▬	........Swimming Pool
⅂	.... Beach	▲	.... Mountain	◒	.... Transport

Note: not all symbols displayed above appear in this book

Introduction

A reef such as is here spoke of is scarcely known in Europe. It is a wall of Coral Rock rising almost perpendicular out of the unfathomable ocean.

Lt James Cook RN, 1770

The Great Barrier Reef stretches for 2000km along the coast of Queensland, Australia – an area of stunning natural beauty and great scientific interest. The reef starts around Gladstone and the Tropic of Capricorn. At first it is a wide scattering of individual reefs around 200km out from the coast, but as you move north it becomes more and more continuous and also gets closer and closer to the coast while still containing a scattering of individual reefs in the inner lagoon. North of Cairns the reef is an almost continuous barrier to the Coral Sea.

Along the reef there are many islands, most of them uninhabited. Some are true coral cays – tiny outcrops of sand and hardy vegetation gradually accumulated after a reef has stayed consistently above sea level. Other islands are larger 'continental' islands, the drowned mountain tops of an ancient coastal range.

The islands have interesting vegetation and many are home for a wide variety of birds but it's the waters around the islands where the reef's real excitement lies. Nowhere else is such a diversity, and such a colourful diversity, of life found.

There are numerous islands, offering the widest range of possibilities imaginable, along the reef. If you're after real seclusion try the exclusive small resorts like Bedarra or Lizard, or relaxed and quiet Hinchinbrook. For a big international resort with a wide range of activities you can head for Hamilton and if you're young and have energy to burn then Great Keppel is aimed right at you. If you're a scuba fan then islands like Heron, Lady Elliot or Lizard specialise in catering for your needs.

If you want to get away from small children then head for Lizard, Orpheus and Bedarra, where kids are not allowed; to the contrary, Daydream and South Molle take great pains to cater for kids' interests. If you have lots of money to spare you can run through a fortune on fine food and expensive activities on some islands. However, if you're penniless you can get a national park camping permit – you'll find plenty of places where you can camp for next to nothing and there will be absolutely nothing to spend money on when you get there!

Facts about the Great Barrier Reef

The Great Barrier Reef extends 2000km in length. It starts slightly south of the Tropic of Capricorn, somewhere out from Bundaberg or Gladstone, and it ends in the Torres Strait, just south of Papua New Guinea. This huge length makes it not only the most extensive reef system in the world but also the biggest structure made by living organisms. At its southern end the reef is up to 300km from the mainland, but at the northern end it runs much closer to the coast, has a more continuous nature and can be up to 80km across. In the 'lagoon' between the outer reef and the coast the waters are dotted with smaller reefs, cays and islands. Drilling on the reef has indicated that in places the coral can be over 500m thick.

The Great Barrier Reef encompasses around 2500 named individual reefs, more than 600 islands in all, 250 named continental islands and 70 named coral cays. Only about 20 of these islands have resort facilities although it is possible to camp on many. Most of the resort islands are partly or completely national park and the resort area is leased to the resort operators.

HISTORY

The history of the Great Barrier Reef is a comparatively short one by geological standards. At the time of the last ice age the sea level was probably over 100m lower than it is today. The continental shelf leading out from the present coast to the outer Barrier Reef was dry land 18,000 years ago and islands like the Whitsundays were hills rising from this coastal plain.

Then the ice started to melt, the sea started to rise and by 12,000 years ago the coastal plain had become a submerged continental shelf. By 8000 to 9000 years ago the outer edge of reef, built up during previous cycles of thaw and freeze, was also submerged and by 6000 to 7000 years ago the sea had reached its present level. The reef, building on the base established by preceding ancient reefs, began to assume its present shape.

The formation of the Great Barrier Reef is so recent that humans were already on the scene. It's thought that the ancestors of Australia's Aborigines started to arrive in Australia more than 40,000 years ago and they certainly knew about the reef and made use of its islands. In some cases they actually lived on islands along the reef but at other times made periodic forays out to the islands from the mainland. Shell middens, the accumulated reminders of countless Aboriginal shellfish feasts, can be found on many Great Barrier Reef islands. Captain Cook, in the log of his pioneering voyage along the coast, commented a number of times about the Aborigines he had seen on the islands or sailing in their canoes between the islands, and on evidence he had seen that they had visited the islands in the past. Today there are few islands populated by Aborigines. One of the exceptions is Palm Island, in the Palm Island group north of Townsville.

The Spanish mariner Luis Váez de Torres was the first European known to have sailed through the strait at the northern tip of Australia. He did this in 1606, although in order to protect their newly discovered route between Europe and the Orient, the Spanish kept the fact a secret until 1764.

With the arrival of Europeans little more than 200 years ago, humankind's relationship with the Great Barrier Reef took on a new form as the reef was extensively explored and charted. For the first European navigators the reef was initially a fearsome place; Captain Cook was mightily glad to escape from its clutches, but soon afterwards even happier to return to its protection (see the Lizard Island to Cape York chapter).

After completing a scientific expedition to Tahiti to observe the transit of Venus, Cook's intructions from the British Admiralty were to search for the Great South Land, which he sighted on 19 April 1770. Cook's voyage up the east coast remained, largely, the only detailed exploration for some time. In the seven years after the First Fleet sailed into Botany Bay, less than 100 miles of the new colony's coastline had been explored. In 1789, William Bligh, who did not know a colony had been established, landed on the eastern side of Cape York while on his epic voyage to Timor after being evicted from the *Bounty*. Bligh charted the coast as he and the other loyal members of his crew sailed north, but did not add significantly to the knowledge of the coastline.

In 1795 Matthew Flinders and George Bass arrived in Port Jackson and soon after began charting the coast in their spare time. However, it wasn't until 1802, when Flinders circumnavigated Australia in the *Investigator*, that the coast we now know as Queensland was charted with more precision. Flinders followed the coast inside the reef until he found a passage through it (offshore from modern-day Ayr), which until 1981 was the most southerly of the few safe passages through. After that he sailed clear of the Barrier Reef until Torres Strait.

A more complete charting of the coast and reefs was not accomplished until 1815, when Charles Jeffreys sailed the entire length of the Barrier Reef coast *inside* the reef. Jeffreys was sailing to Ceylon (modern-day Sri Lanka) in the *Kangaroo* and followed Cook's wake until Endeavour Reef, and then pioneered a new route inside the reef until picking up Bligh's course further north.

Phillip King continued the work of charting the coast and reef in 1819 and following his surveys the 'inside passage' soon supplanted the 'outside passage' as the safest and fastest route along the east coast. Further surveys continued in the 1840s and the advent of steamships and the completion of the Suez Canal in 1869 made the route around the north of Australia and inside the Great Barrier Reef a far faster and shorter voyage from Europe than the old

Captain James Cook was the first known explorer to chart the Queensland coast and the Great Barrier Reef

route around the southern tip of Africa and the south of Australia.

Today a steady stream of cargo ships continues to move up and down the carefully plotted channels inside the reef but it was not until this century that the reef's potential as a tourist attraction began to emerge. EJ Banfield's well known sojourn on Dunk Island at the turn of the century excited a great deal of interest in the reef islands and between WWI and WWII a number of popular island resorts were established, some of which still operate today.

To the early explorers the colourful and intriguing world beneath the surface was a complete mystery and although pearl diving became an important activity before the turn of the century it has only been since WWII that snorkelling and scuba diving have taken off as recreational activities.

Today visitors to the reef come for a variety of reasons. They may be simply passing through on commercial ships,

Shipwrecks

Even today, with sophisticated navigation equipment and reliable charts, ships still get wrecked on the Great Barrier Reef, so it shouldn't come as any surprise that the reef was once a real nightmare for early explorers, back in the days when Terra Australis was a big blank on the map. Captain Cook with his ship the *Endeavour* was, of course, the first recorded European explorer to tangle with the reef, but Cook made a lucky escape, repaired his damaged ship at the site of modern-day Cooktown and sailed back to report his finds. The cannons and ballast he jettisoned during his escape from the reef have been recovered by divers.

HMS *Pandora*, which sunk in 1791 while bringing captured mutineers from the *Bounty* back to England, wasn't so lucky and its discovery and investigation has made it one of the most interesting Barrier Reef wrecks. See the Lizard Island to Cape York chapter for more details.

Ships sailing along the Queensland coast basically had two choices. They could hug the coast and enjoy the protection the reef offered from the open ocean, though the prospect of meeting an uncharted reef was the principal danger for this route. The other alternative was to sail outside the reef and then enter the Torres Strait, north of Cape York, via the Great North-East Channel or Raine Island Entrance and Blackwood Channel. Again, careful navigation was required and attempts to enter the reef at other points were fraught with danger.

Both routes saw numerous shipwrecks over the years. The Capricorn-Bunker Group, at the southern end of the reef, claimed many boats while others, like *Pandora*, failed to find the key to Raine Island Entrance. Some of the interesting Great Barrier Reef wrecks from south to north include:

Golden City This US built clipper had operated as an immigrant ship from England to Australia and New Zealand but was wrecked on Lady Elliot Island while loading guano in 1865.

America A little further north, after leaving its load of female convicts in Hobart, the convict transport *America* was sailing north to Batavia (modern-day Jakarta) in the Dutch East

cruise liners or yachts. They may be actually working the waters of the reef in prawn trawlers or other fishing vessels, or they may be there to simply marvel at one of the great wonders of the natural world. Keeping these conflicting demands in balance is the greatest challenge into the next century.

GEOGRAPHY
Reef Types

Basically, reefs are either fringing or barrier. You will find fringing reefs around many of the Great Barrier Reef's islands. Barrier reefs are further out to sea and usually enclose a 'lagoon' of deep water. The Great Barrier Reef is out at the edge of the Australian continental shelf and the channel between the reef and the coast can be 60m deep. In places the reef rises straight up from that depth. This raises the question of how the reef built up from that depth when coral cannot survive below 30m. One theory is that the reef gradually grew as the seabed subsided, and that the reef was able to keep pace with the rate of sinkage. The alternative is that the sea level very gradually rose, and the coral was able to keep pace.

Island Types

Let's admit right away that this book, like most books and articles about 'Barrier Reef islands' is not really accurate. Most of the reef islands are not really on the Great

Indies when she struck a reef. The ship was abandoned on Wreck Island reef in the Capricorn Group in 1831.

Yongala This passenger steamer sank in a cyclone off Cape Bowling Green, south of Townsville, in 1911. All 120 people on board were drowned and it was not until WWII that the mystery of the ship's disappearance was finally solved. The ship lies in 30m of water and is a very popular dive site.

Foam This blackbirding schooner was wrecked on Myrmidon Reef, north of Townsville, in 1893. 'Blackbirding' was the collecting of Pacific Islanders to work on Queensland plantations. Supposedly the islanders were recruited voluntarily and were free to return to their home islands at the end of their period of indenture but in practice they were often 'recruited' forcibly and worked under conditions of near slavery. The islanders on the *Foam* were being returned home and all aboard were saved.

SS Gothenburg Originally named the *Celt*, this iron steamer also operated for a time as a three-masted schooner and was carrying passengers, cargo and gold from the Pine Creek gold site, near modern-day Darwin. She hit Old Reef off Ayr and sank taking 106 people with her.

HMS Mermaid In 1829 this Calcutta-built teak schooner sank south of Trinity Inlet, Cairns. She had been used to survey the Australian coast between 1818 and 1820.

Morning Star Carrying cargo from early Australian colonies, this brig sunk near Temple Bay, towards the top of Cape York, in 1814. The wreck has not yet been found.

Quetta The *Quetta* sank off Mt Adolphus island, near Cape York, in 1890 when it ran straight into an uncharted rock in the channel south of the island. She sank in less than three minutes, taking 133 of her 290 passengers and crew with her.

Barrier Reef at all, they're between the reef and the mainland. Of course there are real reef islands but in general they tend to be very small and the major islands are not actually on the reef. The islands covered in this book are islands on or within the Barrier Reef – Queensland has other islands such as Fraser Island or Moreton Island which lie south of the reef.

There are two types of islands along the Barrier Reef. The larger islands, like those of the Whitsunday group, are the tops of flooded mountains. At one time these would have been the high points of a range running along the coast, but rising sea levels submerged the range. These islands have vegetation like the adjacent mainland.

Other islands may actually be on the reef, like Heron Island near Gladstone, or may be isolated coral cays, like Green Island near Cairns. These cays are formed when the growth of coral is such that the reef is above the sea level even at low tide. Dead coral is ground down by water action to form sand and eventually hardier vegetation takes root. Coral cays are low-lying, unlike the often hilly islands closer to the coast.

Most of the islands, continental or cays, suffer from water shortages and resort construction has often required desalination plants, shipping in water or other expensive solutions. Only three islands with resorts – Dunk, Bedarra and Hinchinbrook – are moist enough to have rainforest cover.

Coral Cays

Coral cays are low islands, formed by the growth of a coral reef and the collection of debris from the reef. This entirely natural creation of new land is a fascinating story.

As a reef grows it eventually forms a reef flat that breaks the surface of the water at low tide. The coral cannot continue to grow above water level as it has to be covered by water to survive, although it can survive a few hours out of water at low tide. Waves break off sticks of branching coral and storms may cause more widespread destruction. This coral debris collects on the reef flat and if the prevailing wave action piles up debris in a particular area of the reef flat, an island, continually above sea level, is gradually formed.

At this stage the island is a very fragile creation. A severe storm or cyclone can scatter the collected material across the flat and it may be years before regular wave action again collects it in one area. Gradually, the waves grind the debris down to create shingle and sand and eventually a sand cay forms. This is usually very unstable and shifts back and forth around the reef as weather conditions alter. There are over 200 totally unvegetated sand cays along the Great Barrier Reef.

Over time the sand stabilises and when it is consistently above water level seabirds start to nest on it. Hardy plants now start to grow on the sand, some washed ashore, others transported by the birds either by being stuck to their feathers or in their digestive tracts. This early and limited vegetation adds to the cay's stability and decomposing vegetable matter and bird droppings start to change the sand into a richer soil, providing a suitable environment for a wider range of plant life. Even at this stage cays are not truly stable and a particularly severe cyclone can wipe them out. There are 65 vegetated sand cays along the Great Barrier Reef.

MICHAEL AW

Lady Musgrave Island

Cays are not uniformly distributed along the reef. Vegetated sand cays are only found in the south, particularly in the Capricorn-Bunker groups, and in the north, starting with Green Island off Cairns. For over 600km in the central section of the Great Barrier Reef there are no vegetated sand cays at all. The great tidal variation here may well be a factor – wave action at one tide level may move debris to one area, only for the action at another level to move it somewhere else. Cyclones in this region are also more severe than further north or further south and are therefore more likely to scatter whatever debris has built up.

Only in the south are vegetated shingle cays found; these require stronger but consistent ocean swells to move the larger coral debris. On the other hand, low wooded islands are only found north of Cairns. On these a leeward sand cay and shingle ridges around the edge of the reef flat combine to create a central reef area where mangroves can grow. The Low Isles off Port Douglas are a good example of this pattern. All the Great Barrier Reef coral cays are relatively young in the geological sense, as it was only about 6000 years ago that the sea's level stabilised at about its present level and the development of cays could commence.

CLIMATE

The Great Barrier Reef is completely in the tropics. The reef commences in the south around the Tropic of Capricorn and extends 2000km north so it's always warm – warmer as you move further north of course. A good season to visit is over the southern hemisphere winter, except in the extreme south where it can be a little chilly at the height of winter (in June, July and August). Near Cairns and further north, the water is pleasant all year, around the Whitsundays and to the south you wouldn't want to spend too long in the water in the middle of winter unless you're wearing a wetsuit.

Over the summer it can sometimes be too hot for comfort and tropical thunderstorms can bring heavy rain. The reef islands are in the cyclone (hurricane) belt and every few years a cyclone does come by and cause some damage. Summer is cyclone season and late summer (February and March) tends to be the wettest time – if you're unlucky you may get a string of rainy days. The rain gets progressively heavier as you move north but the distinction between the dry season and the wet season also becomes clearer. By the time you get to the north of Cape York peninsula the wet season is very wet and the dry season completely dry.

The rainfall probably has more influence than the temperature; it's hard to enjoy a tropical island when the sky's grey and the rain is pelting down. The peak monthly rainfall is about 175mm in Rockhampton, twice as high in Mackay or Townsville and nearly three times as high by the time you get to Cairns and Cape York.

REEF MANAGEMENT

In 1975 the Great Barrier Reef Marine Park (GBRMP) was established. It is administered by the Great Barrier Reef Marine Park Authority (GBRMPA), PO Box 1379, Townsville, Qld 4810. In 1981 the reef was added to the World Heritage List by the United Nations Education, Scientific & Cultural Organization (UNESCO). The GBRMP is not a national park although Queensland National Parks & Wildlife, part of the Department of Environment, handles the 'in the field' management of the marine park.

The GBRMPA coordinates different activities and uses of the Great Barrier Reef and a complete zoning of the 344,000 sq km of the reef has been completed. The zoning

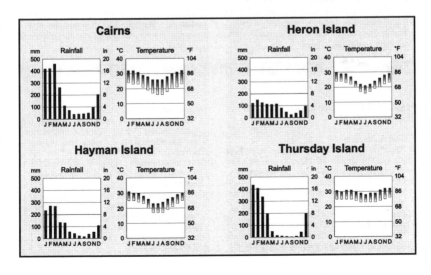

Crown-of-Thorns

The monster that ate the Barrier Reef – the crown-of-thorns starfish has managed to build itself a fearsome reputation since the early 1960s. At that time it was noticed that the crown-of-thorns starfish was multiplying rapidly and it was thought that in certain areas it could prove a grave danger to the reef as its favourite food was living coral.

The crown-of-thorns is a large, 'thorny', brown-coloured starfish. When it finds a patch of coral to its liking it turns its stomach out through its mouth, an activity known as 'stomach eversion', wraps it around the coral and digests the living coral polyps. When the stomach is drawn back in and the starfish moves on to the next tasty coral patch, all that's left is the limestone coral skeleton. A hungry crown-of-thorns can work its way through five square metres of coral in a year.

The problem is exacerbated by the apparent ability of the starfish to alert other starfishes to the presence of a tasty coral reef. Eventually huge numbers of starfish concentrate on one area and when this happens they start to feed day and night instead of hiding during the daylight hours.

While this has meant pockets of the reef have been killed off by the crown-of-thorns, there remains some conjecture as to the harmful effects of it on the reef as a whole.

The coordinator of the Great Barrier Reef Marine Park Authority's study into the crown-of-thorns, Udo Engelhardt, concluded in 1997 that he believed huge outbreaks of the starfish might be a natural part of the reef's lifecycle – in a similar way to how a bushfire regenerates growth in a forest.

Others are less sure, and in some areas you can help to physically remove the crown-of-thorns from the reef.

Either way, the number of crown-of-thorns on the Barrier Reef has declined since the last major outbreak ended in the early 1990s, and institutions like the GBRMPA and the Australian Institute of Marine Sciences continue to monitor the situation and conduct regular surveys of their numbers.

---

breaks the Great Barrier Reef up into six classes:

Preservation Zone
Areas of the reef that are intended to be kept completely untouched. Entry is only allowed in an emergency or for scientific research.

Scientific Research Zone
Areas set aside exclusively for scientific research.

Marine National Park B Zone
A 'look but don't take' zone intended to be kept in a relatively undisturbed state. Fishing and shell collecting are not permitted.

Marine National Park A Zone
Recreational use of these areas is permitted, which means fishing with one line and one hook is allowed but no commercial fishing.

General Use B Zone
Reasonable recreational and commercial uses are permitted but not trawling or shipping.

General Use A Zone
All reasonable uses are permitted including trawling and shipping. Mining, oil drilling, commercial spearfishing and spearfishing with scuba equipment are not permitted in these zones, or anywhere else in the Great Barrier Reef Marine Park.

The Great Barrier Reef is one of Australia's greatest natural assets and one of the country's ultimate playgrounds. The region is usually blessed with picture perfect weather, making it ideal for travellers to get out and enjoy the many activities on offer, ranging from snorkelling and sailing to simply lounging in the sun.

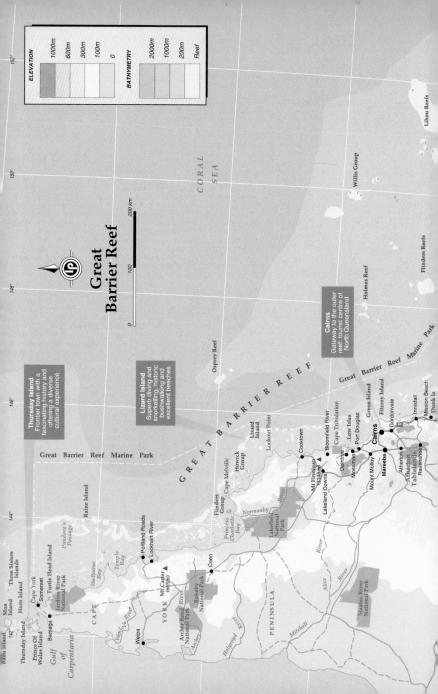

Great Barrier Reef

ELEVATION
1000m
600m
300m
100m
0

BATHYMETRY
2000m
1000m
200m
Reef

0   100   200 km

Thursday Island
Frontier town with a fascinating history and offering a diverse cultural experience

Lizard Island
Superb diving and snorkelling, historic bushwalking and excellent beaches

Cairns
Gateway to the outer reef: tourist centre of North Queensland

CORAL SEA

Lihou Reefs

Willis Group

Flinders Reefs

Holmes Reef

Osprey Reef

Great Barrier Reef Marine Park

GREAT BARRIER REEF

Great Barrier Reef Marine Park

Raine Island

Pandora's Passage

Portland Roads
Lockhart River

Temple Bay

Shelburne Bay

McCoy's (445m)

Coen

Archer River

Rokeby National Park

Archer Bend National Park

Weipa

Wenlock River

Holroyd River

Mitchell River

Alice River

Staaten River National Park

Mitchell River

CAPE YORK PENINSULA

Flinders Group
Cape Melville

Howick Group

Princess Charlotte Bay

Normanby River

Lakefield National Park

Lizard Island

Lookout Point

Cooktown

Bloomfield River
Cape Tribulation
Daintree
Mossman
Low Isles
Port Douglas
Mount Molloy
Mareeba
Atherton
Atherton Tablelands
Ravenshoe

Mt Finnigan (1148m)

Lakeland Downs

Green Island
Cairns
Gordonvale
Fitzroy Island
Innisfail
Mission Beach
Dunk Is

River

Badu Island
Moa Island
Three Sisters Islands
Cape York
Somerset
Turtle Head Island
Horn Island
Prince Of Wales Island
Bamaga
Jardine River National Park
Thursday Island
Gulf of Carpentaria

Fish of the Great Barrier Reef

Blue-lined surgeonfish

Blue tang

Blue-barred parrotfish

Semicircle angelfish

Flutefish

Cleaner wrasse

Weedy scorpion fish

Butterfly cod

Stonefish

Diagonal-banded sweetlip

Saddled butterfly fish

Moorish idol

Coral cod

Damselfish

Black-backed butterfly fish

Harlequin tuskfish

Blue angelfish

Boxfish

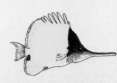

Long-snouted butterfly fish

Information on the GBRMPA zoning can be obtained from the authority. The GBRMPA produces *Reef Notes*, a series of pamphlets that cover various aspects of the reef and the marine life. The authority also operates Great Barrier Reef Wonderland, probably the best aquarium in Australia, at its headquarters in Townsville.

FLORA & FAUNA

The Barrier Reef islands are fascinating places for anybody with an interest in wildlife, whether it's strange and exotic sea creatures or the many species of birds that make the islands their home. The Barrier Reef would just be a very big breakwater if it wasn't for the colourful and highly varied reef life.

Reef Life

Coral reefs provide a home and shelter for an enormous variety of life. Most evident, of course, are the often fantastically colourful reef fish – but fish are only one of a host of species to be seen. Reef walks, glass-bottom or semi-submersible boat trips, snorkelling or, best of all, scuba diving, will all help to open the door to the magical world below the surface.

See the Reef Life chapter for full details of the amazing array of creatures that lives in this marine habitat.

Sex & Coral

Coral's sex life may be infrequent (happening only once a year) but when it happens it's certainly spectacular. Some coral polyps are all male or all female, while other colonies' polyps are hermaphrodite (both male and female). In a few types of coral these polyps can produce their own young. In most cases, however, an hermaphrodite polyp's sperm cannot fertilise its own eggs or other eggs from the same colony.

Although the mass spawning that creates new coral only takes place once a year, the build up lasts for six months or more. During that time the polyps ripen their eggs, which are initially white but then change to pink, red, orange and other bright colours. At the same time the male testes form in the polyps and develop the sperm.

The spawning period comes in late spring or early summer, beginning a night or two after a full moon and building to a crescendo on the fourth, fifth and sixth nights. At this time the water temperature is right and tidal variation is at a minimum. Within the coral the eggs and sperm are formed into bundles and a half-hour before spawning time the bundles are 'set' at the mouth of the polyp, clearly visible through the thin tissue.

The remarkable thing is that this spawning takes place at the same time all over the reef. Different colonies release their egg and sperm bundles, single sex polyps eject their sperm or their eggs, everything floats up. The egg and sperm bundles, big enough to be seen with the naked eye, are a spectacular sight. It's been described as looking like a fireworks display and, because it can be so accurately predicted, divers are often able to witness it.

Once on the surface the bundles break up and the sperm swim off to find eggs of the same coral type. It's obviously far from easy for an individual sperm to find the right egg, but experts believe this mass spawning is timed to reduce the risk of the eggs/sperm being consumed by other marine creatures. By spawning soon after the full moon the reduced tidal variation means there is more time for fertilisation to take place before waves and currents sweep them away.

Once fertilisation has taken place the egg cells begin to divide and within a day have become swimming coral larvae known as planulae. These are swept along by the sea for a few days, before sinking to the bottom and, if the right spot is found, the tiny larva becomes a coral polyp and a new coral colony is begun.

Reef Fish & Sex

There's unlikely to ever be a need to tell reef fish those nice straightforward 'birds and the bees' stories – a high proportion of the fish you see around the Great Barrier Reef are able to change their sex at some time in their life. Some of them are protandry, they start as males then switch to become females, others are protogyny, which means they start as females and switch to become males. Some fish are monandric, meaning they are all born one sex and only switch to the other sex later, while others may be born either sex and able to change sex later.

The tiny blue and gold angelfish is an example of protogyny. These fish normally live in small groups of four to seven in a territory of several square metres. The group usually consists of one larger dominant male with a 'harem' of female fish, although there may sometimes be a smaller 'bachelor' male fish present. The dominant male guards the group's territory and warns off any intruding angelfish. At mating time the male mates with all the females in the group. If the dominant male dies the largest female changes sex and takes over. It appears to be the dominant male that prevents females from changing sex earlier.

MICHAEL AW

Clown anemone fish

The male 'dominates' and harasses the larger females and somehow this affects their hormone balance and prevents them changing sex. As soon as the male is removed the largest and most aggressive female is able to switch sexes.

The opposite situation can be observed in the familiar clown anemone fish. The small group that shelters around a protective anemone usually consists of a large adult female and a group of smaller males. The female mates with only one of the males and this chief male keeps all the other 'bachelor' anemone fish in line. If something happens to the female then the chief male switches sex and becomes the new female, while the most dominant and aggressive of the other males takes over as the new chief male.

Scientists believe there are a number of reasons for this strange state of affairs. Competition on the reef is fierce and by staking out their own small territory and defending it against intruders the small groups of fish ensure their own survival. If changing sex were not possible and the sole male or female in the group dies then the group cannot reproduce. However, as it is there's a quick change of sex on the part of one fish and life continues as normal.

Island Life

Not all the life along the Great Barrier Reef is found underwater – the islands of the reef also harbour a great variety of land-dwelling creatures.

Island Flora The island flora varies with the islands found along the reef. At one extreme there are the vegetated coral cays, sandy islands recently emerged from the depths. Plant life here is limited and hardy but of great interest as it takes hold and begins to flourish.

At the other extreme there are the rainforest islands where rich soil and heavy monsoonal rain cloaks the landscape in a jungle of deep, moist plant life. In between are the other continental islands where plant life is rich and varied but without the dense rainforest growth found on the wetter islands. Several islands also have mangrove forests and this provides another interesting insight into the power of nature to adapt to often hostile environments.

Birds Even on the smaller islands there is a surprising diversity of birdlife. Some of the smaller cays support a limited variety of birdlife, however, during breeding season these populations increase at a phenomenal rate. The southern reef islands are noted particularly for their huge breeding populations and there are other islands, like Michaelmas Cay off Cairns, with similarly huge populations. Larger continental islands like the Whitsundays, Hinchinbrook or Dunk support a wide variety of birdlife.

Certain islands are closely linked with a particular type of bird, eg Heron Island takes its name from the reef herons that are common on the island. The haunting 'weeloo' call of the bush stone curlew is a familiar sound on many islands, particularly Magnetic.

Over 200 species of birds have been sighted on Hinchinbrook Island, while the nearby Brook islands are noted for the huge nesting colonies of Torresian imperial pigeons. Dunk Island's bird population was closely studied by EJ Banfield, Dunk's famous reclusive 'beachcomber', and this is one of a number of islands where you can see the mound-building megapode, or jungle fowl.

Other birds that island visitors will soon recognise are the colourful but raucous little rainbow lorikeets; attendees to the bird-feeding tables that so many resorts provide. Jaunty little silvereyes are a feature on many islands where they shamelessly scrounge off the restaurant tables. The tiny hummingbird-like sunbirds are a delight wherever you see them.

Insects Dunk and Bedarra's most colourful fliers are insects rather than birds. On these islands of the Family Group the huge and bright blue Ulysses butterflies are a truly spectacular sight.

Animals The animal life on the reef islands is, of course, rather restricted but even some of the smallest islands manage to support some mammals. Flying foxes or fruit bats, one of the largest types of bats, can be seen flapping away over many islands at sunset; even Lizard Island supports a small flying fox colony. A number of islands, Hinchinbrook in particular, have wallabies while Magnetic Island has a large koala population and an extremely fearless collection of possums. Even Orpheus has its resident population of tiny bandicoots.

Facts for the Visitor

PLANNING
When To Go
The best seasons to visit the Great Barrier Reef are probably during the southern hemisphere's autumn (from March to May) and spring (from September to November). During winter, the southern sections of the reef can be quite chilly, and during summer in the tropics you'll have to contend with the extremes of heat, humidity and tropical rainstorms. See the Climate section in the Facts about the Region chapter for more details.

Apart from the climate there's another influence on when to visit and that is Australian holiday patterns. During school holidays the resorts can be very crowded except, of course, for those that accept adults only.

The main annual holiday period in Australia is from mid-December through to the end of January. This is Christmas, New Year and school summer vacation all rolled into one and, although it's not the best time of year on the reef, it can get crowded there nevertheless.

Other school vacations come in two week bursts, but because there's some variation from state to state in Australia the danger period is more like three weeks. Approximately, the school holidays are around the last two weeks in April, the first two weeks in July, and the last two weeks in September. Lots of families head north to escape the winter weather in southern Australia at these times, particularly over the July holiday.

Maps
The *Great Barrier Reef* by Travelog Maps is a handy map of the whole reef. This same map, or a close variant of it, seems to appear in a number of publications on the reef. Travelog also produces *Whitsunday Passage*, a 1:100,000 map of the Whitsunday Islands. This is the best general tourist map of the Whitsundays. Sunmaps, the Queensland Government mapping organisation, has *Australia's Whitsundays*, but the Travelog map is superior.

What To Bring
Most of the resorts are very casual and have few rules, although at some of the more expensive resorts there is some dressing up for dinner. Otherwise, dressing up usually means a change from swimsuit to shorts and T-shirt.

Most resorts specify shirts for men and no bare feet or thongs at dinner time. Hayman actually suggests (but doesn't expect) jackets and long trousers in their fancier restaurants. For the most part, Barrier Reef resort wear is cool and casual. Almost all the resorts have laundry facilities so you can always wash clothes if necessary.

Come prepared for the tropical sun. A T-shirt to slip over a swimsuit – even when swimming if you're planning to do a lot of snorkelling – is a good idea, as is a hat and sunglasses. Don't forget good sun-protection lotion or cream as well.

Bring comfortable sandals or thongs for times when the sand is too hot for comfort, if you plan to do much walking then running shoes will be necessary. An old pair of running shoes is also essential for reef walking – walking on the reef barefoot is neither comfortable or safe.

Most of the year, even in the evenings, you're unlikely to need anything as warm as a long-sleeved shirt. If you are visiting the reef in midwinter (from June to August) particularly further south, then a sweater or light jacket will probably be a good idea for the occasional chilly evening.

If you are visiting there in the middle of the summer rainy season, be prepared for lots of rain. You might want to bring an umbrella or even a waterproof poncho, particularly for visiting wet rainforest islands like Hinchinbrook or Dunk.

Choosing an Island

The Barrier Reef has a great selection of islands and they're extremely variable in what they are and what they have to offer. Don't let the catchword 'reef island' suck you in. Only a few of the islands along the coast are real coral cays on the reef. Most of the popular resort islands are actually continental islands and some are well south of the Great Barrier Reef.

It's not necessarily important since many of them will still have fringing reefs and in any case a bigger continental island will have other attractions that a tiny, dot-on-the-map coral cay is simply too small for: like hills to climb, bushwalks, and secluded beaches where you can get away from your fellow island-lovers.

The islands vary considerably in their accessibility – Magnetic Island is a short trip by a regular commuter ferry, some other islands are also reasonably close to the mainland while Lady Elliot and Lizard are a long way out and require an aircraft flight to get there. If you actually want to stay on an island rather than just make a day trip from the mainland, that too can vary widely in cost.

If you want to stay on the islands the choice is generally between resorts or camping. Most visitors at the resorts will be staying on all-inclusive package deals. Many of the islands are national parks and have camping sites; a few, such as Great Keppel, Dunk, Hook, Lizard and Hinchinbrook, have both resorts and camping sites. Some islands have proper sites with toilets and fresh water on tap while, at the other extreme, on others you'll even have to bring drinking water and a cooking stove with you.

HIGHLIGHTS

The Great Barrier Reef is one big highlight that offers something for everybody, whether it be scuba diving, kicking back on a sandy, deserted beach or bushwalking through spectacular island scenery.

Divers are spoilt for choice, but it's hard to go past the resorts on **Heron Island** and **Lizard Island**. The three best dive spots on the reef are the **Cod Hole** and **Pixie Bommie** (both close to Lizard Island), and the *Yongala* wreck off Townsville.

Many people are disappointed with the **beaches** found in this part of the world. Most of the islands do in fact have coral rather than sand beaches and these can be coarse and unpleasant to lie on. The same cannot be said for **Whitehaven Beach** on Whitsunday Island. This is one of those picture-postcard white-sand beaches and is a deservedly popular day-trip destination from many of the Whitsunday islands resorts.

For bushwalkers the choices range from a short stroll to a four day trek, and the highlight among these is the picturesque and challenging **Thorsborne Trail** on Hinchinbrook Island. Spending a few days walking this trail offers a superb wilderness experience.

INFORMATION

There are a number of potential sources for information on the Great Barrier Reef.

Australian Tourist Commission

The Australian Tourist Commission (ATC) is the government body intended to inform potential visitors about the country. There's a very definite split between promotion outside and inside Australia. The ATC is strictly an external operator; it does minimal promotion within the country and has little contact with visitors to Australia. Within the country, tourist promotion is handled by state or local tourist offices.

The Australian Tourist Commission maintains a good web site at www.aussie.net.au/.

The ATC also maintains a number of Helplines (often toll-free), which independent travellers can ring or fax to get specific information about Australia. All requests for information should be directed through these numbers:

France
   ☎ toll-free 0591 5626
Germany
   ☎ toll-free 0130 825 182

Hong Kong
☎ 2802 7817; fax 2802 8211
Japan
☎ /fax (03) 5229 0021
New Zealand
☎ toll-free 0800 650 303
Singapore
☎ 250 6277; fax 253 8431
UK
☎ 0990 022 000
USA
☎ (847) 296 4900; fax 635 3718

Queensland Government Travel Centres

The Great Barrier Reef lies entirely within the state of Queensland and no effort is spared to promote the state's greatest tourist attraction. The QGTC are primarily booking of-fices rather than information centres but you can still find out a great deal about the reef and its resorts. There are offices of the QGTC in a number of overseas countries and also in each state:

Germany
(☎ (089) 2317 7177) Neuhauserstrasse 27, 4th Floor, 80331 Munich
Hong Kong
(☎ 2827 4322) Room 2209, 22nd Floor, Harbour Centre, 25 Harbour Rd, Wanchai
Japan
(☎ (03) 3214 4931) Suite 1301, Yurakucho Denki Building North Wing, 7-1 Yurakucho 1 Chome, Chiyoda-ku, Tokyo 100
Korea
(☎ 756 9011) Suite 301B, Hotel President 188-3, Ulchiro 1-Ka, Chung-Ku, Seoul 100-191
New Zealand
(☎ (09) 377 9053) 9th Floor, Quay Tower, 29 Customs St West, Auckland
Singapore
(☎ 253 2811) 101 Thompson Rd, No 07-04, United Square, Singapore 307591
Taiwan
(☎ (02) 2723 0656) Suite 2601, 26th Floor, International Trade Building, 333 Keelung Rd, Section 1, Taipei 10548
UK
(☎ (0181) 780 2227) Queensland House, 392/3 Strand, London WC2R OLZ
USA
(☎ (310) 788 0997) Northrop Plaza, Suite 330, 1800 Century Park East, Los Angeles, CA 90067

The QGTC also has offices throughout Australia. Contact them on their central contact number (☎ 131 801), or visit them on the net at www.qttc.com.au or send an email to qldtravl@ozemail.com.au.

Australian Capital Territory
(fax (02) 6257 4160) 25 Garema St, Canberra, ACT 2601
New South Wales
Chatswood: (fax (02) 9411 6079) Shop 2, 376 Victoria Ave, Chatswood, NSW 2067
Newcastle: (fax (02) 4929 6774) 97 Hunter St, Newcastle, NSW 2300
Parramatta: (fax (02) 9865 8444) Shop 2158, Westfield Shoppingtown, Parramatta, NSW 2150
Sydney: (fax (02) 9209 8686) 156 Castlereagh St, Sydney, NSW 2000
Queensland
(fax (07) 3221 5320) Corner Edward & Adelaide Sts, Brisbane, Qld 4000
South Australia
(fax (08) 8211 8841) 10 Grenfell St, Adelaide, SA 5000
Victoria
(fax (03) 9206 4577) 257 Collins St, Melbourne, Vic 3000
Western Australia
(☎ (08) 9322 1800) Shop 6, 777 Hay St, Perth, WA 6000

Department of Environment

Most of the Great Barrier Reef islands are completely (or largely) national parks and the 'on site' management is handled by Queensland National Parks & Wildlife (QNPW), part of the Department of Environment (www.env.qld.gov.au). They have interesting brochures and publications on many of the islands or on wildlife and plant life found on and around the islands. The department also handles permits if you want to camp on a national park island.

Contact the relevant Department of Environment offices at:

Brisbane
(☎ 3227 8186) 160 Anne St, Qld 4000; PO Box 155, Brisbane Albert St, Qld 4002
Cairns
(☎ 4052 3096) 10-12 McLeod St; PO Box 2066, Cairns, Qld 4870

Cardwell
(☎ 4066 8601) Rainforest & Reef Centre, Bruce Highway; PO Box 74, Cardwell, Qld 4816

Gladstone
(☎ 4972 6055) Park Lane Plaza, corner of Goondoon & Tank Sts, PO Box 5065, Gladstone, Qld 4680

Mackay
(☎ 4951 8788) Corner of River & Wood Sts; PO Box 623, Mackay, Qld 4740

Rockhampton
(☎ 4936 0511) Corner of Yeppoon & Norman Rds, Qld 4700; PO Box 3130, North Rockhampton, Qld 4701

Townsville
(☎ 4721 2399) Great Barrier Reef Wonderland office, Flinders St East, PO Box 5391, Townsville, Qld 4810

Whitsundays
(☎ 4946 7022) Whitsunday Information Centre, corner of Shute Harbour & Mandalay Rds, Airlie Beach; PO Box 332, Airlie Beach, Qld 4802

Great Barrier Reef Marine Park Authority

If QNPW looks after the islands then it's the Great Barrier Reef Marine Park Authority (GBRMPA, and known locally as 'g-broom-pa') that looks after the water around the islands. In actual fact the division is not so straightforward and there's some overlap, and a great deal of cooperation, between the two organisations. The GBRMPA's aim is to increase people's understanding of the reef and ensure that it is used in the most enjoyable and least harmful fashion.

Great Barrier Reef Marine Park Authority (☎ 4750 0700; fax 4772 6093; www.gbrmpa .gov.au) Great Barrier Reef Wonderland, Flinders St East, PO Box 1379, Townsville, Qld 4810

Other Sources

There is a host of other organisations that can provide information about the Great Barrier Reef. Many towns have local tourist offices that provide a great deal of information about local tourist facilities and actively promote their islands.

The two national domestic airlines have

a great interest in the Great Barrier Reef because they bring many of the visitors to the reef and they own or are linked with a number of the resorts along the reef. In particular Qantas owns Great! Keppel and Lizard, while Ansett owns or has links with Hayman, South Molle and Hook. Finally the resorts themselves can tell you about their own facilities and attractions.

VISAS & DOCUMENTS
Visas

All visitors to Australia need a visa. Only New Zealand nationals are exempt, and even they receive a 'special category' visa on arrival.

Tourist visas are issued by Australian consular offices abroad; they are the most common visa and are generally valid for a stay of either three or six months. The three month visas are free; for the six month visa there is a $35 fee. The visa is valid for use within 12 months of the date of issue and can be used to enter and leave Australia several times within that 12 months.

Young, single visitors from the UK, Canada, Korea, Holland and Japan may be eligible for a 'working holiday' visa. 'Young' is fairly loosely interpreted as around 18 to 25, although exceptions are made and people up to 30, and young married couples without children, may be given a working holiday visa, but it's far from guaranteed. See the section on Work later in this chapter for details of what might be available and where.

The maximum stay allowed to visitors is one year, including extensions.

Electronic Travel Authority (ETA) Visitors who require a tourist visa of three months or less can make the application through an IATA-registered travel agent (no form required), who can then make the application direct and issue the traveller with an ETA, which replaces the usual visa stamped in your passport. This system was only introduced in late 1997, and the nationalities to which it is available is so far limited, but includes passport holders of the

UK, the USA, most European and Scandinavian countries, Malaysia and Singapore, and the list is likely to grow rapidly.

Travel Insurance

A travel insurance policy to cover theft, loss and medical problems is a good idea. The policies handled by STA Travel and other student travel organisations are usually good value. Some policies offer lower and higher medical-expense options; the higher ones are chiefly for countries such as the USA, which have extremely high medical costs. There is a wide variety of policies available so check the small print.

Some policies specifically exclude 'dangerous activities', which can include scuba diving, motorcycling, even trekking. A locally acquired motorcycle licence is not valid under some policies.

You may prefer a policy that pays doctors or hospitals direct rather than you having to pay on the spot and claim later. If you have to claim later make sure you keep all documentation. Some policies ask you to call back (reverse charges) to a centre in your home country where an assessment of your problem is made.

Check that the policy covers ambulances or an emergency flight home.

EMBASSIES
Australian Embassies Abroad
Australian consular offices overseas include:

Canada
  (☎ (613) 236 0841; fax 236 4376) Suite 710, 50 O'Connor St, Ottawa, Ontario K1P 6L2; consulate also in Vancouver
France
  (☎ 01 40 59 33 00; fax 40 59 33 10) 4 Rue Jean Rey, 75015 Cedex 15, Paris
Germany
  (☎ (0228) 81 030; fax 373 145) Godesberger-allee 107, Bonn 53175

Indonesia
  Jakarta: (☎ (021) 522 7111; fax 522 7101) Jalan HR Rasuna Said Kav C15-16, Kuningan, Jakarta Selatan 12940
  Bali: (☎ (0361) 23 5002; fax 23 1990) Jalan Prof Moh Yamin 4, Renon, Denpasar
Ireland
  (☎ (01) 676 1517; fax 661 3576) 6 Fitzwilton House, Wilton Terrace, Dublin 2
Italy
  (☎ (06) 85 2721; fax 8527 2400) Via Alessandria 215, Rome 00198
Japan
  Tokyo: (☎ (03) 5232 4111; fax 5232 4178) 2-1-14 Mita, Minato-ku, Tokyo 108
  Osaka: (☎ (06) 941 8601; fax 941 8602) Twin 21 MID Tower, 29th floor, 2-1-61 Shiromi, Chuo-ku, Osaka 540
Malaysia
  (☎ (03) 242 3122; fax 241 4495) 6 Jalan Yap Kwan Seng, Kuala Lumpur 50450
Netherlands
  (☎ (070) 310 8200; fax 364 3807) Carnegie-laan 4, The Hague 2517 KH
New Zealand
  Wellington: (☎ (04) 473 6411; fax 498 7103) 72-78 Hobson St, Thorndon
  Auckland: (☎ (09) 303 2429; fax 303 2431) Union House, 32-38 Quay St
Papua New Guinea
  (☎ 325 9333; fax 325 3528) Godwit St, Waigani, Hohola, Port Moresby
Philippines
  (☎ (02) 750 2850; fax 287 2029) Dona Salustiana Ty Tower, 104 Paseo de Roxas Ave, Makati, Metro Manila
Singapore
  (☎ 737 9311; fax 735 1242) 25 Napier Rd, Singapore 258507
South Africa
  (☎ (012) 342 3740; fax 342 4222) 292 Orient St, Arcadia, Pretoria 0083
UK
  (☎ (0171) 379 4334; fax 465 8218) Australia House, The Strand, London WC2B 4LA; consulate also in Manchester
USA
  (☎ (202) 797 3000; fax 797 3100) 1601 Massachusetts Ave NW, Washington DC 20036-2273; consulates also in Los Angeles and New York

Foreign Embassies in Australia
The principal diplomatic representations to Australia are based in Canberra. There are

also representatives in Brisbane, particularly from countries with major connections with Australia like the UK or New Zealand, although visa applications are generally handled in Canberra. Addresses of important offices follow (look under Consulates & Legations in the *Yellow Pages* telephone book for more):

Canada
  (☎ (02) 6273 3844) Commonwealth Ave, Yarralumla, ACT 2600
France
  Canberra: (☎ (02) 6216 0100) 6 Perth Ave, Yarralumla, ACT 2600
  Brisbane: (☎ (07) 3229 8201) 10 Market St, Brisbane, Qld 4000
Germany
  (☎ (02) 6270 1911) 119 Empire Circuit, Yarralumla, ACT 2600
Indonesia
  (☎ (02) 6250 8600) 8 Darwin Ave, Yarralumla, ACT 2600
Ireland
  (☎ (02) 6273 3022) 20 Arkana St, Yarralumla, ACT 2600
Malaysia
  (☎ (02) 6273 1543) 7 Perth Ave, Yarralumla, ACT 2600
Netherlands
  Canberra: (☎ (02) 6273 3111) 120 Empire Circuit, Yarralumla, ACT 2600
  Brisbane: (☎ (07) 3839 9644) 5th Floor, 101 Wickham Terrace, Brisbane, Qld 4000
New Zealand
  Sydney: (☎ (02) 9247 1511) Level 14, 1 Alfred St, Circular Quay, Sydney, NSW 2000
  Brisbane: (☎ (07) 3221 9933) 288 Edward St, Brisbane, Qld 4000
Papua New Guinea
  Canberra: (☎ (02) 6273 3322) 39-41 Forster Crescent, Yarralumla, ACT 2600
  Cairns: (☎ (070) 521 033) Level 15, 15 Lake St, Cairns, Qld 4870
Singapore
  (☎ (02) 6273 3944) 17 Forster Crescent, Yarralumla, ACT 2600
Thailand
  Canberra: (☎ (02) 6273 1149) 111 Empire Circuit, Yarralumla, ACT 2600
  Brisbane: (☎ (07) 3832 1999) 5th Floor, 101 Wickham Terrace, Brisbane, Qld 4000
UK
  Canberra: (☎ (02) 6270 6666) Commonwealth Ave, Yarralumla, ACT 2600
  Brisbane: (☎ (07) 3236 2575) Level 26, 1 Eagle St, Brisbane, Qld 4000
USA
  (☎ (02) 6270 5000) 21 Moonah Place, Yarralumla, ACT 2600

CUSTOMS

When entering Australia you can bring most articles in free of duty provided Customs is satisfied they are for personal use and that you'll be taking them with you when you leave. There's also a duty-free per person quota of 1125mL of alcohol, 250 cigarettes and dutiable goods up to the value of A$400.

With regard to prohibited goods, there are two areas that need particular attention. Number one is, of course, drugs – Australian Customs are serious about the stuff and can be extremely efficient when it comes to finding it.

Problem two is animal and plant quarantine. You will be asked to declare all goods of animal or vegetable origin – wooden spoons, straw hats, the lot – and show them to an official. The authorities are naturally keen to prevent weeds, pests or diseases getting into the country – Australia has so far managed to escape many of the agricultural pests and diseases prevalent in other parts of the world. Fresh food is also unpopular, particularly meat, sausage, fruit, vegetables and flowers.

Weapons and firearms are either prohibited or require a permit and safety testing. Other restricted goods include products (such as ivory) made from protected wildlife species, non-approved telecommunications devices and live animals.

MONEY
Costs

The cost of visiting Barrier Reef islands can vary enormously. At one extreme you can camp on national park islands for no more than a few dollars for a camping permit. You bring your own food, and on many islands your own water as well, and there's absolutely nothing to spend money on even if you wanted to. At the other extreme there are resorts like Bedarra where the daily cost per person is around $1000. In between there's everything from backpackers hostels where a bunk bed will cost you from $12 to $20 a night or lower key resorts where the per person costs could be anything from $100 to $250 a night.

If you want to enjoy the reef islands without spending the national budget there are several alternatives. One is to stay on the mainland and make a day trip out. Cairns is a particularly good place for this as there are many reefs and cays easily accessible from the mainland and a great many trips operate out to them. In the Whitsundays, on the other hand, the reefs are further out but there are a variety of resort islands, many of which actively encourage day-trippers.

The other way of getting to the islands on the cheap is to look for special deals and standby packages. Some of the resorts never discount their rates and you're also unlikely to find anything at peak holiday times but when things are quiet, or during the off season, many resorts will offer standby rates.

If you just happen to be at Airlie Beach, the jumping-off point for Whitsunday trips, at a quiet time you may find the travel agencies promoting all sorts of special standby deals at much lower rates than usual and often including transport out and back.

Travellers Cheques & Credit Cards

Travellers cheques and credit cards are widely accepted at most resorts and major mainland towns along the Queensland coast. While it is possible to pay for resort accommodation with travellers cheques, chances are the rate you will receive will be less than spectacular; credit cards are the preferred option. Visa, MasterCard, Diners Club and American Express are all widely accepted.

Cash advances from credit cards are available from mainland banks, from many automatic teller machines (ATMs) and from places with EFTPOS (Electronic Funds Transfer at Point Of Sale) facility, which is quite widespread these days.

Currency

Australia's currency is the Australian dollar, which comprises 100 cents. There are coins for 5, 10, 20, 50 cents, $1 and $2, and notes for $5, $10, $20, $50 and $100.

Although the smallest coin in circulation is 5 cents, prices are still marked in single cents, and then rounded to the nearest 5 cents when you come to pay.

There are no notable restrictions on importing or exporting travellers cheques. Cash amounts in excess of the equivalent of A$5000 (any currency) must be declared on arrival or departure.

Currency Exchange

The Australian dollar fluctuates quite markedly against the US dollar, but it seems to stay pretty much in the 70 to 80 cent range, although recently it has been hovering around 65 cents, which is great news for visitors with foreign currency.

Canada	C$1	=	$1.05
France	FFr10	=	$2.44
Germany	DM1	=	$0.82
Hong Kong	HK$10	=	$1.92
Japan	¥100	=	$1.16
New Zealand	NZ$1	=	$0.87
South Africa	SAR1	=	$0.30
UK	UK£1	=	$2.47
USA	US$1	=	$1.49

Tipping

In Australia tipping isn't entrenched. It's only customary to tip in more expensive restaurants and only then if you feel it's necessary. If the service has been especially good and you decide to leave a tip, 10% of the bill is an acceptable amount.

POST & COMMUNICATIONS
Post

Australia's postal services are relatively efficient but not altogether inexpensive. All the resorts sell postcards and stamps and will handle incoming and outgoing mail. Hamilton, Magnetic and Thursday islands actually have post offices, and many of the other resorts have postal agencies.

Telephone

The resort reef islands generally are on the main trunk dialling network and calls can be dialled directly. The phone numbers given in this book are in the Queensland code area, which is 07. Note that if the number you want to ring does not have the same two first digits as the number you are ringing from, then you still need to dial the 07 area code before the eight digit phone number. This does not apply after March 1999 when all numbers to and from anywhere within the 07 area can be dialled without using the 07 code.

A number of the islands are close enough to the coast to be within mobile phone range, but if this is important to you check in advance.

BOOKS
Guides

For the complete story on the Barrier Reef's creatures and creations, liberally illustrated with a great number of superb colour plates the number one book is undoubtedly the *Reader's Digest Book of the Great Barrier Reef* (1990). This is not, however, a book to take with you to the islands to casually leaf through while lying on the beach. It's a hefty volume, nearly as big as the reef itself. An abbreviated version of this book has also been produced. If you want the full story make sure you get the original.

100 Magic Miles of the Great Barrier Reef – The Whitsunday Islands by David Colfelt (1993) concentrates on the Whitsunday area. This large format paperback guide, now in its 4th edition, could be subtitled 'everything you could possibly want to know about the Whitsundays'. There are photographs and articles on the resorts; features on diving, sailing, fishing, and even camping; natural history; an exhaustive collection of aerial photographs and charts; and descriptions of boat anchorages all around the islands. A new edition was scheduled for 1998.

Discover the Great Barrier Reef Marine Park by Lesley Murdoch (1992) is a simple and colourful book on the reef, its creatures, its islands and the Great Barrier Reef Marine Park Authority.

The *Insight Guide to the Great Barrier Reef*, edited by John Borthwick and David McGonigal (1992), features a collection of excellent colour photos and descriptive text as well as a section of travel tips and useful information, and would be a handy primer for (or souvenir of) a trip to the reef.

Scuba Divers Guide to the Great Barrier Reef by Tom Byron is a series of books specifically for divers, with undersea maps, colour photos and descriptions of dives. There are separate books to the southern, northern, central and Whitsunday areas of the reef. Also for divers is *Dive Sites of the Great Barrier Reef & the Coral Sea* by Neville Coleman. This a glossy, thoroughly researched book. The Pisces guide *Australia: Coral Sea and Great Barrier Reef* by Carl Roessler is also worth a look.

The Missing Coast – Queensland Takes Shape by JCH Gill is a fascinating account of the European exploration of the Queensland coast starting with the Portuguese, Spanish and Dutch visitors and continuing with Cook, Bligh, Flinders et al.

For yachties the bible is *Cruising the Coral Coast* by Alan Lucas (1995). First published in the 1960s, this book has been through several editions and is an indispensable guide to anchorages, facilities and navigation along the Barrier Reef.

See the Dunk Island section for information on EJ Banfield's classic book *The Confessions of a Beachcomber* and Michael Noonan's fascinating biography of Banfield, *A Different Drummer*. Other books on individual islands or groups are covered in the relevant chapters.

Field Guides There are a number of books that can help you identify the amazing array of corals, fish, shells and other marine life you're likely to come across on a visit to the reef.

Among the best all-round guides is *Coral Reef Field Guide* by Dr Gerald R Allan & Roger Steene.

The Collins *Pocket Guide of Coral Reef*

Fishes is another handy reference, although it is not specific to the Great Barrier Reef. Also useful are the *Guide to Sea Fishes of Australia* by Rudie H Kuiter, and *Marine Fishes of the Great Barrier Reef* by Gerry Allen.

The *Field Guide to Crustaceans of Australian Waters* by Diana Jones & Gary Morgan is the book to get hold of if this is your area of interest.

INTERNET RESOURCES

Web surfers will find plenty of interesting material relevant to the reef. Good places to start are the Great Barrier Reef Marine Park Authority (www.gbrmpa.gov.au) and the Great Barrier Reef Aquarium (www.aquarium.gbrmpa.gov.au) sites, both of which have links to other sites of interest.

VIDEO SYSTEMS

Australia uses the PAL system, so prerecorded videos purchased in Australia may be incompatible with overseas systems. Check this before you buy.

PHOTOGRAPHY & VIDEO

There are lots of photographic possibilities on the Great Barrier Reef but also a number of photographic challenges. Light on the islands or out on the reef can often be very tricky. The time proven rule for photography in tropical light applies to the Queensland coast: shoot early or late as the sun is often high overhead between around 10 am and 3 pm and photos taken at that time tend to be flat or washed out. At the best of times exposure settings can be critical. It's very easy to end up with overexposed photos and you should beware of backlighting from bright sunlight and of reflected light. A polarising filter can work wonders when photographing over the sea.

At the other extreme, lack of light can also be a problem. On rainforest islands like Dunk or Hinchinbrook it can be remarkably gloomy in the forests and you will need a high-speed film for good results. The contrast between dark and light can also pose difficulties. If your picture has brightly lit and shadowed areas you must choose to expose only one or the other area correctly.

Film is available at the resort islands but is generally expensive. In major cities Kodachrome or Fujichrome 36 exposure slide film including processing can be bought from around $20 a roll. If you're simply taking snapshots and want to see the results quickly a number of the larger resorts offer fast-turn-around photo developing.

Underwater Photography

Of course the urge to take underwater photographs is going to come upon many Great Barrier Reef snorkellers and divers. In recent years, underwater photography has become a much easier activity. At one time it required complex and expensive equipment whereas now there is a variety of reasonably priced and easy-to-use underwater cameras available. Very often it's possible to rent cameras, including underwater video cameras, from diving operators on the reef. The cheapest and most convenient option for most people are the 'disposable' one roll underwater cameras. These cost around $25 and are widely available at shops and resort.

As with basic cameras above surface level, the best photos taken with the simplest underwater cameras are likely to be straightforward snapshots. You are not going to get superb photographs of fish and marine life with a small, cheap camera but, on the other hand, photos of your fellow snorkellers or divers can often be terrific.

More than with other types of photography, the results achieved underwater can improve dramatically if you spend more on equipment, particularly on artificial lighting. As you descend natural colours are quickly absorbed, starting with the red end of the spectrum. You can see the same result with a picture or poster that has been left in bright sunlight for too long, with the colours faded until everything looks blue. It's the same underwater, the deeper you go the bluer things look. Red virtually disappears by the time you're 10m down. The human brain fools us to some extent by automatically compensating for this colour change, but the camera doesn't lie. If you are at any depth your pictures will look cold and blue.

To put the colour back in, you need a flash and to work effectively underwater it has to be a much more powerful and complicated flash than you'd use above water. Thus newcomers to serious underwater photography soon find that having bought a Nikonos camera they have to lay out as much money again for flash equipment to go with it. With the right experience and equipment the results can be superb. Generally the Nikonos cameras work best with 28 or 35mm lenses; longer lenses do not work so well underwater. Although objects appear closer underwater with these short focal lengths you have to get close to achieve good results. Patience and practice will eventually enable you to move in close to otherwise wary fish. Underwater photography opens up whole new fields of interest to divers and the results can often be startling. Flash photography can reveal colours that simply aren't there for the naked eye.

TIME
Australian Eastern Time is 10 hours ahead of GMT (UTC) so when it is noon on the Barrier Reef islands it is 2 am in London and 6 pm the previous day on the US west coast.

In Queensland, Australian Eastern time applies all year round. Meanwhile, daylight saving time operates on the rest of the east coast, which means that from late October until early March, New South Wales, Victoria, and Tasmania are all 11 hours ahead of GMT/UTC.

Heron Island is the oddity here as it operates on daylight saving time year round, and so is always one hour ahead of the rest of Queensland.

ELECTRICITY
Electricity supply in Australia is 240V, 60 Hz cycle. The resort islands all have electricity, usually provided through a generator. The sockets are three-pin with the two live pins in a position that you can usually fit US two-prong plugs if you twist the prongs to the required angle.

Some US plugs now have one prong longer than the other which may cause difficulties so, if you're packing a lot of electrical gadgets, a converter plug may be a good idea. Don't try plugging 120V appliances into 240V even if the plug fits.

If you plan to camp out on the uninhabited islands bring some candles or a lamp.

HEALTH
Australia is a remarkably healthy country in which to travel, considering such a large portion of it lies in the tropics. Tropical diseases such as malaria and yellow fever are unknown, diseases of insanitation such as cholera and typhoid are unheard of, and even some animal diseases such as rabies and foot-and-mouth disease have yet to be recorded.

Travel health depends on your predeparture preparations, your daily health care while travelling and how you handle any medical problem that does develop. Few travellers experience anything more than upset stomachs.

Health Insurance
Make sure that you have adequate health insurance. See the Travel Insurance boxed text in this chapter for details.

Environmental Hazards
Fungal Infections Fungal infections occur more commonly in hot weather and are usually found on the scalp, between the toes or fingers, in the groin and on the body (ringworm). You get ringworm (which is a fungal infection, not a worm) from infected animals or other people. Moisture encourages these infections.

To prevent fungal infections wear loose, comfortable clothes, avoid artificial fibres, wash frequently and dry carefully. If you do get an infection, wash the infected area at least daily with a disinfectant or medicated soap and water, and rinse and dry well. Apply an antifungal cream or powder like tolnaftate (Tinaderm). Try to expose the infected area to air or sunlight as much as possible and wash all towels and underwear in hot water, change them often and let them dry in the sun.

Heat Exhaustion Dehydration and salt deficiency can cause heat exhaustion. Take time to acclimatise to high temperatures, drink sufficient liquids and do not do anything too physically demanding.

Salt deficiency is characterised by fatigue, lethargy, headaches, giddiness and muscle cramps; salt tablets may help, but adding extra salt to your food is better.

Heat Stroke This serious, occasionally fatal, condition can occur if the body's heat-regulating mechanism breaks down and the body temperature rises to dangerous levels. Long, continuous periods of exposure to high temperatures and insufficient fluids can leave you vulnerable to heat stroke.

The symptoms are feeling unwell, not sweating very much (or at all) and a high body temperature (39 to 41°C or 102 to 106°F). Where sweating has ceased the skin becomes flushed and red. Severe, throbbing headaches and lack of coordination will also occur, and the sufferer may be confused or aggressive. Eventually the victim will become delirious or convulse. Hospitalisation is essential, but in the interim get victims out of the sun, remove their clothing, cover them with a wet sheet or towel and then fan continually. Give fluids if they are conscious.

Motion Sickness Eating lightly before and during a trip will reduce the chances of motion sickness. If you are prone to motion sickness try to find a place that minimises movement – near the wing on aircraft, close to midships on boats. Fresh air usually helps; reading and cigarette smoke don't. Commercial motion sickness preparations, which can cause drowsiness, have to be taken before the trip commences. Ginger (available in capsule form) and peppermint (including mint-flavoured sweets) are natural preventatives, and these are usually offered free of charge by the large reef operators such as Fantasea (Whitsundays) and Great Adventures (Cairns).

Prickly Heat Prickly heat is an itchy rash caused by excessive perspiration trapped under the skin. It usually strikes people who have just arrived in a hot climate. Keeping cool, bathing often, drying the skin and using a mild talcum or prickly heat powder or resorting to an air-conditioned environment may help.

Sunburn In the tropics you can get sunburnt surprisingly quickly, even through cloud. Use a sunscreen, hat, and barrier cream for your nose and lips. Calamine lotion or Stingose are good for mild sunburn. Protect your eyes with good quality sunglasses.

Don't think that lazing on the beach is the only way to get sunburnt. Snorkelling, for example, is an ideal way to burn your back. If you're going to be snorkelling for a prolonged period wear a T-shirt or Lycra suit.

Insect Bites & Stings

Bee and wasp stings are usually painful rather than dangerous. However, in people who are allergic to them severe breathing difficulties may occur and require urgent medical care. Calamine lotion or Stingose spray will give relief and ice packs will reduce the pain and swelling. There are some spiders with dangerous bites but antivenins are usually available. Scorpion stings are notoriously painful. Scorpions often shelter in shoes or clothing.

Certain cone shells found in Australia can sting dangerously, even fatally. There are various fish and other sea creatures that can sting or bite dangerously or which are dangerous to eat. Local advice is the best suggestion.

Japanese Encephalitis Japanese encephalitis is a viral disease that has been spreading through Asia and the Pacific over the last few decades, and has recently been reported in the Torres Strait islands. This potentially fatal disease is transmitted by mosquitoes. Vaccination against it is not routinely required for travel to northern Queensland, however, travellers should use precautions to avoid all mosquito bites.

Ross River Fever This viral disease, properly known as epidemic polyarthritis, is transmitted by some species of mosquitoes. Outbreaks of the disease have been reported in the Townsville area and are most likely to occur in January and February, but risk of infection is very low. Flu-like symptoms (muscle and joint pain, rashes, fever, headache, tiredness) are possible indicators, but blood tests are necessary for positive detection. Unfortunately there is no treatment for Ross River Fever, although relief of symptoms can be achieved. Conventional wisdom has it that the symptoms do not last more than a few months, although there are now serious doubts about this, with some people still feeling the affects (mainly chronic fatigue) some years after contracting the disease. Avoid mozzie bites is the best advice.

Cuts & Scratches
Wash well and treat any cut with an antiseptic. Where possible avoid bandages and Band-Aids, which can keep wounds wet. Coral cuts are notoriously slow to heal and if they are not adequately cleaned small pieces of coral may remain embedded in the wound. Clean any cut thoroughly with an antiseptic. Severe pain, throbbing, redness, fever or generally feeling unwell suggest infection and the need for antibiotics, as coral cuts may result in serious infections.

Women's Health
Gynaecological Problems Sexually transmitted diseases are a major cause of vaginal problems. Symptoms include a smelly discharge, painful intercourse and sometimes a burning sensation when urinating. Male sexual partners must also be treated. Medical attention should be sought and in addition to these diseases HIV or hepatitis B may also be acquired during exposure. Besides abstinence, the best thing is to practise safe sex by using condoms.

Antibiotic use, synthetic underwear, sweating and contraceptive pills can lead to fungal vaginal infections in hot climates. Maintaining good personal hygiene, and loose fitting clothes and cotton underwear will help to prevent these infections.

Fungal infections, characterised by a rash, itch and discharge, can be treated with a vinegar or lemon juice douche, or with yoghurt. Nystatin, miconazole or clotrimazole pessaries or vaginal cream are the usual treatment.

WOMEN TRAVELLERS
Queensland's coastal region is generally a safe place for women travellers, although you should avoid hitchhiking. Sexual harassment is rare, although the Aussie bloke culture does have its sexist elements.

GAY & LESBIAN TRAVELLERS
Australia is a popular destination for gay and lesbian travellers. Certainly the profile of gay and lesbian travel has risen significantly in the last few years, partly as a result of the publicity surrounding the Gay & Lesbian Mardi Gras in Sydney. Throughout the country, but especially on the east coast, there is a number of tour operators, travel agents, airlines, resorts and accommodation places that are exclusively gay and lesbian, or gay friendly.

There are several gay and lesbian hotels or resorts in Far North Queensland, most of which are around Cairns, and which should be known to the Australian Gay & Lesbian Tourism Association (☎ (02) 9955 6755; fax 9922 6036; aglta.asn.au/index.htm), PO Box 208, Darlinghurst, NSW 2010.

DISABLED TRAVELLERS
Travellers with disabilities may find the Great Barrier Reef a difficult place to holiday. The large resorts, such as Hamilton Island, would be able to accommodate you but very little thought has been given to the

disabled, and things like the absence of access ramps and disabled toilet facilities can make the going pretty tough.

Those places accessed by boat or seaplane are generally going to cause problems, as there is usually a fair bit of scrambling in and out of boats or cramped aircraft cabins. The best way around this is to arrive by helicopter, but this is not always possible and can be expensive.

TRAVEL WITH CHILDREN

The Barrier Reef is one of Australia's top family holiday spots so it comes as no surprise that kids are well catered for at most of the bigger places. This is usually in the form of a Kids' Club or similar, where the children are supervised and distracted for the greater part of the day, leaving the parents free to kick back on the beach. Most of these services are free, and are generally available between about 8 am and 6 pm, although this does vary from island to island.

During the evening the larger resorts can also arrange for babysitters, which typically cost around $10 per hour for one or two children.

At the other end of the scale there are resorts that are resolutely child-free zones, for those who want to escape the noise and general mayhem that kids can often generate. These resorts include Bedarra and Lizard islands, while at Orpheus Island children are 'not catered for', which basically means children are charged full price and there are no special activities.

BUSINESS HOURS

Queensland's shops generally open from 9 am to 5.30 pm on weekdays, and doors stay open until around 9 pm on either Thursday or Friday for late-night shopping. On Saturday, shops open from 9 am to noon, but many of the larger towns now have all-day trading on Saturday. The resort shops on the island tend to have longer and more flexible opening hours.

Banks are open from 9.30 am to 4 pm Monday to Thursday, and until 5 pm on Friday.

PUBLIC HOLIDAYS & SPECIAL EVENTS

As well as the school holidays when Australian families flock to the Great Barrier Reef islands (see the When to Go section) there are also holidays, festivals and events directly related to the islands. Some of the main ones include:

April
  Hamilton Island Race Week features a series of yacht races
October-November
  Marlin season at Lizard Island peaks with the Lizard Island Black Marlin Classic from 30 October
November
  Heron Island Dive Festival brings together divers from all over the world for a week of scuba activity

Public Holidays

The public holidays celebrated in Queensland are:

New Year's Day
  1 January
Australia Day
  26 January
Easter
  Good Friday, and Easter Saturday, Sunday and Monday (March/April)
Anzac Day
  25 April
Labour Day
  1st Monday in May
Queen's Birthday
  2nd Monday in June
Christmas Day
  25 December
Boxing Day
  26 December

ACTIVITIES

The resort islands along the reef have the whole range of typical resort activities from tennis and squash to windsurfing and sailing. There are also some fine bushwalking opportunities on a number of islands but snorkelling, scuba diving and sailing are the Great Barrier Reef's major attractions.

(Continued page 40)

Into the deep blue

GBRMPA

Diving

Scuba diving has always been a big attraction along the Great Barrier Reef. There are diving schools right up and down the coast and most resorts have dive shops and offer diving courses. The main consideration with scuba diving is that it requires knowledge and care. You can sling a mask and snorkel on and be a snorkeller in minutes. Adding an air tank on your back and diving in is asking for trouble. If you want to take up scuba diving you should first complete a good diving course that leads to an approved diving certificate. But the first thing to do is to ensure you are medically fit to dive. For instance, a history of asthma is a contra-indication for scuba diving.

Although learning to scuba dive requires some application, it is not difficult to learn and it does not require any sort of superhuman strength or fitness. In fact one thing you quickly learn is that doing things with the minimum expenditure of energy is what diving is about. Your diving time is limited by your tank of air and the more gently you do things the longer that air is going to last. It's remarkable how much longer the same tank of air will last with an experienced diver compared to a beginner. Women often have an advantage over men in this area, they don't breathe so much air.

GBRMPA

Divers receiving instruction on Lizard Island

Diving Courses

Full time diving courses last about a week and can cost anywhere from $250 to $450. A good course will include classroom instruction and underwater experience in a pool, followed by some real dives in the sea. The best way of finding out if the course is good is to ask somebody else who has done it. Resorts, with a reputation to protect, usually ensure their dive school operators know what they're about.

If you're a backpacker making your way up the Queensland coast there are many dive schools, often loosely associated with the popular backpackers' hostels. Word of mouth should let you know which ones are good. Of course you can also learn about diving before you leave home. Diving courses in your home town are likely to be part time rather than full time.

What do you learn in a diving course? 'One thousand ways to kill yourself underwater' was one succinct description. Actually it's the reverse of that; a diving course should teach you to anticipate possible problems and avoid them. Much of the course is designed to drum into you things that have to become second nature when you're underwater – always keep breathing, don't hold your breath as you ascend, how to adjust your buoyancy; all these soon become straightforward techniques. Of course you also spend some time learning how to grapple with those tricky decompression tables.

Certificates

The end result of your diving course is not just a basic knowledge of scuba diving it's also a certificate to prove you know it. A certificate is like a driving licence. You can't walk into a rent-a-car agency and rent a

MICHAEL AW

A diver gets up close and personal with a school of inquisitive hussar snapper

car without a driving licence, nor can you go out on a diving trip without a diving certificate. Once you have a recognised certificate, however, you'll be welcomed by diving operators all over the world. Certificates in Australia are generally issued by PADI (Professional Association of Diving Instructors) or FAUI (Federation of Australian Underwater Instructors). PADI is the larger and is better known internationally but either certificate is quite acceptable.

As well as successfully completing the course you must have a diving medical examination before your certificate can be issued. Certain medical conditions, such as asthma, do not go with diving.

Don't let having a certificate lull you into thinking you know everything. As with any activity, experience is vitally important. As well as your diving certificate every diver has a log book in which they should record every dive they make. If a proposed dive is

QUEENSLAND TOURIST & TRAVEL CORPORATION

Colourful surprises greet divers around every corner

deep or difficult a good dive operator should check your log book to ensure your experience is sufficient. A high proportion of diving accidents happen to inexperienced divers 'getting out of their depth'.

Equipment

Dive operators can rent out all diving gear but most divers prefer to have at least some of their own equipment. The usual minimum is mask, snorkel, fins and boots. These are items most divers have personal preferences for and are happiest using their own equipment. These things are also relatively light and compact to pack.

Other necessary scuba diving equipment includes:

• Air cylinders – don't bother bringing your own
• Buoyancy vest – readily available but some divers prefer to have their own
• Depth gauge & tank pressure gauge – readily available but again some divers like their own familiar equipment
• Regulator – many divers like to have their own regulator with which they are familiar and confident
• Weight belt & weights – there is absolutely no reason to bring lead weights with you to the reef
• Wetsuit – the waters of the Great Barrier Reef may be warm but a wetsuit is still necessary for comfortable diving, particularly in the southern part of the reef. Having a properly fitting wetsuit is also important, gushes of cold water rushing down your back are never comfortable. On the other hand a wetsuit is relatively bulky to carry around and if you normally dive in colder waters your regular suit may be too thick for the reef.

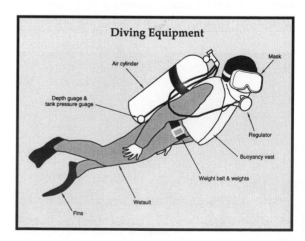

Diving Equipment

Air cylinder

Mask

Depth guage &
tank pressure guage

Regulator

Buoyancy vest

Weight belt & weights

Wetsuit

Fins

Responsible Diving

The popularity of diving is placing immense pressure on many sites. Please consider the following tips when diving and help preserve the ecology and beauty of reefs:

- Do not use anchors on the reef, and take care not to ground boats on coral. Encourage dive operators and regulatory bodies to establish permanent moorings at popular dive sites.
- Avoid touching living marine organisms with your body or dragging gauges or other gear across the reef. Polyps can be damaged by even the gentlest contact. Never stand on corals, even if they look solid and robust. If you must secure yourself to the reef, only hold fast to exposed rock or dead coral.
- Be conscious of your fins. Even without contact the surge from heavy fin strokes near the reef can damage delicate organisms. When treading water in shallow reef areas, take care not to kick up clouds of sand. Settling sand can easily smother the delicate organisms of the reef.
- Practise and maintain proper buoyancy control. Major damage can be done by divers descending too fast and colliding with the reef. Make sure you are correctly weighted and that your weight belt is positioned so that you stay horizontal. If you have not dived for a while, have a practice dive in a pool before taking to the reef. Be aware that buoyancy can change over the period of an extended trip; initially you may breathe harder and need more weighting; a few days later you may breathe more easily and need less weight.
- Take great care in underwater caves. Spend as little time within them as possible as your air bubbles may be caught within the roof and thereby leave previously submerged organisms high and dry. Taking turns to inspect the interior of a small cave will lessen the chances of damaging contact.
- Resist the temptation to collect or buy corals or shells. Aside from the ecological damage, taking home marine souvenirs depletes the beauty of a site and spoils the enjoyment of others. The same applies for marine archaeological sites (mainly shipwrecks). Respect their integrity; they may even be protected from looting by law.
- Ensure that you take home all your rubbish, and any litter you may find as well. Plastics in particular are a serious threat to marine life. Turtles will mistake plastic for jellyfish and eat it.
- Resist the temptation to feed fish. You may disturb their normal eating habits, encourage aggressive behaviour or feed them food that is detrimental to their health.
- Minimise your disturbance of marine animals. In particular, do not ride on the backs of turtles or hang onto whales as this causes them great anxiety.

Shipwreck Diving

Shipwrecks are the main 'artificial' diving attractions on the Great Barrier Reef. Queensland has several of the world's best shipwrecks for diving, although certainly none of them can be ranked among the most accessible or easiest of wreck dives.

The most popular is the *Yongala* (max depth 30m). It is accessible from a number of locations along the North Queensland coast. Mainly from Townsville and from Airlie Beach where several dive shops offer tours to the wreck. Tours range from day trips to live-on-board trips lasting several days, which include visits to other dive locations in the general area.

Another wreck accessible from Townsville and Airlie Beach is the *Gothenburg* (max depth 18m), lost on Old Reef off Bowen in 1875. Although not as spectacular, nor as challenging as the *Yongala*, the *Gothenburg* is an interesting dive and a better location for novice wreck divers to practice wreck diving skills.

Much further north, in fact almost at the very end of the east coast, lies the *Quetta* (1890; max depth 24m), another passenger ship which, like the *Yongala* and the *Gothenburg*, was wrecked with the loss of hundreds of lives. Seasoned wreck divers argue whether the *Quetta* isn't actually a better wreck dive than the *Yongala*. Access to the *Quetta* is difficult (and expensive), not only because of its remote location but mainly because it lies in waters which are exposed to strong currents. Novice divers should be very wary here! Unless you have a private vessel, getting there is easiest by dive charter boat.

Two recently discovered wrecks lie off Cardwell and Cairns. Neither has been positively identified, but the one off Cardwell is thought to be the coal carrier *Lady Bowen* (1894). The one off Cairns is referred to as the 'Green Island wreck'; it appears to be a vessel which was scrapped and stripped of all its fittings before it was deliberately scuttled. Both are deep dives (max depth 32m) and lie in open waters, susceptible to strong currents.

At considerably less depth (6m) lies the *Tambaroora*, on Polmaise Reef off Gladstone in the Southern Great Barrier Reef. It is relatively easy to get to, but because it was wrecked on the exposed side of the reef, it is only really accessible during calm weather when swells breaking on the reef do not cause too much turbulence. For more information on many of the ships wrecked on the Barrier Reef see the Shipwrecks boxed text in Facts about the Great Barrier Reef chapter.

Shipwreck Dive Considerations

All shipwrecks off the Australian coast wrecked more than 75 years ago are considered to be of historic value; consequently these are protected under Commonwealth legislation. The Historic Shipwrecks Act (1976) provides for two levels of protection: free access and restricted access. Some wrecks of exceptional cultural significance (for instance, the *Pandora* and the *Yongala*) have been placed within a special zone and are therefore restricted access wrecks. As such, you can only dive on them with a permit. Most dive charter operators are aware of this and usually have permits for their vessels. However, if you are on a private vessel you should make sure you get a permit before visiting.

Permits can be obtained from The Director, Queensland Museum, PO Box 3300, South Brisbane, Qld 4101, or by phoning the Queensland Museum's Maritime Archaeology Section (☎ 07 3840 7675) or Townsville (☎ 07 4721 1662). Permit applications take about a week to process. You are required to provide registration details for the vessel you are on, the number of divers it is carrying and, as the applicant, you must be willing to accept responsibility for ensuring that the permit conditions are complied with.

Permit applications are very rarely refused, even for sites which are of exceptional historic significance. Permits stipulate special conditions, which vary at each wreck. However, one condition that never varies, even at free access wreck sites, is that a historic wreck, its 'goodies' and its flora and fauna may not be disturbed. This applies to all wrecks, even the ones not within a special zone. It also means that artefacts are not to be touched or removed and marine life on or around the wreck not to be unduly disturbed. Some divers, inveterate 'wreck ratters', consider this condition as evidence of a greedy government, or greedy state museums, intent on 'keeping everything for themselves'! But the real reason for this condition is that it reflects a growing recognition that shipwrecks are part of Australia's cultural heritage and deserve to be protected for everybody to enjoy and appreciate on-site in perpetuity.

Under the Historic Shipwrecks Act a number of Australian museums and heritage protection agencies have been appointed as custodians of Australia's maritime heritage (including shipwrecks). For wrecks in Great Barrier Reef waters this is the Queensland Museum.

In addition to displays and information about wrecks off Queensland's coast, the Queensland Museum's Maritime Archaeology Section also offers internationally accredited (AIMA/NAS) courses in maritime archaeology for qualified scuba divers. Some of the courses are run in conjunction with dive charter operators (for instance with Undersea Explorer in Port Douglas) and include six day, live-on-board tours to the wrecks of the *Foam*, *Gothenburg* and *Yongala* off Townsville.

The museum is currently involved in an extensive maritime archaeological excavation of the *Pandora* historic shipwreck. A comprehensive display of the *Pandora* excavation is planned for a new wing of the Museum of Tropical Queensland in Townsville, which is due to open in early 2000.

(From page 32)

Snorkelling

If you can swim then you can also snorkel and the Great Barrier Reef is simply one of the best places in the world for this activity. Some islands are much better than others for snorkelling: at some there's virtually no snorkelling to speak of while at others there's a wonderland waiting just a few steps out from the beach. Everywhere there will be snorkelling and diving trips on offer, however. Trips out to the outer reef will always offer an opportunity to do some snorkelling, and scuba diving trips will often take snorkellers along as well.

Every resort will have snorkelling equipment that you can borrow or rent. Of course if you've got your own that certainly makes life somewhat easier and you won't face the risk of finding that you've got an odd-shaped face that most masks won't fit.

Snorkelling Equipment There are only three pieces of equipment for snorkelling.

Mask First and most essential there's the mask, which lets you see underwater. The reason you can't see underwater normally is that your eyes won't focus in water. Fish eyes were designed to focus underwater, ours weren't. The mask introduces an air space in front of your eyes so you can focus.

Masks cost anything from $10 to hundreds of dollars and, as with most things, you get what you pay for. Any mask, however, no matter how cheap, should have a shatterproof lens. That's the one essential to check before you try a mask on.

Next you must make sure it fits and this is highly dependent on the shape of your face. Some people find almost any mask fits easily, others find oval masks fit better, others square ones. If the mask doesn't fit well, it will gradually fill with water and you'll have to stop periodically to clear the water out, which can be annoying. To check if a mask fits well, simply fit it to your face without the strap around the back of your head. Breathe in through your nose and if the fit is good the suction should hold the mask on your face.

If you're shortsighted and serious about snorkelling or scuba diving you can get the mask lens ground to your optical prescription or, rather easier, get a stick-on optical lens to attach to the inside of the mask lens. If you wear contact lenses you can wear these with a mask, although there is the risk of losing them if your mask is accidentally flooded. Actually, the altered focal length of light underwater often compensates quite well for shortsightedness.

Snorkel With your mask on you can now see fine underwater, but every time you want to breathe you must raise your head out of the water. This will be the instant that the fish you were quietly observing shoots for cover. A snorkel lets you breathe with your face down in the water. It's simply a curved tube with a mouthpiece, which you grip in your teeth. The tube curves round beside your head and you breathe in and out through your mouth. When you dive underwater the snorkel tube fills with water, which you expel, once back on the surface, by simply blowing out forcefully. The snorkel tube has to be long enough to reach above the surface of the water but should not be either too long or too wide. If it is too big then you have more water to expel when you come to the surface and it's not pleasant to find that first gulp of fresh air is mostly seawater. Also, each breath out leaves a snorkel full of used air. Normally, this only slightly dilutes the fresh air you breathe in but if the snorkel is too big you could breathe in too much carbon dioxide.

Fins The third part of a snorkeller's equipment is not absolutely necessary. If fins are available it's always nice to use them, but if not you can still snorkel without them. As with masks, fin selection is very much a matter of personal preference. What fits and suits one person another person simply cannot get along with. Fins either fit completely over your foot or have an open back with a strap around your heel. The latter generally offer more adjustment and are more comfortable. If you're serious about your underwater activities then you should really buy fins in conjunction with wet-suit boots. These boots make the fins more comfortable and a better fit and they can also be used for walking across reefs.

Reef Walking
Reef walking has always been a popular alternative to snorkelling or diving on the Great Barrier Reef; however, as harmless as walking over a stretch of reef at low tide may seem it can cause substantial damage, which takes the reef years to recover from, and we recommend travellers don't do it.

However, if you *must* walk on the reef please consider the following essential rules to lessen your impact on the reef and its impact on you:

- Observe warnings – some sections of the reef are already fragile and if warned by resort staff or other operators not to walk on a particular section please follow their advice.
- Take care of the reef – walk gently, avoid breaking coral, replace any rocks that you move (it could be some creature's home) and be aware of the regulations regarding collecting.
- Wear strong soled shoes (an old pair of sturdy runners is ideal) – coral cuts can be difficult to heal, urchin spines are difficult to remove and you certainly don't want to find out what happens when you step on a stonefish. Ankle and leg protection is also a good idea.
- Wear a hat, a shirt and apply a sunscreen – it's easy to get sunburnt
- Take care at all times – watch for the turn of the tides, you may only be centimetres above sea level and tides can flood in rapidly; be careful what you pick up.

Viewing the Reef
The cheapest way to get a good look at the reef is to do a day trip from somewhere like Cairns, where the reef is relatively close to the coast. Other options are to go to one of the islands on a package deal that includes boat and snorkelling trips or take a one or two day island trip and make reef trips from there independently. See the Mainland Gateways chapter for complete details on the mainland jumping-off points.

Boating
Sailing is a popular Great Barrier Reef activity whether it's cruising the length of the reef in your own yacht, taking a turn round the bay in a resort catamaran or chartering a bareboat for a week. Bareboat means you rent the fully equipped boat which you then provision and sail yourself. The vast majority of bareboat chartering on the Great Barrier Reef is in the Whitsundays. If you don't have the experience or the inclination to go sailing, it's also possible to charter cruisers and again, the Whitsundays is the most popular place to do it. See the Whitsunday Islands chapter for more information on boating on the reef, including contacts for the main bareboat rental operators.

Shell Collecting
Limited shell collecting, which the Great Barrier Reef Marine Park Authority defines as collecting by hand of not more than five examples of a particular unprotected species in any 28 day period, is only permitted in areas of the Great Barrier Reef zoned General Use A or B. Many of the areas around national park islands on the reef where resorts are located are zoned Marine National Park A or B, where collecting is not permitted. Collecting in the Far North Section (ie north of Lizard Island) without a permit is prohibited.

Reef souvenir shell collectors are asked only to collect dead specimens of unprotected species. Living shells are a vital part of the marine ecosystem.

The following guidelines should also be followed:

- Do not break or damage coral to look for shells
- If you have to, take shells only in accordance with the GBRMPA guidelines
- Replace overturned rocks (with care) to their original position
- Minimise disturbance to shell's habitat
- Do not remove juvenile shells or live shells with eggs on them

Marine Dangers

For some people coral reefs conjure visions of hungry sharks, fierce moray eels, stinging jellyfish and other aquatic menaces. In actual fact the dangers are slight and in most cases it's simply a matter of avoiding touching or picking up things that are best left alone. The basic rules of reef safety are:

1. Don't walk on reefs or in the shallow water between reefs without wearing shoes with strong soles.
2. Don't eat fish you don't know about or can't identify.
3. Don't pick up cone shells.
4. Don't swim in murky water, try to swim in bright sunlight.

Sharks Hungry sharks are the stereotypical aquatic nasties but for sharks on the Great Barrier Reef there is no shortage of meals that are far tastier and more conveniently bite-sized than humans. Tiger sharks and whaler sharks are found on the reef but generally on drop-offs from the outer reef. Sharks are a negligible danger.

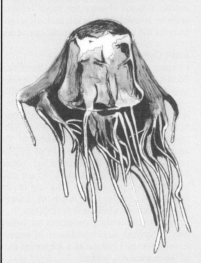

Jellyfish Australia has a very dangerous jellyfish, the box jellyfish or sea wasp. Fortunately the chances of meeting this creature on the reef or islands is remote, although on some of the islands close to the coast this jellyfish can still pose a danger. It is chiefly found around river mouths or in other muddy, shallow water, and only during the summer months. It is possible that a box jellyfish could drift out from the mainland to one of the closer islands but it's most unlikely.

Vinegar neutralises stinging cells that may have adhered to the skin but not actually fired. Don't peel off adhering tentacles, this will cause more of the stinging cells to fire. Death from a box jellyfish sting is due to respiratory arrest so keeping the victim breathing, if necessary by applying artificial respiration, is most important. Medical help should be sought as quickly as possible. An antivenin is available.

Butterfly Cod & Stonefish These two fish are closely related and have a series of poisonous spines down their back. The butterfly cod, also known as the lionfish or firefish, is an incredibly beautiful and slow-moving creature – it's as if it knows it's deadly and doesn't worry about possible enemies. Even brushing against the spines can be painful but a stab from them could be fatal. Fortunately it's hard to miss a butterfly cod, so unless you stepped on one or deliberately hit one, the danger is remote.

Stonefish are the ugly sibling of the beautiful butterfly cod. They lie on the bottom, where they merge into the background. When you step on a stonefish, the 13 sharp dorsal spines pop up and inject a venom that causes intense pain and can cause death. Fortunately stonefish are usually found in shallow, muddy water, but they can also be found on rocky and coral bottoms.

Wearing shoes with strong soles is the best protection but if you are unlucky, bathing the wound in very hot water reduces the pain and the effects of the venom. An antivenin is available and medical attention should be sought as the aftereffects can be very long lasting.

Cone Shells Cone shells kill their prey by firing a poisonous barb. Several of these shells are so poisonous that they have caused human deaths. Although the barb is fired from the pointed end of the shell it's possible to get stung from any angle. The geographer cone is particularly dangerous. Cone shells are very  pretty but any Great Barrier Reef shell, and particularly the cone shells, should be handled with great caution.

Pressure immobilisation, as for snake bites, is the recommended treatment. The affected limb should be tightly bound with bandages (not a tourniquet) and tied to a splint or in some way immobilised.

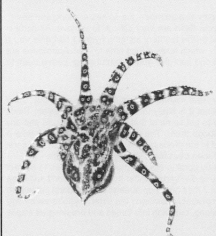

Blue-Ringed Octopus The blue-ringed octopus, which is found in a smaller southern variety and a large tropical type, can inflict a potentially deadly bite with its beak. The pretty little blue-ring is the world's only deadly octopus. To be bitten by an octopus you must first pick it up so the easy solution is not to do this. Unwary people, especially curious children, occasionally pick up octopuses that have been stranded by the tide in rock pools. The blue-ringed octopus is easily identified by the bright blue circles that appear when it is threatened.

Pressure immobilisation is the preferred treatment and medical attention should be sought as quickly as possible. The poison can result in respiratory failure so keeping the victim breathing is most important.

Fish Poisoning 'Human bites fish' can be just as dangerous as 'fish bites human'. Ciguatera poison is a poison that seems to accumulate in certain types of fish due to the consumption of certain types of algae by grazing fish. The poison seems to concentrate the further up the food chain it goes so it isn't the original algae-eating fish that poses the danger, it's the fish that eats the fish that eats the algae-eating fish. The danger is remote, though recovery, although usually complete, is very slow. Chinaman-fish, red bass, large rock cod and moray eels have all been implicated.

One fish that is poisonous all the time is the pufferfish – don't go dining on it unless you're a Japanese *fugu* fan.

Stingrays Stepping on stingrays is also not a good idea. They lie on sandy bottoms and if you step on one, its barbed tail can whip up into your leg and cause a nasty, poisoned wound. Furthermore sand tends to drift over stingrays so they can become all but invisible while basking on the bottom. Fortunately, although they may be invisible to you, you are certainly not invisible to them and stingrays will usually wake up and zoom away as you approach. If you're out walking in the sort of sandy shallows that rays like it's wise to shuffle along and make some noise. Bathing the affected area in hot water is the best treatment and medical attention should be sought to ensure the wound is properly cleaned.

Sea Snakes Sea snakes are deadly poisonous and they have the scary habit of being extremely curious. The last thing you want is something potentially fatal winding itself around your arm in order to sneak a peek inside your diving mask. Fortunately the sea snake's curiosity is usually friendly rather than malevolent and people unfortunate enough to get bitten by one are usually fishers who have pulled them out of the water – which is enough to make any sea creature see red.

Other Stinging Things Don't step on spiny sea urchins – the spines are long and sharp, break off easily and once embedded in your flesh are very difficult to remove. All coral is poisonous and brushing against fire coral or the feathery stinging hydroid can give you a surprisingly painful sting and an itchy rash, which takes a long time to heal. Anemones are also poisonous and putting your arm into one can give you a painful sting. Leave them to the clown fish.

Coral Cuts The most likely Great Barrier Reef marine injury is the simple coral cut. Coral is nasty, sharp stuff and brushing up against it is likely to cause a cut or abrasion. Since coral kills its prey with poison you're likely to get some of that poison in the wound and tiny grains of broken coral are also likely to lodge there. The result is a small cut can take a long, long time to heal and be very painful in the process. The answer is to wash any coral cuts very thoroughly with fresh water and then treat them liberally with antiseptic.

An even better answer is not to get cut by coral in the first place. Wear shoes to protect your feet if you're walking over coral. If you're diving remember that wetsuits don't just keep scuba divers warm, they also protect them if they brush up against coral. A coral cut is also a two-way thing, in cutting yourself you've probably damaged the coral. If you're swimming through a coral garden try not to blunder along, bumping into things and breaking off fragile branching coral.

Other Marine Dangers If you go out of your way looking for trouble it's certainly possible to find it and lots of fish will bite if you put your fingers in their mouths. Lots of scuba divers find this out when they're handfeeding fish but, fortunately, a bite from most small fish is nothing more than a playful nip. A bite from a moray eel is said to be a much more serious affair but eventually every Barrier Reef scuba diver seems to get the opportunity to tickle a friendly moray eel under the chin and they never seem to bite anybody.

Fishing

Although much of the Great Barrier Reef waters are marine park there is an important fishing industry. Prawn trawling is the most important commercial fishing operation along the coast, with prawn trawlers operating the entire length of the east coast of Australia and around into the Gulf of Carpentaria. Scallop trawling is also important in the southern reef waters. Fish like barramundi, salmon, coral trout, red emperor and sweetlip are all economically important, and fish for aquariums are also caught on the reef. Queensland's revered mud crab, a gourmet delight, is also harvested from these waters.

Of course there is more than just commercial fishing along the reef. Queensland has a huge sport-fishing industry ranging from hanging a line off a dinghy to chasing marlin off Cairns; traditional Aboriginal and Torres Strait Islander fishing is another area; and the Great Barrier Reef also suffers from a variety of illegal fishing activities. Over the years Queensland has acquired quite a fleet of confiscated Asian fishing vessels, caught illegally poaching in Australian territorial waters. The protected giant clams are a favourite for some of these fishermen and if you visit the underwater observatory off Great Keppel Island you can see a confiscated Taiwanese fishing boat, sunk beside the observatory to provide a haven for fish.

Recreational Fishing Recreational line fishing is permitted in General Use A and B zones, Habitat Protection zones and Estuarine Conservation zones. Limited line fishing is also allowed in some Marine National Park A zones.

Spearfishing while scuba diving is prohibited, but it is allowed in some General Use sections when snorkelling.

Zoning maps and information are available from GBRMPA or Department of Environment offices (see the Information section earlier in this chapter).

Be aware that catch quotas and minimum legal lengths apply to a variety of fish and shellfish. Make sure you know what is legal and what is not. For further information contact the Queensland Fish Management Authority (☎ 3227 6250) in Brisbane. To report any illegal fishing activities, contact the Fisheries Enforcement Hotline on 1800 017 116.

Other Activities

Most island resorts will have a range of watersports equipment available for resort guests and day-trippers. This typically includes windsurfers, catamarans, jet skis, paddleboats and fishing dinghies. Parasailing and waterskiing are also popular, or if you need a major adrenalin fix you can even try tandem skydiving in some places.

Cruising the reef in a glass-bottomed boat or a semi-submersible is another popular activity – it's a bit like going snorkelling, but without getting wet.

WORK

The Great Barrier Reef resorts employ lots of short-term and temporary staff and many move from job to job and resort to resort, although getting a foot in the door initially can be difficult. There tends to be a very high staff turnover at many resorts, partly because the staff are fairly footloose and partly because the work is very seasonal. Many resorts work on the NBO (next boat out) principle, sacking excess staff as soon as times go slack, taking more on when school holidays roll around.

See the Visa section earlier in this chapter for details about working visas and who is eligible for them.

ACCOMMODATION
Resort Types

The division between active or passive seems to be the main distinction between the island resorts. Some places can run you ragged from dawn to long after dusk with a wide variety of activities, like at islands like Lizard or Heron, to the assiduous pursuit of the opposite sex at young people's resorts like Great! Keppel. Other resorts are passive with the emphasis on fine food and wine and luxurious accommodation – Hayman and Bedarra are good examples of this type of island. Of course every resort is a bit of both: any island vacation entails some lazing on the beach and navel contemplation; similarly nobody is going to get this close to the reef without at least thinking about strapping on a mask and snorkel and having a closer look.

There are two important considerations about the resorts – how you pay and what happens with children. Some of the resorts are all-inclusive – the daily tariff covers your room, all meals and most activities. Drinks and powered watersport activities are the usual extras but at Bedarra 'all-inclusive' really means that – even drinks, whether you have mineral water or Moet & Chandon, are included. Some resorts, however, are room or bed and breakfast only – everything else costs extra. Hamilton and Hayman islands, where you can really run up an impressive bill, are in this category.

Attitudes to children at the resorts are ambivalent. Some places, like Bedarra, ban them completely, others, like Lizard, have a minimum age limit. Most places welcome children with open arms. It's surprising how many of the resorts – notably Daydream, Great! Keppel, Hayman and South Molle – become family resorts come school holiday time.

The island resorts fit into the following categories:

Diving Specialists – Heron, Lady Elliot and Lizard

Rainforest Islands – Bedarra, Dunk and Hinchinbrook

Young People's – Great! Keppel, Club Crocodile (Long) and Club Med (Lindeman)

Coral Cays – Green, Heron and Lady Elliot

Activities for Kids – Brampton, Great! Keppel, Hayman, Club Med (Lindeman), Dunk, Daydream and South Molle

Small Resorts – Bedarra, Hinchinbrook, Whitsunday Wilderness Lodge (Long) and Orpheus

Big Resorts – Brampton, Dunk, Great! Keppel, Hamilton, Daydream and South Molle

Exclusive & Expensive – Bedarra, Hayman, Lizard, Green and Orpheus

Mass Market – Great! Keppel, Daydream, Club Crocodile (Long), and South Molle

Cheap & Cheerful – Lady Elliot, Magnetic, Palm Bay Hideaway (Long) and Fitzroy

Good Food – Bedarra, Hayman and Hinchinbrook

Eco-resorts – Whitsunday Wilderness Lodge (Long)

Cheap if you Camp – Dunk, Great Keppel, Hinchinbrook, Magnetic, Hook and numerous islands without resorts

Best Beaches – Great Keppel and Lizard

Resort Accommodation

Although the resort accommodation varies quite widely most places emphasise 'getting away from it all' by not having too many telephones, radios, TVs or other contact with the outside world. At some resorts there may be only one or two phones on the entire island.

Otherwise the usual amenities of an Australian hotel/motel are generally available. This means that, almost without exception, every room will have tea and coffee-making equipment plus supplies of tea and coffee. Many rooms will have a fridge (to keep the beer cold), and laundry facilities including irons are usually available.

Costs & Bookings Accommodation costs at the resorts vary widely from resort to resort and season to season. The midwinter school holidays (June and July) is usually the peak cost time. Daily costs at the 'all-inclusive' resorts typically run from $150 per person per day at lower key resorts like Great! Keppel or South Molle right up to $1000 per day at Bedarra. Non-inclusive costs can range from $20 for a bunk bed on Hook (and fix your own meals) to $490 to $600 for a room at Hayman Island (and with meals your costs can soon head towards the Bedarra level). Of course most visitors to these resorts will be on some sort of package deal including airfares.

At a number of resorts standby deals are an interesting possibility. Heron, South Molle, Daydream, Hamilton, Hayman, Club Crocodile (Long Island), Club Med

(Lindeman) and Hinchinbrook resorts are some of the places offering standby rates during off-peak periods. These are usually available only from agents in the mainland jumping-off points. There will be various restrictions such as when bookings can be made and how long they can be made for, but the bottom line is often half price or less and very often includes transfers to and from the island. If you just happen to be up the coast and fancy a few days on an island, these deals can be worth watching out for.

Similarly, when business is slack on the reef, special packages are often offered in the southern capitals – seven days on island X at $Y including airfare from Sydney might be the deal.

Any cheap deal is, of course, only going to be available at the quiet times of year.

When a chilly June wind blows over Melbourne and the kids are on school vacation many Great Barrier Reef resorts will be posting 100% occupancy rates. If you plan to visit the reef at that time of year *book ahead*.

Other Accommodation Alternatives

If your credit cards aren't strong enough to support resort living there are a number of alternatives to still enjoy this magnificent part of the world, apart from camping. Great Keppel, Magnetic, Hook and Fitzroy islands have hostels or backpacker accommodation, while several other islands have cabins or permanent tents.

Magnetic Island also has a large number and wide variety of hotels, motels and other accommodation.

Island Camping

Camping on islands of the Great Barrier Reef offers the chance for a great Robinson Crusoe experience and is an opportunity not to be missed. Most of the islands are national parks, and so permits are required before you can land on them. Facilities on the islands range from absolutely nil to shower blocks and picnic tables.

The ecosystems of the reef islands are very fragile and so campers need to take special care that they don't do anything to upset the balance. As the islands are also isolated, careful preparation is also required. The following guidelines may help:

NICK TAPP

- All plants and animals on the islands are protected
- Engine-driven equipment is banned on most islands
- Camp in designated areas only
- Fires are generally banned, and so you need to bring a fuel stove. Where fires are allowed, you'll need to bring firewood as all trees and driftwood are protected.
- Litter is a real problem on the islands. All your litter must be taken back to the mainland with you.
- Water is often scarce, completely unavailable or not suitable for drinking. Bring supplies with you where necessary – count on 5L per person per day, plus three days extra supply.
- Be aware that the island you are on could be isolated by rough weather or strong winds. Carry emergency supplies in case of an enforced stay of an extra day or two. A mobile phone can be handy if the island you are on is within range (many are).

Camping

While staying on the Barrier Reef islands costs some people hundreds of dollars a day others have just as good a time for only a few dollars a day. The latter are camping and there is an amazing variety of camping possibilities along the reef. Many of the islands are national parks and with a permit from the Department of Environment you are able to camp on a wide variety of islands at minimal cost. A few islands have resorts and campsites. At Great Keppel, for example, you can camp for $8 a night and still wander up the beach and get wrecked at the Anchorage Bar disco, just like the resort guests.

Camping facilities vary widely – sites like Great Keppel, Dunk or Fitzroy are just like mainland commercial camping sites with running water, flush toilets, shops and supplies. Others may have minimal facilities – perhaps just pit toilets and freshwater. Others may have virtually nothing at all – bring a shovel for toilet use, water for drinking and a stove and fuel for cooking.

Camping is not allowed on all national park islands but on those where it is, a permit is required. The following chart details the possible camping islands or island groups and which Department of Environment (D of E) office handles permit requests. In some groups, like the Whitsundays, there are a great number of possible camping areas. See the island chapters for more details.

Islands from south to north:

Camping Islands	T	D	D of E
Capricorn Group	✓	–	Gladstone
Keppel Group	✓	–	Rockhampton
Cumberland Group	–	–	Mackay
Whitsunday Islands			Whitsunday
Orpheus Island	✓	–	Cardwell
Hinchinbrook Island	✓	✓	Cardwell
Family Islands	–	–	Cardwell
Dunk Island	✓	✓	Cardwell
Lizard Island Group	✓	✓	Cairns

T – toilets; D – drinking water; D of E – office for bookings & information.

See the Information section earlier in this chapter for addresses and phone numbers of the relevant Department of Environment offices.

Permits for camping on national park islands cost $3.50 per person. The permits should be applied for at least six weeks in advance. Since there are limits on the maximum number of campers on most islands, at peak times of year it's possible that an island can be booked right out.

Enclose a stamped self-addressed envelope when applying for a permit and give the group leader's name and address, boat number if you have your own boat, number in the party, expected date of arrival and proposed length of stay, and desired site or alternatives. If you've left it too late to apply in writing it's worth phoning, so long as there are still vacancies, the relevant office as it may be possible to get a permit number over the phone.

A problem with many of the national park camping islands is getting out to them. It's no problem from resort islands like Great Keppel or Dunk where transport is regular and reasonably priced but if you don't have your own boat it's more problematic from some other islands. In some cases there are regular day trips that can get you out to the islands; in the Whitsundays you can often arrange to be dropped off and later picked up from one of the regular 'moseying around the islands' day trips. On other islands the only way to do it may be by chartering a boat, in which case you'll probably want to get a group of people together in order to share the costs. For more details see under the individual islands.

FOOD

With the exception of Hamilton and Magnetic islands, where accommodation is room-only and there is a wide variety of restaurants to sample, the food situation on the islands usually follows two opposite extremes. Either you bring everything yourself (if you're camping out on an island for example) or everything is included in the price (most resort islands quote all-inclusive tariffs, which include all your meals). At some resorts the meals package is an optional extra.

Don't plan to lose weight on a Great Barrier Reef resort visit – they usually feed you very well. Breakfast will typically include fruit, cereals and a cooked breakfast too if you can manage it. At most larger resorts lunch will be help-yourself buffet-style and at dinner time there'll be a four-course meal.

Seafood

Of course there will be some emphasis on fresh seafood although, surprisingly, the fish may not come from around your island getaway. It's likely that your island is zoned as part of the marine park where commercial fishing is not allowed. So while you may be able to catch a fish yourself and ask the chef to cook it for you, the resort can't go out and catch a fish for all their guests. Nevertheless there will be seafood and it will be fresh.

Some seafood specialities you may encounter include barramundi (one of the best eating fish) found in rivers and estuaries in northern Australia. The coral trout is probably the best eating fish on the reef, and also one of the prettiest. Other popular fish caught along the reef include tuna, sweetlips, bream and mangrove jack.

A great number of prawns are caught along the Queensland coast – many are then frozen and exported, although a fair number are served up fresh. You'll see the prawn trawlers anchored off some reef resorts as the crew usually trawl by night and sleep by day. Moreton Bay is in the south of the state near Brisbane, and Moreton Bay bugs (what an off-putting name) are a sort of miniature lobster or giant-size prawn. They rarely get over 15cm long but whatever size they're delicious and often feature on Queensland menus. So do mud crabs, also known as mangrove crabs. These monsters can grow to a couple of kilograms and are indeed fond of mud. They've got big bodies, big claws, which means they have plenty of meat, and are very tasty.

Fruit

Fresh Queensland fruit will often feature on the menu come dessert time and it's become much more interesting since attention has been turned to growing exotic tropical fruits in north Queensland. The exotic tropical fruits found in South-East Asia take a long time to establish but many Australians have come back from Indonesia, Malaysia, Singapore or Thailand with a taste for rambutans, mangosteens and other delicacies that are starting to appear in Queensland fruit salads. It certainly makes a difference to the great Australian dessert, the pavlova – a concoction of meringue, whipped cream and fruit.

DRINKS

Resort bars will have a wide variety of Australian wines, champagnes and beers. The wine lists usually include a good selection of popular and very good Australian wines, which will usually be sold by the bottle, but may also be sold by the glass.

Beer is a chauvinistic subject in Queensland and as well as the familiar 'southern' brands like Tooheys, VB and Foster's you'll also find Cairns NQ, XXXX (Fourex) and Powers. Boutique beers have also caught on in a big way in Australia and there are also popular specialist brands like Cascade and Redback. A cold beer goes down well after a hot day on the reef.

THINGS TO BUY

Resort stores generally have toiletries, suntan lotion, insect repellent, magazines, books, film, souvenirs and the like. Although most of those essential but easily forgotten items are there, they are generally more expensive than on the mainland.

If you need a souvenir of the islands, the resort T-shirts are probably the best buys. There's usually a boutique or at least a boutique section in the resort stores that often have an excellent selection of summery clothes and swim gear. Surprisingly, the prices are often not too outrageous and if you need a new swimsuit you may well find the choice is better than back home.

Shells, shell jewellery and coral jewellery are sold at many resorts. With strict regulations about shell collecting you can be sure these shells have been properly collected. Nevertheless, shells are still best left in the sea.

Getting There & Away

Getting to the Barrier Reef islands may involve two moves – from overseas to Australia and then from within Australia to the various jumping-off points to the reef islands. You can fly directly from overseas to two major reef jumping-off points – Cairns and Townsville – but other places will require further travel within Australia.

To Australia

AIR

Basically getting to Australia means flying. Once upon a time the traditional transport between Europe and Australia was by ship but those days have ended. Infrequent and expensive cruise ships apart, there are no regular shipping services to Australia. It is, however, sometimes possible to hitch a ride on a yacht to or from Australia – you'll certainly see plenty of cruising yachts sailing through the Great Barrier Reef.

Australia is a long way from anywhere. Coming from Asia, Europe or North America there are lots of competing airlines and a wide variety of airfares but there's no way you can get around those great distances. If you want to fly to Australia at a particularly popular time of year (the middle of summer, ie Christmas time, is notoriously difficult) or on a particularly popular route (like Singapore-Sydney) then plan well ahead.

Australia has a large number of international gateways but if you're heading for the reef the most convenient ones will be Cairns or Townsville, right on the reef coast; followed by Brisbane, the capital of the state of Queensland; and then Sydney. Although Sydney is Australia's busiest gateway it makes a lot of sense to avoid arriving or departing there. Sydney's airport is stretched way beyond its capacity and flights are frequently delayed on arrival and departure. If you can organise your flights to avoid Sydney it's a wise idea.

Tickets

Discount Tickets Buying airline tickets these days is like shopping for a car, a stereo or a camera – five different travel agents will quote you five different prices. Rule number one if you're looking for a cheap ticket is to go to an agent, not directly to the airline. The airline will often only quote you the absolutely straight-up-and-down, by-the-rulebook regular fare. An agent, on the other hand, can offer all sorts of special deals particularly on competitive routes.

Ideally an airline would like to fly all their flights with every seat in use and every passenger paying the highest fare possible. Fortunately life usually isn't like that and airlines would rather have a half-price passenger than an empty seat. Since the airline itself can't very well offer seats at two different prices what they do when faced with the problem of too many seats is let agents sell them at cut prices.

Of course what's available and what it costs depends on what time of year it is, what route you're flying and who you're flying with. If you want to go to Australia at the most popular time of year, on one of the very popular routes or via a route where there is little alternative competition, you are likely to have to pay more. Similarly the dirt-cheap fares are likely to be less conveniently scheduled, to go by a less convenient route or be with a less popular airline.

Round-the-World Tickets Round-the-world (RTW) tickets are very popular and many of these will take you through Australia. The airline RTW tickets are often real bargains and, since Australia is pretty much at the other side of the world from Europe or North America, it can work out no more expensive or can be even cheaper to keep going in the same direction right round the world rather than U-turn when you return.

The official airline RTW tickets are put together usually by a combination of two airlines, and permit you to fly anywhere you want on their route systems so long as you don't backtrack. Other restrictions are that you (usually) must book the first sector in advance and cancellation penalties then apply. There may be restrictions on how many stops you are permitted and usually the tickets are valid for 90 days up to a year.

An alternative type of RTW ticket is one put together by a travel agent using a combination of discounted tickets. A UK agent like Trailfinders can put together interesting London to London RTW combinations including Australia.

Circle Pacific Tickets Circle Pacific fares, a similar idea to RTW tickets use a combination of airlines to circle the Pacific – combining Australia, New Zealand, North America and Asia. As with RTW tickets there are advance purchase restrictions and limits on how many stopovers you can take. A possible Circle Pacific route would fly Los Angeles-Honolulu-Auckland-Sydney-Bangkok-Hong Kong-Los Angeles.

Europe
The cheapest tickets in London are from the numerous 'bucket shops' (discount ticket agencies) that advertise in magazines and papers like *Time Out* or *Australasian Express*. Pick up one or two of these publications and ring round a few bucket shops to find the best deal. The magazine *Business Traveller* also has a great deal of good advice on airfare bargains. Most bucket shops are trustworthy and reliable but the occasional sharp operator appears – *Time Out* and *Business Traveller* give some useful advice on precautions to take.

Trailfinders (☎ (071) 938 3366) at 46 Earls Court Rd, London W8, and STA Travel (☎ (071) 581 1022) at 74 Old Brompton Rd, London SW7, and 117 Euston Rd, London NW1 (☎ (071) 465 0484), are good reliable agents for cheap tickets.

The cheapest flights from London to the east coast are usually only available if you leave London in the low season, from March to June. In September and mid-December, fares go up about 30% while the rest of the year they're somewhere in between.

Many cheap tickets allow stopovers on the way to or from Australia. Rules regarding how many stopovers you can take, how long you can stay away, how far in advance you have to decide your return date and so on, vary from time to time and ticket to ticket, but recently most return tickets have allowed you to stay away for any period between 14 days and one year, with stopovers permitted anywhere along your route. As usual with heavily discounted tickets the less you pay the less you get in terms of convenience and popular airlines.

Apart from regular by-the-book fares there are all sorts of ticketing variations and rules including advance purchase periods, seasonal variations in fare and so on.

North America
There are a variety of connections across the Pacific from Los Angeles, San Francisco and Vancouver to Australia, including direct flights, flights via New Zealand, island-hopping routes or more circuitous Pacific rim routes via nations in Asia. Qantas, Air New Zealand, American, United and Continental all have USA-Australia flights. Qantas and Canadian Airlines International operate between Canada and Australia.

To find good fares to Australia check the travel ads in the Sunday travel sections of papers like the *Los Angeles Times, San Francisco Chronicle-Examiner, New York Times* or Toronto's *Globe & Mail*. You can typically get a one-way/return ticket from the west coast for US$998/1498 in the low season, US$1058/1558 in the high season (Australian summer/Christmas period), or from the east coast for US$1179/1378 one way/return in the low season and US$1609/1878 in the high season.

In the USA good agents for discounted tickets are the two student travel operators

Council Travel and STA, both of which have offices around the country. Canadian west coast fares out of Vancouver will be similar to those from the US west coast.

New Zealand

Air New Zealand and Qantas operate a network of trans-Tasman flights linking Auckland, Wellington and Christchurch in New Zealand with most major Australian gateway cities. You can fly directly between a lot of places in New Zealand and a lot of places in Australia including directly to the Barrier Reef gateways of Cairns and Townsville.

Fares vary depending on which cities you fly between and when you do it. One-way fares are not much cheaper than return ones but there is a lot of competition on this route – with United, Continental and British Airways all flying it as well as Qantas and Air New Zealand – so there is bound to be some good discounting going on.

Asia

Ticket discounting is widespread in Asia, particularly in Singapore, Hong Kong, Bangkok and Penang. There are a lot of fly-by-nights in the Asian ticketing scene so a little care is required. Also, the Asian routes have been particularly caught up in the capacity shortages on flights to Australia. Flights between Hong Kong and Australia are notoriously heavily booked while flights to or from Bangkok and Singapore are often part of the longer Europe-Australia route, so they are also frequently very full. Plan ahead.

Africa & South America

The flight possibilities from these continents are not so varied and you're much more likely to have to pay the full fare. There is only one direct route between Africa and Australia and that is the Harare (Zimbabwe)-Perth-Sydney route, flown by Qantas and South African Airways. An alternative from east Africa is to fly from Nairobi to India and South-East Asia and connect from there to Australia.

Two routes operate between South America and Australia. The long running Chile connection involves a Lan Chile flight Santiago-Easter Island-Tahiti from where you fly Qantas or on another airline to Australia. Alternatively Aerolóneas Argentina has a Buenos Aires-Auckland-Sydney route across the Antarctic. This is operated in conjunction with Qantas.

DEPARTURE TAXES

A departure tax of $27 is already included in the price of your ticket so there is nothing to pay when leaving the country.

To Queensland & the Reef

Having arrived in Australia you then have to make your way to the jumping-off points from where you go out to the reef islands. There are five major coastal towns from where you transfer to the islands, plus a number of lesser starting points. The major centres are, from south to north, Rockhampton, Mackay, Airlie Beach, Townsville and Cairns. You can fly to all of these centres and they can also be reached by car, bus or rail. In addition there is one island, Hamilton in the Whitsundays, with a large airstrip and flights from other major centres.

AIR

Australia's two major domestic airlines, Qantas and Ansett, both connect the main coastal centres with other major cities in Australia and Ansett also has direct flights to Hamilton Island from the eastern state capitals. You can usually book connecting flights from these arrival ports directly to many of the reef islands. See the Mainland Gateways chapter for information about transport from the coastal cities to the islands.

Both airlines have centralised bookings

and reservations numbers – for Ansett phone ☎ 13 1300, for Qantas phone ☎ 13 1313.

Airfares are identical on Ansett or Qantas. Regular economy one-way fares to the coastal entry point cities from other major centres are listed below.

Apart from the regular one-way economy fares, there are a variety of other fares. You can pay more and fly business class or there are a variety of discount fares available. Both airlines offer a range of five day (or longer) deals, including flights and accommodation, to their respective resorts that include flights and accommodation – prices vary according to when you are going.

There are also airpasses available with Ansett that allow 6000km of travel for $949 or 10,000km for $1499. Overseas visitors can get a discount of around 30% on the regular airfare with either airline, although this often works out no cheaper than the best discounted fares.

LAND
Bus
Greyhound Pioneer (☎ 13 2030) and Mc-Cafferty's (☎ 13 1499) are the two major companies, and they have services that run the full length of the east coast, connecting in the north with Darwin and in the south with Melbourne and Adelaide.

Approximate fares and travel times to Brisbane include: Sydney $71 (15 to 16 hours); Melbourne $141 (20 to 25 hours); Adelaide $183 (26 to 32 hours). See the Getting Around chapter for information on bus travel up the coast.

Train
You can also get to Brisbane by train. The national booking phone number is ☎ 13 2232. The fare from Sydney ranges from $56 to $93, depending on season and advance purchase conditions. For a 1st class seat it's $78 to $130.

Hitching
Hitching is never entirely safe in any country in the world, and we don't recommend it. Travellers who decide to hitch should understand that they are taking a small but potentially serious risk. People who do choose to hitch will be safer if they travel in pairs and let someone know where they are planning to go.

Getting Around

Having arrived in Queensland you then have to get out to your island, which usually means getting to the appropriate mainland jumping-off point. There are very few direct connections from one reef island to another; you will almost always have to go back to the mainland and on to the next mainland departure point – Hamilton Island is the most obvious exception. Specific information on transport to each island is with the relevant chapter, an overview follows.

AIR

Hamilton Island in the Whitsundays has an airport capable of taking Boeing 767s and similar sized wide-body jets. This is the one island you can fly directly to from a state capital city and Ansett has direct connections with major centres around Australia, mostly via Brisbane but including some direct flights to and from Sydney and Melbourne.

Other airlines useful for getting to the mainland jumping-off points or out to the reef islands include the following.

Sunstate

Sunstate, a Qantas affiliate, is the major regional airline. It has flights to and from Brisbane and between the major towns along the coast, including Bundaberg, Gladstone, Rockhampton, Mackay, Proserpine (for Airlie Beach), Townsville and Cairns. It also flies to a number of islands, including Thursday and Lizard islands from Cairns, to Dunk island from Cairns and Townsville, to Great Keppel from Rockhampton, to Brampton from Mackay, and to Lady Elliot from Bundaberg. For information and bookings on Sunstate contact Qantas.

Flight West

Flight West flies from Cairns to Cooktown and numerous other destinations throughout Queensland. For information and bookings phone ☎ 13 2392.

Helijet Air Services

Helijet operates helicopters, light planes and amphibious aircraft mainly in the southern section of the reef. Phone ☎ 4957 3574 for flight details.

Island Air Taxis

Island Air Taxis connects Lindeman Island with Mackay and the Whitsundays (Airlie Beach). Phone ☎ 4946 9933.

BUS

Greyhound Pioneer (☎ 13 2030) and McCafferty's (☎ 13 1499) operate up and down the coast between Brisbane and Cairns. Travel times and approximate fares are:

Brisbane-Bundaberg	6 hours	$43
Bundaberg-Rockhampton	3½ hours	$42
Rockhampton-Mackay	3¾ hours	$39
Mackay-Airlie Beach	1½ hours	$25
Airlie Beach-Townsville	3 hours	$36
Townsville-Cairns	4½ hours	$38

TRAIN

There's a rail service from Brisbane up the coast to Cairns. The trains are slower and more expensive than buses but generally more comfortable. The trains are almost all air-conditioned and you can get sleeping berths on most trains for $30 a night in economy or $50 in 1st class.

CAR

The Bruce Highway, which runs 1728km from Brisbane to Cairns, is a good, well-surfaced road; driving along the Great Barrier Reef coast presents no problems or surprises. Unfortunately the road very rarely runs right on the coast and some of the towns that act as jumping-off points for the reef are actually some distance off the main road.

Rental cars are available from the major nationwide operators (like Avis, Budget, Hertz and Thrifty) at all the main centres as well as at tourist centres like Airlie Beach. It is possible to rent cars on a one-way basis with the major operators. Usually there is no repositioning charge so long as you rent for a minimum of three days.

BOAT

Boat services operate out to the reef islands and the reef itself from towns up and down the coast. High-speed catamarans have become the standard transport for most reef-resort transfers.

Travelling by private or chartered boat is very popular along the Queensland coast. If you don't have your own boat, there are a number of charter operators in various places, with the highest concentration being in Airlie beach in the Whitsundays. See the Boating section of the Whitsundays chapter for details.

Reef Life

The Great Barrier Reef is the largest coral reef in the world. Every element of its 2000km length teems with life: on the shore of every coral cay, under every rock, in every tidal pool, on every barrier rampart ... colourful and unique creatures abound. This stunning kaleidoscope of life-forms, and the perfect weather that goes hand in hand with it, is what draws so many travellers to this fascinating region.

PHOTO BY SIMON FOALE

Coral

The coral that makes up the vast network of the Great Barrier Reef is formed by a primitive animal, a marine polyp – a tiny tube-like fleshy cylinder that looks very much like its close relations the sea anemones of the family Coelenterata. These polyps form a hard exterior surface by excreting lime; when a polyp dies its 'skeleton' remains and then new polyps grow on their dead predecessors and continually add to the reef.

Tree fern soft coral

Corals catch their prey by means of stinging nematocysts (some of which can give humans a painful sting, such as the fern-like stinging hydroid). The top of the cylinder of a polyp opens and is ringed by waving tentacles that sting and draw into the polyp's stomach (the open space within the cylinder) any passing prey.

Each polyp is an individual creature, but can reproduce by splitting to form a coral colony of separate but closely related polyps. Although each polyp catches and digests its own food, the nutrition passes between the polyps to the whole colony. During the day most coral polyps withdraw into their skeletons and it is only at night that a coral reef can be seen in its full, colourful glory.

Coral needs a number of preconditions for healthy growth. Firstly, the water temperature must not drop below 17.5°C – which is why the Barrier Reef does not continue further south into cooler water. Also, the water must be clear to allow sunlight to penetrate, and it must also be salty. Coral will not grow below 30m depth because the sunlight does not penetrate sufficiently, and it will not grow around river mouths.

Left: Sea fan
Middle: Giant brain coral
Right: Tubastraea coral

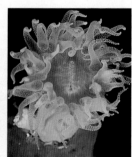

PHOTOS BY MICHAEL AW

Coral is usually stationary and often looks decidedly flowery, but is in fact an animal and a hungry carnivorous animal at that. Hard corals take many forms. One of the most common and easiest to recognise is the staghorn coral, which grows by budding off new branches from the tips. Brain corals are huge and round with a surface looking very

PHOTOS BY MICHAEL AW

much like a human brain. They grow by adding new base levels of skeletal matter and expanding outwards. Flat or sheet corals, like plate coral, expand at their outer edges. Many corals can take different shapes depending on their environment. Staghorn coral can branch out in all directions in deeper water or form flat tables when it grows in shallow water.

Left: Staghorn coral
Right: Plate coral

Like their reef-building relatives, soft coral is made up of individual polyps, but does not form a hard limestone skeleton. Without the protective skeleton hard corals have it would seem likely that soft coral would fall prey to fish, but this is not the case. Soft coral seems to remain relatively immune to predators, either due to toxic substances in its tissues or to the presence of sharp limestone needles, which protect the polyps. Soft corals can move around and will sometimes engulf and kill off a hard coral.

Left: Red whip coral
Bottom: Massive coral
Below: Soft coral

SIMON FOALE

MICHAEL AW

SIMON FOALE

Fish

The Great Barrier Reef has around 2000 species of fish, including everything from tiny gobies, the smallest backboned animals, to huge whale sharks. Some fish are seen in the day while others shelter in crevices and caverns in the coral and only emerge at night. Some are grazers, other hunters. Some huddle together in groups for protection, some are territorial, guarding their own patch of reef fiercely, while others are free ranging.

Reef fish are remarkable for their brilliant and exotic colours and patterns, and for the unique shapes and fascinating behaviours that have helped them adapt to life on the reef.

Left: Clown anemone fish

Right: Blackspotted wrasse

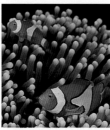

PHOTOS BY SIMON FOALE

Anemone fish, members of the damselfish family, live close to large sea anemones, which normally sting any small fish that come too close. In this symbiotic relationship, however, the fish helps to keep the anemone clean and in return it can swim or nestle among the anemone's deadly tentacles without being stung.

The cleanerfish are **wrasses** that perform an essential cleaning service for other fish, nibbling away at parasites on their bodies (even inside their mouths) and so helping them to stay healthy. The cleanerfish stays at its 'station' while other fish requiring its cleaning services wait their turn.

Angelfish are brilliantly patterned in mainly blue and yellow and tend to live in caves and crevices. Related to the **butterfly fish**,

Below: Emperor angelfish

Right: Spotted boxfish (male)

both species are abundant on the reef. Sometimes the two species interbreed and produce hybrid (sterile) offspring.

In some reef fish, the sexes have very different coloured markings – usually,

PHOTOS BY MICHAEL AW

PHOTOS BY MICHAEL AW

the male is the more attractive. The vivid blue male boxfish, for example, is much more striking than its rather dull female partner.

Many reef fish are hermaphroditic, possessing both male and female reproductive tissues and changing from one sex to another during their lifetime. The **fairy basslet**, **parrotfish**, cleanerfish, angelfish and some anemone fish are capable of sex changes. (See the Reef Fish & Sex boxed text in the Facts about the Region chapter.)

Most reef fish are harmless, but some are best left alone. Despite its pretty blue-and-yellow striped appearance, the **blue-lined surgeonfish** has an aggressive streak, jealously guarding its territory to protect the seaweed it feeds on. Its venomous spines can cause painful injuries.

Members of the spiky-looking scorpionfish family, including the **stonefish** and the **butterfly cod** (or firefish), should also be avoided – their poisonous fin spines can cause death.

Eels are long snake-like fish with sharp teeth and mostly brown or black spotted or striped markings. There are several different types of **moray eels**, mostly living in the crevices of coral reefs. **Snake eels** generally burrow in the sand and are sometimes mistaken for sea snakes. **Garden eels** also live in sandy burrows, usually in large colonies.

Left: Saddled butterfly fish

Middle: Striped surgeonfish

Right: Whitemouth moray eel

PHOTOS BY SIMON FOALE

Left: Redfin anthias

Right: Ragged-finned firefish

Sharks

The mere mention of the word 'shark' often causes people's hearts to skip a beat, although divers and marine biologists have long marvelled at these primitive fishes' sleek, practical and highly streamlined shape. One of nature's most efficient killing machines, sharks are a primitive form of fish with a cartilaginous skeleton. They generally have poor eyesight and hunt food with a highly developed form of sonar.

White-tipped reef shark

There are a variety of sharks found around the reef, although it is unlikely you'll see them unless you seek them out especially. The **white-tipped reef shark** is a small, unaggressive territorial shark rarely more than 1.5m long and often seen over areas of coral or off reef edges. **Black-tipped reef sharks** are also timid, shallow-water dwellers. Even more retiring is the **tessellated wobbegong**, which is sometimes found in reef pools and lies still, relying on its camouflage, rather than trying to escape danger. **Whale sharks** are sometimes seen off the outer reef and can reach over 15m in length. They are the largest fish in the sea but are harmless, feeding on plankton and tiny fish.

Usually sharks are either shy and timid and disappear at first sight or, more often, they simply ignore humans. However, not all are harmless. **Whaler sharks** are common around the reef and can be threatening and very aggressive towards humans and should be treated with caution. A rare sight around the reef is the **tiger shark**, which can grow up to 5m in length. If you do see one of these magnificent creatures on the reef, it's probably time to get out of the water.

Whale shark

PHOTOS BY MICHAEL AW

Stingrays & Manta Rays

Rays are essentially flattened sharks, but their feeding habits are very different to sharks. Stingrays feed on the ocean floor, and are equipped with crushing teeth to grind the molluscs and crustaceans they sift out of the sand. They are very common along the Great Barrier Reef, often lying motionless on the sandy bottom of their favourite shallow bays. It's fun to wade across such a bay, watching them suddenly rise up from the bottom and glide smoothly away. Be wary though, as stingrays are less than impressed when a human foot pins them to the bottom – that barbed and poisonous tail can then swing up and into your leg with painful efficiency.

Manta rays are among the largest fish found on the Great Barrier Reef and a firm favourite of scuba divers. There's nothing quite like the feeling of sensing a shadow passing over the sun and looking up to see a couple of tons of manta ray swooping smoothly through the water above you. They are quite harmless, feeding only on plankton and small fishes, and in some places seem quite relaxed about divers approaching them closely. Manta rays are sometimes seen to leap completely out of the water, landing back with a tremendous splash.

Rays, like sharks, generally give birth to live young. A baby manta ray is born neatly wrapped up in its bat-like wings.

Manta ray

Echinoderms

The echinoderm family consists of five distinct creatures: sea urchins, starfish, brittle stars, feather stars and sea cucumbers (or bêches-de-mer). It is difficult to believe that creatures as different in appearance as the starfish and the sea cucumber are closely related, but the group all share three distinct characteristics. They all have a five-armed body plan, a skeleton of plates, and tube feet that are operated by hydraulic pressure. The five-armed plan of the starfish is easy to see, but it is harder to identify in the sea cucumber.

Echinoidea sea urchin

Sea Urchins

It's the spiny sea urchins that give the echinoderm family its name: in Greek *echino* is spiny and *derm* is skin. With a ball-like body, the sea urchin is covered in spines that can vary considerably from the short blunt spines of the slate-pencil urchin to the long, sharp black spines of *Diadema* urchins.

The sea urchin's mouth at the bottom is a complex structure known as Aristotle's lantern and with this the urchin grazes as it crawls across the sea bottom. Despite the formidable protection of its spines, urchins hide away during daylight and come out to feed at night. Spines or not, some triggerfish will eat sea urchins and in some countries, but not in Australia, sea urchins are a delicacy for human consumption.

Sea urchins taking over a reef

PHOTOS BY MICHAEL AW

Starfish

Starfish, or asteroids, like most echinoderms, are ocean floor dwellers and because they are often brightly coloured and slow moving are relatively easy to spot on the reef. Generally, they have five distinct arms, although some may have more – **crown-of-thorns starfish** usually have 15 or 16 but may also have more. In other starfish, like the rotund-looking **pincushion sea star**, the arms are not distinct at all, but the five-cornered shape is still immediately apparent.

Pincushion sea star

SIMON FOALE

The five arms of a starfish each contain the full quota of organs for respiration, digestion, motion and reproduction. Along the underside of each arm is a groove from where the tiny tube feet emerge. These hydraulically operated feet are the starfish's actual means of locomotion, not the much larger arms. The starfish's mouth, with a surprisingly complex jaw, is at the bottom centre, but some starfish, including the crown-of-thorns, can also consume their prey by a method known as 'stomach eversion'. The stomach is pulled out through the mouth and wrapped over the prey, which is digested before the stomach is pulled back inside.

Echinoderms in general have strong powers of regeneration and can often regenerate the entire creature from an unattached arm.

The vivid **blue starfish** are widespread throughout the Pacific and easily recognisable by their distinct colouring, but the **brown sea star** is probably the most common.

Left: Linkia sea star, growing a new leg

Right: Fromia sea star

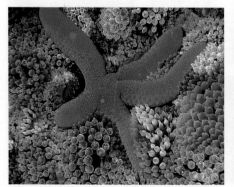

PHOTOS BY MICHAEL AW

Crown-of-thorns starfish

The **crown-of-thorns starfish** is the best known of the Great Barrier Reef's starfish. Once dubbed 'the monster that ate the Great Barrier Reef', recent research seems to indicate that the crown-of-thorns is a natural part of the reef's lifecycle.

Brittle Stars & Feather Stars

Brittle stars and feather stars are two more examples of the incredible variety of echinoderms. The small circular body of the **brittle star** contains the main organs, unlike starfish where each arm has a full complement of organs. The brittle star's arms are constructed of segmented sections of 'skeleton', rather like the vertebrae in a mammal's backbone. It's the arms that give the brittle star its name as they are indeed very brittle and will break off if the creature is mishandled.

Feather stars, or crinoids, are the most primitive of the echinoderm group and look much more like a plant than an animal. At one time crinoids were the dominant form of sea life, but feather stars are the only species in the family still found. Although feather stars can move around they usually stay firmly attached in one place, holding on to the coral, rock or some other suitable anchor with their cirri (tentacle or filament), while the arms wave in the water and their numerous pinnules give them their characteristic feather-like appearance.

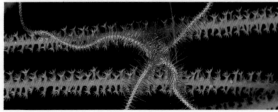

Left & right: Two different but equally brilliant feather stars

Bottom: A brittle star on several sea whips

PHOTOS BY MICHAEL AW

Crustaceans

SIMON FOALE

Crustaceans – the hard-shelled creatures like crabs, shrimps and lobsters – are one of the most varied group of animals found on the Great Barrier Reef. Crabs scuttling across rocks or island beaches may be quite a familiar sight but many of the marine crustaceans are nocturnal creatures and are rarely seen. For many reef visitors the most commonly seen crustaceans are the ones that decorate their plates at meal time.

Barnacles and a variety of other small creatures are also members of the crustacean family, but it is the decapods – crabs, shrimps, prawns and lobsters – that are the best known. They are characterised by their hard outer covering known as an exoskeleton. Since this cannot grow, crustaceans must shed their skin from time to time and then go through a rapid period of growth before the newly exposed skin hardens. Decapods have five pairs of legs with nippers or large claws called chelae on the front legs. They vary in size from minute shrimps, best seen under a microscope, to large spiny lobsters.

Shrimps

The smallest of this group, shrimps are amazingly diverse with even the smallest reefs harbouring several hundred species. Many shrimps live symbiotically with other creatures. There are various cleaner shrimps that offer a cleaning service to larger fish. Some shelter on coral or among the spines of sea urchins. **Prawns**, so important to commercial fishers along the coast, are found in shallow tropical waters but are not common on the reefs.

MICHAEL AW

Hinge beak shrimp

Lobsters

The panulirid lobsters are the largest crustaceans found on the reef. These spiny lobsters are confusingly known by a host of names including rock lobsters, crays and, most commonly, crayfish. They are tasty creatures that unfortunately tend to be difficult to catch – unlike like the cold water lobsters found further south, they will not enter traps.

Lobster

Crabs

The Great Barrier Reef region is home to a great variety of crabs. **Hermit crabs**, which shelter in abandoned gastropod shells in order to protect their soft abdomens, are a common and amusing sight. Some types of hermit crab live on dry land while others live permanently in the water. Whereas other crustaceans shed their hard skins as they grow, hermit crabs simply switch shells. When their current abode becomes too small, hermit crabs inspect a variety of new residences before quickly abandoning one and moving in to another. Sometimes a hermit crab will try to move into a shell that is simply too big, and after discovering the huge effort needed to move it around will change to a less grand mansion. The shell doesn't necessarily have to be empty before the move – if necessary a hermit crab will drag a resident mollusc out of its shell like a landlord evicting a tenant.

Hermit crab

PHOTOS BY MICHAEL AW

Ghost or **sand crabs** are often seen on sandy beaches scavenging for that has washed up on the beach. They're a great danger to vulnerable, recently hatched turtles. Ghost crabs scuttle across the sand at surprisingly high speed and live in long burrows, up to 1m underground. **Fiddler crabs** are another shore-based crab.

The **sponge crab** has tiny claws on its back legs that it uses to clutch a sponge, holding it like an umbrella to disguise its presence. The long-legged and slow-moving **spider**

Decorator crab

crab also relies on camouflage and disguise to evade its enemies. This group also includes the **decorator crab**, which covers itself in bits of debris and vegetation in order to blend into the background.

PHOTOS BY MICHAEL AW

Spider crab

Swimming crabs and **rock crabs** are the most common crabs found on the reef. Swimming crabs include the Queensland gourmet delight, the **mud crab**, which is found in mangroves. Brightly coloured **rock crabs** are very common around branching coral on the reef. Some varieties are even supposed to protect coral from the crown-of-thorns starfish by nipping the starfish's arms.

SIMON FOALE

Spotted reef crab

Molluscs

Invertebrate creatures that inhabit shells are all in the group *Mollusca*, although not all molluscs have shells. The group is a huge one including creatures as diverse as common garden snails at one extreme and octopus at the other. The variety found on the Great Barrier Reef is also immense and falls into several categories.

Cocks comb oyster

Bivalves & Clams

Bivalves, which include oysters and scallops, have a two-half shell that can be closed by powerful muscles. Some bivalves embed themselves in rocks and others can swim, but most live in mud or sand. Great Barrier Reef bivalve shells are generally much more colourful than their cousins from the colder waters further south.

Clams are a common sight on reef flats. The colourful boring clam is the most familiar on the Great Barrier Reef. They gradually grind away coral boulders until they are completely embedded. All bivalves are covered by a flap of skin known as the mantle. The edge of the mantle meets the edge of the shell and creates the shell by adding layer after layer of calcium carbonate along its edge. Only the fleshy shape of the open mantle is visible and it comes in many different colours and makes a fascinating sight for reef walkers.

The giant clam, found in the far north of the Great Barrier Reef, is the largest bivalve in the world. It can reach over 1m in length and weigh over 200kg. Stories abound of divers inadvertently

Variable thorny oyster

PHOTOS BY SIMON FOALE

putting their foot into the shell and being unable to escape when it shut – this is obviously a myth, as the clams shut slowly and none too tightly. Their adductor muscles are certainly strong, however, and persuading a closed clam to reopen is not easy.

Clams are a popular delicacy in parts of Asia and the Pacific. As a result many Pacific reefs have been stripped bare of clams. At Orpheus Island, the marine research station is breeding and raising clams, initially with the intention to repopulate overfished reefs, but also with a view to commercially farming them – dried adductor muscles are worth over US$100 a kilogram in parts of Asia.

A giant clam can reach 50cm in length in less than seven years, and a 50 year old clam has reached a venerable age. The clams start out as microscopic swimming larvae then settle down as minute clams only 0.2mm long. By six months of age, artificially reared clams reach about 1.5cm in length and can be transferred to the sea in protective cages.

Nudibranches

Coming in an amazing variety of colours and shapes – some look like snails minus their shells, while others resemble seaweed – there are four main types of nudibranches. Each type is different, but each has an exposed respiratory organ on its back, the tentacle-like gills are either a small outcrop or stretch the entire length of the body. Most nudibranches range in size from microscopic to just a few centimetres, and their diets can include anemones, hydroids, corals, sponges, fish eggs and crustaceans. A few species are essentially solar-powered, producing carbohydrates through photosynthesis.

Left & right: Nudibranches come in a large array of colours and shapes

PHOTOS BY MICHAEL AW

Gastropods or Univalves

Consisting of everything from snails, limpets and slugs right through to the colourful shells of interest to collectors. (See the Activities section in the Facts for the Visitor chapter for more on shell collecting.)

Cowrie shells are noted for their gently rounded shape, their beautiful patterns and their glossy surface. They are a firm favourite among amateur shell collectors but living examples are mainly seen at night, when they come out in search of food.

Volute shells are also brightly coloured and vary considerably in size. Like cowries they mainly emerge at night when they hunt bivalves and other molluscs. During daylight hours they usually bury themselves in the sand in coral lagoons although volutes can sometimes be seen crawling across the sandy bottom on dull days. The largest of the Great Barrier Reef volutes is the huge **baler shell** (sometimes called a melon shell), which can weigh up to 2kg and reach 40cm in length. It takes its name from its use by Aborigines as a water baler.

Cone shells are also beautiful, but quite dangerous – the cone can shoot out a barbed dart known as a radular tooth. A potent venom is then forced down this hollow tooth and although it is usually used to kill the carnivorous shell's prey, cone shells have caused human deaths. *Conus geographus* is the particularly dangerous cone shell, but all cone shells should be treated with great caution.

Left: Cone shell
Right: Bat volute shell

PHOTOS BY MICHAEL AW

Strombs have a strong foot that is used to close off the shell opening when the creature is inside. The spider shell is a particularly popular stromb with collectors.

Octopus & Squid

It scarcely seems credible that cephalopods, the tentacled octopus and squid, should be related to oysters, clams, cowries and cone shells, yet all are molluscs. The eight-tentacled octopus usually shelters in a cavity or cave in the coral, coming out to grab unwary fish or crustaceans, which it kills with an often venomous bite from its beak-like jaws. The **common Great Barrier Reef octopus** spans about 60cm across its tentacles, but the only variety that is dangerous to humans is the tiny **blue-ringed octopus**. This pretty little octopus is instantly identi-

Ornate octopus

MARK NORMAN

fiable by the bright blue rings that appear all over its head and legs when it is disturbed. Although it only grows to about 15cm across, its bite can cause death from respiratory arrest.

Squid are rather like a longer, streamlined version of an octopus. Like an octopus, they move by a form of jet propulsion, squirting out the water they take over their gills. They can move at remarkable speed and catch their prey, usually small fish and crustaceans, by shooting out two long tentacles. Like octopus they are also masters of disguise, able to change their colour by squeezing or flattening out cells that contain coloured material.

Cuttlefish are like a larger squid and, along with speed and the ability to change colour, they also perform a

Big fin reef squid

type of smokescreen trick. When threatened they turn a dark colour then shoot out a blob of dark ink that takes a cuttlefish-like shape. The real cuttlefish then rapidly turns a lighter colour and shoots away, leaving the predator to grab at its ghost. The familiar cuttlebone found washed up on beaches is a cuttlefish's internal skeleton. This skeleton is made up of dozens of thin layers, and by filling the space between these layers with gas the cuttlefish is able to float.

Octopus and squid have evolved from earlier cephalopods that had external shells. The **nautilus** is the best known and most spectacular survivor of these creatures. Its large brown and white shell is divided into chambers and the tentacled creature can vary its buoyancy by changing the amount of gas and liquid in individual chambers. These creatures avoid the light and warm waters and usually live on the external slopes of the reef at depths up to 500m. Feeding on crabs and shrimps, the nautilus uses its many tentacles (about 90 around the mouth) to feed and protect itself.

Cuttlefish

PHOTOS BY MICHAEL AW

Marine Mammals

R CHARLTON

Whales & Dolphins

Cetaceans, the family of marine mammals that includes dolphins, porpoises and whales, are frequently found along the Great Barrier Reef. Some, like dolphins, live continuously in the reef waters, while others migrate through the reef or come to the reef to breed. There are about 50 species of cetaceans found in Australian waters, and around 25 of these frequent the waters of the Great Barrier Reef.

Whales can be divided into two groups: *Odontocetes*, or toothed whales, are predators that hunt fish and other creatures; and *Mysticetes*, or baleen whales, which strain vast amounts of water through the hairy baleen plates in their mouth. This 'filter' system strains out the tiny fish and krill (planktonic crustaceans) on which the whale lives. It's a curiosity that these largest of living creatures live by consuming such minute ones.

MICHAEL AW

Bottlenose dolphin

Toothed Whales Best known of this group are **dolphins**, which are often seen frolicking around, leaping the bow wave of your boat and engaging in other typical dolphin-like amusements. Dolphin species seen around the reef include the **bottlenose**, the **spinner**, the **Irrawaddy River dolphin** and the **Indo-Pacific humpback dolphin**. The spinner generally stays some distance from the coast, while the other dolphins come close to the shore, often in small groups.

Baleen Whales Eight species of baleen whale are seen in Australian waters and the most visible and spectacular of these are the great **humpback whales** that come north from the Antarctic between July and October to enjoy the warm waters of the Great Barrier Reef. The humpback's activities are a delight to watch. Most spectacular of all is a 'breach', when a 40 tonne, 15m-long whale makes a stupendous splash as it leaps out of the water. Apart from their physical activities, which also includes swimming lazily on one side flapping a huge pectoral fin above the water, humpbacks are also known for the complex 'songs' with which they communicate. They are the most vocal of the great whales.

Humpbacks breed while they are around the Great Barrier Reef. The gestation period is about a year and the newborn whales are around 5m long and weigh about 1.5 tonnes. A mother whale provides her new baby with about 500L of milk a day, and during the first weeks, the whale calf puts on 50 to 100kg of weight per day.

At one time whales were hunted off the Queensland coast and the whaling station at Tangalooma on Moreton Island took over 7000 whales in the 10 years prior to its closure in 1962, by which time humpback whales had almost disappeared from the coast. As many as 10,000 whales were estimated to visit the Great Barrier Reef waters each year prior to whaling, as few as 200 when whaling finally stopped. Whales are now protected and their numbers are slowly recovering; today there are thought to be about 600 whales around the Great Barrier Reef during the winter months. Whale watching (as the whales migrate through the waters of the Southern Reef islands) is becoming a major tourist activity.

GBRMPA

ROBERT CHARLTON

Left: Dugongs
Right: Humpback whale

Dugongs

The dugong, also known as a sirenian or sea cow, looks rather like a decidedly overweight and lethargic dolphin. Like dolphins, dugongs are mammals that have adapted to spending their entire lives in water. Unlike dolphins, which are carnivorous predators, dugongs live mainly on sea grass. It is thought that dugongs may have inspired the ancient seamen's tales of mermaids.

The Great Barrier Reef is probably the world's major habitat of this rare and endangered creature. They are a protected species, except for hunting by Aboriginals and Torres Strait Islanders. Such hunting does not impact on their numbers: the dugong's greatest threat is from fishing nets and shark-proof netting off swimming beaches. Once caught in these nets they frequently drown before being freed.

Dugongs live to about 70 years of age and breed very slowly. A calf is produced every three to seven years and stays with its mother for the first two years of its life. Dugongs suckle their young from mammary glands under each flipper, positioned much like human breasts.

Reptiles

R CHARLTON

Sea Snakes

Sea snakes, a marine adaption of the land snake, are found in many places along the Great Barrier Reef and are frequently seen by divers and snorkellers. They have evolved paddle-like tails to propel themselves through the water, as well as a means of sealing their nostrils when they are submerged. Sea snakes generally come to the surface to breathe every 20 to 30 minutes. The different hunting technique required underwater has also resulted in the development of extremely potent venom. On land, a snake can bite its victim and then follow the wounded creatures scent until it dies.

MICHAEL AW

Olive sea snake

Following disabled prey is not so easy underwater and there is always some other predator ready to jump in and grab an easy meal. So sea snakes have developed a venom that guarantees instant death.

Fortunately for divers, sea snakes are retiring creatures and most unlikely to pose any danger to humans unless they are molested. Fishers take note: sea snakes do not like to be netted or hooked on fishing lines. Extremely curious, especially to divers, the **olive sea snake** has given more than a few people momentary cause for concern. Having a highly venomous creature stare in your face mask or wrap itself around your limbs is likely to make you nervous, even if you know its intentions are friendly.

Turtles

The Great Barrier Reef is a very important habitat for sea turtles. They nest on a number of islands including Heron, Lady Elliot, and the other islands of the Southern Reef groups, but most particularly on Raine Island in the far north.

There are three types of turtles found on the reef – **loggerhead**, **hawksbill** and **green turtles**. Three other types are found near the mainland or further out, beyond the outer edge of the reef. Remarkably little is known about the life cycle of turtles. Although turtles bred in captivity may mature in less than 10 years, in the wild this may take up to 50 years. Mature turtles are a common sight along the reef and actually breed here, but after hatching the baby turtles simply disappear and are rarely seen in reef waters again until they have grown to about 40cm in length.

At one time turtles were harvested for food or, in the case of the hawksbill turtle, for its shell. As turtles take a long time to reach maturity and because a very high proportion of them die along the way, commercial exploitation can have disastrous effects. Today, turtles are protected except for hunting by people from indigenous communities. Nevertheless, the turtles' survival is still threatened by commercial development (loss of the beaches where they lay their eggs) and by prawn trawlers, which accidentally catch and drown them in their nets.

The islands of the Southern Reef group are important breeding sites for turtles and visitors regularly see them on Lady Elliot and Heron islands during the November to March nesting season. The turtles come ashore at night, crawl laboriously up the beach, dig a hole with their flippers and bury a clutch of eggs (ranging in number from 50 for a flatback to 120 for a loggerhead or green turtle). It's possible to tell from the tracks if a turtle was a green or a loggerhead: green turtles crawl breaststroke-fashion with both flippers at once, while loggerheads alternate flippers, like freestyle swimmers. Sea turtles return several times each season to lay more eggs. A green turtle will come back up to eight times at 13 day intervals, but they then take a rest of several years before nesting again.

The warmth of the sand incubates the eggs, which typically take eight or nine weeks to hatch, although in the cooler sand of the early part of the season, or if there is a wet spell, this may stretch to 12 weeks. Turtle eggs are not sex-determined when they are laid: the heat of the sand determines the turtle's sex – sand warmer than 27°C produces more females; cooler sand, more males.

The eggs hatch at night and the tiny turtles make a dash for the relative safety of the sea; waiting crabs or seagulls can easily pick them off in those dangerous first moments. The lighter sky over

Hawksbill turtle

MICHAEL AW

the horizon guides the turtles on this important first voyage – guests at the Lady Elliot and Heron resorts are warned not to leave more lights on than necessary as this can distract them. Each year turtles are lured to their death by the lighthouse on Lady Elliot.

Green turtle

MICHAEL AW

It's important not to disturb the turtles if you are turtle-watching. Don't shine lights on them or use a camera flash until they are actually laying. Prior to that they can turn around and head straight back to sea, even with their egg hole almost dug. Protect turtle hatchlings from predators by all means – chase seagulls off, keep hatchlings together etc – but don't carry them all the way to the sea. They need some crawling time across the sand.

Important nesting sites for green turtles are North West, Hoskyn and Wreck islands. The most important island for loggerheads are Erskine, Masthead, Tryon and Wreck. It's possible to camp on North West Island during the nesting season, but Heron and Lady Elliot, with their resorts, are the islands where most visitors see turtles. On Heron there are typically 50 green turtles nesting every night during the peak season, and over 1000 turtles have nested there in one summer. North West can have several thousand in a good season, and as many as 400 may make it ashore in a single night. Loggerheads are much rarer on Heron, with less than 100 typically in a season and rarely more than six on any one night. Wreck Island will get over 1000 loggerheads in a good season. Hawksbills also visit the Capricorn waters, but don't nest there.

Other Marine Life

SIMON FOALE

Jellyfish

A variety of jellyfish are found in reef waters. While most jellyfish do not pose serious dangers, several are potentially lethal. The **Portuguese man-of-war**, actually a hydrozoan colony rather than an individual jellyfish, is not common in Great Barrier Reef waters and, although the large **lion's mane jellyfish** can cause injury, the deadly box jellyfish is Australia's real aquatic horror story. There are other jellyfish that can give you a painful sting, but none approach the box jellyfish for simple lethal danger. All these jellyfish live in coastal waters and are more likely to appear when the water is warmer – late summer is the worst time.

Box Jellyfish Also known as the **sea wasp**, the box jellyfish is found in northern Australian waters during the summer months. The polyp stage lives in rivers and estuaries during winter, and the mature jellyfish stage, or medusa, emerges in early summer to feed along the shallow coastal waters of the mainland. Only found north of the Tropic of Capricorn, box jellyfish don't generally pose a danger out on the Great Barrier Reef or reef islands, although they have been found at some of the islands close to the coast. On Magnetic Island, several swimming areas have been netted.

The box jellyfish lives on prawns, which it paralyses in shallow water, particularly near river or creek outlets. An adult box jellyfish has enough poison to kill a vast number of prawns, or three or four adult humans. The 'box' name comes from the four-sided bell from which tentacles hang at each corner. The near-transparent jellyfish can trail as many as 60 tentacles up to 3m long. These tentacles have millions of little capsules, some of which

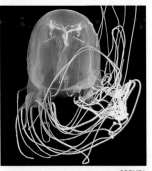

GBRMPA

Box jellyfish

contain a substance that sticks to its victim and others with stinging cells that inject the deadly venom. People who get entangled in a box jellyfish describe an intense pain immediately on contact, quickly followed by the paralytic effect of the poison, which can kill within three minutes by stopping the heart and respiration. The complex venom also destroys red blood cells and damages skin tissue.

While it is wise to be prepared to deal with box jellyfish it's highly unlikely to be necessary since, as noted above, they are found close to the coast, not out on the reef islands. Mysteriously, when the summer ends so do the box jellyfish. Even aquariums have been unable to keep them alive beyond the end of the summer.

Massive leafy sponge

MICHAEL AW

Sponges

Sponges are among the most primitive of multi-celled creatures. In fact, reefs were very probably formed from sponge skeletons long before coral took over the reef construction business.

Sponges feed by filtering bacteria out of the water, which they do in amazing volume and with phenomenal efficiency. A sponge can typically handle its own volume of water every five to 20 seconds and continues doing so for 24 hours a day. As the water passes through its body up to 99% of the bacteria is filtered out.

Despite this efficiency, sponges often draw on additional means to get the nutrition they need. Some sponges have a form rather like a chimney and passing currents draw water up through the sponge. Most sponges also act as a home to blue-green algae, which symbiotically repay their host by providing a share of its photosynthetic nutrient production. Other less welcome tenants also find that sponges make a good home – small crabs, shrimps, worms and even brittle stars often take up residence in a sponge's tubes and passages.

Worms

Left: Flatworm

Middle: Feather duster worms

Right: Christmas tree worm

The reef is home to many species of marine worms. Some live in burrows bored into dead coral, some in the sand or mud, and some in the reef plankton (the millions of tiny organisms drifting just below the surface). They are an important food source for many fish.

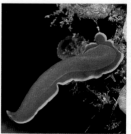

MICHAEL AW

MICHAEL AW

SIMON FOALE

Mainland Gateways

MAINLAND GATEWAYS

Highlights
- Visit the aquarium at the Great Barrier Reef Wonderland in Townsville
- Try a few of Cairns' other activities: white-water rafting, canoeing, horse riding, bungee jumping or sky diving

A number of cities on the coast are major 'gateways' to the Barrier Reef; cities most reef visitors will visit. From south to north these cities, and the reef islands and areas they give access to, are:

Airlie Beach
Whitsunday Islands, outer reef
Townsville
Hinchinbrook Island, Magnetic Island, Orpheus Island
Cairns
Bedarra Island, Dunk Island, Fitzroy Island, Green Island, Hinchinbrook Island, Lizard Island, Thursday Island, Orpheus Island, Low Isles, many outer reef areas

Airlie Beach

Airlie Beach, 25km north-west of Proserpine off the Bruce Highway, is the gateway to the Whitsunday Islands. It's a small but lively centre that has grown phenomenally since the mid-1980s. The whole town revolves around tourism and pleasure boating.

Airlie Beach also has a reputation as a centre for learning to scuba dive. A wide assortment of travel agents and tour operators are based here, and most boats to the islands leave from Shute Harbour, 8km east of Airlie Beach, or from the Abel Point Marina, 1km west.

Whale watching boat trips, between July and September, are another attraction.

Information
There's a tourist office (☎ 4945 3711) on the Bruce Highway at Proserpine, near the turn-off to Airlie Beach.

In Airlie Beach, nearly everything of importance is on the main road, Shute Harbour Rd. There are numerous privately run 'information centres' (ie booking agencies) along Shute Harbour Rd, including Destination Whitsunday (☎ 1800 644 563) and the Airlie Beach Tourist Information Centre (☎ 4946 6665).

The Department of Environment office (☎ 4946 7022) is 3km past Airlie Beach towards Shute Harbour, and is open weekdays from 8 am to 5 pm and at varying weekend hours. This office deals with camping bookings and permits for the Whitsunday Islands national parks.

Diving
Four outfits in and around Airlie Beach offer five to seven day scuba-diving certificate courses. All the companies also offer diving trips for certified divers. Book where

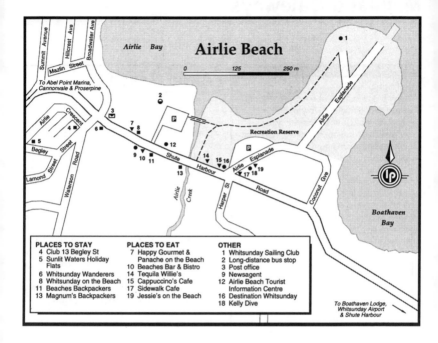

PLACES TO STAY
4 Club 13 Begley St
5 Sunlit Waters Holiday
   Flats
6 Whitsunday Wanderers
8 Whitsunday on the Beach
11 Beaches Backpackers
13 Magnum's Backpackers

PLACES TO EAT
7 Happy Gourmet &
   Panache on the Beach
10 Beaches Bar & Bistro
14 Tequila Willie's
15 Cappuccino's Cafe
17 Sidewalk Cafe
19 Jessie's on the Beach

OTHER
1 Whitsunday Sailing Club
2 Long-distance bus stop
3 Post office
9 Newsagent
12 Airlie Beach Tourist
   Information Centre
16 Destination Whitsunday
18 Kelly Dive

you are staying or at one of the agencies on
the main road in Airlie Beach.

The companies include: Oceania Dive
(☎ 1800 075 035), Pro-Dive (☎ 1800 075
120), True Blue (☎ 1800 635 889) and
Kelly Dive (☎ 1800 063 454) – all of which
have offices/shops in Airlie Beach.

Places to Stay

Hostels Right in the centre, *Magnum's
Backpackers* (☎ 4946 6266) is a huge place,
set out in a very pleasant tropical garden
with two pools. The cheapest dorms are the
eight-share units at $12 a night; four-share
is $14.

Also in the centre is *Beaches Backpackers* (☎ 4946 6244), another big place with a
party attitude and its own bar and restaurant. Beds cost $14 a night ($13 VIP).

Club 13 Begley St (☎ 4946 7376) has
great views over the bay from the hill just
above the centre. Beds are $14 ($13 VIP,

YHA), including breakfast. This place gets
consistently good reports from travellers.

Holiday Flats & Resorts In the centre at
26 Shute Harbour Rd, *Whitsunday on the
Beach* (☎ 4946 6359) has small, brightly
renovated studio apartments from $75 to
$85.

Up the hill on the corner of Begley St and
Airlie Crescent, *Sunlit Waters* Holiday Flats
(☎ 4946 6352) has budget studio flats at
$40 a double plus $8 for extra adults.
Boathaven Lodge (☎ 4946 6421), a couple
of hundred metres east of the centre at 440
Shute Harbour Rd, has units overlooking
Boathaven Bay from $50 a double plus $10
for extras.

Of the numerous resorts, *Whitsunday
Wanderers* (☎ 4946 6446), on Shute Harbour Rd, has Melanesian-style units for $38
to $54 per person, depending on the season.
Club Crocodile (☎ 1800 075 125), in

Cannonvale, 2km west of Airlie Beach, has modern units around a central courtyard and costs $55 per person including a 'tropical' breakfast.

Places to Eat

Beaches Bar & Bistro is almost always crowded with both travellers and locals looking for a good, cheap filling feed. *Magnum's Bar & Grill* is also popular and has a similar set-up, with pool tables and a video screen. Meals start at $6.

The *Happy Gourmet*, 263 Shute Harbour Rd, is a great place for lunch, while *Cappuccino's Cafe* in a breezy arcade has focaccias and serious coffee.

The *Sidewalk Cafe* on Airlie Esplanade has great fish and chips ($4), while *Jessie's on the Beach* does good breakfasts.

Panache on the Beach is a very pleasant open-air place with pasta from $12 to $14 and other mains from $18 to $22.

If it's Mexican you want, *Tequila Willie's* is open for lunch and dinner and is good value at $9 for main courses, from $13 to $18 for grills.

Getting There & Away

Air The closest major airports are at Proserpine and Hamilton Island (Ansett only).

There are a few operators based at the Whitsunday airport, a small airfield about 6km past Airlie Beach towards Shute Harbour. Island Air Taxis (☎ 4946 9933) flies to Hamilton ($45) and Lindeman ($55) islands. Heli Reef (☎ 4946 9102), Coral Air Whitsunday (☎ 4946 9111) and Island Air Taxis all do joy flights out over the reef.

Bus Sampson's (☎ 4945 2377) runs local bus services from Proserpine to Airlie Beach ($6.50) and Shute Harbour ($8.40); buses operate daily from 6 am to 7 pm. Sampson's also meets all flights at Proserpine airport and goes to Airlie Beach ($11) and Shute Harbour ($13).

Boat The sailing club is at the end of Airlie Esplanade. There are noticeboards at the Abel Point Marina showing when rides or crewing are available. Ask around Airlie Beach or Shute Harbour.

See the Whitsunday Islands chapter for details of ferry services from Shute Harbour and around the islands.

Townsville

The fourth largest city in Queensland, Townsville is the only departure point for Magnetic Island (20 minutes away by ferry), and the Barrier Reef is about 1¼ hours away by fast catamaran.

The city's main attraction is the excellent aquarium at the Great Barrier Reef Wonderland.

Orientation

The transit centre, the arrival and departure point for long-distance buses, is on Palmer St, just south of Ross Creek. The city centre is immediately to the north of the creek, over the Dean St bridge. Flinders St Mall stretches to the left from the northern side of the bridge, towards the train station. To the right of the bridge is the Flinders St East area, which contains many of the town's oldest buildings, plus cafes, restaurants, the Great Barrier Reef Wonderland and the ferry terminal.

Information

Townsville Enterprises' main tourist information office (☎ 4778 3555) is on the Bruce Highway, 8km south of the city centre. There's also a more convenient information booth (☎ 4721 3660) in the middle of Flinders St Mall, between Stokes and Denham Sts. There's also a Department of Environment information office (☎ 4721 2399) at the Wonderland.

Great Barrier Reef Wonderland

Townsville's top attraction is at the end of Flinders St East, beside Ross Creek. Although its impressive aquarium is the highlight, there are several other sections

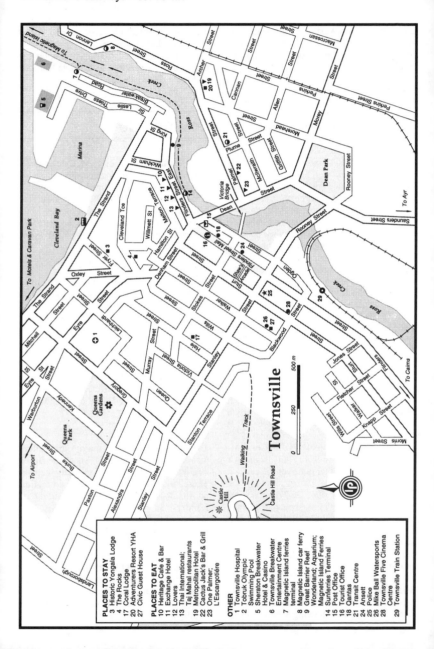

Townsville

PLACES TO STAY
3 Historic Yongala Lodge
4 The Rocks
17 Coral Lodge
20 Adventurers Resort YHA
27 Civic Guest House

PLACES TO EAT
10 Heritage Café & Bar
11 Exchange Hotel
12 Lovers
13 Thai International;
   Taj Mahal restaurants
19 Metropolitan Hotel
22 Cactus Jack's Bar & Grill
23 One Palmer;
   L'Escargotière

OTHER
1 Townsville Hospital
2 Tobruk Olympic
   Swimming Pool
5 Sheraton Breakwater
   Hotel & Casino
6 Townsville Breakwater
   Entertainment Centre
7 Magnetic Island ferries
   terminal
8 Magnetic Island car ferry
9 Great Barrier Reef
   Wonderland; Aquarium;
   Magnetic Island Ferries
14 Sunferries Terminal
15 Post Office
16 Tourist Office
18 Qantas
21 Transit Centre
24 Ansett
25 Police
26 Mike Ball Watersports
28 Townsville Five Cinema
   Centre
29 Townsville Train Station

including a theatre, a museum, shops, the Great Barrier Reef Marine Park Authority office, and a terminal for ferries to Magnetic Island.

Aquarium The huge main tank has a living coral reef and hundreds of reef fish, sharks, rays and other marine life, and you can walk beneath the tank through a clear domed tunnel. To maintain the natural conditions needed to keep this community alive, a wave machine simulates the ebb and flow of the ocean, circular currents keep the water in motion and marine algae are used in the purification system. The aquarium also has several smaller tanks, extensive displays on the history and life of the reef, and a theatrette where slide-shows on the reef are shown, plus regular guided tours. It's open daily from 9 am to 5 pm and admission is $13 ($6.50 children).

Omnimax Theatre This is a cinema with angled seating and a dome-shaped screen for a 3-D effect. Hour-long films on the reef and various other topics such as outer space alternate through the day from 9.30 am till 4.30 pm. Admission to one film is $11.50 ($6).

Diving
Townsville has four or five diving schools, including Mike Ball Watersports (☎ 4772 3022), 252 Walker St, and Pro-Dive (☎ 4721 1760), another well-regarded dive school, with an office in the Great Barrier Reef Wonderland.

Cruises
Pure Pleasure Cruises (☎ 4721 3555) has five trips each week out to Kelso Reef on the outer reef. The cost of $130 (children $65) includes lunch and snorkelling gear; scuba dives are an optional extra.

Places to Stay
On the south side of Ross Creek, and conveniently close to the transit centre but a bit isolated from the town centre, is the huge *Adventurers Resort YHA* (☎ 4721 1522) at 79 Palmer St. Accommodation in a four-bunk dorm costs $14 for YHA members, and singles/doubles cost $24/32. Non-members pay an extra $3 per person.

On the other side of the river is the *Civic Guest House* (☎ 4771 5381) at 262 Walker St. This clean and easy-going hostel has three or four-bed dorms for $14, six-bed dorms with bathroom and air-con for $16, and pleasant singles/doubles from $28/33, or $48 with air-con and private bathroom. Its courtesy bus does pick-ups and there's a free BBQ on Friday night.

At 32 Hale St, the *Coral Lodge* (☎ 4771 5512) is a neat, friendly guesthouse in a renovated Queenslander building, with air-con rooms from $38/48 and self-contained units from $48, including a light breakfast.

The Rocks (☎ 4771 5700), 20 Cleveland Terrace, is a superb, renovated historic home with great views over the bay. All the rooms have period furnishings and are great value at $78/88 including breakfast. Evening meals are available on request.

The *Historic Yongala Lodge* (☎ 4772 4633), 11 Fryer St, has modern motel units and self-contained rooms from $69/79, and heritage-style units from $80, as well as a good Greek restaurant at the front (see Places to Eat).

The *Townsville Seaside Apartments* (☎ 4721 3155), 105 The Strand, has renovated 1960s air-con one-bedroom apartments from $55 a double or two-bedroom from $90.

The high-rise *Aquarius on the Beach* (☎ 4772 4255) at 75 The Strand has excellent self-contained suites, complete with great views, from $110 for two.

Places to Eat
Flinders St East is the main area for eateries, and it offers plenty of choice. The *Heritage Cafe & Bar* is a modern, cosy place with light meals (pasta etc) from $8 to $10; other mains are slightly more.

The *Thai International Restaurant*, upstairs at No 235, has fine soups for $6, a good range of vegetarian dishes from $6 to $9, and other mains from $10 to $14.

Downstairs is the *Taj Mahal*, an Indian and Persian restaurant with vegetarian dishes from $11 to $14, others are from $15 to $18.

On the same street is *Lovers*, a trendy cafe/restaurant with a downstairs licensed cafe section (main courses $12 to $15) and a slightly more formal upstairs section ($17 to $20). The Exchange Hotel has the pleasant *Thai Exchange* upstairs on the balcony (mains from $9 to $14) and the casual *Portraits Wine Bar* with bistro-type meals.

South of the river, Palmer St also has some good pubs and eateries. *One Palmer*, on the corner of Palmer and Dean Sts, is a modern licensed cafe (mains from $14 to $18), while next door is *L'Escargotiére*, a simple BYO French restaurant.

At No 21 is *Cactus Jack's Bar & Grill* (☎ 4721 1478), a lively licensed Mexican place with main courses in the $10 to $14 range; you'll need to book on weekends. The *Metropole Hotel*, next to the YHA, has good bistro meals in the rear beer garden, or there's more formal dining in the *La Met* restaurant.

Getting There & Away
Air Sunstate has flights to Dunk Island ($135). Townsville airport is 5km northwest of the city at Garbutt; a taxi to the city centre costs $10. The Airport Shuttle (☎ 4775 5544) services all main arrivals and departures. It costs $5/8 one way/return and will drop you off or pick you up almost anywhere fairly central.

Bus All long-distance buses operate from the transit centre on Palmer St. Both Greyhound Pioneer and McCafferty's have frequent services up and down the coastal Bruce Highway.

Boat There are two terminals for the ferries to Magnetic Island. Sunferries (☎ 4771 3855) operates about 10 services a day between 6.20 am and 7.15 pm from its terminal on Flinders St East. The trip takes about 20 minutes and costs $7/13 one way/return.

Magnetic Island Ferries (☎ 4772 7122) runs a similar service from its terminal at the breakwater on Sir Leslie Thiess Dve, near the casino. The trip takes about 15 minutes and the return fare is $14 ($11 for students).

Bicycles are carried free on all ferries.

Cairns

The 'capital' of the far north, Cairns is firmly established as one of Australia's top travellers destinations. It is a centre for a whole host of activities – not only reef trips and scuba diving but white-water rafting, canoeing, horse riding, bungee jumping and sky diving.

Cairns is also the centre for a great number of boating connections, day trips and scuba diving trips. Fitzroy, Green and the Frankland islands are all reached from Cairns. Because the reef is closer to the mainland here, Cairns is particularly popular for scuba trips. Boats also operate from Cairns on cruises to Lizard Island, Cape York and Thursday Island.

Orientation
The centre of Cairns is a relatively compact area running back from the Esplanade. Off Wharf St (the southern continuation of the Esplanade), you'll find Great Adventures Wharf, Marlin Jetty and the Pier – the main departure points for reef trips. Further around is Trinity Wharf (a cruise-liner dock with shops and cafes) and the transit centre, where long-distance buses arrive and depart.

Information
The Wet Tropics Information Centre, on the Esplanade across from the Shields St corner, combines information with displays on the environment and rainforests of the far north. It's open daily from 9.30 am to 5.30 pm.

There are literally dozens of privately run

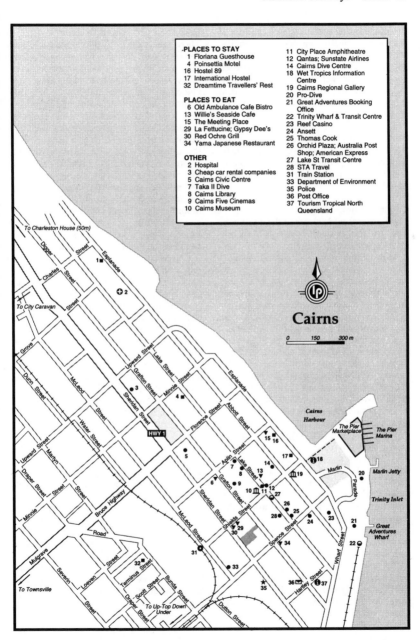

PLACES TO STAY
1 Floriana Guesthouse
4 Poinsettia Motel
16 Hostel 89
17 International Hostel
32 Dreamtime Travellers' Rest

PLACES TO EAT
6 Old Ambulance Cafe Bistro
13 Willie's Seaside Cafe
15 The Meeting Place
29 La Fettucine; Gypsy Dee's
30 Red Ochre Grill
34 Yama Japanese Restaurant

OTHER
2 Hospital
3 Cheap car rental companies
5 Cairns Civic Centre
7 Taka II Dive
8 Cairns Library
9 Cairns Five Cinemas
10 Cairns Museum
11 City Place Amphitheatre
12 Qantas; Sunstate Airlines
14 Cairns Dive Centre
18 Wet Tropics Information Centre
19 Cairns Regional Gallery
20 Pro-Dive
21 Great Adventures Booking Office
22 Trinity Wharf & Transit Centre
23 Reef Casino
24 Ansett
25 Thomas Cook
26 Orchid Plaza; Australia Post Shop; American Express
27 Lake St Transit Centre
28 STA Travel
31 Train Station
33 Department of Environment
35 Police
36 Post Office
37 Tourism Tropical North Queensland

Cairns

0   150   300 m

'information centres' in Cairns, and these places are basically tour-booking agencies. Most of the backpackers hostels also have helpful tour-booking desks. Note that each booking agent will be pushing different tours, depending on the commission deal they have with the tour companies, so shop around.

The Department of Environment office (☎ 4052 3096), 10 McLeod St, is open on weekdays from 8.30 am to 4.30 pm; it deals with camping permits and information on the region's national parks, including islands.

Diving & Snorkelling

The Barrier Reef is closer to the coast here than it is further south, making Cairns one of the scuba-diving capitals.

Most people look for a course that takes them to the outer Barrier Reef rather than the reefs around Green or Fitzroy islands. Some places give you more time on the reef than others but you may prefer an extra day in the pool and classroom before venturing out. A chat with people who have already done a course can tell you some of the pros and cons. A good teacher can make all the difference to your confidence and the amount of fun you have. Another factor is how big the groups are – the smaller the better if you want personal attention.

The main schools include: Deep Sea Divers Den (☎ 4031 2223), 319 Draper St; Pro-Dive (☎ 4031 5255), Marlin Jetty; Down Under Dive (☎ 4031 1288), 155 Sheridan St; Cairns Dive Centre (☎ 1800 642 591), 135 Abbott St; Tusa Dive (☎ 4031 1248), 93 The Esplanade; and Taka II Dive (☎ 4051 8722), 131 Lake St. Most of these operators can also be booked through the hostels.

If you want to learn about the reef before you dive, Reef Teach offers an entertaining and educational lecture at Boland's Centre, 14 Spence St, every night (except Sunday) from 6.15 to 8.30 pm. The lectures are well worth attending and get good reports from travellers. The cost is $10 – for more details phone ☎ 4051 6882.

Barrier Reef & Island Cruises

There are dozens of options available for day trips to the reef. It's worth asking a few questions before you book, such as how many passengers the boat takes, what's included in the price and how much the 'extras' (such as wetsuit hire and introductory dives) cost, and exactly where the boat is going. Some companies have a dubious definition of 'outer reef'; as a general rule, the further out you go, the better the diving.

Great Adventures (☎ 1800 079 080) is the major operator with the biggest boats and a wide range of combination cruises, including a day trip to either Norman or Moore reefs. You get about three hours on a pontoon at the reef itself, lunch, snorkelling gear, and a semi-submersible and glass-bottom boat ride thrown in.

Compass (☎ 1800 815 811) and Noah's Ark Cruises (☎ 4051 5666) have popular day trips to Hastings Reef and Michaelmas Cay for $55, including boom netting, snorkelling gear and lunch. Certified divers can take two dives for an extra $45.

Falla (☎ 4031 3488), *Seahorse* (☎ 4031 4692) and *Passions of Paradise* (☎ 4050 0676) are all ocean-going yachts that 'sail' out to Upolo Cay, Green Island and Paradise Reef daily for about $50, which includes lunch and snorkelling gear.

There are many, many other boats and operators, so shop around.

Places to Stay

Near the corner of Shields St and the Esplanade, the *International Hostel* (☎ 4031 1424) is a big, old multi-level place with about 200 beds. Fan-cooled four, six and eight-bed dorms are $12, twin rooms are $28, and doubles range from $28 to $36 with either air-con and TV or a bathroom.

At No 89 is *Hostel 89* (☎ 1800 061 712), one of the better Esplanade hostels. It's a smallish and helpful place, with twin and double rooms and a few three ($18) or four-bed ($17) dorms, all air-conditioned. Singles/doubles are from $36/44. Security is good, with a locked grille at the street entrance.

Three blocks further along the Esplanade is another cluster of hostels.

Dreamtime Travellers' Rest (☎ 4031 6753), 4 Terminus St, is a small guesthouse run by a friendly and enthusiastic young couple. It's in a brightly renovated timber Queenslander and has a good pool, double rooms from $35, and three or four-bed (no bunks) rooms at $15 per person.

The Art Deco *Floriana Guesthouse* (☎ 4051 7886), 183 the Esplanade, has four self-contained units with polished timber floors, TVs, en suites and kitchenettes. This place is excellent value at $55 to $70 for up to four. The old building next door has 24 simple rooms with communal facilities at $28 to $42 for doubles, some with air-con, or $48 with appealing ocean views (book ahead).

The *18-24 James* (☎ 1800 621 824) at, funnily enough, 18-24 James St, is an exclusively gay and lesbian hotel with four-share rooms at $50 per person or singles/doubles at $95/109, all including a tropical breakfast.

There are a few budget motels around the centre: the *Poinsettia Motel* (☎ 4051 2144), 169 Lake St, has decent budget rooms from $46/50.

Places to Eat

The Esplanade, between Shields and Aplin Sts, is basically wall-to-wall eateries with plenty of variety – Italian and Chinese food, burgers, kebabs, pizzas, seafood and ice cream – and is open all hours. The *Night Markets*, in the thick of it, is a modern hawker-style food court with plenty of choices. Better is the *The Meeting Place*, around the corner in Aplin St.

Willie's Seaside Cafe is a bright and airy (if misnamed) cafe right by City Square, and so is good for catching the lunch-time performances given in the amphitheatre

there. A de rigeur focaccia and cafe latte lunch costs $6.50.

On the corner of Grafton and Aplin Sts, the *Old Ambulance Cafe Bistro* is a chic new place in, as the name suggests, the old ambulance station. It's a popular place and has great coffee and filled croissants.

La Fettucini, a narrow bistro at 43 Shields St, has great home-made pasta at $12 and Italian mains for about $16; it's BYO. Next door is the dim and exotic *Gypsy Dee's*, with a bar, live acoustic music nightly and mains in the $12 to $18 range.

On the corner of Shields and Sheridan Sts, the *Red Ochre Grill* is a stylish restaurant with innovative Aussie bush tucker, but it's not cheap with mains ranging from $17 to $25.

For Japanese food, try *Yama* on the corner of Spence and Grafton Sts – it has good value lunches and dinners.

Getting There & Away

Air Sunstate flies to Lizard Island ($200) and Thursday Island ($324). The Australia Coach shuttle bus (☎ 4031 3555) meets all incoming flights and runs a regular pick-up and drop-off service between the airport and town; the one-way fare is $4.50. A taxi is about $11.

Bus All the bus companies operate from the transit centre at Trinity Wharf. Most of the backpackers hostels have courtesy buses that meet the arriving buses.

Boat The daily *Quicksilver* (☎ 4099 5500) fast-catamaran service links Cairns with Port Douglas. The trip takes 1½ hours and costs $20 one way, and $30 return.

See the Green Island section in the Islands Off Cairns chapter and the Lizard Island to Cape York chapter for details of services to those islands.

Southern Reef Islands

The Capricorn Marine Park, known as Capricornia or the Southern Reef Islands, is the southernmost part of the Great Barrier Reef. It begins north-east of Bundaberg with Lady Elliot Island and stretches about 140km north up to Tryon Island, east of Rockhampton. There are 300-plus cays on the whole Barrier Reef and many of the most accessible are in the Capricornia section. Although Capricornia is inshore from the main outer reef these are real coral reef islands, formed from reef debris, as opposed to the continental islands like Great Keppel, the Whitsundays or Hinchinbrook, which generally lie closer to the mainland and are the tops of submerged hills. Most of the cays are surrounded by calm lagoons formed by the coral reefs that they top.

Several vegetated cays in the Capricornia section are open to visitors for camping or day trips and two of them even have resorts. They are excellent places to go snorkelling and diving and just getting back to nature – though reaching them is generally more expensive than reaching islands nearer the coast.

Apart from Lady Elliot Island, isolated at the south end, the Capricornia islands fall into two main groups: the Bunker group, which includes Lady Musgrave and the Fairfax and Hoskyn islands; and further north the Capricorn Group, which includes Heron, Masthead, Wilson, Tryon and North West islands. Many of these cays are national parks. The Tropic of Capricorn runs through the Capricorn Group, passing very close to Heron Island.

Several of the islands are important breeding grounds for turtles, including the endangered green turtle. Turtles arrive at night from late October to early February to lay their eggs, and the young emerge from mid-January to April. Seabirds also breed on the islands and at nesting time some islands are home to massive numbers of

SOUTHERN REEF ISLANDS

Highlights
- Go turtle watching (November to February) on Heron Island
- Feed the butterfly fish and sergeant-majors while snorkelling in the 'fish pond' on Lady Elliot Island
- Dive right off the beach on Lady Elliot

mutton birds, terns and other birds. Humpback whales also pass through the waters of Capricornia on their annual migration from the Antarctic. Whale watching trips operate from Bundaberg between mid-August and mid-October.

The Southern Reef Calendar

With whales migrating north and south, turtles nesting, birds mating and hatching, there's plenty of activity year round on the islands of the Southern Reef section of the Great Barrier Reef.

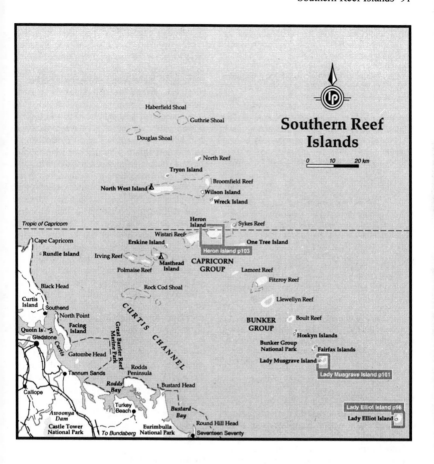

Southern Reef Islands

January, February, March and from May to June are usually the wettest months of the year. It can get surprisingly chilly on these islands during the winter months; you certainly need a good wetsuit if diving in June and July.

A calendar of significant events in this area follows:

January – peak breeding season for Heron Island's reef herons. Turtle hatchlings have started to appear in late December and continue through to late March or early April.

February – mutton bird chicks start to hatch

March – this is the end of the turtle-nesting season, and migratory birds like the ruddy turnstones and eastern golden plovers start to depart, heading for the Arctic. Buff-banded rails and black noddy terns have started to nest.

April – adult mutton birds start to leave the islands and, soon after, their abandoned chicks emerge from their burrows. Most of the noddy terns leave the islands.

May – the young mutton birds are busy teaching themselves to fly and by the end of the month should all have left the islands, in pursuit of their parents. The last of the baby turtles have made the dangerous trek down to the sea.

June – humpback whales start to pass through the Southern Reef Islands on their migration north from the Antarctic

July – humpback whales are seen more regularly. This is the coldest month of the year with average water temperatures around 18 to 23°C

August – the cold winter water is starting to warm up

September – black noddy terns start to return and nest while migratory birds from the northern hemisphere start to arrive. Turtles may be seen mating in the sea.

October – the humpback whales that have given birth to their calves while in the warm waters of the Great Barrier Reef can now be seen heading south back to the Antarctic for the summer. The mutton birds return to the island to nest and the jaunty little silvereyes, which are resident on the islands year-round, start to nest.

November – the female turtles start to come ashore to lay their eggs while the mutton birds clean out and repair their burrows. Black noddies' eggs start to appear in their precarious and shoddily built nests. This is usually the month when corals spawn; the exact date is related to the lunar month and may be in December.

December – the birdlife will be noisy and active as black noddy tern chicks start to hatch and mutton birds lay their eggs. Turtles continue to lay their eggs and the season's first new turtle hatchlings start to appear and head for the protection of the sea.

Places to Stay

On the three islands in the Capricornia Cays National Park where camping is allowed (Lady Musgrave, Masthead and North West islands) campers must be totally self-sufficient. There are no reliable water supplies and all garbage should be taken when you leave. The number of campers is limited so it's advisable to apply well ahead for your camping permit. You can book six months ahead for these islands instead of the usual six to 12 weeks for other Queensland national parks. The busiest times for bookings are December and January, school holiday periods, and May and November when the diving is at its best. For information and permits contact the Department of Environment (☎ 4972 6055), Tank St, Gladstone, or at PO Box 5065, Gladstone, Qld 4680.

When you receive your permit you'll also receive information on any rules such as restrictions on the use of generators, and on how not to harm the wildlife. Turtles nest on these islands between October and February and care should be taken not to disturb them.

A variety of seabirds nest on the Capricornia cays, particularly between October and May, and campers should take great care not to disturb or harm them. Some birds, especially the black noddy terns, are easily disturbed and may abandon their nests, which can result in the loss of their eggs or chicks to scavenging gulls. Mutton birds dig burrows that can collapse under the weight of unwary walkers, with dire results for any bird in the burrow at the time. Also, their long wings make it difficult for them to make sudden changes in direction when coming in to land, so don't get in their way and don't camp on their 'runways'. Feeding seagulls can disturb the islands' ecological balance as gulls often wreak havoc on their less aggressive neighbours.

Co-existing with the cays' birdlife can have a less salubrious side. The birds, in particular the noddies, play a vital role in the cays' lifecycle by fertilising the soil with their droppings. As a result, if you decide to set up camp under the pisonia trees, especially during the noddies nesting season, this can result in your tent getting a very healthy coating of droppings.

Getting There & Away

Access to the Capricornia islands is from Bundaberg, Gladstone or Rosslyn Bay, near Rockhampton. Information on regular transport services to the islands is covered under the individual islands themselves later in this chapter.

It's possible to charter boats for day trips or drop-offs to the islands. Operators tend to come and go, and boats frequently change hands, but Gladstone Area Promotion & Development (☎ 4972 4000) at the ferry terminal has an up-to-date list of charter operators registered with them.

Birds of the Southern Reef Islands

The islands of the Capricorn Group generally support a similar but diverse birdlife. They are also amazingly prolific in number, some visitors to Heron Island, where there can be a constant night-time caterwauling of mutton birds, might feel they are *too prolific*.

Noddies

One of the most common of the Capricornia seabirds is the white-capped or black noddy. They nest in the pisonia trees in great numbers on many of the cays between October and March. December is the peak nesting season and the Capricornia cays are among the most important nesting sites for these birds in the south-west Pacific. At the height of the nesting season Heron Island may have as many as 100,000 noddies on the island. Their smell pervades the island and their droppings fall so regularly that at this time of year you're strongly advised to wear a wide brimmed hat while walking the island's trails. The birds remain on the island throughout the year.

When mating season approaches, noddies go through an elaborate mating ritual. The female bird sits in the tree where the nest will be built while the male carefully selects an appropriate leaf to use for building the nest. Having checked the leaf from every perspective he reverently hands it to his potential mate who disdainfully discards it. This process is repeated until a pile of discarded leaves litters the ground. Finally, he hands her the right leaf, and she defecates on it. This leaf then forms the keystone of the nest, constructed from the previously discarded leaves cemented together with droppings.

Reaching adulthood is especially challenging for noddy chicks. They have to balance in a shoddy nest, and if they fall out they are abandoned.

The ritual far exceeds the quality of the resulting nest, however. Into the shallow depression on this grotty little nest a single egg is laid and incubated for an average of 35 days. Sometimes the egg simply falls out of the nest, and the birds just start all over again. Unfortunately, chicks are also prone to falling out of the nest and when this happens they, too, are simply abandoned. A storm during nesting time can wreak havoc upon a noddy colony.

Once the chicks are old enough to leave the nest they wander round in groups that are known as creches. During the day their parents venture far out to sea hunting small fish that swim close to the surface. When they return at night they call to their offspring, which recognise their parents' call and break away from the creche to be fed on regurgitated stomach contents. Soon the young

ROBERT CHARLTON

birds also start to leave the islands each morning, at first returning earlier than their parents, which continue to feed them.

Noddy droppings are a vital element in fertilising a cay's soil and help to account for the often surprising lush vegetation found on small cays. It is the countless thousands of years of bird droppings that build up the high-phosphate guano deposits for which many coral cays have been exploited.

Mutton Birds

While the noddies nest in trees mutton birds, or wedge-tailed shearwaters, live in burrows in the sand. Many noddies stay on the islands year-round but mutton birds are only seen (and more definitely heard) during the mating and nesting season. From their winter homes the male mutton birds return to the southern reef islands regular as clockwork in early October. They return to exactly the same burrow as in previous years and clean things up in preparation for the arrival of their mates.

ROBERT CHARLTON

The mutton bird's disproportionately large wingspan is great for flying, but makes the birds ungainly when it comes to take-offs and landings.

Mutton birds mate for life and when their companion, unseen for the past year, turns up all hell breaks loose. From dawn to dusk they shriek, wail, groan and howl to each other. The whole colony seems to get together on this and the noise builds up to an absolute crescendo before suddenly ceasing. But just as island visitors at this time of year heave a sigh of relief and decide they can finally get to sleep a single groan will recommence the whole symphony. You soon get used to it. It's said that sailors became convinced that certain islands were haunted. All night long this horrible, almost human-like noise would be heard, but come dawn the island would be found empty. The mutton birds had set out just before dawn to spend the day fishing.

Mutton birds have a wingspan disproportionately large compared to their body size. This makes for easy flying but difficult take-offs and landings. On the islands the birds have well defined 'runways', where they line up to make their pre-dawn departure. When coming in to land, once they're committed on their final approach they have great difficulty in making changes of direction and have been known to collide with trees, buildings or casual strollers if they get it wrong. A mutton bird's nest is usually in the outer fringe of an island's central pisonia growth, while the `runways' lead through the fringing vegetation towards the beach.

Apart from the tiring noise, island visitors should also take care to keep away from their nesting area. The nesting burrows are liable to collapse under a walker's weight and the unfortunate birds may be killed. The single egg is incubated for about 50 days and the chick is fed so energetically that it may eventually grow to be bigger than its parents! Then the parents abandon their off-spring and fly off, leaving their well-fed chick to survive on its body fat, learn to fly and follow its parents. It's been suggested that mutton birds' lousy take-off and landing abilities are not unrelated to the fact that their parents leave them to learn this vital skill by trial and error.

Silvereyes

The tiny olive-green silvereyes, named after the whitish-silver ring around their eyes, are one of the cheekiest of the islands' birds. On Lady Elliot and Heron islands they've learnt to exploit the advantages of a handy resort and can often be seen inspecting the food offerings. At Heron they even learned to lift the lid off sugar bowls by concerted group efforts, forcing a changeover to sugar sachets. These tiny birds are continuous residents, they don't come and go from the islands and are not identical to their slightly smaller mainland cousins. This interesting small captive population has been studied on Heron for over 20 years. Unlike their island neighbours the noddies, whose nest is nothing if not jerry-built, the silvereyes build a nest that is a model of craftsmanship. The neat little cup-shaped nest is constructed of pandanus leaves, bound together with spider webs!

GBRMPA

Stop – sugar thief! The silvereyes on Heron Island learned to lift the lids off sugar bowls, causing locals to switch to sachets

Other Birds

A variety of terns are found on the islands. Bridled terns have a white eyebrow line but are otherwise predominantly brown. They nest from October to March and their nests are scattered indiscriminately across the island. Their eggs often hidden in grass or fringe vegetation. When alarmed, bridled terns make a noise like a dog's bark. Elegant black-naped terns are also found on some of the islands and visitors should take care not to disturb these nervous birds. On Heron Island they've taken such a dislike to human contact that they've all moved off the island and now nest on the harbour breakwater, the rusting old *Protector*. Roseate terns are also notoriously shy and are generally only found on

HOLGER LEUE

Seen stalking along the water's edge at low tide, the elegant reef herons gave Heron Island its name.

islands where human visits are few.

Heron Island's elegant reef herons gave their name to the island, although they are more correctly known as eastern reef egrets. They can be seen stalking imperiously along the water's edge at low tide, or hanging around at the top of the beach. The grey and white varieties are simply a colour variation.

Banded land-rails are found on several of the Capricornia islands. The hen-like birds are able to fly but prefer to stay on the ground. They've adapted well to human contact and can be seen scrounging around the resort at Heron. Bar-shouldered doves are also often seen with the rails. Sooty oystercatchers have totally sooty-black plumage, contrasting nicely with their red eyes, bright orange-red bill and pink legs. Oysters are a principal part of their diet. They distract would-be predators from their young by putting on an elaborate act, which can include pretending they have broken a wing or even rolling on the ground as if they are on the point of death.

Ruddy turnstones have been appropriately named – they wander along the waters edge flipping over stones, shells or bits of weed to see if there's anything interesting underneath. These birds breed in the Arctic and migrate here for the Australian summer (September to April). Many of the young birds also spend their first winter in Australia before attempting the long migration flight for the first time.

One feathered friend found on the islands that is not such a welcome sight is that unscrupulous though efficient scavenger, that `feathered cockroach', the seagull. Seagull numbers have multiplied dramatically since the arrival of Europeans in Australia. An island like Heron would typically support about 200 seagulls without the presence of humans; a few years ago the seagull population was more like 5000. However, efforts to reduce the dumping of garbage (food scraps are now shipped back to the mainland rather than being dumped at sea) had brought the population back to about 1000. That's still too many, and they pose a danger to other birds – seagulls will seize unprotected noddy eggs or chicks – and to turtle hatchlings.

Although the bird populations are essentially the same from island to island there are often unusual sightings. Since the mid-1980s Lady Elliot Island has even had a handful of rare redtailed tropic birds nesting on the island. Raine Island, far to the north, is the only other known nesting site for this bird on the east coast of Australia.

Top Left & Right: Quiet beaches and a superb fringing reef greet the traveller to Heron Island
Bottom: The rusting wreck of the *Protector* guards the channel entrance inside
   Heron's fringing reef

ROBERT CHARLTON

ROBERT CHARLTON

MICHAEL AW

ROBERT CHARLTON

QUEENSLAND TOURIST AND TRAVEL CORPORATION

Top: Lady Musgrave Island
Middle Left: Let's hit the surf!
Middle Centre: Black noddies are a common sight on the Southern Reef islands
Middle Right: The automatic light beacon on Lady Musgrave Island
Bottom: Lady Elliot Island

Lady Elliot Island

Area:	0.42 sq km
Type:	coral cay
High point:	3m
Max visitors:	130

Right at the southern end of the marine park and the Great Barrier Reef, Lady Elliot Island, dubbed Queensland's 'Shipwreck Islands', is very popular with divers and has been the scene of numerous shipwrecks.

The island was the starting point for Australia's bêche-de-mer industry during the last century. Early explorer Matthew Flinders was shipwrecked on Wreck Reef (not Wreck Island in the Capricorn Group)

170km from Lady Elliot in 1803. Following the survivors' period on the reef, James Aickin, an early trader in this region, went there looking for these Oriental delicacies. He failed to find them on the reef in commercially viable quantities but did find them on Lady Elliot Island. In the following years, collecting bêches-de-mer became an important activity right up the coast. If Aickin's bêche-de-mer island was indeed Lady Elliot he didn't bother to name it or chart its position. The island had to wait another 13 years for a name, which was given to it by Captain Thomas Abbott of the ship *Lady Elliot* in 1816. The *Lady Elliot* was en route from Calcutta to Sydney but on her return voyage, heading for Batavia (now Jakarta) in the Dutch East Indies, ran aground on a reef off Hinchinbrook Island but was refloated. The reef also bears the ship's name.

Shipwrecks

Ships started ploughing into Lady Elliot Island at an early stage in Australia's colonial history and the activity has still not come to a halt. There were numerous wrecks in the 1970s and 80s and bits and pieces of various ships can be found all around the island.

Lady Elliot shipwrecks probably started with the 620 ton cargo ship *Bolton Abbey*, which sank off the island in 1851. Its remains were only recently located. The cargo steamer *Port St John*, which ran aground here in 1938, was one of the largest ships claimed by the island.

The year 1975 was a bad year for island wrecks, with groundings, including the 18m *Vansittart*, which later managed to get off the reef and continue its journey north. The 15m cutter *Tahuna* was not so lucky when it struck the reef and was later washed up onto the beach.

Another bad year was 1980. The schooner *Thisby*, crippled by a cyclone, washed ashore early in the year. The heavy timbers from this old boat were used to construct the resort's Thisby bar and it's easy to identify the chunks of the wreckage around the eastern point. The island's most famous, and probably most expensive, wreck followed six weeks later. The 19m *Apollo I*, designed by America's Cup designer Ben Lexcen and skippered by a Sydney millionaire who had made a mint through gambling machines, ploughed straight into the island in a 20-knot wind while leading the Brisbane to Gladstone Yacht Race. They'd been led astray by the lights of a catamaran that also went on to the reef, but had managed to extricate itself. The yacht's bow forms a servery between the resort's bar and dining room.

More wrecks followed including, in April 1989, the Fremantle yacht *Tenggara II* (*tenggara* is Indonesian for 'south-east'). She hit the reef during bad weather in the middle of the night and was washed right up on the reef and eventually abandoned. A small yacht that hit the reef in 1992 is now the centrepiece of the resort's children's playground. These days wrecked yachties are supposed to clear up any mess their wrecked boats make, as bits and pieces of boat soon end up spread right across the reef flat.

Later, in the 1860s, the island was exploited for its guano deposits and, coupled with overgrazing by goats, has never totally recovered from this Victorian-era degradation. Since the airstrip was built in 1969, the vegetation has recovered amazingly, as a comparison with photographs of the island earlier this century or even at the time the airstrip was built will show, but it's still rather bare compared to some other densely vegetated Capricornia islands. The small stand of pisonia trees in the resort area is the only one to be found on the island. The picturesque lighthouse dates from 1873, but it lost some of its romance when it was converted to automatic operation.

In 1843 Joseph Beete Jukes, naturalist on HMS *Fly*, which was surveying the Great Barrier Reef, visited Lady Elliot Island and made some interesting notes on its natural history. W Saville-Kent, another naturalist, visited the island in 1892 and commented on the rich marine life as well as the destruction of the tree cover and the scarcity of birds and turtles due to the activities of the guano miners and the lighthouse operators. Fortunately the wildlife is returning today.

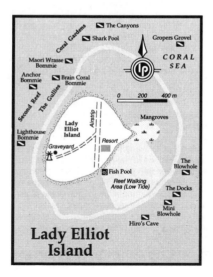

Lady Elliot Island

Information

Reservations can be made through the Sunstate Travel Centre (☎ 4152 2322 or ☎ 1800 072 200) or write to the Lady Elliot Resort, PO Box 206, Torquay, Hervey Bay, Qld 4655.

The resort's phone and fax number is ☎/fax 4125 5344. The resort has a shop with general supplies.

Around the Island

You can stroll gently right round the island in less than an hour, but it's easy to get distracted. The beach is composed of pounded coral and sand, and the glints of rainbow colours hint at the coral reef around you. If it's low tide and you're prepared to get your feet wet you can start exploring the reef. Fish, crabs, octopus, eels and cowrie shells are all waiting for the keen observer, and blue-spotted rays or wobbegong sharks, lying motionless on the sandy bottom, can also be seen. At low tide look for parrot fish, which often come in large schools into surprisingly shallow water near the shore.

The island is also a bird sanctuary and a popular stopping place for migrating species. Look for the bright blue wings of sacred kingfishers, or eastern reef herons and white-faced herons searching the shallows for fish. Turtles nest on the island in the summer and their offspring hatch out and make for the sea in the autumn.

The Lighthouse

A temporary lighthouse was built on the island in 1866 but a storm blew it down six years later. A sturdier replacement, one of the state's first steel-frame lighthouses, was completed in 1873. In 1988 it was converted to automatic operation but it's a facility that seems to have done remarkably little to warn sailors of the dangers of the Great Barrier Reef's first island. The lighthouse keepers' cottages, which are beside the lighthouse, are now used as staff accommodation for the resort.

Just inland from the lighthouse is a tiny fenced-in graveyard with two graves. One is that of Miss Phoebe Phillips, a lighthouse keeper's rather reclusive 30 year old daughter who died on the island from pneumonia in 1896. The other is Susannah McKee's, a lighthouse keeper's wife who drowned herself in 1907.

Diving

Glass-bottom boats are available on the island, friendly fish come up to be fed in the coral pools and there's good snorkelling. As the island does not suffer from heavy boat traffic or strong currents, the underwater visibility is usually extremely good and the coral is excellent. In the 'fish pond', a favourite snorkelling locale, butterfly fish and sergeant-majors will gather around snorkellers to snatch bits of bread. Many other fish can be seen in the coral around this pool, just a few steps from the shore on the resort side.

A real advantage of the island for scuba divers is that there is superb diving straight off the beach. The coral gardens area on the opposite side of the island from the resort offers wonderful diving right along the western side of the island. Divers walk round there, pulling little trolley carts containing their gear. From the edge of the reef you can fin out to attractions like the Canyons, Shark Pool, Maori Wrasse Bommie (a bommie is a submerged coral outcrop), Brain Coral Bommie and the Gullies. Sharks may indeed be seen in the Shark Pool, where they gather before moving out at the change of tide. Huge (and harmless) manta rays are often seen serenely winging past and turtles are regularly spotted around the reef.

Around the Anchor Bommie, also on the western side of the island, a number of old anchors can be seen. It's thought they belonged to the guano ships that used to anchor here during the time when the island was mined for guano. When a sudden wind shift put the guano boats in danger of being blown onto the reef they would sometimes have to cut their anchors in order to escape. Off the lighthouse at the south-west corner of the island, the Lighthouse Bommies are another shore-dive attraction.

Dives off the eastern side of the island have to be made from a boat and the winds have to be cooperative in order for you to dive here. Hiro's Cave, the Mini Blowholes and the Docks are popular dives here but the Blowhole is probably Lady Elliot's premier dive. You enter the blowhole at about 14m in depth and follow it down and around to emerge horizontally on the reef drop-off at 23m.

The island rises up from water 40m deep. The resort has good diving facilities and you can take certificate courses, which start on the 1st of each month, last five days and cost $440. All equipment is available for hire. It costs $25 for each shore dive, $35 for a boat dive, and $45 for a night dive. They're diving crazy on this island so it's often possible to do more than two dives a day. Because you have to fly out of the island there are restrictions on when you can make your last dive before departure.

Places to Stay

The small resort was just a campsite for divers until extensive development in 1985. It's still a very straightforward place with two styles of accommodation. Costs include breakfast and dinner, and children aged from three to 14 years pay half the adult rate.

The solid looking safari-style tents are basically permanently erected. Toilet and shower facilities are shared and costs are $115 per person per night for two to four adults. There's a $60 supplement to take a tent as a single.

The 'Reef Units' are simple motel-type rooms with a common vèranda area out the front and attached bathrooms. Nightly costs are $150 per person for up to four adults, and again, there's a $60 supplement for single occupancy.

One and two-bedroom suites come with a separate lounge and kitchen, and these cost $170 per person.

All rates are inclusive of dinner and breakfast.

There's no swimming pool or heavily organised entertainment but there's usually something going on in the evening, and there is a table tennis table and a video recorder. Basically, however, this is a place to get away from civilisation and concentrate on the diving.

Places to Eat

There's a dining room where the food is as simple and straightforward as the accommodation. Lady Elliot is not going to win any Great Barrier Reef cuisine awards. Never mind, diving gives you a phenomenal appetite and, since many of the resort guests are here for the diving, there are unlikely to be many complaints as any shortfalls in culinary quality are overshadowed by the large quantities of food.

The adjoining Lagoon bar's sturdy top is made from timbers from the wreck of the *Thisby*. The wine list also has a good selection of reasonably priced Australian wines.

Getting There & Away

Lady Elliot Island is the only coral cay on the reef with an airstrip. You can fly here from Bundaberg or Hervey Bay with Whitaker Air Charters – for bookings phone the Sunstate Travel Centre (☎ 4152 2322). Flight times are 30 minutes from Bundaberg and 40 minutes from Hervey Bay, and the return trip costs around $130 for resort guests.

There is a 10kg baggage weight limit, which is only rigidly enforced if the flight has weight problems. You can also do a day trip for $135 from Bundaberg, Hervey Bay or Gladstone that includes the return flight, a picnic lunch and snorkelling.

Anchorages for visiting yachts at Lady Elliot are difficult to negotiate and generally poor unless the wind is being very cooperative.

Getting supplies out to the island is also a problem: a barge comes out from the mainland, which brings non-perishable supplies – all fresh food has to come out by light aircraft. The barge has to be parked over the reef at the change of tide and then the supplies are manually carted ashore at low tide.

The Bunker Group

The Bunker Group starts with Lady Musgrave Island, which is only about 40km north of Lady Elliot Island.

If the visibility is good it's possible to see the islands as you are flying to or from Lady Elliot. The group takes its name from Captain Ebenezer Bunker, a legendary whaler, who sailed through the island group aboard his ship the *Albion* in 1803. Flinders had seen at least one of the group from afar in 1802, and in 1770 Captain Cook suspected that islands lay off the coast because of the large number of sea birds seen hunting in these waters.

LADY MUSGRAVE ISLAND

The tiny, uninhabited Lady Musgrave cay, about 100km north-east of Bundaberg, is part of the Capricornia Cays National Park. The island sits at the western end of a huge lagoon measuring 5km from end to end and occupying 12 sq km. It's the southernmost of the Bunker group, but seems like only a stone's throw south of the Fairfax and Hoskyn islands. The island was charted in 1843 and its name comes from Queensland governor Sir Anthony Musgrave's wife, Jeannie.

The perfect lagoon is one of the very few along the entire Barrier Reef where ships can safely enter – a fact which is taken advantage of by many visiting yachties.

In the early 1900s goats were released on the island, part of a British Admiralty plan to provide a food source for shipwrecked sailors. Whether any unfortunate seamen did manage to run down a sure-footed goat and butcher it for survival rations is unknown but what is more certain is that the goats totally overran the island and stripped it bare of vegetation. The goats were cleared off in 1971 and since then the vegetation has recovered remarkably. The depredations of guano miners must have been much less severe than on Lady Elliot for Lady Musgrave's vegetation, particularly the pisonia trees, is much denser.

Lady Musgrave Island

0   0.5   1 km

Boulders
The Cliff
Entrance Bommie
Triggerfish Bay
The Slotz
Gullies
Coral Gardens
Coral Canyons
Lagoon
Battery Bommie
Aquarium Pool
Staghorn Shoals
Lady Musgrave Island
Tabletops
Manta Ray Bommie
Plate Coral Slope

In the typical fashion of the southern reef cays, the tangled central pisonia growth is surrounded by hardy casuarinas and pandanus. It takes about half an hour to walk right round the island, and there's also a trail leading across from the usual landing place to the campsite and the western end of the island. The island is an important nesting ground for mutton birds and white-capped noddies, while green and loggerhead turtles also come here to lay their eggs.

Despite an automatic light beacon, which was installed on the island in 1974, Lady Musgrave has also had its share of passing ships colliding into it. In 1985 the 35,000 tonne bulk carrier *TNT Alltrans* ran aground on the reef but was refloated a day later, having suffered fairly extensive damage to its bottom, although fortunately not losing fuel or cargo.

Diving

Lady Musgrave offers some excellent diving opportunities, often enjoyed by day trip visitors. The lagoon offers excellent snorkelling and some good shallower scuba dives for beginners. The fish have become so used to being fed that they virtually mob divers and snorkellers and it's a good idea to wear gloves if you're going to be handing out goodies.

Diving outside the reef is usually on the northern side of the lagoon, because it is much quicker to reach from the lagoon anchorage and also because this side is sheltered from the prevailing winds and currents. Dives along this face of the reef are usually to around 12m in depth, but there are two deeper, popular dives at opposite ends of the reef. Manta Ray Bommie at the western corner is about 17m deep and, yes, there are indeed frequent sightings of manta rays here.

Just outside the lagoon entrance the Entrance Bommie is a superb dive with a maximum depth of just over 20m. The bommie has a swim-through and a number of resident fish, including two elderly and surprisingly large lionfish, which regularly come out to greet divers. The only catch with this dive is that it can only be made at the turn of the tide, due to the rapid currents sweeping in or out of the lagoon entrance at other times. A dive, if you've come out to the cay with the *Lady Musgrave*, costs $40 including a full tank and all gear, or $60 for an introductory dive.

Places to Stay

With a national parks permit you can camp on the island but the only facilities are some surprisingly luxurious bush toilets. Campers – a maximum of 50 at any one time – must be totally self-sufficient in drinking water and fuel. The enormous amount of fallen pisonia wood around the island must be very tempting but, no doubt, it would soon be gone if campers were allowed to burn it. Generators cannot be run on the island between 9 pm and 7 am.

The large centipedes on the island, which usually appear after dark on rainy days, are harmless but if you're unlucky enough to get a bird tick they should be removed. These tiny ticks, carried by noddies, will cause itching, but are not a serious problem unless you have a reaction to them. The easiest way to avoid them is not to camp under the pisonia trees where noddies nest.

Getting There & Away
You can reach Lady Musgrave Island by the fast catamaran MV *Lady Musgrave* from Bundaberg. It's operated by Lady Musgrave Barrier Reef Cruises (☎ 4152 9011) at 1 Quay St in Bundaberg. The cost is $105 ($53 for a child), which includes lunch, snorkel gear and a glass-bottom boat ride. The trip takes 2½ hours each way and you have about four hours on the island. The boat leaves from Port Bundaberg near Bundaberg at 8.30 am on Monday, Tuesday, Wednesday and Saturday and you return at 5.45 pm. You can also use this service for a camping drop-off and pick-up at a cost of $200. A connecting bus service, which costs $8 for morning pick-up and evening drop-off, is also operated from Bundaberg and Bargara.

Captain Cook Great Barrier Reef Cruises (☎ 4974 9077) also operate trips out of Seventeen Seventy three times a week on its vessel MV *Spirit of 1770*. The trips visit Lady Musgrave and include all the usuals, such as snorkelling, glass-bottom boat trip and coral viewing, but fishing is also included. The cost is $105 ($53). They also do camping transfers to the island.

Lady Musgrave is one of the few cays on the Barrier Reef where visiting yachts can safely anchor within the lagoon. At most cays the water within the reef is too shallow or there is no suitable entrance. Anchoring outside a cay's reef is seldom practicable.

OTHER BUNKER GROUP ISLANDS
The **Fairfax Islands** are two tiny cays north of Lady Musgrave Island. These cays were, unfortunately, devastated by practice bombing during WWII, grazing by goats, and guano mining. They are no longer open to visitors.

Slightly north again are the **Hoskyn Islands**, also national parks and the most unspoiled of the group. They are presently closed to day visitors. The western of the

two Hoskyn islands is almost completely vegetated by pandanus, apart from a few pisonia. The Hoskyn and Fairfax islands are the southernmost recorded nesting ground for gannets, which come here from September to January.

North again are the Boult, Llewellyn and Fitzroy reefs, before you reach the Capricorn Group. The **Fitzroy Reef**, 30km northwest of Lady Musgrave, is another coral lagoon where visiting yachts can safely enter and anchor. It's rather like the lagoon at Lady Musgrave, but without an island in the lagoon. **Boult Reef** has an enclosed lagoon and a very conspicuous trawler wreck, perched on the eastern edge of the reef. **Llewellyn Reef** has a deep and extensive enclosed lagoon.

The Capricorn Group

North of the Bunker Group and straddling the Tropic of Capricorn are the islands and reefs of the Capricorn Group. These islands include Masthead, North West, Tryon – all popular camping islands – and Heron Island, with its resort, is probably the most popular diver's island on the Great Barrier Reef.

HERON ISLAND

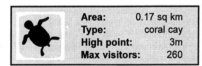

Area:	0.17 sq km
Type:	coral cay
High point:	3m
Max visitors:	260

Heron is a real coral cay and the Tropic of Capricorn virtually runs through the island. The tiny island rises only 3m above sea level although it's quite densely vegetated with pisonia trees, which can reach 15m high. Although the tiny island is less than a kilometre long it's surrounded by 24 sq km of reef where keen divers will find a vast

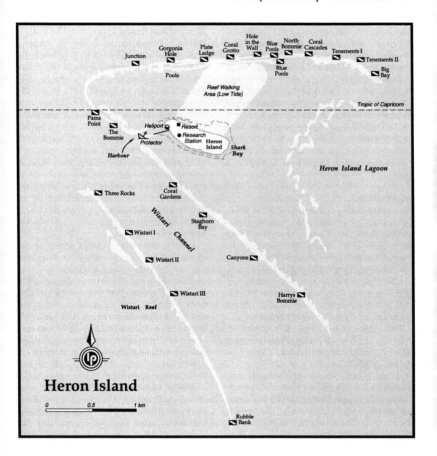

Heron Island

0   0.5   1 km

variety of marine life. The island takes its name from the distinctive reef herons seen here. The resort covers the north-eastern third of the island and, although the rest is national park and includes a marine research station, you cannot camp here.

The island has had a varied and interesting history. HMS *Fly*, which did so much of the surveying of the Southern Reef Islands, anchored off Heron Island in 1843 and Joseph Beete Jukes, the expedition's naturalist, noted the island's many reef herons and named it in their honour. In 1910 and

several times in subsequent years, ornithologists visited the island to study its birdlife, but in 1925 a lease was granted to establish a turtle soup factory on Heron Island. The initial company failed two years later without commencing operations but another company took over the lease. By 1930 turtles were already becoming very scarce and this company ceased operations shortly after.

In 1932 Captain Christian Poulson commenced work on converting the turtle soup cannery into a small resort. The Poulson family was to play a major part in the development of Heron Island as a resort. After WWII Captain Poulson started flights to Heron from Brisbane. He purchased three ex-RAAF Catalina flying boats and cobbled them together to make one useable 28 seat aircraft. Landings were made either within the shallow Heron lagoon or between Heron and Wistari reefs. Unfortunately, in 1947 Captain Poulson drowned while returning to the resort from a boat moored offshore.

The resort was taken over by P&O in 1973.

Information

The resort phone number is ☎ 4978 1488, the fax number is 4978 1457, and the postal address is Heron Island Resort, via Gladstone, Qld 4680. Reservations should be made through P&O Resorts (☎ 13 2469), 160 Sussex Street, Sydney, NSW 2000.

There are a couple of pay phones by the reception area. There are no banking facilities, but the resort can exchange foreign currency and cash travellers cheques.

The Queensland National Parks & Wildlife Service has an information centre (☎ 4972 5690) on the island, and this is staffed by the resort.

Heron Island time is permanently one hour ahead of Australian Eastern Standard Time, which can make for confusing transfers to and from the mainland.

Books The resort shop and the diving shop both have an interesting selection of books on the Barrier Reef for sale.

An interesting series of $1 booklets is also available from the resort shop. Look for *Reef Walking*, *Sea Turtles of Heron Island* and *The Birds of Heron Island*.

Dangers & Annoyances If you have an aversion to noisy birds Heron may be a bit much in the nesting season. The noddies twitter day and night; the mutton birds wail ceaselessly and crash into roofs, walls, and resort guests when making their inept landings. Plus you'll be lucky if you don't suffer at least a few direct hits by bird droppings.

Around the Island

Heron's a fascinating island to wander around and you can walk right around the beach or take the stroll through the dense pisonia forest in the centre of the island. There's usually an island walk organised every day.

Heron follows a very similar pattern to other cays in the Southern Reef group – a fine sand beach with patches of beach rock encircles the island. Beyond the high-water mark you first find the hardier she-oaks and pandanus trees, able to withstand the wind and salt spray. Further inland are the stately pisonia trees with their cooling canopy of light green leaves. And everywhere there's the noise and odour of the island's huge bird population.

Keep to the walking tracks when you're exploring the island – straying from the tracks can easily lead to stepping on a mutton bird's burrow, with potentially dire results to any occupant and to yourself. The main walking track meanders from the resort through the centre of the island to Shark Bay at the eastern end. Here you will often see gummy sharks or small rays basking on the sandy bottom of the bay.

Heron's harbour is a controversial subject. Like on many other cays, getting boats in is a problem and in Heron's case it was solved by dredging a harbour and building a jetty. Unfortunately silt from the harbour has affected the coral in places, and the harbour is also causing changes to the water flow right across the reef. Normally as the tide drops, water spills off the reef in all directions, but now there's a natural drain for it to run out and this is sucking the sand off the northern edge of the island near the resort area.

The rusting old wreck beside the harbour entrance is the *Protector*. Launched in England in 1884, she was originally built for the South Australian Navy, when Australia was still composed of a number of separate colonies. The *Protector* saw service during the Boxer Rebellion and, then named the *Sidney*, was to be used by the US Army in WWII in New Guinea, however, following a collision with a tug was abandoned on Facing Island near Gladstone. In 1943 she was towed out to Heron Island to make a breakwater, long before the harbour entrance existed, and has been there ever since. The *Protector* is a picturesque part of Heron to some eyes – an ugly, rusting eyesore to others. A number of birds nest on the *Protector*, including the shy black-naped terns that have abandoned the island itself.

Heron Island Research Centre

Originally established in 1951, the research station is now run by the University of Queensland. The station conducts work on numerous projects connected with the islands and reef and has laboratories, workshops, aquarium facilities, a library, boats and diving equipment together with accommodation facilities. Apart from researchers actually working on projects at the station there are often conventions and other academic gatherings, plus visits by groups of secondary and tertiary students. Visits to the station can be arranged through the resort, although the level of activity fluctuates considerably through the year.

Activities

Heron is a diver's island and night-time activities take second place, although there is a bar and disco. Other facilities include tennis courts and two small swimming pools. If you have to have a TV, the resort does have one – it's in the departure lounge. **Guided reef walks** (viewing tubes and reef shoes provided) and **nature walks** around the cay, led by the resort staff, are popular daytime activities and there are also **slide shows** and lectures on the reef and its management by scientists from the island's research station. **Fishing trips** are another activity at Heron (\$35 for half a day).

Turtle watching is also extremely popular, and this offers a rare chance to view these creatures at close quarters. Green, loggerhead and hawksbill turtles are seasonal visitors to Heron, and the green and loggerhead actually nest on the island. During the nesting season (November through February) it's possible to walk along the beach at night (no torches, as these disturb the turtles) and observe the turtles crawling up the beach, digging huge holes and laying their eggs, before they return to the sea. Flash photography is allowed during certain stages of the pro cess; check with the information centre for more details. While the turtles generally stay away from the resort, they occasionally wander off course, and have been known to end up in the swimming pool, perhaps wondering why the ocean is suddenly so small.

Diving & Snorkelling Heron Island, which is a national park, is famed for its superb scuba diving and each October or November the week-long Heron Island Dive Festival includes a host of diving seminars, lectures and other activities. (Accommodation can be tight during this time, so plan ahead.) Spear fishing is banned and the reef here is fortunate to have escaped attacks by the crown-of-thorns starfish, which has caused so much damage further north. Although diving is very popular there are also semi-submersible boat trips for the less energetic (\$24; one hour), and even walking (very carefully) across the reef flats at low tide will provide lots of interest.

It's only a few steps out to the reef for snorkellers and only 15 minutes on the resort's dive boat (\$14) out to various good diving sites. All diving is from boats; there is no shore diving at Heron.

There are some superb diving spots around Heron, starting with the famed dive known as the Bommie, right outside the harbour entrance. It's not just 'a bommie' but a whole series of huge bommies (submerged coral outcrops) going step by step down the reef slope from around 10 to 18m in depth. The Bommie is particularly well known for Harry and Fang, two of Heron's three 'tame' moray eels that live in the bommies and regularly come out to meet divers. Just east of the bommies is a large anchor; there's no history to it – the anchor was simply put there to add some interest.

Around the north side of the reef Gorgonia Hole with its dramatic drop-off, the Coral Grotto at 10m, Hole in the Wall at 15 to 18m, Coral Cascades at the same depth, and Tenements I and Tenements II are other popular dives. There are more dives along the north-east edge of Wistari Reef.

Two dives a day are usually possible, and sometimes you can also fit in a night dive (although these are often heavily booked). Day dives cost $38 including the boat trip and diving equipment, night dives are $60. All equipment can be hired from Heron's comprehensively equipped dive shop. June is a good month for diving at Heron because your airfills and boat charges are free. Heron is a popular place to learn diving. A six day certificate diving course cost $395.

Places to Stay

Accommodation on Heron Island consists of lodges or suites, and all prices are inclusive of meals. The 30 Turtle Cabins are basically simple little bunkrooms with beds enough for four people and shared toilet and bathroom facilities. There's nothing special about the cabins but most people staying here will be worrying about the diving, not the creature comforts. Daily cost in a cabin is $158 per person ($126 per person for a group of four) but, although you can book a single bed, sole use of a cabin is not available. If the resort is uncrowded you may get a room to yourself, if it's busy you may find yourself making some new friends.

In the other rooms costs are per person but you can take a room by yourself for a $65 surcharge. There are 38 Reef Suites at $224 per person, 44 spacious Heron Suites at $246 per person, and four Point Suites and one Beach House at $306 per person. The suites are all comfortable, modern, well equipped and have all the mod cons you could ask for, although Heron makes a point of not having telephones or TVs. Children aged from three to 14 years pay half the adult rate, those under three stay free.

All rooms have access to guest laundries, which are at various locations around the resort.

Out of season there are often special deals to Heron Island which can reduce the cost of a diving holiday. If you're in Gladstone it's worth inquiring about standby rates. Traveland Gladstone (☎ 4972 2288) and Harvey World Travel (☎ 4972 3488) can both offer standby rates if rooms are available. Standby helicopter and catamaran transfers are also available.

Places to Eat

There's just one place to eat at Heron; breakfast and lunch are buffet style while at dinner time you order from a menu. On day one you're assigned a table and although nobody makes a fuss about it you're supposed to stick to that table throughout your stay. Heron is not an island for romantic tête-à-têtes and, let's face it, a lot of the conversation is diving talk. Never mind, your meal companions tend to change from day to day as people come and go. And the food really is pretty good. Of course the diving-honed appetites tend to be decidedly healthy ones, but even if you haven't been burning up your energy metres below the surface you still won't be disappointed with the food.

The menu typically includes a soup, followed by a choice of a couple of starters, three main courses (one of them seafood), then a couple of desserts. There's a separate vegetarian menu, plus serve-yourself salads, fruit salad, cheese and biscuits, and coffee. Nobody goes hungry and generally there's praise for the quality as well as the quantity. Adding to the atmosphere are the buff-banded rails, which wander nonchalantly through the dining room in search of scraps.

The drinks list includes beers at around $3.50, wine by the glass for $4.50 to $7.50 and by the bottle for around $20 to $40.

Getting There & Away

Offshore, 72km east of Gladstone or about 100km from Rockhampton, Heron Island is a real reef island. Due to its distance from the mainland it's one of the more expensive islands to get out to.

Flying to Heron

Flying to Heron Island has had a slightly dramatic history although, fortunately, only once have regular fare-paying passengers come to grief. Perhaps it's a spin-off from those lousy landers the mutton birds, whose arrival attempts are often more crashdown than touchdown. Back in WWII a RAAF Avro Anson aircraft, on a training flight, made slightly too low a pass over the island, clipping the tops of the pisonia trees and crashing, killing four of the five crew.

The Poulson's Catalina flying boats services to the island passed without serious mishap, but helicopter flights to Heron have had a few problems over the years. In 1969 a helicopter crashed on take-off from Gladstone, seriously injuring one passenger. Three years later a helicopter crashed, after taking off from the resort to investigate a distress flare, killing the pilot, resort manager and a resort employee.

Only a year later there were three helicopter mishaps in the space of two months. First a chopper made an emergency landing at sea near Polmaise Reef. A second helicopter dropped its passengers off on Masthead Island then returned to the stricken helicopter only to sink after puncturing a float while landing, fortunately without harm to the passengers. The third incident again took place near Polmaise Reef. The undamaged helicopter was towed to near Masthead Island where the passengers were transferred to a boat – but as the tow continued, the helicopter turned over and sank.

Air The sophisticated way of getting to Heron is by helicopter – the catch is that it costs you $240 one way or $396 return. The trip, of about 30 minutes, whisks you out to Heron and provides spectacular views over Polmaise Reef, Masthead and Erskine islands and finally Wistari Reef. A quick circuit of Heron Island, on arrival or departure, completes the trip. If you're going out to Heron by chopper phone Marine Helicopters (☎ 4978 1177) the day before to check departure time. A standby fare of $114 one way is also available.

Sea The resort's *Reef Adventurer* high-speed catamaran will take you out to the island from Gladstone in less than two hours for $75 ($150 return). The crossing can be choppy – pop those seasickness pills.

There are basically no anchorages for visiting yachts and day visitors to Heron are not welcome.

ONE TREE ISLAND

South-east of Heron Island, this island is another national park and, like Heron Island, it has a marine research station, operated in this case by Sydney University. No visitors are permitted on this desolate island – and it has rather more than one tree.

The island was originally named by officers on HMS *Fly* during its 1843 visit and they noted a sea eagle's nest on the island that is still there today. North of One Tree and east of Heron is Sykes Reef with its very small lagoon.

MASTHEAD & ERSKINE ISLANDS

Masthead Island was named by officers on HMS *Beagle* when it sailed by in 1839. It's an uninhabited national park island slightly south-west of Heron Island. Camping is permitted, with limits of 30 people in the summer bird-nesting season and 60 people in winter, but there are no facilities and campers have to be completely self-sufficient. It's also a 'silent' island, ie no radios or generators are permitted. The island has a dense central forest of pisonia trees, one of the largest stands of this interesting tree in the Capricornia islands. Masthead is an important nesting ground for green turtles.

Mutton birds and black noddies and a number of other birds also nest here.

Erskine Island is just north of Masthead and only day visits are permitted. Even these are discouraged from October to March because of the many birds that nest here.

You see both these islands from the *Reef Adventurer*, en route to Wistari Reef or Heron Island, and get superb views of them from the helicopter. Irving Reef, west of Polmaise Reef, usually has sufficient water cover for boats to sail right over it.

WILSON ISLAND

North of Heron Island, Wilson is a national park and a popular day trip ($45) for Heron guests looking for a break from diving. They spend a pleasant day there swimming off the island's excellent beaches and enjoying a BBQ lunch. There's superb snorkelling around Wilson Island, which does not have the extensive surrounding reef area found on most other Capricornia islands. Not everybody enjoys the visitors: it's said the island's roseate terns abandoned the island when visitors started to turn up regularly. The birds have since returned, but it's still important for people to avoid disturbing them.

WRECK ISLAND

Just to the south-east of Wilson Island, Wreck Island is a Preservation Zone and no access is permitted. The island is a major rookery for loggerhead turtles and roseate terns and has had an interesting history. One of the first shipwrecks in the Southern Reef Islands, that of the *America* in 1831 took place here. The 391 ton *America* was built in Quebec in 1827 and was bound from Sydney to Batavia (Jakarta) when she ran hard onto a reef. For a time it was thought that the location might have been off Lady Elliot Island, but in 1843 Captain Blackwood of HMS *Fly* reported the remains of a wreck on the Wreck Island reef and found inscriptions on trees stating 'The *America*, June 1831' as well as from the ship *Nelson*, which played a follow up part in the

America saga. The island was named by Captain Blackwood after the wreckage he noted there. More recently hand-hewn ballast stone has been found on the reef flat.

The survivors from the *America* eventually made their way to Moreton Bay, a fraught journey taking a month or more. The wreckage was sold at auction and later that year the *Caledonia* sailed north to retrieve whatever could be scavenged from the reef. The unfortunate *Caledonia* arrived too late, as the whaler *Nelson* had already done a salvage job on the wreckage and sailed on to Sydney.

Matters were to turn distinctly worse for the unfortunate *Caledonia*: when it arrived at Moreton Bay a convict escape took place and the ship was hijacked, together with the ship's master, Captain Browning, who was taken along to navigate. The *Caledonia* eventually ended up in Tonga, over two months later, where the ship was scuttled. By this time only two or three of the original 15 escapees were still with the ship. Browning eventually escaped and was rescued by the barque *Oldham*. None of the convicts were brought back to Australia.

NORTH REEF ISLAND

North of Wilson and Wreck Islands is tiny North Reef Island where a lighthouse was completed in 1878. It was noted at the time that the island 'is composed of nothing but dead coral, which shifts more or less during heavy gales, its total extent not exceeding 200 by 80 yards'. Over the years the island certainly has shifted. The lighthouse started off right in the middle but gradually 'moved' along the island until it hung right off one end, at which point the island about turned and moved back until the lighthouse is once more in the middle. Sensibly the lighthouse was bedded right into the solid rock, beneath the moving coral debris that formed the island.

Today the lighthouse is an automatic one but it didn't save the 3879 ton steamship *Cooma*, which was wrecked on the eastern side of the reef in 1926. The wreck is visible at low water and the reef offers great diving.

Broomfield Reef with its high sandbank is about midway between North Reef, to the north, and Wilson and Wreck islands to the south.

NORTH WEST ISLAND

At 0.9 sq km, North West Island is the biggest cay on the Great Barrier Reef. Guano was mined on the island from 1894 to 1900 and at times there were over 100 people living and working here. Over 4000 tons of guano had been exported (mostly to New Zealand) from the island when guano mining ceased. A picket fence encloses the tiny grave of Dorothea Sundvall, daughter of the captain of the guano ship *Limari*. She was born at sea in 1899, died a few days later and was buried on the island at the north-western end. There are said to be other graves on the island including those of two Japanese divers but any markers have now disappeared.

Turtles were also killed and processed into turtle soup on the island, an activity that continued intermittently right up until 1928. A few bits and pieces of rusting equipment remain from the turtle soup days and the island is infested with cats and chickens from that period. Today turtles, now fully protected, have returned to North West and it is the most important site for green turtles in the Capricorn Group.

Places to Stay

The island is all national park and independent camping is allowed with a permit. Often fully booked during holiday periods the island has a camping limit of 150 people. There are pit toilets and the hut on the island (the *Tanby Hilton*) may have some water although campers are advised to take their own. A track runs across the island from the hut.

Getting There & Away

There are no scheduled services to North West, so without your own boat it's a matter of finding a charter from Gladstone or Rosslyn Bay, near Rockhampton.

TRYON ISLAND

Immediately north of North West Island this minute (only about 11 hectares or a tenth of a sq km) national park island is a typical cay that has largely remained undisturbed by humans, although it may have been briefly exploited for guano. There is much birdlife on the island including shy black-naped and bridled terns. Mutton birds also nest here, as do green turtles. The north-facing beach on Tryon has many cordia trees with their bright orange flowers, and despite the island's tiny size there is a small stand of pisonia trees in the centre.

Camping is permitted on Tryon, but there are no facilities.

SWAINS REEF

Offshore from the Capricornia area, on the main outer reef, the Swains Reef area is claimed to have some of the best fishing on the Great Barrier Reef. Coral trout, red emperors and Spanish mackerel are common here.

Great Keppel Island

Great Keppel was named (by Captain Cook when he sailed by in May 1770) after Rear Admiral Augustus Keppel. Cook did a great deal of naming as he cruised the east coast of Australia. The first European known to visit the island was a naturalist named McGillivray, who arrived on the *Rattlesnake* in 1847. At that time Aboriginals lived on the island, which they named Wapparaburra, thought to mean 'resting place'.

First settled by Europeans in 1906 the early residents were a disreputable bunch who poisoned the Aboriginals' flour with strychnine after some of their sheep were killed. From the 1920s through the 1940s the Leeke family grazed sheep on the island and gave their name to Leeke's Beach and Leeke's Creek. You can still see their restored homestead, which makes a popular walk destination from the resort. The island resort opened in 1967, but it is not the only occupant of the island. The Svendsen family at the northern end are professional fishers.

Although it's not on the reef, Great Keppel is a fine island, big enough that you won't see all of it in an afternoon but small enough to explore over a few days. Its 28km coastline includes 18km of very fine beaches. Great Keppel is only 13km off the coast and there's a variety of reasonably priced air and sea transport out to it. Coupled with this, a good choice of cheaper places to stay makes Great Keppel an unbeatable destination for budget travellers.

Information

There are pay phones at the resort and outside reception at Keppel Haven, and both places also have EFTPOS facilities. The resort Island Shop has some clothes, sunscreen, magazines and newspapers, toiletries, a postal agency with postcards and stamps, and maps of the island. The kiosk at Keppel Haven also sells a limited range of groceries.

GREAT KEPPEL ISLAND

Highlights
- Pack a picnic and soak up the sun on your own private stretch of superb white-sand beach
- Order home-made scones and chat to the owner of the Shell House
- Go for a walk on one of Great Keppel's many interesting trails

Area:	14 sq km
Type:	continental
High point:	175m
Max visitors:	400m

Zoning Most of the waters around Great Keppel are zoned General Use A or B but the area off Fisherman's Beach is all Marine National Park A, which allows line fishing but prohibits shell or coral collecting. The waters around Middle Island are zoned the more restrictive Marine National Park B.

Great Keppel Island

CORAL SEA

Big Peninsula

Half Tide Rocks

Little Peninsula

Butterfish Bay

Big Sandhills Beach

Svendsens Beach

Second Beach

Wreck Beach

0   1   2 km

Middle Island

Passage Rocks

Leeke's Beach

Wreck Bay

Bald Rock

Underwater Observatory

Putney Beach

Leeke's Creek

Homestead

Dam

Bald Rock Point

Ferry Landing

Fisherman's Beach

The Valley

Great Keppel Island

Red Beach

Putney Creek

Mt Wyndham

Clam Bay

Airstrip

Wyndham Cove

Shelving Beach

Coconut Point

Monkey Beach

Long Beach

Little Monkey Point

Monkey Point

Halfway Island

Cathedral Rock

Humpy Island

1 Keppel Haven & Keppel Kamp-Out
2 Dive Shop
3 Keppel Haven Bar & Bistro
4 Great Keppel YHA Hostel
5 Island Pizza
6 Shell House
7 Keppel Lodge
8 Great! Keppel Resort

Activities

Resort With its motto of 'Forget the Rest', the resort promotes Great Keppel as the 'active island'. Many of the activities on offer are free for house guests, including use of the squash courts, tennis courts, a six hole golf course, a playground, windsurfers, catamarans and a couple of swimming pools. Resort guests are also kept busy with archery, aerobics, volleyball and other organised activities. They don't want you to get bored.

To encourage guests to keep active (and spend more money), the resort has a Legends Club. Every activity is allocated a certain number of points, and when you reach 2500 points you become an automatic 'legend', which gets you a T-shirt and certificate. The highest point-scorer is tandem skydiving – for $250 ($320 with a video) you get to jump out of a light plane at 7000 feet.

The Keppel Kids' Klub, for three to 14 year olds, can keep kids occupied all day, and babysitting services are usually available for the younger ones. The resort also organises overnight Kids' Campouts to the Homestead (the old Leeke family home), where they set up their own tents, cook damper and have singalongs around the campfire. Finally, like almost every resort up the coast, Great Keppel has a lorikeet-feeding table where the colourful birds appear for a feed every morning. Possums can appear around the resort at any time.

The resort has a separate section for day-trippers with a small pool, bar, outdoor tables and umbrellas, a char-grill restaurant and a takeaway cafe.

Watersports Two places hire out water-sports equipment – Keppel Watersports on Fisherman's Beach is run by the resort, or there's the Beach Shed on Putney Beach, run by Keppel Haven. Both have snorkelling gear, jet skis, windsurfers, cata-marans, motorboats, fuel, tackle and bait. Non-powered equipment like aqua bikes, catamarans, sailboards, paddle skis and snorkelling gear is free to guests but it's also available, for a charge, to non-residents. The Beach Shed has slightly cheaper rates.

Keppel Watersports has motorboats for $20 per hour. There are limits on how far you can take a motorboat, generally only as far as Leeke's Beach in the north and Long Beach in the south. You can also take a paraflight with Keppel Watersports for $40; you're only up for about seven minutes but that must be long enough as it's so popular you need to book on arrival if you're not staying on the island overnight. Waterskiing ($20 for 10 minutes), tube rides ($10) and catamarans ($10 an hour) are also available.

Diving The Great Barrier Reef is a long way out at this latitude but there's good diving much closer to Great Keppel, and you can go diving with Keppel Reef Scuba Adventures (☎ 4939 5022), on Putney Beach just down from the Beach Shed. The company has a five day diving course on demand (minimum two) for $420 – all in-clusive except for a medical certificate. It also offers introductory dives ($80) and dives for certified divers ($55 for one, $100 for two).

Dive companies on the mainland, includ-ing Capricorn Reef Diving (☎ 4922 7720) and Rockhampton Dive (☎ 4928 0433), both in Rockhampton, and Tropicana Dives (☎ 4939 4642) in Yeppoon, do trips to various locations around the islands from Rosslyn Bay.

Close to Great Keppel itself, Man & Wife Rocks and Bald Rock are two popular diving attractions. The water off the south-ern end of Halfway Island and the shallow Middle Island Reef between Putney Point and Middle Island also has good coral and sea snakes. Parker's Bommie, off the south-eastern tip of Great Keppel is believed to offer the best diving around the island, so long as the weather is calm. The bombora rises almost to the surface from water about 20m deep and is surrounded by a great variety of sea ferns, sponges, coral and a great number of fish.

See the Other Keppel Bay Islands section later in this chapter for more information on diving in the area.

Beaches & Snorkelling It only takes a short stroll from the main resort area to find your own deserted stretch of white-sand beach. These are among the best beaches on any of the resort islands and it's remarkable how many people make no effort to try any of them apart from Fisherman's Beach, the one right in front of the resort, and nearby Putney Beach. Small Shelving Beach is only a few minutes walk from the resort or, further afield, is Long Beach and Leeke's Beach are also pleasant. Some beaches, like Red Beach near the lighthouse, are only ac-cessible by boat.

The water around the island is clear, warm and beautiful, and there is good coral at many points, especially at Shelving Beach and Monkey Beach. Much of the coral around Great Keppel has been killed over the years by fresh water flooding from the Fitzroy River, most recently in 1991. Worst affected areas are Shelving and Monkey beaches, with Passage Rocks least severely affected. Further out there's more good coral between Great Keppel and Humpy Island to the south, particularly around Halfway Island.

The resort hires out watersports equipment through Keppel Watersports on Fisherman's Beach. Snorkelling equipment is free to resort guests. Snorkelling equipment can be hired from the Beach Shed on Putney Beach ($10 full day) or from the YHA hostel manager ($8).

Boats & Cruises Keppel Tourist Services (☎ 4933 6744) runs various cruises, mainly in the *Reefcat*. Its island cruise departs daily from Rosslyn Bay at 9.15 am and from Fisherman's Beach at 9.50 am, and continues on a three hour cruise to the company's large floating pontoon moored 50m offshore from the northern tip of the island. The cruise includes boomnetting and snorkelling, and a visit to the underwater observatory. It returns to the mainland at 4.30 pm; the cruise costs $70 from Rosslyn Bay or $33 if you're already on the island.

Several vessels are available for longer diving, fishing or cruising trips – ask at Rockhampton tourist office or Rosslyn Bay harbour.

Walks There are a number of fine bushwalking tracks but don't underestimate the island – some of the walks can take the whole day and you'll need water as it can be very hot and dry. During its farming period some parts of the island were treated with less than good care and in a few places ugly garbage dumps and other eyesores could do with a good clean up. The goats you may see around the island are a legacy of the farming days.

It takes about 20 minutes to walk the length of the airstrip to Long Beach and you can make a circuit of it by walking back around the coast via Monkey Point, Monkey Beach and Shelving Beach.

It's nearly 3km to the old Leeke homestead; count on about an hour each way. The walk starts from near the Shell House and climbs up to a lookout before dropping down to the homestead near Leeke's Creek. You can make this a partial round trip by taking the turning down to Leeke's Beach and walking along the beach and over the headland to Putney Beach.

The more energetic can make the climb to Mt Wyndham, at 175m it is the highest point on the island. The trail branches off the homestead route and the summit is clearly visible from the resort, rising up to the east of the airstrip. It takes about 1½ hours from the resort to the top.

There are two longer walks that continue on beyond the homestead. It's nearly 8km to the lighthouse: climb up to the ridge line beyond the homestead and Leeke's Creek, then follow the ridge to its 170m high point and head down to Bald Rock Point and the lighthouse. The walk takes 2½ hours each way so allow the whole day. At the top of the ridge you can turn north-west instead of south-east and walk down to Big Sandhills Beach on Butterfish Bay.

Places to Stay
The Great! Keppel Resort is so well known that it's easy to forget there are some excellent budget-priced alternatives. At the resort the great majority of visitors will be on some sort of all inclusive package but Great Keppel also has cabins and campsites, a small lodge and a youth hostel so it's one of the limited number of resort islands where backpackers can stay at a reasonable cost.

Great! Keppel Resort The resort phone number is ☎ 4939 5044, the fax number is 4939 1775, and the postal address is Great! Keppel Island Resort, PMB North Rockhampton, QLD 4701. Reservations can be made with Australian Resorts (☎ 13 1415).

The 190 unit resort, which was renovated in the early 1990s, is quite stylish and comfortable without being sophisticated. The older Beachfront and Garden units are essentially the same, only the location differs. They're plain and straightforward motel-type units, all with a queen and a single bed, ceiling fan, TV, telephone, bar fridge, and tea/coffee-making facilities. The rooms have a veranda out the front and there are laundry facilities in each block. The newer Hillside Villas are more upmarket, with split-level design, all-white decor and great views. These rooms also have air-conditioning.

Surprisingly, noise doesn't seem to be a real problem – the disco and other centres of disturbance are kept down at one end of the grounds. In the older rooms, ventilation can, if the wind's blowing the wrong way, be more of a problem; the room design doesn't encourage breezes to blow through. Interconnecting rooms are available for families.

Daily costs are officially $270 for the Garden Units, $300 for the Beachfront Units, and $380 for the Hillside Villas. Rates are cheaper for five nights or more, and cheaper standby rates are available (typically around 50% discount if you book three days in advance). The standard rates include breakfast and include quite a few activities, and you have the option of taking a lunch and dinner package for another $38.

Qantas has a variety of package tours to Great Keppel – prices include accommodation and return airfares and vary depending on where you start from. Outside peak periods such as school holidays, seven day packages cost from around $590 per person from Brisbane, and around $735 from Melbourne. Ring Qantas Australian Holidays (☎ 13 1415) for details.

Hostel The *Great Keppel YHA Hostel* (☎ 4939 4341), a short walk behind Keppel Haven, has room for 48 people. The main building has two 16-bed dorms, a kitchen, bathrooms and a laundry, and there are two separate eight-bed units with their own bathrooms. A bed costs $16 in the dorms, $17 in the cabins, non-members pay another $3. Overall the hostel is rather shabby but that doesn't stop it being very popular and it's often booked out for weeks ahead. Book through the Rockhampton Youth Hostel or the YHA head office in Brisbane (☎ 3236 1680). The hostel's $79 deal ($89 non-members) is good value –

you get one night in Rocky, two nights on the island and bus and boat transfers.

Lodge *Keppel Lodge* (☎ 4939 4251), midway between the resort and Keppel Haven, is a very pleasant little place with four spacious motel-style units, each with their own bathroom. In the centre of the building there's a large communal lounge room with a good kitchen, and there's also a BBQ area outside for guests. The rooms sleep up to five people, and the nightly cost is $90 for a double or twin plus $30 for each additional person, or $15 for kids under 12.

Cabins & Campsites At *Keppel Haven* (☎ 4933 6744) there are pre-erected tents that sleep up to four people. The tents come complete with mattresses and cost $25 per person.

The Tent Village has undercover cooking and washing-up facilities and a fridge and BBQ – you need to bring your own cutlery etc. There are also 12 self-contained six-bed cabins at $110 a double, plus $30 for each extra person. The cabins have full kitchen facilities, laundry and bedding, but communal bathrooms. By mainland standards the cabins aren't cheap but for the islands they're a bargain.

Right next door to Keppel Haven is *Keppel Kamp-Out* (☎ 4939 2131), an almost identical tent village (in outward appearance). However, the concept (and price) is different. It's geared to the 18 to 35 age bracket with organised activities and the cost of $69 per person includes twin-share tent accommodation, three meals (wine with dinner), and all activities such as watersports, parties and video nights. The tents are large, the gardens are lovely and the staff are friendly. A standby rate of $49 is usually available.

Places to Eat
The Resort If you're staying at the resort you have the option of taking the meal package ($38 for lunch and dinner) or buying your meals individually. The main dining room is the *Admiral Keppel Restau-*

rant. To start the day you can have either a continental or full buffet-style breakfast. Lunches consist of grills and salad buffet at the outdoor *Anchorage Char-grill* by the pool, and dinner alternates between good old buffet-style (Monday is Italian, Thai on Wednesday, Aussie BBQ on Thursday, seafood on Friday, and roasts on Sunday) and an à la carte menu on the other nights.

The *Anchorage Char-grill*, in the day-tripper's section of the resort, opens for lunch from noon to 2 pm and for dinner from 6.15 to 8.15 pm. You can get char-grilled steaks or fish with salad and chips for around $12.

The outdoor *Keppel Cafe*, next to the resort shop, is open from 8 am to 9 pm and is the best eating option for day-trippers. Burgers are available from $4 to $5, sandwiches from $3 to $5 and pizzas (evening only) from $11 to $15.

Other Possibilities Halfway between the resort and Keppel Haven, along the path, the *Shell House* has a good shell collection and sells excellent home-made scones and rock cakes. A Devonshire tea costs $4.50. The owner is an interesting character who's lived on Keppel for many years and worked as a chef in the resort's early days. He's happy to chat about the island's history and his tropical garden offers a pleasant break from the sun.

Further along the path, just in front of the hostel, you'll come to *Island Pizza*, open Wednesday to Sunday for lunch and dinner. This place is run by a friendly young couple and has hot dogs for $2.70, subs for $4.20, pastas from $3.50 and good pizzas ranging from $10 to $26.

The *Keppel Haven Bar & Bistro* is a bit pricey with burgers from $6 to $7, sandwiches at $4, grills at $15, and breakfast from $6 to $9.

Self Catering If you want to cook your own food it's best to bring provisions from the mainland as there is not much for sale on the island itself. The kiosk at Keppel Haven has a few basic supplies.

Entertainment
Night-time entertainment is a big deal at Great Keppel and getting wrecked in the resort's *Neptune's Bar*, with a live band or disco, is very popular. It's open to all comers between 10 pm and 2 am, and there's no cover charge. The *Keppel Haven Bar* also has live entertainment on Wednesday and Saturday nights.

The *Sunset Lounge* cocktail bar is an alternative place for a drink at the resort.

Getting There & Away
Air Sunstate (Qantas) Airlines flies at least twice daily between Rockhampton and Great Keppel. The 50km flight costs $82 one way and there are usually connections with Qantas flights up and down the coast.

Sea Ferries for the half-hour trip to Great Keppel leave from Rosslyn Bay Harbour on the Capricorn Coast, south of Yeppoon. You can book the ferries through your accommodation or agents in Rockhampton or the Capricorn Coast. The youth hostel in Rockhampton often has special deals on bus, ferry and accommodation packages. There is no jetty at Great Keppel; the ferries just pull in to the northern end of Fisherman's Beach, right by Keppel Haven, and a ramp is lowered onto the sand.

Some of the cruise and ferry operators have connecting buses to Rockhampton, otherwise Young's Bus Service (☎ 4922 3813) and Rotheby's (☎ 4922 4320) both have services to Rosslyn Bay and Yeppoon. If you're driving to Rosslyn Bay there's a free day carpark at the harbour, or the Kempsea Car Park (☎ 4933 6670), on the main road just north of the harbour turn-off, charges $6 a day (overnight is charged as two days), $2 for motorbikes or $48 a week, and runs a free bus to and from the harbour.

Keppel Tourist Services (☎ 4933 6744) operates two boats, the *Reefcat* and the *Spirit of Keppel*. The *Reefcat* leaves Rosslyn Bay at 9.15 am and returns from Great Keppel at 4.30 pm, and costs $25 return. The *Spirit of Keppel* leaves Rosslyn Bay at 11.30 am and 3.30 pm, and returns from Great Keppel at 8.15 am and 2 pm. The *Reefcat* also goes on to a pontoon on the north side of the island (see Boats & Cruises earlier), or you can buy a $39 package to the island that includes lunch at the resort and a 10% discount on watersports.

If you come to Great Keppel Island with your own boat, the anchorages around the island are reasonable although rather unprotected. Svendsen's Beach is a popular anchorage. The island is also a good place to pick up a ride on a yacht heading north to the Whitsundays or beyond; check the noticeboard at the Keppel haven kiosk.

Other Keppel Bay Islands

Great Keppel is only the biggest of the 18 continental islands dotted around Keppel Bay, all within 20km of the coast. The other islands in the Keppel group are all virtually undeveloped. Part of the reason for this is lack of water – only Great Keppel has a permanent water supply from wells. You may get to visit Middle Island, with its underwater observatory, or Halfway or Humpy islands if you're staying on Great Keppel.

Some of the islands are national parks where you can maroon yourself for a few days of self-sufficient camping, while Pumpkin Island is privately owned and has a few cabins where you can get away from it all in a little bit more comfort. Most of the islands have clean white beaches and several (notably Halfway) have fringing coral reefs that are excellent for snorkelling or diving.

Diving

There are a number of good diving spots around the Keppel Bay islands. Visibility is generally clear, and is usually at its best in the June through August winter months. Large manta rays are often seen in these

waters and sea snakes are quite common around the reefs. The olive sea snakes are inquisitive creatures and often give divers a scare by peering into their face masks or winding around their legs. Sea snakes are poisonous but harmless as long as you don't annoy them.

Although there is some good diving around Great Keppel itself the water tends to be clearer and deeper around the outer islands where manta rays, turtles and other larger species are seen more frequently. Barren Island and The Child are particularly popular with divers.

Places to Stay

To camp on a national park island you need to take all your own supplies including a stove, fuel and water – on North Keppel and Humpy islands water is only available for washing, and on most others there's none at all. You also need a camping permit, and since camping numbers are restricted these can be hard to come by for some islands. You can get information and permits from the Rockhampton Department of Environment office (☎ 4936 0511) on the corner of Norman and Yeppoon Rds, just after the turn-off to Yeppoon, or the ranger base at Rosslyn Bay harbour (☎ 4933 6595), PO Box 770, Yeppoon, Qld 4703.

Getting There & Away

The Keppel Bay Marina (☎ 4933 6244) can organise a water taxi for camping drop-off services from Rosslyn Bay to the islands; prices start from $300 return for up to four people, plus $40 for each extra person.

For transport to North West Island and the Capricorn Group islands on the Barrier Reef beyond Keppel Bay, see the Southern Reef Islands section.

BARREN ISLAND & THE CHILD

Rising sheer from the water Barren Island is indeed rather barren but here, on the outer edge of Keppel Bay, the water is generally clear and there is a great variety of marine life. The Child is a smaller rock thrusting up from the sea just north of Barren Island.

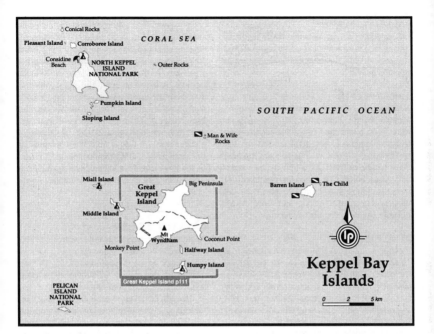

Keppel Bay Islands

The narrow channel separating the two islands has a steeply sided gully that offers fascinating diving.

NORTH KEPPEL ISLAND

The second largest island in the group and one of the most northerly, the 6.3 sq km North Keppel Island is a national park. The most popular camping spot is Considine Beach on the north-west coast, where there are toilets and well-water for washing but not drinking. The camping limit is 100. The mosquitoes and other six-legged wildlife can be fierce on North Keppel.

PUMPKIN ISLAND

Just south of North Keppel, tiny Pumpkin Island has beaches, reefs, mangroves and some fine views. Five cabins here accommodate five to six people each at a cost of around $130 per night for the whole cabin. There's water and solar electricity. Each cabin has a cooking area with stove and fridge, a bathroom with shower, one double bed and three single beds. You need to take your own food and drinks. Camping is also available at $12 per person. Phone ☎ 4939 2431 for information and bookings.

MIALL & MIDDLE ISLANDS

These two small islands just north-west of Great Keppel are national parks and have no facilities and tight limits on the numbers of people who can camp there – 18 on Middle, six on Miall.

Just off Middle Island is the underwater observatory (☎ 4939 4191), which is visited by cruises from Rosslyn Bay and from Great Keppel. A confiscated Taiwanese fishing junk was sunk next to the observatory to provide a haven for fish and there's usually plenty to see. A visit to the observatory costs $10, and the trips leave Great Keppel at 12.15 pm.

HALFWAY ISLAND

Just south of Great Keppel, little Halfway Island is a national park with a good reef but no facilities, and access is restricted to day use only.

HUMPY ISLAND

A short way south of Halfway Island, 65 hectare Humpy Island has little shade as its vegetation bears the brunt of the south-east winds. There's a beautiful beach on the north-western side, with good fringing reef close to the shore. Like Halfway, it's a national park and a popular snorkelling ground. There's a camping limit of 50 people. There are toilets, and bore water suitable for washing and drinking.

OTHER ISLANDS

Further south are **Pelican**, **Divided** and **Peak islands**. Camping is not permitted on Peak Island during the turtle season, while Pelican and Divided islands are very rocky. There are limited anchorages and few beaches on these three islands. None of them has any facilities. **Wedge** and **Hummocky islands** are privately owned.

Duke Islands

Lying halfway between Yeppoon and Mackay, many of the Duke Islands are privately owned. Few people stop here and even most yachties skip the group altogether (the anchorages are not very good) and head for the Percy Isles instead. Another problem with the Duke Islands is that access to Stanage Bay, the most obvious jumping-off point for private boats, is by a long stretch of dirt road. The Shoalwater Bay Military Training Area is a further restriction on access and the islands also suffer from 7m tides. Wild Duck Island has an airstrip but attempts to set up a resort there have been so unsuccessful that it is known locally as Lame Duck Island.

Percy Isles

The Percy Isles – Middle Percy, North East and South Percy – are also difficult to reach without your own boat, but as Middle Percy is about halfway between the Keppel islands and the Whitsundays it's a popular rest stop for yachties. Surrounded by sandy bays the island is a good anchorage with washing and shower facilities for visitors.

Andy Martin lives on the island and lets people stay in his A-frame building on the west side; you can contact him by writing care of Mackay Post Office, Qld 4740. Pine Islet, just to the west of Middle Percy, had a staffed lighthouse until 1987 when it was converted to automatic operation.

Brampton & the Cumberland Islands

Newry and Brampton, have resorts and with a national parks permit you can camp on a number of the islands.

The local Ngaro Aboriginal people once visited the islands, paddling flimsy bark canoes out from the mainland. Aboriginal middens have been found on Brampton and other islands. The group was named after the Duke of Cumberland, brother of King George III, by Captain Cook when he sailed through in 1770. His mind must have been far away in the Lake District of northern England on that day as he named a number of the islands in the group after towns in the region.

Around the turn of the century Europeans began to settle some of the islands and use them for grazing. Apart from the resort islands, there are still residents on Farrier, Keswick and St Bees.

Newry Island Group

The Newry Island Group comprises half a dozen islands, three of which you can camp on. Rabbit Island, to the west, is the largest of the group and has a campsite at its southeast tip. Next to it is Newry Island itself, with the small resort on the eastern-most point. Outer Newry Island flanks Newry Island to the east and also has a campsite. Immediately south of the three larger islands, between them and the mainland, are the smaller Stone, Acacia, Mausoleum and Rocky islands. The islands are close enough to the mainland for box jellyfish to be found in the summer months, so swimmers should beware.

The continental islands are rocky and wild-looking, but Rabbit Island has a series of sandy beaches along much of its eastern side. Five of the islands – Rabbit, Newry, Outer Newry, Acacia and Mausoleum – are

The Cumberland Islands are sometimes referred to as the southern Whitsundays, because that's where they lie. Indeed the line that separates the Cumberlands from the Whitsundays is really an arbitrary one – the islands are similar in appearance and continue straight from one group to the next. The islands are all designated national parks except for Keswick, St Bees and part of tiny Farrier Island, just to the west of Goldsmith Island. Two of the islands,

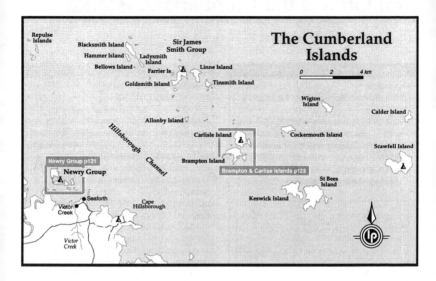

national parks. These national park islands have grassy open forests and isolated small patches of rainforest. The towering hoop pines, Mackay cedars, tulip oaks, mountain ash, blue gums, ironbarks and bloodwoods are the prevalent trees.

The islands have many possums and echidnas, and koalas, which were introduced here, have thrived. Observant walkers may also see holes scratched by bandicoots and large mounds scraped together by scrub fowl to incubate their eggs. Patches of seagrass around the island are grazed by gentle dugongs but you would have to be very lucky to spot one. Between November and January green turtles come up on the beaches of Rabbit Island to lay their eggs.

Places to Stay
Rabbit Island has the main national park campsite with BBQs, tables and toilets. Although there is a water tank here, water may be in short supply during the summer months. The site on Outer Newry's western beach also has toilets, tables and water. Camping is also possible on Rocky and

Mausoleum islands. The resort on Newry, which has campsites as well, will boat you over to Rabbit or Outer Newry islands. Camping permits for the national park sites are obtained from the Department of Environment (☎ 4951 8788), corner of River and Wood Sts, Mackay. The postal address is PO Box 623, Mackay, Qld 4740.

NEWRY ISLAND
There are day trips from Victor Creek to pleasant Newry Island, a little known island very close to the coast. There's good swimming, bushwalks and plenty of koalas but this is certainly not a big bucks tourist resort; most of the visitors are local cane cockies and fishers or visitors from Mackay.

Information
The resort phone number is ☎ 4959 0214, or write to Newry Island Resort, PO Box 3, Seaforth, Qld 4741.

Activities
There's a superb walk through patches of rainforest to a picnic site at Fish Point on

the other side of the island, overlooking the Rabbit Island camping area. You may see koalas along the way and they have been known to swim between Newry and nearby Rabbit and the Outer Newry islands. The walk starts at the Rotunda Lookout and is about 2km long. Unfortunately, the island's beaches are not very good. Fishing and oystering are the main activities on Newry. There are practically no activities – although, you can go waterskiing – but there is no nightlife to speak of.

Places to Stay & Eat

The small resort accommodates only 40 people but has a licensed bar. There are eight basic cabins, all with showers, toilets and tea/coffee-making equipment. These cost $20 per person per night (maximum $60). There are also 20 campsites at the resort, which is the only place where camping is allowed, and costs $7 per tent.

Meals are also available at the resort – breakfast costs around $5 and dinner around $12.

Getting There & Away

Newry Island is close to the mainland just north of Seaforth. The resort picks up people from Victor Creek, near Seaforth, a coastal holiday town north of Mackay. The cost is $15 return (maximum $60, up to 10 people) and you can ring the resort for pickups. A bus runs from Mackay to Seaforth on school days – if that's not convenient the resort can usually arrange transport from Mackay at other times.

The resort also operates day trips on a frequent basis, so inquire at reception when you arrive. There's no jetty at Newry Island; you'll have to jump off the boat into (about) knee-deep water – it adds to the island experience, but it's usually a good idea to wear shorts and slip-on shoes.

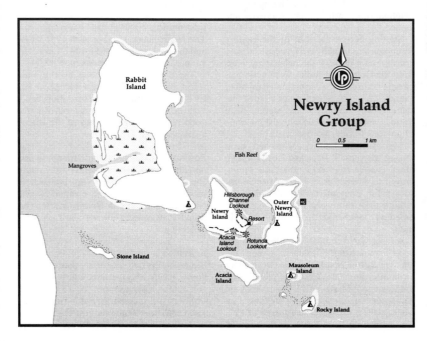

Brampton Island

Area:	4.6 sq km
Type:	continental
High point:	219m
Max visitors:	240

Mountainous Brampton Island is a national park and wildlife sanctuary with lush forests surrounded by coral reefs. It is part of the Cumberland Group and is connected to nearby Carlisle Island by a sand bar that you can walk across at low tide. You can also walk out to tiny Pelican Island at low tide. Essentially Brampton is just like the islands of the Whitsundays, which are just to the north. Although Cook named some of the other islands in the Cumberland Group it was not until 1879 that Brampton and neighbouring Carlisle were surveyed and named.

Starting before the turn of the century Brampton was used by the Queensland government as a nursery for palm trees. Nuts from the Dutch East Indies were germinated here before they were replanted on other islands, hence the island's particularly fine stand of this tropical island staple! Sisal hemp, planted on Carlisle with the intention of producing rope, has become a pest.

The Busuttin family, who had been raising sheep on St Bees and Keswick, two other islands in the Cumberland group, moved to Brampton in 1916. After an unsuccessful attempt to breed chinchilla rabbits they turned to raising goats and breeding horses for the British army in India.

A resort was established on the island in 1933, soon after Lindeman's, and the massive fig tree beside the older fresh water swimming pool dates from that year. At that time you could have an 11 day holiday on Brampton Island, including steamer fare from Sydney, for the princely sum of £27. Guests making the 10 minute flight or 45

minute high-speed catamaran trip out to Brampton from Mackay might pause to think that in those days it was a six hour boat crossing on the old *Woy Woy*, whose wheel now hangs in the resort's Nautilus Lounge. In those days guests could indulge themselves in turtle and dugong hunting and other activities that would definitely be frowned on today.

Since the war the farming activity has ceased and the sheep and cattle have been replaced with more and more guests. The Busuttin family sold the resort in 1959 and it eventually ended up with the Roylen group, which still operates the boat service between Mackay and Brampton. The bone-shaking mini-railway that transports visitors from the all-tide wharf to the resort was built in 1966. In 1998 Brampton was bought by P&O Resorts, after having been run by Australian Airlines (part of Qantas) since 1985. Apart from the resort area the island is all national park.

Information

The resort phone number is ☎ 4951 4499, and the fax number is 4951 4097. For reservations contact P&O Resorts on ☎ 13 2469.

There is a pay telephone by the main resort complex. The resort reception has EFTPOS facilities. The resort shop has a very limited supply of books, but it has a good aerial photograph map of the island, available in poster form.

Zoning The waters around Brampton and neighbouring Carlisle islands are mainly zoned General Use B, but the waters between the two islands are zoned Marine National Park A and B. Neither Marine National Park zoning allows shell or coral collecting.

Activities

Brampton has two swimming pools (one for house guests only), tennis courts, a small golf course, a games room and a TV lounge. Children are catered for with free supervised activities throughout the day.

Day visitors to the island are welcome

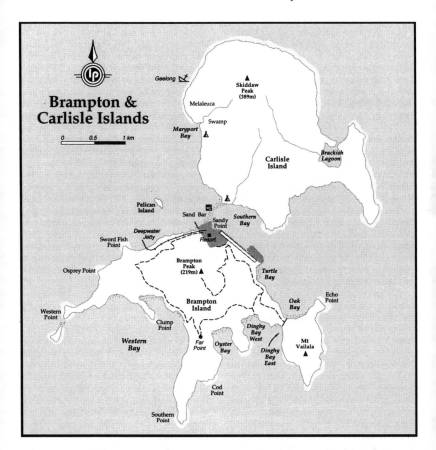

Brampton & Carlisle Islands

0   0.5   1 km

Geelong

Skiddaw Peak (389m)

Melaleuca

Swamp

Maryport Bay

Carlisle Island

Brackish Lagoon

Pelican Island

Sand Bar

Sandy Point

Southern Bay

Deepwater Jetty

Sword Fish Point

Resort

Osprey Point

Brampton Peak (219m)

Turtle Bay

Echo Point

Oak Bay

Brampton Island

Western Point

Clump Point

Western Bay

Far Point

Oyster Bay

Dinghy Bay West

Dinghy Bay East

Mt Vailala

Cod Point

Southern Point

and can use some of the guest facilities but they don't come over in such numbers that they over-run the resort.

Watersports equipment, including surf skis ($5 per hour), snorkelling gear ($10), catamarans ($15) and windsurfers ($10) can be hired from a shed on the main beach – all of which are free to house guests. Powered watersports include waterskiing ($20), tube rides ($10) and glass-bottom waterbikes ($25).

Water and showers are also available for passing yachties.

Beaches, Snorkelling & Diving Although there are beaches scattered right around the island, Dinghy Bay and Oyster Bay are particularly pleasant, and Sandy Point right in front of the resort is just fine. There's good snorkelling at low tide over the coral in the narrow channel between Brampton and Carlisle islands, again right in front of the resort.

Brampton is not a divers' island but the trips out of Mackay to the outer reef stop at Brampton to drop off day-trippers and pick up Brampton guests. The Roylen's *Spirit of*

Roylen (☎ 4955 3066) cruises to Credlin Reef every Monday, Wednesday and Friday, costing $100 from Mackay or $85 from Brampton, including lunch. At the reef there's a pontoon with underwater observatory and a semi-submersible. Diving ($65) and snorkelling ($5) facilities are offered on these trips.

Walks Trails lead from the resort to quiet bays on the other sides of the island or to the lookout at the island's high point. The circuit walk is one of the best on any resort island and takes you through great stands of Moreton Bay ash and poplar, gum forests, giant grass trees, past coral beach and offers sweeping panoramas. There are basically two walks, the 7km island circuit, with side tracks leading off to Dinghy Bay and Oak Bay, and the 2km ascent to the top of Brampton Peak (219m). Both walks start from near the resort golf course.

A variety of wildlife can be seen on the island: scrubfowl (and their huge nesting mounds), sand goannas, grey kangaroos and koalas can all be found here. Fruit bats roost in trees near Turtle Bay.

Island Circuit The track climbs up the slopes of Brampton Peak and follows alongside the airstrip until it descends towards the shoreline. There's a picnic area here at Turtle Bay and for a few steps the route is on the beach before climbing back up above the shoreline and turning south. A side track branches off and descends to Dinghy Bay East and Oak Bay, and another side track soon after goes down to Dinghy Bay West.

The main track here runs well above Dinghy Bay and Oyster Bay with superb views across the grassy slopes, punctuated with grass-trees, to the twin bays with their sandy beaches. The grassy areas of Brampton are probably a result of the goats that were once grazed here. Finally the track climbs up an open grassy slope to Far Point from where there are great views to the east over Oyster and Dinghy bays and to the north-west over Western Bay.

Far Point is the halfway mark on the circuit track and from here the track soon descends into dense vegetation, which it remains in for the rest of the track. The walk descends steeply to Western Bay, crosses a short stretch of beach and then continues round to a second strip of beach beside Clump Point, where there is a picnic area. Soon after this the walk crosses a vehicle track again then climbs up and over a ridge line before reaching the vehicle track again, between the resort and the deepwater jetty.

If you follow this track anticlockwise instead of clockwise it's possible to miss some of the signs, which are more aligned to clockwise walkers. In a couple of places the walk follows 4WD vehicle tracks then suddenly diverges off them. It's possible to miss these turnings if you aren't alert. The full circuit is about 7km and takes two to three hours.

Brampton Peak The start of the walk to the island's highest point is also near the resort golf course. It follows the island circuit route for just a couple of hundred metres before turning sharply off at a well-signposted junction. From here the path switchbacks gently uphill to the Carlisle Lookout, which gives wonderful views over the resort area, Carlisle Island and the north-west. From near the top an alternative spur runs a short distance to Cape Hillsborough Lookout with views over the south of the island.

This pleasant and gentle stroll takes about two hours (for the round trip) at an easy pace and the views from the top are well worth the effort.

Places to Stay

Brampton Island, run by P&O Resorts, is a very pleasant mid-range resort that attracts couples, families, honeymooners, in fact, just about everyone except the 'young singles' crowd – it's definitely not a party island. The resort is at Sandy Point at the north central point of the island, looking across the narrow strait to larger Carlisle Island. The accommodation consists of

Garden and Beachfront Units, or the older, smaller and cheaper Carlisle Units, which date back to 1981 (and it shows). All rooms have a double and a single bed, attached bathroom, air-con, tea/coffee-making equipment, fridge, TV, video and telephone. The attractive units are in compact two storey blocks and most rooms have their own veranda or balcony. As the name suggests, the Beachfront Units are right by the beach.

Daily costs are $280 for a single, twin or double in the Carlisle Units; or $300/350 in the Garden/Beachfront Units, all including breakfast. Lunch and dinner costs $48 ($25 for children). Rates are cheaper for five or more nights, and discounted standby rates are available (starting at around $70 per person twin share not including meals). Rates include use of all non-powered activities equipment, including golf, tennis, windsurfing, catamarans and the like. There's an additional charge for waterskiing and other activities requiring power.

Places to Eat
Guests have the option of buying a lunch and dinner package ($48) or paying for each meal separately, with a choice between the restaurant and the cafe. The main dining area is the upstairs *Carlisle Restaurant*, where a buffet lunch is good value at $15, and dinner is $35 for four courses, or à la carte main dishes are around $21 to $24. The food at Brampton is not going to send any gastronomes into fits of rapture; it's unadventurous but varied enough to keep most people happy, although vegetarians aren't given much thought. On Saturday nights there's that Great Barrier Reef essential, a seafood smorgasbord, and on other nights there are the usual theme buffets, with Thursday being Aussie BBQ night. The wine list is varied enough to suit most palates and budgets, with bottles ranging from $20 to $36.

For guests not on the meals package or for day visitors, there's also the somewhat gloomy *Rocks Sandwich Bar* downstairs in the main resort complex. It serves drinks and ice creams as well as good sandwiches

($5), salads and light meals ($10 to $13), and is open all day.

Getting There & Away
Air Sunstate will fly you over from Mackay airport in just 10 minutes for a one-way fare of $80.

Sea McLean's Roylen Cruises (☎ 4955 3066) has two fast cats, the *Spirit of Roylen* and *Sunbird*, which take turns to make the 55 minute run to Brampton. The boat leaves Mackay harbour every day at 9 am; the crossing can be rough in heavy seas. Return fare is $50 with lunch or $35 without. On Monday, Wednesday and Friday the *Spirit of Roylen* continues from Brampton out to Credlin Reef on the outer reef – return fares are $100 from Mackay and $85 from Brampton, again including lunch.

Other Cumberland Islands

There are 70-odd islands in the Cumberland Group and, in addition to the Newry Island Group, it is also possible to camp on Carlisle, Cockermouth, Goldsmith and Scawfell islands. For camping permits contact the Mackay Department of Environment office (☎ 4951 8788; fax 4957 2036) on the corner of River and Woods St (PO Box 623).

Getting There & Away
Check with Tourism Mackay (☎ 4952 2677), Nebo Rd, Mackay, for information on boat and plane charters out of Mackay. Air Pioneer (☎ 4957 6661) and Fredrickson's Air Services (☎ 4942 3161) both offer seaplane flights from Mackay out to the reef for snorkelling and diving.

CARLISLE ISLAND
Carlisle is just a stone's throw from Brampton Island. Campers can sit on the beach

and watch the resort activities on Brampton separated only by the narrow channel between the two islands. Indeed at low tide a sand bar emerges between the island and you can walk between them. With an area of just over 5 sq km and Skiddaw Peak soaring to 389m, Carlisle is both larger than its near neighbour and also looks down on it.

The island is covered in dense eucalypt forest and there are no walking tracks. Patches of rainforest are found in the gullies while there is a melaleuca (paperbark) swamp at the western end of the island, which lies below sea level. There's a good area of rainforest behind the swamp. The small lagoon at the island's eastern end attracts pelicans, herons and other waterbirds.

SS Geelong
In 1888 the 431 ton iron steamship SS *Geelong* (originally named the *Thomas Powell*) sheltered behind Carlisle Island during a severe storm. After being there for more than a day a sudden shift of wind forced the captain to run the ship onto the beach. In getting a rope ashore two of the crew were swept off and drowned but no passengers were lost. It was impossible to salvage the ship. The bow of the ship still lies on the beach today and has trees growing through it. A section of hull with brick ballast can also be seen. At low tide snorkellers can find another 13m of the keel in just 5m of water.

Places to Stay
There are sites for 15 people at Southern Bay, directly across from the Brampton Island resort, and another site further north at Maryport Bay. Both sites are completely undeveloped and there are no facilities or water. The national parks office warns that you cannot get water from Brampton; no doubt you could stroll over and buy a cold beer at low tide, however.

Getting There & Away
You can get to Carlisle Island by private boat. Although you could also walk to it from Brampton at low tide.

SCAWFELL ISLAND
Lying about 115km north-west of Middle Percy, 50km north-east of Mackay, and 10km directly east of Brampton, Scawfell has a safe anchorage in Refuge Bay on its northern side. The 11 sq km island is the largest in the group and is a popular resting place for yachts sailing between the Percy and the Whitsunday islands. Refuge Bay has a beach and a campsite but there are no facilities and water is only available during the wetter summer months. The island's coastline ends in granite cliffs while large patches of rainforest can be found on the steep mountain slopes.

ST BEES & KESWICK ISLANDS
St Bees and Keswick are separated by a narrow channel. Both are privately owned; St Bees was once a sheep property owned by the Busuttin family, original owners of the Brampton Island resort. Off to the west of Keswick is Singapore Rock, named after the *Singapore*, which was wrecked on it while en route from Shanghai to Sydney in 1877. The lighthouse steamer *Llewellyn* also went down somewhere near St Bees in 1919, while in 1943 the Dutch ship *Cremer*, being used to transport troops between New Guinea and Australia, ran into the island itself and was totally wrecked.

COCKERMOUTH ISLAND
Cockermouth Island has a good anchorage and sandy beach on its western side and campsites on the north-western beach, but there are no facilities or fresh water. The hilly island is mainly covered with open grassland.

GOLDSMITH & FARRIER ISLANDS
North-west of Cockermouth in the Sir James Smith Group there is a good anchorage and campsite on the north-western side of Goldsmith Island. The island has excellent beaches backed by pandanus and she-oaks, while inland there is open woodland with brush box, wattle trees and grass-trees. The campsite has toilets, BBQ fireplaces and tables, but no fresh water.

Tiny Farrier Island is immediately to the west of Goldsmith – it's safe to sail between the two islands. There is no traditional accommodation on Farrier, but there are quite a few privately owned cabins on the south-east shore. And usually the owners or occupiers of these cabins like their privacy.

THE REPULSE ISLANDS

Well to the west of the Sir James Smith Group is South Repulse Island. It has a campsite on the western beach, which is similar to Goldsmith, but again there is no water. East and North Repulse islands are just to the north.

Whitsunday Islands

The 70-odd islands of the Whitsunday Group are probably the best known and most developed of the Barrier Reef islands. The group was named by Captain Cook who sailed through here on 3 July 1770. The islands are scattered on both sides of the Whitsunday Passage, within 50km of Shute Harbour, the jumping-off point for many of the cruises through the group.

The actual Barrier Reef is at least 60km out from Shute Harbour; Hook Reef is the nearest part of the reef. Many of the Whitsunday islands are national parks. The large block of mainland national park opposite them, stretching from Airlie Beach south to Conway, is known as Conway National Park. All the islands of the group are high continental islands and on most of them the beaches are not that special. There are large tidal variations in the Whitsundays and when the tide is way out, exposing large mudflats in front of some of the resorts, it's time to head for the resort swimming pool.

Whitsunday or Not?

Curiously, the Whitsundays are, in fact, misnamed – Captain Cook didn't actually sail through them on Whitsunday as he thought. Cook forgot to allow for the international date line and his meticulously kept log was one day out, something he only realised when he got back to England.

As he sailed through the Whitsundays and on further north, Cook was also unaware of the existence of the Barrier Reef, although he realised there was something to the east of his ship making the water unusually calm. It wasn't until he ran aground on Endeavour Reef, near Cooktown, that he finally found out about the Great Barrier Reef.

WHITSUNDAY ISLANDS

Highlights
- Hire a yacht for a week and set your own agenda
- Spend a lazy day on the pristine white sands of Whitehaven Beach
- Go camping on one of the many secluded national park islands

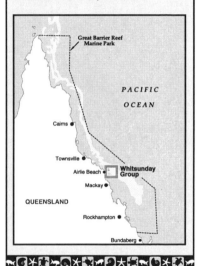

Information

Airlie Beach is the mainland centre for the Whitsundays, and there are plenty of shops, banks, travel agents and tour operators. You can also find out all about cruises, trips, standby rates at resorts and so on there.

All but five of the Whitsunday islands are national parks; in all, over 95% of the island land area is park. The Whitsunday Information Centre (☎ 4946 7022) is 2km past Airlie Beach towards Shute Harbour, and is open from 8 am to 5 pm Monday to Friday, and on weekend. This office deals with

Top: Great Keppel Island has 28km of quiet, sand beaches
Middle Left: Taking a tube ride, Great Keppel Island
Middle Right: Water skiing, Brampton
Bottom: Brampton Island resort

HOLGER LEUE

The Great Barrier Reef encompasses around 2500 individual and named reefs and more than 600 islands in all – of which, 250 continental islands and 70 coral cays have been named. This is Black Island (Bali Ha'i), a popular sailing destination from nearby Hayman Island in the Whitsundays.

bookings and permits for Conway and the Whitsunday islands national parks.

Further Reading The Queensland National Parks & Wildlife Service produces the useful *Whitsunday Islands National Parks* camping guide leaflet.

Two of the best maps to this area are the Travelog *Great Barrier Reef* map, which has a *Whitsunday Passage* map on the back; and Sunmap's *Australia's Whitsundays*. A comprehensive guide to the Whitsundays is *100 Magic Miles of the Reef – The Whitsun-*

days, with charts and aerial photographs. *Whitsunday Islands: A Historical Dictionary*, by Ray Blackwood (1997), is a useful reference for island and regional history.

Zoning Most of the waters around the Whitsundays are zoned General Use A and B with some important exceptions around the islands – in these areas Marine National Park A and B zoning applies. The main difference for visitors is Zone A permits limited fishing whereas Zone B permits no fishing at all.

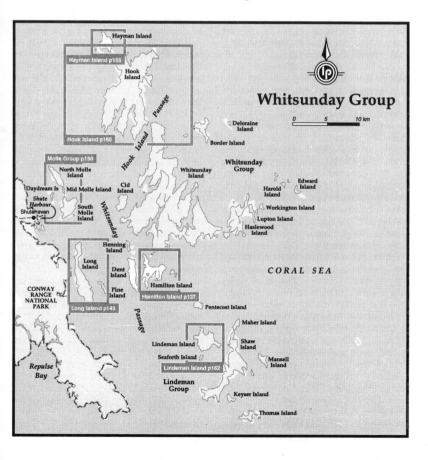

Zone A applies to the waters around Long Island, the Molle islands, Lindeman Island, Hamilton Island, Cid Harbour, Henning Island, and the waters between Whitsunday and Haslewood islands. It also included Nara Inlet and Saba Bay on Hook Island, and the area around Hayman Island, Black and Langford islands, and across from there to Hook Island.

The more restrictive Zone B applies to Butterfly Bay and the other bays at the north of Hook Island, to Border Island and to Lupton Island, and the east side of Haslewood Island. The outer reef off the Whitsundays is also a mix of zones. The main reefs visited from the islands are Marine National Park A (Bait and Hook reefs) and B (Hardy Reef).

Islands & Wildlife

The Whitsunday islands are essentially drowned mountains with peaks rising clear of the sea. The islands were initially formed by volcanic eruption – the unmistakable shape of Pentecost Island is the remains of the plug of rock from a volcano cone. The sea level was about 100m lower during the last ice age, when, 18,000 years ago, the Whitsundays would have been hills beyond which a plain stretched out to the coastal limestone hills, which are now the Great Barrier Reef. As the polar ice caps melted about 10,000 years ago, the sea rose and the 'hills' became the Whitsunday islands.

Although the Whitsundays are not technically reef islands, many of them have fine fringing reef systems. The great range between low and high tide in the Whitsundays creates fast flowing currents between the islands and in turn the nutrients carried by these currents feed a healthy variety of corals. Closer to the shore there are crabs, oysters, snails and worms, and a variety of birds of prey that patrol the coastal strip.

Inland there are vine forests and the distinctive hoop pines found on most of the Whitsunday islands. Eucalypts and acacias predominate on the drier slopes while the grass-tree is a familiar understorey sight. There are not as many animals on the islands as on the adjacent mainland, but on some islands goannas and bush-tailed possums have learnt to raid campers' provisions. Rock wallabies are found on Whitsunday Island, and the unusual Proserpine rock wallaby on Gloucester Island. There are plenty of birds – 156 different species have been recorded.

Diving & Snorkelling

The water in the Whitsundays tends to be clearer at the northern end of the outer islands – Hook, Border, Deloraine and Langford are particularly popular snorkelling and diving locations. Regular diving tours are made to the outer Barrier Reef.

Island & Reef Cruises & Flights

Cruises If you're not simply transferring to an island, there are all types of boat trips out to the islands of the Whitsundays and beyond them to the Barrier Reef. Most trips originate at Shute Harbour (the end of the road from Airlie Beach), or at the Abel Point Marina. Some of these pick up from islands on the way, and others originate from the islands, particularly Hamilton.

You can divide the trips into several categories. First of all there are the straightforward go-see-the-islands cruises. You go to resort island A, have an hour or two there to sample the beach, pool and bar, then carry on to do the same at island B. Somewhere along the line you usually get a BBQ lunch thrown in. An excursion to the underwater observatory at Hook Island is often part of the picture. Typical prices for these cruises are around $35. They're great if you want to make an on-the-spot assessment of the resort swimming pools.

A variation on these resort island trips is one that just takes you out to one island and leaves you there for the day. Whitsunday Allover Water Taxis (☎ 4946 6900) and Seatrek (☎ 4946 5255) have shuttle trips to South Molle ($18), Long ($15) and Daydream ($20) islands; and Fantasea Cruises (☎ 4946 5111) have day trips to Hamilton Island ($39).

Category two is the nowhere-in-particular trips, usually in smaller boats. You usually stay away from the resort islands, perhaps try a beach here, a bit of snorkelling there, maybe some fishing somewhere else. Many of the boats operating these trips are yachts. For example, a day on the former America's Cup contender *Gretel* is yours for $65.

There are also outer reef trips where you power out to the outer reef for a spot of snorkelling or diving. The high-speed catamarans used for these trips get you out there in about two hours. Beware of seasickness, as the trips can often be surprisingly bumpy. Out on the reef the major operators all have their own pontoons with glass-bottom boats, semi-submersibles, diving facilities, snorkelling equipment and all waiting for you. These outer reef trips are generally more expensive (around $100 to $120, with lunch) but getting out to the reef is really an other-world experience that, if you can afford it, should not be missed.

Another option is to take an overnight or longer cruise around the islands. Meals and snorkelling gear are usually included, and you either sleep on board or in tents on an island. There are plenty of variations on this theme – overnight cruises from $160, two-night/three-day trips from $275, and three-night/four-day trips from $400.

Finally, there are all sorts of do-your-own-thing odds and ends. You can get yourself dropped off on an island to camp or you can charter a bareboat yacht and sail yourself. Some typical Whitsunday boat trips include the following:

Fantasea
Outer Great Barrier Reef cruises on the high-speed catamaran *Fantasea 2000* cost $117, including smorgasbord lunch, snorkelling and rides in a semi-submersible. Phone ☎ 4946 5111 for bookings.

Nari
The twin-keeled *Nari* operates sailing cruises to Nari Beach in Cid Harbour, costing $49 including lunch and snorkelling gear ($59 for divers). Phone ☎ 4946 6224 for details.

Apollo
Famous Sydney-to-Hobart veteran 80 foot racer, does day trips to Langford Reef or Whitehaven Beach for $49 each or $80 for both. Phone ☎ 1800 635 334 for details.

Providence V
This modern replica of the old gaff-rigged Gloucester schooners sails around the islands for three days for a cost of $250, which includes all meals and snorkelling gear. Phone ☎ 1800 655 346 for bookings.

Jade
Popular 46 foot sailing catamaran does cruises to South Molle, Sunlovers Reef and Daydream Island for $55, or to Langford Reef, also for $55, or $85 for both trips. Phone ☎ 4946 6848.

Flights Air Whitsundays Seaplanes (☎ 4946 9130), based at the Whitsunday airport, has the only day trip to exclusive Hayman Island. For $150 per person, they'll fly in one of their seaplanes from the mainland to the island, where you have use of all the resort facilities for the day and a $30 credit towards your lunch. They also do three-hour trips to Hardy Reef ($175) and 1½ hour trips to beautiful Whitehaven Beach ($120), or you can combine the two in one day for $225.

Also based at the Whitsunday airport, Helireef (☎ 4946 9102) has helicopter flights out to Fantasea's huge Reef World pontoon on the outer reef. The fare is $195, which includes snorkelling gear, rides in the glass-bottomed boat and semi-submersible, lunch, and the Fantasea fast-cat back to Shute Harbour. To fly both ways it's $295.

Sailing
Sailing through the Whitsunday Passage in 1770, Cook wrote that 'the whole passage is one continued safe harbour'. In actual fact, stiff breezes and fast flowing tides can produce some tricky conditions for small craft but, with a little care, the Whitsundays offer superb sailing and bareboat charters have become enormously popular. 'Bareboat' doesn't refer to what you wear on board – it simply means that you rent the boat without skipper, crew or provisions.

Most charter companies don't require potential renters to have any previous sailing experience. If book in advance (and some book up to two years ahead!) some charter

Sailing – The Basics

Picture this: the sun's already risen to another beautiful day in the Whitsundays. After an al fresco breakfast on deck with your companions you hoist the mainsail and head for Whitsunday Island, where you spend a lazy day on the white-crystal sand of Whitehaven Beach.

Sounds ideal, doesn't it? And the best thing about this picture is you can be in it, even if you don't know how to sail.

You don't have to be Dennis Connor to hire a yacht on the Whitsundays. A lot of the people who hire yachts here have little or no sailing experience when they start. The bareboat charter companies can teach you all you need to know before you set sail.

Getting the basics of sailing is not so difficult – we're not talking about entering the America's Cup here – and the following will give you insight into what to expect:

Wind One thing you'll learn quickly about sailing is that the wind is rarely constant and from the same direction. It requires constant attention. Take note of where the wind is coming from. Look up to the top of the mast, there should be a flag or some other wind indicator up there. Good sailors don't need to look, they can feel it on their face – practise that, but look up to make sure.

Also, look for wind changes on the water's surface: a darkening of the water indicates an increase in wind strength.

Terminology If this is going to be your only sailing experience then you're not going to need to know all the terminology. The US Navy uses left (port) and right (starboard), so you can do the same. Windward (the side the wind is coming from) and leeward (opposite) are important to know, and you should know what a mainsail and headsail are. After a few hours with an experienced yachtie you'll learn a sheet is a line (or rope), a shroud is a wire line holding the rigging in place, trimming (the sails) has nothing to do with your waistline, and luff (forward edge of the sail) may have four letters but the kids can safely say it without offending anybody.

Sails The boat will come with a basic rig of a mainsail and headsail, and there won't be any need to change these. Usually, the headsail will be self-furling, which means that it doesn't need to be pulled down when not it use (it simply rolls up like a blind).

Safety Most of the charter companies require you to report in by radio twice daily. This provides plenty of opportunity to get answers to any sailing questions and also report any problems – one company we spoke to said, typically, they had only one boat sustain hull damage a year. There is also an emergency service based at Airlie Beach that you can reach by radio 24 hours a day. When you hire the boat ensure it has appropriate emergency gear and you are familiar with where it is and how to use it.

If somebody falls overboard shout out 'MAN OVERBOARD' straightaway to get all crew on deck. Somebody other than the helmsman (the person steering) should point to the person in the water all the time, never losing sight of them. If you feel confident handling the boat you'll need to tack back around; otherwise drop your sail and turn the engine on to pick the person up.

Steering Usually, the smaller/older boats have a tiller (a steering arm attached to the rudder), although the bigger boats will likely have a steering wheel. When steering with a tiller the boat will move in the opposite direction to the way you move it: move it to the right and the boat will move left, move it to the left and it'll go right. However, with a steering wheel it works just like your car, steer right and you go right, etc. The best way to ensure you steer a straight line is to pick an object off in the distance (most of the time you'll be surrounded by islands on the Whitsundays) and aim for it.

The object of sailing is to harness the wind, not sail straight into it. Turn into wind if you're in trouble of capsizing, but in the normal course of steering you should avoid the 45° either side of true wind. If you're sailing at about 45° then you're sailing 'close to the wind' (on the fastest course).

On each of the sails there are several tell-tales (pieces of wool, hanging off it like loose threads) that should, ideally, be streaming aft (to the back). If they aren't, you're pointing the boat too close to the wind or too far off it and you'll need to make a course correction.

Keeping Balance The keel under the boat helps keep it balanced when the sails are full of wind and prevent it from capsizing. If there is a lot of wind it will be necessary to position the crew on the windward side of the boat to help with the counterbalance. If you don't want so much wind you can steer slightly towards the wind (called luffing) until the gust eases, or you can limit its effect by easing the mainsail.

Navigation No, you won't need to break out the sextant, but you will have to know how to read a map (which will be provided with the boat). The degree of navigational skills you'll need will depend on your objective. Most of the time you'll be able to navigate visually – you'll be amazed how much the 'skyscrapers' on Hamilton Island stand out.

Trimming Getting a sail properly trimmed is

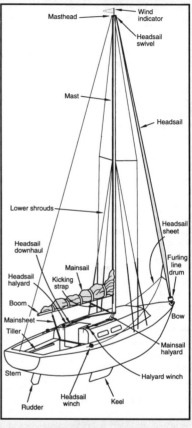

important for efficiency and can be a complicated business to get right. Not all the tell-tales (woollen threads) on the sails are for checking the boat's course – the precise tell-tales we're talking about here should be pointed out to you during your training on the boat – some are for checking the sail's trim (tightness). A sail can be too tight and too loose; getting it right will improve your boat speed. Generally, you should trim the headsail first and adjust the mainsail's trim (possibly by also adjusting the mainsheet – the rope holding down the boom, at the back) to match it.

Anchoring After the tension of sailing 'solo' for the first time you shouldn't relax completely when you reach your mooring and simply drop anchor. Anchoring needs to be handled well, both because of the damage you can do to the boat if it slips during the night and because of the potential damage you can do to the environment on the sea floor. You'll be given detailed advice on how to do this tricky procedure when you hire the boat.

Tacking Tacking is how you get a boat upwind, and is achieved by a zig-zagging motion. When setting up for a tack try not to tack into a wave, instead look for a flat piece of water – it'll give the least resistance to the turn.

❶ Alert everybody on board about what you're doing and ensure they understand. Push the tiller (slowly at first and more firmly as the boat turns) towards the sails, or turn the wheel away.

❷ Release the headsail sheets (lines) just prior to turning straight into the wind.

❸ As the boat points into the wind you'll need to trim the mainsail, and then let it out again when you cross the wind.

❹ As the sails cross the centreline of the boat, begin to ease the angle of the rudder – although it's better to go beyond the 45° of the tack to get the sails full, before bringing it back closer to the wind – and start to trim the sails. Wait until back up to speed before tacking again.

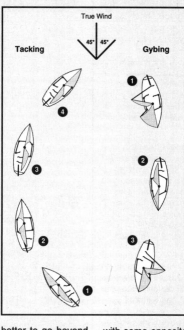

True Wind

45° 45°

Tacking   Gybing

Gybing A gybe is essentially the reverse of a tack, although it's a slightly trickier manoeuvre. If you find yourself heading in the wrong direction on a downwind leg you gybe to bring the wind in from the other side.

❶ Alert everybody on board about what you're doing and ensure they understand. Pull the tiller (slowly at first and more firmly as the boat turns) away from the sails, or turn the wheel towards the sails. At the same time start to recover the mainsail, pulling in about half of the mainsheet (mainsail line).

❷ Look out for the boom (and control it) as the sails cross the centre of the boat.

❸ The tiller needs to be centralised – if this is done late it might be necessary to check the boat with some opposite rudder for a second or two. As the wind hits the mainsail, ease the mainsheet out to take some of its force – it's easy to sustain rigging damage if you simply let the mainsail go. Trim the sails.

---

companies will start teaching you the basics by sending out a briefing kit, which can include detailed literature and/or a video on what to expect. Boat hire usually commences at noon, and for most of the remainder of the first day you'll be shown over the boat's gear and taught the basics of how to use the radio, anchoring and the basics of sailing. If you're not confident at

that point you can hire a skipper for a few more days, although most people don't.

The operators usually require a $500 bond, payable on arrival and refunded after the boat is returned undamaged. Bedding is usually supplied. Most companies have a minimum hire of five days and the daily rate drops considerably if you hire for 10 days or more.

Most of the charter companies have a wide range of yachts and cruisers available. You'll pay around $240 a day in the high season for a Holland 25 yacht that sleeps two people, around $380 a day for a Robertson 950 yacht that sleeps up to four, around $530 a day for a Hunter 376 that sleeps up to six people, and around $400 a day for a Flybridge 35 cruiser that sleeps up to eight people.

There are a number of bareboat charter companies at Airlie Beach, including:

Australian Bareboat Charters
   (☎ 4946 9381 or 1800 075 000; fax 4946 9220; www.ozemail.com.au/~bareboat) PO Box 357, Airlie Beach, Qld 4802
Mandalay Boat Charters
   (☎ 4946 6298 or 1800 075 123) PO Box 273, Airlie Beach, Qld 4802
Prosail Whitsunday
   (☎ 4946 7533) 386 Shute Harbour Rd, Airlie Beach, Qld 4802
Sail Whitsunday
   (☎ 4946 7070 or 1800 075 045) PO Box 929, Airlie Beach, Qld 4802
Whitsunday Escape
   (☎ 4946 7367 or 1800 075 145) PO Box 719, Airlie Beach, Qld 4802

Camping on the Islands

Although accommodation in the island resorts is typically expensive, it's possible to camp on several islands. Hook Island has a privately run camping ground, and on a number of the islands (see the following table) you can camp cheaply at national park sites.

Self-sufficiency is the key to camping in national park sites; some have toilets, but only a few have drinking water, and even then not always year-round. You're advised to take 5L of water per person per day, plus three days' extra supply in case you get stuck.

You should also have a fuel stove – wood fires are banned on all islands. There's a national parks leaflet that describes the various sites, and provides detailed information on what to take and do.

Camping permits are available from the Whitsunday Department of Environment office (see the Information Section at the start of this chapter) and cost just $3.50 per person per night; numbers are limited for each camping area.

You can get out to your island with one of the day cruise boats (generally the sail-around ones rather than the island resort boats) or with Whitsunday Allover Water Taxis. Island Camping Connection (☎ 4946 5255) will drop you off at Long, North Molle, South Molle, Planton or Tancred Island for $35 return (minimum of two people).

If you've got camping gear, give it a try – Robinson Crusoeing on your very own island can be a lot of fun. An Esky would be handy to keep the wine cool. The booking offices in Airlie Beach are helpful and can advise on which boats are best to use for your situation.

The possibilities for camping in national parks in the Whitsundays are summarised in the table. Note that some sites are subject to seasonal closures due to bird nesting.

Island	People	Drinking Water
Tancred		
northern end	4	no**
North Molle		
Cockatoo Beach	36	seasonal
Whitsunday		
Dugong Beach	30	yes, but may be seasonal
Sawmill Beach	15	seasonal
Joe's Beach	6	no
Thomas		
Sea Eagle Beach	4	no**
Shaw		
Neck Bay Beach	12	no
South Repulse		
western beach	18	no**
Gloucester*		
Bona Bay	15	yes
Armit*		
western beach	5	no
Saddleback*		
western side	6	no**
Olden*	4	no**
Lindeman		
Boat Port	6	no
Planton	4	no**

Henning		
Northern Spit	20	no
Long Island		
Sandy Bay	6	no
South Molle		
Sandy Bay	15	no
Shaw		
Neck Bay	12	no**
Hook		
Maureen Cove	20	no
Denman	4	no**

* Northern islands like Armit, Gloucester, Olden and Saddleback are harder to reach because the water taxi and cruises from Shute Harbour don't usually go there. Gloucester and Saddleback are best reached from Earlando, Dingo Beach or Bowen.
** Bush campsite. No facilities.

Getting There & Away

Air Most visitors arriving by air fly directly to Hamilton Island (Ansett flights only) and transfer from there to another island, without setting foot on the mainland at all.

Qantas (☎ 13 1313) can only get you to Proserpine, 36km from Shute Harbour.

Land Most of the bus services up and down the Bruce Highway detour into Airlie Beach. It's about 18 hours from Brisbane, 2 hours from Mackay, 4 hours from Townsville or 9 hours from Cairns. See the Getting There & Away chapter for more information.

Sampsons (☎ 4945 2377) has around 20 services daily from Proserpine to Airlie Beach and Shute Harbour between 6 am and about 6 pm. It's $6.50 from Proserpine to Airlie Beach, and $4 from Airlie Beach to Shute Harbour. There are two main bus stops in Airlie Beach, one at the western end of the main street, outside the post office, the other at the other end of town, outside the pub.

If you drive to Shute Harbour, the daily parking charge in the carpark is $7. There's also a lock-up carpark a few hundred metres back along the road, by the Shell service station, costing $5 from 8 am to 5 pm, or $8 for 24 hours.

Boat The Whitsunday Sailing Club is at the end of Airlie Beach Esplanade. Check the noticeboards at the Abel Point Marina for possible rides or crewing opportunities on passing yachts.

Getting Around

Air Lindeman and Hamilton are the only Whitsunday islands with airstrips (a limited international airport in Hamilton's case). Island Air Taxis (☎ 4946 9933) flies from Whitsunday airport at Airlie Beach to Hamilton ($45) and Lindeman ($55) islands.

If you really want to arrive in style, most of the resorts have helicopter landing pads – contact Helireef (☎ 4946 9102). They also do transfers to, among other places, Hayman ($250), Daydream ($50) and Lindeman ($375). Prices are per aircraft for two passengers.

Sea Transfers to the resorts are usually made from Shute Harbour or Hamilton Island. Some of the resorts have their own boats to ferry their guests back and forth.

The water taxis provide much the same service. See the individual island sections for details of regular transfers and the cruises section for information on cruises through the Whitsundays.

Hamilton Island

Area:	6 sq km
Type:	continental
High point:	230m
Max visitors:	1600

Hamilton Island is certainly the most ambitious resort development along the Great Barrier Reef – not only does it have a huge range of accommodation possibilities, shops, restaurants and a 400 boat marina, but also its own international airport.

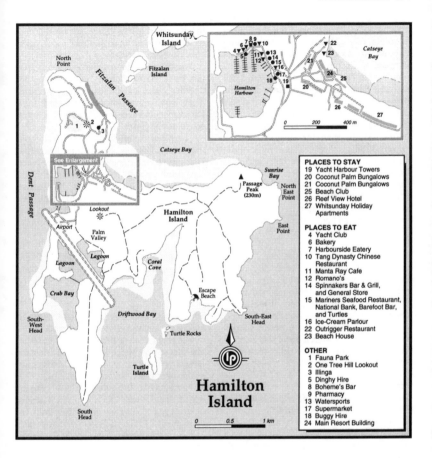

PLACES TO STAY
19 Yacht Harbour Towers
20 Coconut Palm Bungalows
21 Coconut Palm Bungalows
25 Beach Club
26 Reef View Hotel
27 Whitsunday Holiday
   Apartments

PLACES TO EAT
4 Yacht Club
6 Bakery
7 Harbourside Eatery
10 Tang Dynasty Chinese
   Restaurant
11 Manta Ray Cafe
12 Romano's
14 Spinnakers Bar & Grill,
   and General Store
15 Mariners Seafood Restaurant,
   National Bank, Barefoot Bar,
   and Turtles
16 Ice-Cream Parlour
22 Outrigger Restaurant
23 Beach House

OTHER
1 Fauna Park
2 One Tree Hill Lookout
3 Illinga
5 Dinghy Hire
8 Boheme's Bar
9 Pharmacy
13 Watersports
17 Supermarket
18 Buggy Hire
24 Main Resort Building

There's an extensive (and expensive) range of entertainment possibilities, including reef trips, helicopter joy rides, game fishing, parasailing, scuba diving and almost anything else you might care to think of.

Hamilton is fairly hilly, rising to 230m at Passage Peak. The resort includes a fauna reserve, restaurants, shopping facilities, tennis and squash courts, gymnasium and sauna. As well as the resort accommodation there are also condominiums and even some private houses – including one belonging to George Harrison. Hamilton's airport has direct daily flights to and from Cairns, Sydney, Brisbane and Melbourne, as well as international charter flights, making it the major arrival point for guests bound for other Whitsunday islands as well as Hamilton Island itself.

Hamilton was originally the creation of Gold Coast entrepreneur Keith Williams, backed by lots of other investors, including Ansett Airlines – which operates all the large aircraft flights into Hamilton. Keith Williams took a lease on the island for deer farming and later managed the not inconsiderable feat of converting the farming lease to a tourism one. Of course, all sorts of amazing accomplishments were commonplace in Queensland in those pre-1989 National Party days. Work started on his mega-resort in 1982, parts of the resort were in operation in 1984, and by the end of 1986 the show was up and running.

Remarkably even for Queensland, the conservationists kept surprisingly quiet while hilltops were levelled, harbours dredged out, artificial beaches created, runways laid and one 15 storey and two 13-storey apartment blocks were erected. The old 'no higher than a palm tree' dictum was certainly ignored here – the buildings serve as useful yachting landmarks all over the Whitsundays.

After the success of the early years, various adverse circumstances such as the domestic pilots' dispute and an international recession led to Hamilton Island being placed in receivership in May 1992. Eighteen months later, Hamilton Island Ltd was successfully floated on the Australian Stock Exchange, and in March 1994 the international hotel chain Holiday Inns took over management of the resort.

Information

The phone number for the resort is ☎ 4946 9999, the fax number is 4946 8888, and the postal address is Hamilton Island Resort, Private Mail Bag, Hamilton Island Post Office, Qld 4803. Reservations can be made directly by a toll-free call to ☎ 1800 075 110.

The *Hamiltonian* is a regular publicity and information paper produced for the resort.

The development at Hamilton is so big that it's really a small town, not just a large resort. The main areas of Hamilton straddle a narrow neck of land where the resort clusters on the east side (resortside), the marina and shops on the other (harbourside). Most of the services on Hamilton Island – shops, restaurants, boat hire and so on – are operated independently of the resort. Never-

theless, resort guests can charge most things to their room account and pay for it when checking out.

You can even get married on Hamilton – the tiny island church has become yet another piece of the island's marketing. They'll put on a full wedding for $1000. Packaged Japanese Wedding Blessings are especially popular.

There are countless 'events' throughout the year at Hamilton, including the annual Hamilton Island Race Week in August when the yachting fraternity heads to Hamilton en masse. Every December sees the Billfish Bonanza, a game fishing tournament, and each June there's the country's biggest outrigger canoe regatta, with teams coming from California, Hawaii and Tahiti.

Medical Services There's a medical centre with a resident doctor. It's open from 10 am to noon and 4 to 6 pm Monday to Friday, and until noon on Saturday.

Shops Hamilton has a complete range of shops, including a small supermarket, a newsagent, a post office, photo service, pharmacy, fish shop, bakery, delicatessen, ice-cream parlour, hairdresser and beauty salon, boutiques and gift shops.

There's also a National Bank branch, which opens from 10 am to 3 pm Monday to Friday, and also has an ATM. Both reception desks have EFTPOS facilities and can cash travellers cheques and exchange foreign currency.

Things to See

In addition to the usual array of resort activities available, guests can also visit nearby Dent Island or the island's fauna park.

Dent Island Adjacent to Hamilton Island, Dent Island shelters Dent Passage. At the north end of the island you can visit Coral Art run by Bill and Leen Wallace, an elderly couple (she's in her mid-90s!) who first settled on Hamilton Island in 1952. They have lived on Dent for many years, selling coral art and other bric-a-brac. They're a friendly pair and, despite the proximity of Hamilton, aren't overwhelmed by visitors and are often happy to have a chat. (Make arrangements in advance with Watersports at the resort because they have to phone ahead.)

Fauna Park & Wildlife At the northern end of the island there's a fauna park (admission $10, children $5) with koalas, kangaroos, deer and other wildlife. The crocodile feeding at 10.15 am and cockatoo capers show at 10.30 am are both very popular. While walking on the island trails you may well bump into goats.

Hamilton also has plenty of birdlife, including numerous raucous cockatoos, which have realised that tourists are always good for a free hand-out.

Activities

The resort has spas, saunas, tennis courts, pools, squash courts, a recreation room, a gym, a golf driving range and mini-golf course, and other sporting facilities. From Catseye Beach, the main resort beach, you can hire watersports equipment from Jono's Beach Hire – sailboards ($15 per hour), catamarans ($20 per hour), jet skis ($20 for 10 minutes), and other equipment.

Motorised watersports are available from the Watersports shop at Harbourside. Parasailing ($55) is very popular at Hamilton and you can go waterskiing ($25 for 10 minutes) or take tube rides ($10).

For dry land sports you can try the Wire Flyer (a cross between a hang-glider and a flying fox), which is affordable at $25 a flight, a target shooting range with archery butts, a rifle range with clay pigeon shooting, a go-kart track and golf driving range.

The children are attended to as well – the Kids' Club handles children up to 14 years of age from 9 am to 5 pm, and there's no charge. Babysitters can be arranged in the evening.

Diving H_2O Sportz by the harbour is the Hamilton Island dive shop and has introductory dives for $65 (for two dives), or diving gear for hire from $55 a day. One day diving trips cost $120 and go to Bait Reef, Butterfly or Manta Ray bays, north of Whitsunday Island, or you can go on the regular trips out to Bait Reef. Diving trips seem to fill up fast at Hamilton, so book early. A full five-day diving certificate course costs $450.

Cruises A variety of short trips and day cruises operate from Hamilton including Great Barrier Reef trips. The resort has a 'war canoe' for short jaunts across to Coral Art on Dent Island; adventure cruises and sunset cruises; and a small cruise boat that does half-day snorkel safaris for $65. The 20m yacht *Banjo Patterson* also operates day trips from the resort, costing $75 and including a BBQ lunch on a deserted beach. Children's fares are all half the adult price.

Longer cruises, game fishing trips and, if you like your cruising well above sea level, helicopter reef flights ($50) are also available. Whale watching cruises are also run on Tuesday and Friday from July to September, and cost $75.

Boats Dinghies with small outboard motors can be hired from Resort Dinghy Hire (☎ 4946 8259) at the marina and cost $55 for a half day, or $80 for a full day. You can take them across to Dent Island, Henning Island or along one part of Whitsunday Island – basically, you're restricted to the waters of Dent Passage. Fishing is popular, and they will supply you with lines, hooks and bait. Or you can just laze on a beach or visit Coral Art on Dent Island.

The Charter Base (☎ 4946 8226), at Harbourside, has a fleet of larger boats including Benateau 35 to 43 foot yachts and Targa Cat 40 foot power cruisers, both available with or without crew. A range of power boats and game fishing craft are also available for charter.

Walks Hamilton is quite a large island and, despite the size of the development, there is a lot of relatively untouched land on the east side, dominated by the 230m Passage Peak.

Passage Peak Walk This is the best walk on the island. A trail leads around the shore-line of Catseye Bay climbing gently at first, then becoming progressively steeper to the rocky summit of Passage Peak. From the top there are superb views back over the resort, across to Whitsunday Island and south to dramatic Pentecost Island, Linde-man Island and other islands of the southern Whitsundays.

Hamilton was not as comprehensively overgrazed as South Molle or some of the other islands in the Whitsundays, and the vegetation is typical, with hoop pines and grass-trees. Apart from Hamilton's large bird and lizard population you may see some of the handsome goats – relics of the island's grazing days.

Other Walks Most of the other island walks are along bulldozed trails, more suit-able for 4WD vehicles or trail bikes than walkers. You can get to the other walks either by starting out along the Passage Peak trail from the resort or by taking the route round by the airport.

Either way you can get to the Resort Lookout, on top of the flattened hill where the airport navigation equipment is mounted. Technically, you have to ask per-mission before venturing up here, so call the resort operator and ask for the airport safety officer. You must also get permission to walk around the end of the runway to reach the part of the island beyond the airport.

The trail round by the resort side of the airport, not crossing the runway, passes by the small palm grove known as Palm Valley, and winds up and then down to Coral Cove on Driftwood Bay. There's a pleasant sweep of beach here, although, as with Catseye Bay, the water is very shallow. You can also reach Coral Cove from the resort side of the island, or follow the trail to Escape Beach, an even more secluded sandy beach about 45 minutes to an hour's

walk from the resort. You catch tantalising glimpses of Coral Cove from the Escape Beach track.

Places to Stay

Hamilton has a variety of hotel rooms, apartments, lodges, bungalows and other buildings. The Reef View Hotel block is 20 storeys high, but most of the resort accom-modation is generally in lower blocks.

Rates here are for room only, and all rooms have air-conditioning and ceiling fans, TV, an iron and ironing board, tea and coffee-making facilities, hair dryers and minibars.

Flanking the main resort complex with its reception area, restaurants, bars, shops and pools are 60 five-star rooms in the *Beach Club*. Behind the resort complex are 51 in-dividual *Coconut Palm Bungalows*, which cost $235. These have a double and a single bed, air-con and fan, minibar, phone, TV and a small patio.

The large 20 storey *Reef View Hotel* has 386 large rooms and suites. They range from 18 junior rooms at $200 a night, 350 premier rooms at $350 a night, and 18 suites from $745 a night, and $1700 for the two 'Presidential' suites, complete with private pool. The premier rooms have two double beds, air-con, fan, TV, phone, minibar, en suite with separate bath and shower, and superb views from the balcony.

Lastly, there are the *Whitsunday Holiday Apartments*, in the two 13-storey and ad-joining lower blocks. The 168 one-bedroom apartments take four people at $335 a night, while the two-bedroom apartments take five people for $465 a night. The apartments are modern, comfortable and equipped with complete kitchens with cooking utensils, plates, dishes, cups, cutlery and so on. Each apartment has a dining and sitting area and a large balcony. There's even a washing machine and clothes drier in the two-bedroom apartments. The apartment blocks have small swimming pools and spas, or you can use the large pool in the main resort complex.

Much cheaper local rates are often available if the resort is not full. It's worth inquiring if you're on the mainland, since these reduced rates also include transfers between Shute Harbour and Hamilton Island.

If you really need a room and money is no obstacle, then the *Yacht Harbour Towers* has self-contained penthouses accommodating eight people at $2000 a night. Each four-bedroom apartment occupies a whole floor. Or you could rent one of the private houses, such as *Illalangi*, costing around $1250 a night, although $600 is more typical. You can even buy your own Hamilton condo and rent it out when you're not in residence – Hamilton Island even has a real estate agency.

Places to Eat
Accommodation on Hamilton Island is all room-only, but meal packages are available at $80 for three meals or $60 for breakfast and dinner. The restaurants participating in the package are: *Toucan Tango Bar & Cafe*, *Beach House* and the *Outrigger Restaurant* within the resort proper, and the *Manta Ray Cafe*, *Tang Dynasty*, *Mariners Seafood Restaurant* and *Romano's* at harbourside.

Resortside There's a few choices of places to eat, or there's a supermarket and shops if you prepare your own food in the apartments.

The bright, airy and thoroughly modern *Toucan Tango Cafe & Bar* in the main resort complex serves breakfast and dinner indoors or outside beside the pool. Light meals are the focus here, with offerings such as focaccia ($10), salmon and prawn salad ($16) or gnocchi ($12). Wine is available by the bottle ($25 to $50) or the glass. Live entertainment features here most nights.

Another breakfast option is the *Coral Lounge & Breakfast Room* on the ground floor of the Whitsunday Holiday Apartments building.

You can also get drinks, lunch or an early dinner at the pleasant *Beach House*, where you can sit inside or outside on the veranda

overlooking the swimming pool and beach. Main dishes, such as pan-fried scallops with marinated eggplant, go for $24 to $30.

There's also a bar (with swim-up facilities, of course) on the pool island.

The final option in the main resort area is the *Outrigger Restaurant*, which is only open in the evenings for dinner and is a seafood specialist. Main meals range from $19 to $25.

Harbourside The restaurants and shops at harbourside are independently run, so if you don't like the food or service, complain to the operator, not the resort. Although they are individual entities you can still charge all meals at island restaurants to your room and settle the total bill on departure.

There's also a supermarket for those in the apartments preparing their own meals.

Working your way round from the ferry jetty, the first place you come across is the *Ice Cream Parlour*. Next along is *Turtles*, a snack bar and cafe with expensive gourmet pies ($3), lasagne ($5) and sandwiches ($3 to $5). Upstairs here is *Mariners Seafood Restaurant*, which has a great veranda overlooking the harbour. Obviously, seafood is the focus (main dishes $22 to $27), but you can also get grills ($20 to $23). If you're feeling flush try a superb seafood platter ($120 for two). It's open in the evenings only from Monday to Saturday, and is both licensed and BYO.

Next along is the *Barefoot Bar*, with lunch-time pub meals for $5 to $8, and next door again is *Spinnakers Bar & Grill*, above the General Store supermarket. It's an evening place with a pleasant veranda. The menu is fairly unambitious, with steaks from $16, pasta $15 to $18, and seafood for $18 to $20.

Across the road is the formal Italian restaurant, *Romano's*, with a deck built right out over the water. Main dishes are $13 to $18, up to $28 for seafood specialities. Wine is available by the bottle ($20 to $70). On the same side of the road is the *Manta Ray Cafe*, open for breakfast ($6 to $9), lunch and dinner (mains $15 to $20). If you come to Hamilton on a day trip that includes lunch, this is one of the places you can eat at (the other is the Yacht Club, see below).

Turn the marina corner, and back across the road you come to the *Tang Dynasty Chinese Restaurant*. It has a typical Chinese menu upstairs and a takeaway counter, which is also upstairs but at the end of the building. Nothing to write home about, but good, straightforward Chinese dishes. It's open for lunch from Monday to Thursday and dinner every night.

Next along is the *Harbourside Eatery*, which is a basic fish and chip and burger place with tables outside on the footpath. The *Bakery*, next door, turns out fresh bread and the like, and good value sandwiches.

Last in the line is the new and decidedly un-nautical *Yacht Club*, which has a self-cook BBQ buffet with steaks ($12) and kebabs ($8). It is elevated with plenty of space, so it's breezy and has great views.

Entertainment
In the evening there are the bars in the resort and harbourside. The *Toucan Tango* has a pianist in the evenings, or you can head to *Boheme's Bar* at harbourside, which opens from 9 pm with a disco from 11 pm till late.

Getting There & Away
Air The Hamilton Island airport is the main arrival centre for the Whitsundays and takes both domestic flights and international charter flights. This is one place where Australia's twin operators don't neatly split things up – Ansett has an exclusive on the trunk routes to or from Hamilton, and Qantas doesn't fly here.

Ansett flies nonstop to Hamilton from Brisbane ($322 one way), Cairns ($251), Melbourne ($540) and Sydney ($457), though advance purchase fares are much cheaper. There are also shorter flights with Helijet between Hamilton and Mackay ($95), Shute Harbour ($45) or Lindeman Island ($45).

Boat Fantasea's Hamilton Island catamaran or the other launch takes 35 minutes to cross to/from Shute Harbour on the mainland. It costs $39, with children half-fare. Departures from Shute Harbour are at 6.45 and 8.45 am direct, and at 8.15 and 11 am and 2.45 and 4.30 pm via Daydream and South Molle islands. Returns from Hamilton Island are at 7.30 am and 3.45 and 5 pm direct, and at 9.45 am and 1.30 pm via Daydream and South Molle, and at 5.30 pm via Long Island.

With regular daily flights to and from the major capital cities, Hamilton is also the main arrival point for Long, South Molle, Daydream, Hayman and Lindeman islands. Whitsunday Allover (☎ 4946 9499) has services to these islands that meet all incoming and outgoing flights. Boat transfers to South Molle, Daydream and Long islands all cost $41 one way. Transfers to Lindeman Island are usually included in accommodation packages – otherwise it's $44.

There are excellent anchorages for visiting yachts at the Hamilton Island marina and, unlike at many Barrier Reef resorts, visiting yachties are actively encouraged. The catch is the daily cost: $60 for yachts up to 12m, $80 for 18m etc, although this does give you access to all the resort facilities. Hamilton is also a base for bareboat or crewed yacht charters around the Whitsunday islands.

Getting Around
On arrival and departure there's a free bus service for guests between the airport or marina and the resort.

Hamilton is big, no question about it. You can have a room where getting to a restaurant is a major trek, although most of the time, walking presents few problems. There are a few alternatives to fast walking. One is the island shuttle, which connects all points around the island on an hourly (or better) basis between 8 am and 10 pm. The cost is $5 for a 24 hour pass, although this is usually included in package deals.

Next are the taxis, which also shuttle around the island and charge a flat rate of $5 per person regardless of distance.

The other, and much more expensive, alternative is the rent-a-buggies. They're small golf buggies that can be rented for $15 an hour, $40 per day or $55 for 24 hours. For the limited distances involved they're pretty good for Hamilton, although some of the steep hills are too much for them and neither the taxis or the buggies are allowed to go down the unsurfaced roads, like the track round the airport to Coral Cove. Buggies can be rented from the office near reception or from the Charter Base at harbourside.

Long Island

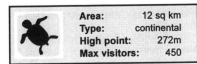

Area:	12 sq km
Type:	continental
High point:	272m
Max visitors:	450

Long Island is the closest of the resort islands to the coast. A channel only 500m wide separates it from the mainland, although some of the swiftest and trickiest currents in the Whitsundays run through this deep stretch of water. The island is about 11km long but no more than 1.5km wide at any point.

The island was originally named Port Molle by Lieutenant Charles Jeffreys in 1815. Jeffreys was en route to Ceylon (now Sri Lanka) at the time and lucky Colonel Molle had his name bestowed on a number of other islands in the Whitsundays. Although North, South and Mid Molle still bear the colonel's name, West Molle is now known as Daydream Island. Port Molle was given its current name by Matthew Flinders.

For many years the island was the most popular anchorage in the Whitsundays for ships travelling along the coast, but all the Molle islands were inhabited by Aborigines and there were a number of often violent clashes between them and the intruders. In the late 19th century timber was cut on the island and taken to the sawmill operating at that time at Cid Harbour on Whitsunday Island. Later, there was a banana plantation on Long Island and it was the base for a mail boat that ran regularly around the Whitsunday islands.

Resorts on Long Island have had a chequered history, with the first ones opening at Palm Bay and Happy Bay in the 1930s. The Happy Bay resort, which even gave its name to the bay, survived right up to 1983 when it changed hands and became Whitsunday 100 in an attempt to make another 'get wrecked' style resort. Despite catchy slogans, it only lasted three years and was then totally redeveloped by the tour operator Contiki and operated as a 'party-hard' resort for the 18 to 35 year old set. In 1990 it changed hands (and names) again and became known as 'The Island'; in 1991 it became the Radisson Long Island Resort, and its most recent incarnation as Club Crocodile dates from January 1994.

Further south it was a cyclone rather than economics that wiped out Palm Bay in the mid-1970s, but it's back in operation as a low-key getaway-style resort, catering for limited numbers. It's a good place to visit if you want to see what the island resorts used to be like before all the developers and up-market hoteliers moved into the Whitsundays.

After some years of uncertainty, the island's third resort, situated in the south of the island at Paradise Bay, has recently re-opened as the Whitsunday Wilderness Lodge. It's a small resort that caters to those who want an alternative to the golf-buggy and jet-ski resort experience.

Information
Club Crocodile The Club Crocodile Resort is towards the northern end of the island. The resort phone number is ☎ 4946 9400 or toll free ☎ 1800 075 125, the fax number is 4946 9555, and the postal address is Club Crocodile Long Island Resort, PO Box 798, Airlie Beach, Qld 4802.

The resort reception has EFTPOS facilities and payphones, and there's a resort shop that sells clothing, swim wear, hats, magazines, toiletries and sunscreen.

Palm Bay The Palm Bay Hideaway Resort is about a third of the way down the island. The resort phone and fax number is ☎ 4946 9233, and the address is Palm Bay Resort, Private Mail Bag, Mackay, Qld 4740.

The resort has no banking facilities, and there's a small shop selling groceries and the bare essentials of island life.

Whitsunday Wilderness Lodge Down at the south of the island is the Whitsunday Wilderness Lodge. The phone number is ☎ 4946 9777, the postal address is PO Box 842, Airlie Beach, Qld 4802, and it has an email address (wilodge@ozemail.com.au).

The resort has no banking facilities or shop, but it does have a payphone (coins only).

Things to See & Do
Club Crocodile The Club Crocodile Resort has two swimming pools, a gym, games room, tennis courts, windsurfers, catamarans and all the other typical Barrier Reef resort equipment; use of all of these is included in the tariffs. You can also hire out dinghies ($80 per day) and jet skis ($50 per half-hour), go waterskiing ($20 for 10 minutes) or parasailing ($49 for 10 minutes), or hire a glass-bottom waterbike ($20 per half hour).

Palm Bay Facilities are rather more limited at the simpler Palm Bay resort. There's a swimming pool, pool table, board games and snorkelling gear, and catamarans ($15 an hour) and windsurfers ($12 an hour) can be hired out. Parasailing, dinghy hire and waterskiing can also be arranged (at Club Crocodile).

Whitsunday Wilderness Lodge In keeping with the lodge's eco-friendly approach, activities here are all non-powered and are included in the tariff. One of the highlights is the sea kayaking day trips along the mangrove estuaries of the nearby Conway National Park. Other than that, pull up a hammock and a good book.

Beaches The mainland (western) beaches tend to be sandy, the eastern beaches are rocky and face the prevailing winds. They're not bad beaches for the Whitsundays, although Long Island suffers even more than most of the islands from the extreme tidal variations. When the tide's out at Happy Bay, it's way out and you might as well head for the pool if you want a swim. Between November and March it's probably an idea to head for the pool anyway as Long Island is close enough to the mainland for box jellyfish (also known as marine stingers or sea wasps) to be a potential hazard. In fact, there have been no fatal incidents in the Whitsundays but nobody wants to be the first victim.

Cutting the channel through the reef and dredging out Palm Bay has made it a good yacht mooring and allows swimming at all tides, but the altered flow pattern has also washed most of the sand off the beach.

The Whitsunday Wilderness Lodge has a picturesque small beach.

Walks Long Island has 13km of walking tracks, although the bottom half of the island has no tracks and is pretty much untouched. Starting from the Club Crocodile resort, there's a 3km trail that loops around the northern end of the island with some good views out to Dent, Hamilton and the other islands to the east. At the northern end of the loop a short spur runs off to an old banyan tree.

Another trail starts near the tennis courts and runs south to Palm Bay, just over 2km away. A short distance along this trail is a junction where trails run west to Humpy Point lookout and east to a 1.5km circuit around the hill. Further on, short spurs run off to Fish Bay and Pandanus Bay, at a point where the island is only 100m wide. Finally, there are glimpses of the Palm Bay Hideaway resort and the yachts moored off it, before the trail drops down into the resort area.

Again the island is only 100 or so metres wide at this point and the trail picks up again on the eastern side of the island and continues 4km south to Sandy Bay – there's an alternative route over the first kilometre or so with some good views to the east. Sandy Bay is a disappointment as a final destination, at least when the tide is in. There is a national parks campsite here.

Wildlife Long Island has some interesting native and introduced wildlife. Just behind the units at the northern end of the Club Crocodile Resort you can see numerous fruit bats hanging in the trees. At sunset hundreds of them flap over the resort, heading for the mainland and a night's gorging.

If you wander the island's bush trails you may come across wallabies and some very healthy-looking goats. Goannas are another island inhabitant, and there are numerous

species of birds, including some very regal looking peacocks around the Palm Bay Hideaway resort. Long Island's scrub fowl are very numerous and remarkably unfussed about humans. There are some spectacularly large incubation mounds around the island, including one beside the Palm Bay to Sandy Bay tracks that is so enormous there's even a bench beside it so you can sit down to admire it.

Shipwrecks Unidentified shipwrecks around Australia have a strange tendency to end up as 'Spanish galleons' and Long Island's own galleon was discovered in the 1970s. Of course, it was a Spaniard who discovered Torres Strait, at the northern end of the Barrier Reef, and gave it his name. Later, other Spanish sailing ships may have used the straits when sailing to or from the Spanish colony at Manila in the Philippines, but there's certainly no evidence that they went further south down the Barrier Reef. It's now believed that the Happy Bay wreck is of the *Valetta*, which went down in 1825, although another source identifies it as the *Louisa*.

Places to Stay & Eat

Camping There's a national parks campsite at Sandy Bay, midway along the western side of the island. There is space here for only six people, and there are no facilities. For permits check with the Whitsunday Department of Environment office in Airlie Beach.

Club Crocodile Behind the long sweep of sand at Happy Bay is the *Club Crocodile Resort*, operated by Club Crocodile Holdings, which runs a similar property near Airlie Beach. It offers an affordable range of accommodation and caters to couples and families, with plenty of activities to keep the kids busy.

The resort has three styles of accommodation. The Beachfront Units, the most expensive rooms, are in two-storey blocks with pleasant, motel-style rooms with attached bathrooms, air-conditioning, a ceiling fan and a balcony. There are facilities for tea and coffee making, TV, fridges and telephones. These cost $190 per person per night, but standby deals are sometimes available. The Garden Units are similar, but lack the beach aspect, and cost $160 per person per night. A meal package is available for $47, or you can pay as you go.

Lastly, there are the Lodge Units, which are basic motel-style twin or double rooms with shared bathrooms and no air-con, costing $25 per person per night, including transfers to and from Shute Harbour.

The tariff in all rooms include entertainment and use of all the non-powered equipment. There's an extra charge for dinghies, jet skis and other equipment that burns fuel. Standby packages from Airlie Beach are often available, and these are significantly cheaper – eg $127 per person in the Garden Units, including three meals.

There are two eating options here: The Palms restaurant and Cafe Paradiso. *The Palms* is the more formal of the two – a large and stylish restaurant with white linen tablecloths. It's open in the mornings with a choice between a continental ($10.50) or a full buffet ($16.50) breakfast. Lunch is a set $12, while at night a three-course set meal costs $24, or à la carte dishes cost from $14 to $20. The more casual *Cafe Paradiso* has both outdoor and indoor tables and opens from 10 am to 9 pm. It offers things like rolls and sandwiches for $6, chicken burgers for $8, Thai noodles for $9.50, as well as snacks, salads and pizzas.

Club Crocodile also has two bars: the *Pool Bar* gives you the choice of sitting by (or in) the pool or overlooking the beach. The *Sand Bar*, which opens at 7 pm, is the resort's entertainment centre and features a resident band and nightly disco until late.

Palm Bay You can actually walk from the Club Crocodile Resort to the *Palm Bay Hideaway Resort,* about 2km south. The island is very narrow at this point and the resort has a sandy beach on the west (mainland) side and a stony one on the other. The resort is very simple, relaxed and low-key,

with 14 individual cabins and bungalows along the sandy sweep of Palm Bay. There are eight basic cabins and six similar but slightly larger bungalows, all with a double bed and four bunks, a kitchenette with a benchtop cooker and fridge, attached bathrooms, and their own little veranda complete with a hammock for lazing the days away in. Just to complete the sense of isolation, there are no TVs or telephones.

In the centre of the resort is a large, island-style building with a high roof and open sides, which serves as the main dining area, lounge and meeting place. Inside there's a small bar, the resort reception desk and a shop. There's also a small swimming pool close by.

This is a good place to stay if you want to experience what the Whitsundays were like in the old days, before it all went upmarket. The only catch is that the prices are certainly no reminder of days gone by. It's expensive yet basic – what you're paying for is the individuality and the smallness of the resort. Nightly costs in the cabins are $146/224 for singles/doubles, and in the bungalows $194/328. Both sleep up to six people; extra adults cost another $35 ($38 in the bungalows), extra children $20 ($25).

At Palm Bay you have a choice of fixing your own food or paying an additional $61 per person per day ($38 for children), which covers breakfast, lunch and dinner – they're straightforward 'home-style' meals. Breakfast is a choice of cereals, fruit or cooked dishes; lunch is often a smorgasbord of salad and cold meats; and dinner consists of a main course (often a BBQ) and dessert. If you opt to fix your own meals, there are cooking facilities, crockery and cutlery in each of the cabins. The resort shop has limited supplies, although, of course, you will find it cheaper to bring your own food over from the mainland. You can also buy meals individually; breakfast costs $10 for the continental and $15 for the cooked, lunch is $17, and dinner $29.

Whitsunday Wilderness Lodge The isolated lodge on the very small Paradise Bay consists of only eight cabins. The spacious but basic cabins contain a double and single bed, and en suite bath. There is no fan or air-con, but the cabins are positioned to make the most of the sea breezes. The solar powered lodge is staffed by a friendly crew of just three, and so informality is the name of the game. The central area consists of a gazebo with comfy chairs and a small library of reference books, and a bar. Meals are buffet style, and most are cooked in camp-ovens over a campfire. The food is simple but filling, and vegetarians are well catered for.

Accommodation is only offered in six-night packages, which run from Monday to Sunday. The cost is $1290 per person, which includes everything (except drinks), and you arrive by helicopter from Hamilton Island.

Getting There & Away

Whitsunday Allover's boats operate to Long Island from Shute Harbour for $15 return. It's a quick trip, just 20 minutes or so. It's only 2km between the Happy Bay and Palm Bay resorts and you can walk it in just 15 to 20 minutes. Departures are from Shute Harbour at 7.15 and 9.15 am, and 1.30, 4 and 5.15 pm. From Club Crocodile they depart at 7.45 and 9.45 am, and 1.50, 4.30 and 5.30 pm. From Palm Bay Hideaway departures are at 8 and 9.30 am, and 4.15 and 5.45 pm.

Fantasea has one service from Hamilton to Long Island at 5 pm, which then leaves Long Island (Club Crocodile) at 5.55 pm for Shute Harbour.

The Happy Bay pier is round at the southern end of the bay, some distance from the resort. A wooden walkway runs over the rocks round the edge of the bay to the resort and guests are shuttled back and forth by little electric vehicles towing a string of trailers like a toy train. There's no pier at Palm Bay, but the resort's launch will run you out to meet the boat, or around to the Happy Bay pier.

Palm Bay and Happy Bay are popular anchorages for yachties. It's the nearest safe anchorage to Shute Harbour, so people

chartering bareboats and leaving late in the day often head here as the conclusion of their first short day's sailing. A channel has been cut through the reef at Palm Bay and there's an anchorage right up by the beach. The nightly mooring cost is $45 at Palm Bay, $40 at Happy Bay.

Daydream Island

Area:	0.17 sq km
Type:	continental
High point:	51m
Max visitors:	750

Formerly known as West Molle, this small island is just over 1km long and only a couple of hundred metres across at its widest point. Daydream is also the closest of the resort islands to Shute Harbour.

The island was first settled in the 1880s when the original grazing leases were issued for the Whitsundays. In 1933 West Molle Island was purchased by Paddy Murray, a retired army major, who renamed it Daydream after his gaff-rigged ketch. The major established the first resort on the island, catering for visitors from passing cruise ships and yachts. In 1947 the aviation pioneer Reginald Ansett (later Sir Reginald) bought the resort and operated it for a few years, bringing visitors out from the mainland by seaplane. But in 1953 he closed the Daydream resort, dismantled all the buildings and equipment and shipped them across to Hayman Island, where he was establishing another new resort.

For over a decade Daydream lay dormant, until it was bought in the mid-1960s by colourful Gold Coast entrepreneur Bernie Elsey, who ran it until 1970 when this resort, along with many others in the area, was levelled by a cyclone. During these years Daydream had acquired a rather risqué reputation, with rumours about outrageous practices like gambling and topless bathing regularly leaking back to the mainland. This was apparently the place to come if you liked your holidays spicy.

More recently, the resort was purchased by the Jennings Group Ltd, which demolished the old buildings in 1989 and spent $100 million on creating a new resort, which opened for business in December 1990 under the management of the Travelodge hotel chain. In the mid-1990s ownership changed once again, to Village Roadshow (the current owner).

The resort is in two parts: at the northern end of the island is the main resort building and facilities, including a mini-marina. At the southern end is the Beach Club, which has a good sandy beach and the facilities here include an excellent kidney-shaped pool, a bar, several shops, a cafe, and a huge outdoor movie screen (which is something of an eyesore even though it does swing up out of the way).

The only drawback with Daydream is its small size – it's not exactly claustrophobic but it does feel pretty cramped.

Information

The resort phone number is ☎ 4948 8488 or ☎ 1800 075 040, the fax number is 4948 8499, and the postal address is Daydream Island Resort, Private Mail Bag 22, Mackay, Qld 4740.

The resort shop sells clothing, books and magazines, sunglasses, swimwear, cosmetics, hats and toiletries. At the Beach Club there's also a photo shop, a souvenir shop, a games room and a clothing and swimwear boutique. A beauty salon and hairdresser are available at the resort on selected days.

Resort reception has EFTPOS facilities and can cash travellers cheques and exchange foreign currency.

Activities

The resort's promotions make much of the fact that many of the activities on the island are free and, apart from activities requiring fuel and trips to the reef or other islands,

most things indeed are. Included in the room tariffs are the use of tennis courts, a gym, sauna and spa, two swimming pools, aerobics classes, snorkelling, beach volleyball, fish feeding and more.

But not everything is free. For a price, the resort can also organise various boat trips for guests including overnight or longer yacht trips, cruises to the outer reef or to other islands, fishing trips, sunset cocktail cruises and guided sea kayak trips.

Daydream does especially well when it comes to looking after children. One of the resort's luxury two storey suites has been converted to accommodate the children's facilities. The Kids Only Club, which opens from 9 am to 10 pm daily, caters for kids from five to 12 years old with a range of (free) daily activities. There's something different on offer every hour, including nature walks, swimming, volleyball and cricket, party games and disco dancing (just to finish them off). The childcare centre is for children up to five years old and is also free.

Watersports All non-powered activities like catamarans, windsurfers, paddleboards and snorkelling equipment are free for house guests. From the Watersports hut on the northern beach you can also hire dinghies ($45 per half-day) and jet skis ($30 an hour), and you can also go waterskiing ($20 for 10 minutes) or parasailing ($49). Snorkelling gear is also available.

Beaches, Diving & Snorkelling There are two main beaches on the island. The tiny Sunlover's Beach is at the north-eastern end of the island, just behind the resort – a short path leads there from the third level of the main resort building. This beach has a 50m-long strip of corally sand, backed by palm trees and low cliffs, and there are some good patches of coral offshore for snorkelling. It seems that the beaches on Daydream aren't as severely affected by the Whitsunday tidal changes as those on some of the other islands, so you can still swim here at low tide. The sand, however, is just as coarse.

Then there's the large, sandy beach on

the south-west side in front of the Beach Club. This beach is also quite good, although not as popular as the northern beach.

The resort's Watersports hut offers a variety of diving courses and services, including introductory resort dives for $65, full gear hire for certified divers for $45 and an open-water certificate course that costs $450.

Walks The main nature walk is a steep, rocky path that climbs up and over the centre of the island and links the Beach Club with the resort. It's a short but strenuous stroll of about 20 minutes, passing through thick vegetation of mainly vine forests and offering some good views out over the Whitsunday waters and across to the mainland. Near the resort another trail deviates off the nature walk and leads down to Sunlover's Beach.

There's also a flat concrete path around the east side of the island – it's a slightly quicker but much less interesting way to get from the Beach Club to the resort. And once you've done these three walks, you've just about covered this island from top to bottom.

Places to Stay

The resort is a modern three level complex with 303 rooms, surrounded by extensive and well-maintained tropical gardens. Obviously a fair proportion of the initial $100 million was spent on landscaping. The overall effect is impressive without being over the top, but with such a large resort on such a small island, it's not the place to come if you're looking for isolation. You certainly won't be lost or lonely on Daydream.

The rooms are your standard motel-style units, all fairly spacious and pleasantly if rather plainly decorated. All rooms have their own bathroom and are fitted out with air-conditioning, telephones, tea and coffee-making facilities and TV. You'll also find a hair dryer, iron and ironing board and a minibar. All the rooms sleep up to four people, with either two double beds or a queen-size bed and a convertible sofa-bed, and interconnecting rooms are available for families. Surprisingly, the rooms don't have balconies.

You have a choice between the Garden Rooms, which look out on the gardens, or the Daydream Rooms, which have ocean views. Garden Rooms cost $175 per person, plus another $25 for each extra child. The Daydream Rooms are $20 more per person. Cheaper weekly and standby rates are also available, so it's worth checking with travel agents. All rates include breakfast.

Places to Eat

There are a couple of eating possibilities in the main resort building. The *Waterfall Cafe* specialises in buffet-style meals and opens for breakfast, lunch and dinner. At breakfast time it can be pretty chaotic if the resort is full, although the staff seem to manage it all quite well. You can get a tropical breakfast for $9 or full buffet breakfast for $17. At lunch time there's a snack menu to choose from ($8 to $10), while at night there's a different theme buffet each evening – it might be Asian, South Pacific, Italian or a good old Aussie BBQ. For $27.50 you get a choice of hot and cold selections, salads, fruit and desserts.

Langford's Lounge, in the centre of the atrium area, serves light snacks and sandwiches, morning and afternoon teas. The *North Pool Bar* is a good spot for lunch, with various snacks and meals, or you can even construct your own sandwich.

Sunlover's restaurant is more formal and only opens for dinner with an à la carte menu offering starters from $9 to $13 and mains from $18 to $25.

Down at the Beach Club end of the island there are a couple of other choices. *Skips' Cafe & Bakery* is a casual little coffee shop and bakery with a great selection of pies, sandwiches and rolls, and an array of very tempting cakes. The *South Pool Bar* also sells hot dogs at lunch time.

If you're planning a day exploring the Whitsundays, the resort can arrange for a picnic hamper to be packed for you.

Getting There & Away

Whitsunday Allover has six daily transfers to Shute Harbour between 7.30 am and 10.30 pm ($24 return), four of them via South Molle Island and Hamilton Island airport ($44 return).

Seatrek also has five services to Shute and South Molle, while Fantasea has two services to Shute Harbour ($16 return), five to South Molle ($16 return) and on to Hamilton ($36 return), and one to Abel Point Marina ($16 return).

South Molle

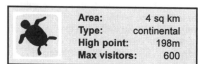

Area:	4 sq km
Type:	continental
High point:	198m
Max visitors:	600

The largest of the Molle group of islands, South Molle is virtually joined to Mid Molle and North Molle islands. You can walk across to Mid Molle any time and Daydream Island seems within arm's reach.

South Molle has long stretches of sandy or coral beach and is criss-crossed by a network of walking tracks. The island has a somewhat central position in the Whitsunday islands and from the highest point, Mt Jeffreys, there are superb views across all the surrounding islands. There are several other excellent viewpoints, particularly Spion Kop and Balancing Rock.

The island was named in 1815 after Colonel George Molle, appointed Lieutenant Governor of the colony of New South in 1814. Later, the Whitsundays were the scene for violent altercations between the new arrivals and the area's Aborigines. In 1864 the schooner *Eva* was driven ashore on the island, but another ship saved the crew.

In 1927 Henry George Lamond settled on

the island and lived here with his wife and three children for the next 10 years. He was the author of a number of books on horses and outback living. If you make the climb up to Lamond Hill, there's a memorial to Hal Lamond, his son.

From 1934 EM Bauer also lived on the island, and the bay in front of the resort is named after him. Bauer and his wife can claim credit for making the first tentative moves towards today's South Molle resort as they used to serve 'teas' to the infrequent visitors who dropped by.

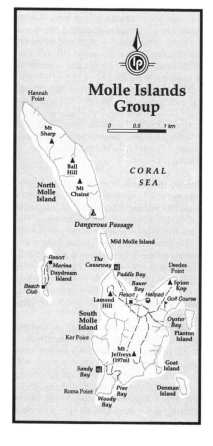

Molle Islands Group

Information

The resort phone number is ☎ 4946 9433 or ☎ 1800 075 080, and the fax number is 4946 9580. Write to South Molle Island Resort, PMB 21, Mackay, Qld 4741.

There's a gift shop with newspapers, cards, clothing, souvenirs, toiletries and the like. A coffee shop sells snacks, ice creams and drinks. There's also a hairdresser.

At reception, you can change travellers cheques and foreign currency. They also have EFTPOS facilities and a postal service.

The Queensland Department of Environment has a *South Molle Island* leaflet.

Wildlife

Well, there are lots of very noisy and very tame lorikeets that will eat out of your hand at their feeding time (3 pm), and some very well trained fish that turn up for a 9 am feed off the pier. Some of the larger fish seem to turn up to feed on the smaller fish, rather than on the resort hand-outs.

Other birdlife is prolific. In addition to the scavenging currawongs, those cheeky, large black and white birds that hang around the swimming pool looking for unattended plates to clean up, you'll see and hear all manner of birds around the resort or while you're walking the trails. You may come across a shy curlew standing by a path and you'll certainly hear their 'weee-loo' call across the golf course at night. The stone curlew is an endangered species on the mainland, but since 1988 when the island's cats and other feral predators were eradicated, the birds have thrived here.

Look for quieter wildlife too: the bright red spiders that sometimes build their intricate webs right across the trails, or the busy green ants that make their neat little shelters by gluing together groups of leaves. You might see them constructing these homes, pulling the leaves together with a 'human chain' of ants and then gluing the leaf edges together with the aid of aphids, which they squeeze the adhesive out of. You'll see these homes in use in the trees or, when the leaves die and drop off, lying on the ground.

Activities

Like a number of Barrier Reef island resorts, the South Molle resort has changed hands a number of times in recent years – most recently in early 1998.

There's a constant buzz of activity, all designed to keep you from getting bored and neatly detailed in a daily activities list. Even the wildlife gets called in to play its part – at 9 am the fish appear by the pier for their daily feeding, and at 3 pm the lorikeets fly in for their feed by the tennis courts.

Children are well catered for here – you can check them in to a pre-school nursery or a school-age activities centre and pretty much forget about them for the day. Actually, a lot of the kids seem happy to forget about their parents, too, and get on with some serious play time.

Sports There's a compact nine hole golf course right behind the resort – watch out for wayward balls hit by visiting beginners. There are a couple of tennis courts, a squash court and a small gymnasium. The activities organisers lay on plenty of competitions and games from cricket matches to golf tournaments, archery contests, and even touch football – the resort band seems to be the resident team. Shock horror, there's a video games room full of buzz-zap-bing-kerwang machines, but most people seem to find the outside diversions more attractive.

Watersports There are surf skis, catamarans, windsurfers and a bunch of other watersports equipment – all free. Windsurfing and sailing lessons are provided free every morning. Powered equipment and activities – dinghies, waterskiing, parasailing, jet skis, watersled rides (all that sort of thing) do have a charge. The resort has one swimming pool with a tiny kiddies pool beside it. The pool – a straightforward rectangle deep at one end, shallower at the other – betrays the resort's age. There's a sauna and spa of similar vintage.

Diving The resort has a PADI dive school that offers a short course for beginners

($80) or a five to six day open-water PADI course ($395). Equipment can be rented for $45 a day with one tank. That gives you about three hours at the reef – time for a couple of good dives.

Beaches & Snorkelling The Whitsundays are not noted for their out-of-this-world beaches and the beach directly in front of the South Molle resort is OK, but only at high tide. When the tide is right out there's an unattractive, rocky mud flat outside the Beachcomber and Reef units that can actually get quite smelly at times. Those beachfront units aren't such an attractive proposition on those occasions.

If you continue round to the west of the resort – either a scramble across the rocks or a 1km stroll on a bush track – you find yourself at Paddle Bay. The beach here is quite pleasant, less crowded than the resort beach and if you swim out over the rocky patch up towards the end of the beach, you'll find some good coral including some interesting bommies.

There's not much else in the way of worthwhile beaches around the island. Oyster Bay is rocky, Pine Bay, on the south side of the island, is very shallow and faces the prevailing winds head on. Also down at the south end of the island, Sandy Bay faces across to Shute Harbour and has some good coral, although it's really stony rather than sandy.

Free snorkelling lessons are provided in the pool most days of the week and snorkelling equipment is also available for free use.

Walks Over much of the central and southern part of the island the bush is quite sparse due to overgrazing in the years prior to the island becoming a national park, but there are still many fine walks. The remaining forest cover is mainly at the north end of the island, around the resort. The middle part of the island is predominantly rolling grassland. At the extreme south of the island, again, there's some very limited remnants of the earlier forest cover, including a patch of hoop pines above Pine Bay.

The walks are easy to follow and very well signposted. Most of them start from up behind the resort golf course. You start by zig-zagging up the hill and the various trails divert off this trail. If you've got tiny children the resort even has baby-carrier backpacks available for free.

Spion Kop The 3km walk to the top of Spion Kop is probably the finest walk on the island. The trail winds along the ridge with fine views down to Planton and Denman islands on the east, and also across to Hamilton; below you on the west side you can see Bauer Bay, the resort and North Molle. Leaving the grasslands the trail climbs onto a forested hillside, dips down briefly onto a saddle and then climbs up again to the rocky outcrop of Spion Kop at the extreme northern point. You can clamber up through the hoop pines to the top of Spion Kop from where there are superb views in all directions, including back down on the resort.

Oyster Bay & Mt Jeffreys Turn south at the junction where the Spion Kop route heads north and after a couple of hundred metres you come to the point where the Oyster Bay trail diverges off and winds its way down to the rock bay on the east coast. Oyster Bay is 2.5km from the resort. Just south of Oyster Bay is Turtle Bay.

The Mt Jeffreys trail continues south, with the trail to the south diverging off it. The Mt Jeffreys trail continues parallel to the east coast, generally through grassland with little original forest cover. There are fine views of the Whitsundays, particularly Hamilton Island with its tell-tale skyscrapers. Finally, the trail winds around to the top of Mt Jeffreys, a bare, grass-covered peak with superb 360° views. From the top you can see across the Molle group, north to Hayman, Hook and Whitsunday islands, south-east to Hamilton, south to Long Island and west to the mainland with Shute Harbour easily identified by its cluster of yachts and boats. It's 3.5km from the resort to the top of Mt Jeffreys.

Sandy Bay & Pine Bay These two bays are at the southern end of the island, 4.7km from the resort. The trail runs through the centre of the island, through forest bush for the first half and then through rolling grassland with grass-trees. The trail curves around the west side of Mt Jeffreys and you can cross down from the Mt Jeffreys trail to this southern trail quite easily. There are some fine views of Long Island and the other islands south of South Molle before you get to the trail junction, from where it is 500m to either bay.

The trail to Pine Bay winds down through a stand of hoop pines. The bay has a wide beach, sloping very gently into the sea and facing due south, which means that the prevailing northerly breezes carry a wide assortment of flotsam and jetsam ashore. In addition to the expected driftwood, there's an amazing assortment of that modern addition – 'driftplastic'. It's a convincing reminder of how indestructible our modern components and containers are.

The alternate trail leads down to Sandy Bay, which is more stony than sandy, but does have some reasonable coral offshore. Right down at the end of the island there's Woody Bay. This southern tip of the island is the only remaining forest cover apart from that around the resort and north end.

Balancing Rock, Lamond Hill & Paddle Bay These trails lead off to the west and north-west from the resort. It's only 1.3km to Balancing Rock – where there is indeed a balancing rock that looks remarkably precarious – and some truly superb views. You can see across to Daydream, across the central area of South Molle and to Mt Jeffreys, and over the resort to Spion Kop. The resort itself seems to be right at your feet.

You can continue on from Balancing Rock to Lamond Hill, which is 3km from the resort. It's a gently rounded hill, not as spectacular as Balancing Rock, but the views are just as good. Just below the summit is a memorial to Hal Lamond, a son of the original European settler, who was killed in action in WWII.

Descend to the main trail and you can either continue on to Paddle Bay, 1km from the resort, or loop back to the resort. Paddle Bay is just before the sand spit across to Mid Molle. There's some good coral just offshore here.

Places to Stay
Camping There is a very basic national parks campsite at Sandy Bay on the island's west side. For permits and bookings check with the Department of Environment office in Airlie Beach.

Resort This is a plain, middle-Australian resort with no pretensions and no special appeal. The rooms are very straightforward, mostly ordinary motel rooms dating from the 1960s, which have been recently refurbished. They come in three categories and, as with many of the reef resorts, costs include all meals.

Most of the accommodation is the middle-priced Reef Units that cost $170. These are side by side rooms facing the sea. They have paper-thin walls, although the beds are (thankfully) commendably quiet. Each unit has a veranda and a bedroom alcove reached by sliding glass doors. The 'family' Reef Units have a second bedroom area separated by a sliding panel. This partition is pleasant if you've got kids, although it does make it rather dark in the back since most of the light comes from the front doors. The ventilation is not too good but the rooms are air-conditioned. Basically they're plain, unpretentious and comfortable, although they make South Molle look like what it is – a resort from 20 years ago.

Cheapest are the Golf Units at $155 per person per day. These provide similar amenities to the Reef Units, but are at the back of the resort by the golf course.

Next up are the Polynesian Units at $170 per person per day. The decor has a few Pacific touches, and they are elevated and located on the hillside further away from the resort, which affords decent views and means they catch the sea breezes.

The Beachcomber Units cost $185 per

person. The units are individual cabins, each with a double and a single bed and a veranda. Some of them are pleasantly isolated, looking out on the beach, and in many ways these are the nicest rooms here.

Finally, there are the Whitsunday Units at $185, a double storey block right on the beach in the centre of the resort. The extra cost buys you the central location, tiles instead of carpet on the floor, and somewhat more luxurious fittings.

All rooms have a fridge, radio, phone and TV. Family rooms have two TVs, which means there are two more TVs in one of these rooms than you'll find in total in some resorts. A large coin-operated laundry provides plenty of opportunities for keeping clothes clean and there is a dry-cleaning service through the gift shop. There's also an ironing board and iron in the rooms.

South Molle often has standby rates, available from Airlie Beach that usually include the return boat trip. They also offer discounted weekend and weekly packages.

Places to Eat

The South Molle food story is equally middle-Australia – good quality pub food is probably the best way to describe it. In the *Island Restaurant*, you start with a breakfast buffet, continue with a lunch time buffet and finish with dinner offering the pub regulars – steak, chicken and fish. You won't starve, but it's no-frills food.

There are some options: most nights there's a poolside BBQ as an alternative to the usual restaurant dinner, and on Friday there's South Molle's Sounds of Polynesia Floorshow feast with an extensive spread of mostly self-service food. The catch is that South Molle welcomes visitors to the island for this occasion, so island guests may well find themselves at the end of a long queue. Fortunately, most things don't run out, although if you're in the late dining group you may well find yourself finishing your meal in total darkness as the show begins.

South Molle also has *Coral's* restaurant as an alternative to the normal dining area, but it's only open three nights a week.

Starters are $12, main courses from $20 to $24, and desserts from the trolley are $3. It's competent but unexciting food, but don't condemn South Molle's eating possibilities out of hand as bland and unadventurous. This is basically a family resort and the kids are well taken care of. While adults are having their dinner in peace the kids can be enjoying themselves at their own dinner, with games to follow until 8.30 pm. Even tiny children can be fed earlier (by parents) and then left in nursery care while the adults eat in peace. Regular babysitting is also available.

Getting There & Away

Hamilton, with its Ansett airport, serves as the main arrival port for South Molle. Whitsundays Allover has four daily boat transfers ($44 return).

Seatrek also has regular services to and from Shute Harbour, leaving Shute Harbour at 9 am and 12.30 and 4 pm, and return trips from South Molle at 7.45 and 10.30 am, and 3.10 and 4.45 pm. The fare is $18 return.

Fantasea has three trips a day to Shute Harbour ($16 return), all via Daydream Island (also $16 return), and five services to Hamilton Island ($36 return).

Hayman Island

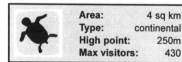

Area:	4 sq km
Type:	continental
High point:	250m
Max visitors:	430

First established in 1950, Hayman Island is one of the oldest Barrier Reef resort islands. The most northerly of the Whitsunday group, the resort is fronted by a wide, shallow reef that emerges from the water at low tide. After a total rebuild, which took nearly two years, Hayman reopened in 1987 as one of the most luxurious resorts on the

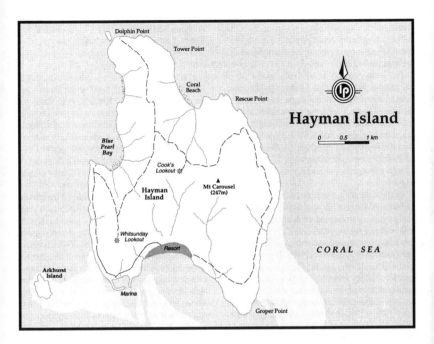

Great Barrier Reef, a position it retains more than a decade later.

The island was named in 1866 after Thomas Hayman, navigator of the naval ship HMS *Salamander*, which spent many years in this area. In 1904 the sawmill in Cid Harbour was replaced by one on Hook Island, operated by Thomas Abel, who at the same time leased Hayman Island for cattle grazing. In 1907 he sold out, handing over the lease and all the goats he had introduced for the sum of £30. In 1935 the island lease changed hands again, this time to the Hallam brothers who set up a fishing resort.

Australian aviation pioneer Reginald Ansett took over 12 years later when he bought Bert Hallam's 1000 goats for £10 a head. The fishing resort, with its solitary coconut palm planted by that well known fishing enthusiast, novelist Zane Grey, was closed in 1948 and it was not until 1950 that the Hayman Resort opened. This phase lasted through to 1985, when it was again rebuilt.

Information

The resort phone number is ☎ 4940 1234 or ☎ 1800 075 175, the fax number is 4940 1567, and the postal address is Hayman Island, Qld 4801.

Hayman's shops are as exclusive as everything else about this resort. There are boutiques, a jewellery shop, a newsagents, and a hairdressing salon. The Club Lounge has a billiard room and also a library.

The reception desk has EFTPOS facilities and can cash travellers cheques and exchange foreign currency.

Resort Redevelopment The 1980s was a time of amazing construction activity on the reef resort islands – new resorts were built (Hamilton being the biggest example), while older ones (such as Daydream) were rebuilt, upgraded or expanded. Hayman is certainly the most ambitious example of the rebuild and upgrade program.

Hayman opened in 1950 and was one of the most luxurious island resorts at the time. For a while they were keen on calling it 'Royal Hayman' because Princess Margaret or some other minor royal had dropped by once. In the early 1980s it was recognised that the resort was no longer in the forefront of development, but throwing $300 million at it has certainly pushed it back towards the top.

What do you get for spending that sort of money? Well, you get 214 rooms, six restaurants (connected to a central kitchen by underground passages), five bars, a hectare of swimming pools, a collection of antiques and arts, an 1840 Herron-Smith billiard table in the Billiard Room, a $3 million luxury launch (the *Sun Goddess*) to whisk you over from the airport on Hamilton, a desalination plant that produces 600,000L of water a day and a fully automatic powerhouse with five generators. And that still left $7 million over to plant 900 coconut palms and over 600,000 other plants. There's even a traditional Japanese garden as the setting for the oriental restaurant, and the main entrance is flanked by a row of stately 9m-high Phoenix palms, transplanted from a convent in Swan Hill, Victoria. There's a resident landscaping staff of 15 to tend these gardens.

The result is a sophisticated international hotel, which is a member of the exclusive 'The Leading Hotels of the World' group. However, 'exclusive' isn't a word they like to hear around here any more. When it first opened, Hayman quickly acquired a reputation for being high-class, ritzy and, yes, exclusive, with much ado being made of the multi-million dollar art works and antiques, grand penthouses and expensive shopping boutiques. But when you've got more than 400 beds to fill, you can't be seen to be *too* exclusive, so in recent years the resort's image has been toned down substantially, which seems more in keeping with its setting – this is the Great Barrier Reef, after all.

Activities

Use of catamarans, windsurfers and paddle skis is free, although most of the other activities attract a charge. You can go parasailing ($55), waterskiing ($60 for 30 minutes) and watersleighing ($25), while on dry land there's a sports centre with tennis courts ($5 for racquets and balls), squash courts ($15 an hour) and a spa and plunge pool. There's also a golf target range and an 18 hole putting green, as well as a very well equipped gymnasium. You can do an unsupervised workout ($10), or hire your own personal trainer ($50 an hour), and then wind down with a massage or a session in the flotation tank ($30 for 30 minutes).

Surprisingly, children are well catered for here. In fact, the daytime children's activities are one of the few things at Hayman that don't get added on to your bill. The Hayman Kidz Club opens from 9 am to 6 pm (to 9 pm during school holidays), catering for kids from five to 14 years old with activities like snorkelling trips, golf, kite flying, swimming and fishing, plaster casting and even etiquette sessions in one of the restaurants! There's a crèche for kids aged up to five years, and babysitting services can also be arranged ($10 an hour). Despite the cost, there are often a lot of kids here during their high seasons (ie the school holidays).

Diving & Snorkelling Hayman has a full-time dive boat where you can get diving instruction in Japanese as well as English. There is good diving at several points around the north of Hayman Island and nearby Hook Island. Hayman is also closer to the outer Barrier Reef than the other, more southerly Whitsunday resorts. It's also only about 30km north-east of Hayman to Hardy and Black reefs.

Bait Reef in particular offers a spectacular variety of diving possibilities, including wall dives, shallow lagoon dives and some excellent drift dives.

Hayman's dive shop is on the marina and offers a variety of diving activities. Trips are made on the *Reef Goddess* and range in cost from a day trip off the island for $120, to day trips to Bait Reef (with two tanks) for $185. Snorkellers are also catered for on these trips. A full range of equipment is available for hire, including underwater cameras.

Boats Hayman is great for local sailing. The wide expanse of water to Langford Island, with its long sand spit and Black Island (Bali Ha'i), are two convenient points to sail to. Beware of the water that funnels through the narrow strait between Hook and Hayman islands because, if the wind is low, you can almost get sucked into the strait. If you sail around Black Island cut well back towards Hayman to avoid the current.

You may see turtles around Langford and Black islands. Stingrays like the shallow, sandy reef flat in front of the resort. You'll often seem them shooting away in front of your boat.

The resort has free hobie cats, windsurfers and paddle skis available from the main beach. You can also hire motorised dinghies for $95 a day, including fishing and snorkelling gear.

Further afield there are cruises to the outer reef or neighbouring islands, game-fishing trips, or you can take an underwater peek in the semi-submersible *Reef Dancer*.

Walks A walk around the resort itself is an eye opener with striking *objets d'art* at every turn – everything from Burmese teak and bronze monastery doors to Moroccan carved stone screens. The gardens are unbelievably lush and a great contrast with the dry bushland of the rest of the island.

There are a number of bushwalks around the island including an 8km circuit (2½ hours), a 3km track across to Blue Pearl Bay (1 hour each way), or the 4.5km trip to Dolphin Point at the northern tip of the island (1½ hours). It's 1.5km from the resort up to the Whitsunday Passage lookout overlooking Arkhurst Island (30 minutes). To get to the start of the walks follow the road round past the marina and through the rather messy maintenance and power station site. Don't take the road that runs off up the hill to the water storage tanks but continue right to the end and take the path up by the old quarried-out area.

All the other trails diverge off the track around the island. First there's the turn down to Blue Pearl Bay and then the turn-off to Whitsunday Lookout. The track continues, rising gently through wooded grassland to the Blue Dolphin turn-off and then climbs through grassland studded with grass-trees to the turn-off to Cook's Lookout. It's a short climb from the main track to the superb views from this point. The resort lies right at your feet and you can clearly see the reef and across to Langford's sweeping spit. There's a small shelter here and a water storage tank, so there may be drinking water if there's been recent rain.

The round-the-island track continues from the lookout turn-off round to the east side of the island, taking several turns down before turning the corner towards the resort.

Other Islands There are a number of small, uninhabited islands very close to Hayman. You can walk out to Arkhurst Island at low tide, or from Langford Island (which has some fine coral around it) you can walk across to Bird Island. Black Island – they like to call it Bali Ha'i – is between Hayman and Hook islands.

Places to Stay

'Not a resort to visit if you're worried about your mortgage payments', was how one magazine report summed up Hayman Island. The old adage about how not being able to afford it if you have to ask the price could also be applied.

The 214 rooms and suites have air-conditioning and ceiling fans, telephones and minibars together with all the usual luxuries, including toiletries, hair dryers, bathrobes and even a personal safe. Each room has its own TV with video player, and there's a free library of video films to choose from. All rooms also have balconies, with all but the cheapest having ocean views. You also have access to 24 hour room service and there are laundry and dry-cleaning services available.

Prices start at $490 for the Palm Garden rooms, some of them recycled from the old resort and not as elegant as the newer ones; they continue up to $690 to $750 for the newer Beachfront, West Wing and East Wing rooms. And prices finally launch through the stratosphere for the $1300 to $1500 West Wing and East Wing suites. Oh, there are 11 individually styled penthouses if you really feel the need to spend up and have a lazy $1800 to $3300 sitting in your bulging wallet.

If you don't have to plan ahead, keep an eye out for standby rates, as these can start as low as $150 per person, including transfers and breakfast.

Places to Eat

With half a dozen dining possibilities to choose from, the resort intends to make the food as important as the accommodation. While the food is not exactly cheap, the service, presentation and attention to detail are absolutely first class. The menus are well thought out and offer great variety. Tours of the huge central kitchen are also held on a regular basis.

Breakfast, which is included in the room tariff, is served buffet-style in the *Coffee House*, a relaxed indoor/outdoor cafe with a great view over the beach. It's open from 7 am to 6 pm. Lunch-time offerings here include a burger for $16, or grilled fish or a steak with vegetables for $20 to $25, or tempura oysters for $16.

Perhaps the best lunch-time option is the *Beach Pavilion*, a casual open-air eatery by the pool, but with excellent beach views. Here you have light lunch options such as pasta ($19), snapper ($19) or a superb seafood platter for two ($50). The resort's other restaurants are only open at night.

La Fontaine is the most formal of the resort's restaurants with, as the name indi-

cates, French cuisine as its speciality – together with a Louis XIV-style dining room with a central fountain, carpets specially woven in China from Australian wool, and Waterford Crystal chandeliers. 'A jacket is preferred', that is a long way from the resorts which only stipulate that you wear shoes, not thongs. Entrees, such as scallops and truffles with crayfish roe sauce, range from $22 to $30; main courses, like pan-fried barramundi with sea urchin sauce, are $36 to $38; while desserts are $13. You could also have the five-course set menu for $98.

The *Oriental Seafood Restaurant* offers Asian cuisine in a Japanese-style restaurant set in a formal Japanese garden. Starters cost around $23, main courses $38 and desserts $11. Alternatively, you could try a lavish banquet at $85 per person. Men are expected to wear long trousers.

La Trattoria is a more casual Italian bistro where you can dine al fresco. It's not much cheaper with pizzas, pastas and antipasto from $16 to $25, main courses around $35, desserts $9.50.

The other dining possibility is the *Planters Restaurant*, with its very non-Australian tropical island theme. The modern Australian menu features entrees such as char-grilled asparagus ($19), main courses such as steak, venison, lamb or seafood ($32 to $36), and desserts at $9.50.

The Hayman wine cellar numbers over 20,000 bottles of Australian and European wine, and *La Fontaine* has an additional 400 choices.

An interesting option is the weekly *Chef's Kitchen*. A large dining table is set up in the middle of the huge Hayman kitchen (actually five separate kitchens), and guests partake of a candle-lit, five-course meal (one course from each of the resort's five restaurants), with each course accompanied by a short explanatory chat by that particular chef. The cost is $165, including drinks.

Afterwards you can recover for a few hours from all that culinary extravagance in the luxurious English-style, wood-panelled Club Lounge.

Entertainment

Most of the entertainment at Hayman takes place in the restaurants, all of which have live music, ranging from a classical pianist to three-piece bands.

Hernando's Nightclub is at the marina and is open from 10 pm to 2 am nightly.

Getting There & Away

Air Helijet has amphibious aircraft services between Hayman and the Whitsunday airport at Shute Harbour.

Sea Hayman guests generally arrive by air at Hamilton Island and are then transferred to the island on the luxury cruisers *Sun Goddess* or *Sun Paradise*. Even the transfers to the island are not like those at other resorts – en route to Hayman you complete registration formalities and sip champagne. Transfers are usually included in room rates.

Guests can also be collected from Shute Harbour. There are twice daily runs that cost $80 return if your package does not include transfers.

Hook Island

Area:		53 sq km
Type:		continental
High point:		443m
Max visitors:		77 in lodge, 70 camping

Nara & Macona Inlets

The bottom half of Hook Island is indented by two very long and narrow fjord-like bays, running a good 5km into the island. The beautiful Nara Inlet is a very popular deep-water anchorage for visiting yachties and you can often see a crowd of them far up the inlet. Several caves with Aboriginal rock paintings have been found in Nara Inlet, and there's a boardwalk to one.

Macona Inlet runs nearly as far into the island and has a national parks campsite.

Underwater Observatory

Underwater observatories have become a little old fashioned with the advent of semi-submersible tourist vehicles, and the high-speed catamarans that whisk visitors out to the real outer reef in a fraction of the time it used to take to get there. Nevertheless, the Hook Island Underwater Observatory is still a popular Whitsunday attraction and a number of the cruises stop here to admire the underwater scenery from 10m below the surface and to enjoy the pleasant beach at the nearby resort. The observatory is open from 10 am to 2 pm daily and admission is $5 (children half-price). The coral displays aren't particularly impressive and it isn't really worth the admission price, although if you're on one of the boat cruises entry is free. The observatory is close to the south-eastern corner of Hook Island, by the narrow channel that separates Hook from Whitsunday Island.

Hook Island Wilderness Resort

Just round the headland from the observatory is the sandy sweep of Yuengee Beach, named after the Aboriginal tribe that once inhabited the Whitsundays. It's a pleasant little beach with good swimming and snorkelling, although you should take care not to swim too far out into the strait – at times the current whips between Hook and Whitsunday islands so swiftly that it produces whitecaps on calm days.

The resort is popular with backpackers and has no fancy facilities or entertainment. Snorkelling gear is available: free for guests, $3 for day-trippers (with a $20 deposit). Apart from this, a volleyball net on the beach and paddle skis are about all the equipment there is on offer. The resort has a small dive shop and offers resort dives, or you can do a complete five day certificate course for $277 including accommodation – one of the cheapest deals around. There's good diving right off the beach if conditions are fair, although the fast current through

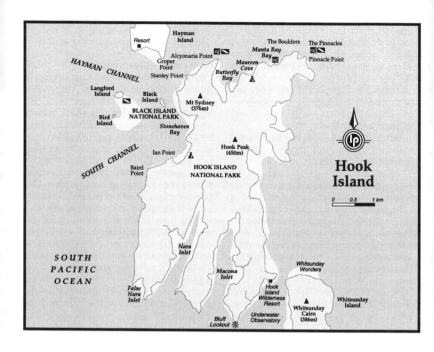

the narrow passage by the resort can stir the water up. Videos on reef topics are sometimes shown in the resort lounge area at night.

Activities

Walks One short walk from the resort site leads to the observatory and round to Back Beach, another gentler track leads straight to the beach. From here you can follow a trail up and over the promontory from the sheltered straits side to Pebble Beach on the ocean side. If you continued through the resort alongside the passage, there are fine views over to Whitsunday Island from Bluff Lookout at the tip of the promontory. From there you could rock hop around the headland to Pebble Beach and come back onto the trail.

Wildlife Hook Island has a wide variety of wildlife, and impressively large goannas are often seen around the resort. Campers are

warned not to leave food in their tents as 'the goannas may chew through to it'.

Northern Diving Spots Hook Island offers some of the best diving and snorkelling locations in the Whitsunday islands. They're mainly at the northern end of the island, which is protected from the prevailing south-easterly winds and are also on the outer edge of the Whitsundays. Alcyonaria Point, Butterfly Bay, The Boulders, Manta Ray Bay and Pinnacle Point are among the most popular spots for diving and snorkelling trips.

Manta Ray Bay is particularly popular because it hasgood snorkelling near the beach and there are a huge variety of small fish. There are also some good diving spots on the western side of the island, particularly at Stonehaven Bay and around Langford and Black islands, between Hook and Hayman islands.

QUEENSLAND TOURIST AND TRAVEL CORPORATION

HOLGER LEUE

QUEENSLAND TOURIST AND TRAVEL CORPORATION

Top: South Molle Island
Left: Whitsunday Island
Right: A snorkeller enjoys the 'underworld' experience of Hardy Reef

HOLGER LEUE

HOLGER LEUE

HUGH FINLAY

HOLGER LEUE

Top: Rush hour on Front Street, Hamilton Island
Left: Bareboat yachting in the Whitsundays
Middle: Hamilton Island harbour
Bottom: Outrigger canoe race, Hamilton Island

Places to Stay & Eat

Camping The observatory doesn't attract big crowds of day-trippers and, in any case, their visits are fleeting, so if you want to get right away from all signs of civilisation there is a camping area at Maureen Cove, on the north side of the island.

Hook Island Resort The *Hook Island Wilderness Resort* (☎ 4946 9380) is the only true budget resort in the Whitsundays. It's a simple, basic lodge with 12 adjoining units, each with either eight bunks or a double bed and four bunks. The lodge is fairly old and spartan, but it's clean, comfortable and cheap at $14 per person per night. Double rooms cost $55. Bedding is provided but you have to supply your own towel.

There are also good camping areas at both ends of the beach and the cost is $9 per person. The toilets and showers, which are by the resort buildings, are shared by the occupants of the cabins as well as by campers. Unfortunately, there are no laundry facilities at the resort.

The resort has a small gift shop, a restaurant and a bar. The restaurant is a very casual affair. Lunch is served from 11 am to 2 pm and offerings vary from sandwiches, to fish and chips, or a burger and chips. Dinner, between 6.30 and 7.30 pm, costs $10 for something like pasta, chicken, baked fish or a BBQ may be on offer for the night.

Alternatively, you can use the BBQs or kitchen area provided for guests. The resort has some basic food supplies available, or you can bring your own over from the mainland. However, if you're caught short for cooking utensils you can borrow one from the resort, although you will need to pay a $10 (fully refundable) deposit.

Getting There & Away

Seatrek (☎ 4946 5255) runs boats to and from Hook Island on a daily basis, leaving Shute Harbour at 8.45 am and returning from the island at 2 pm. The return fare is $25.

Lindeman Island

Area:	8 sq km
Type:	continental
High point:	210m
Max visitors:	300

Back in 1868 the island was named after George Sidney Lindeman, a sub-lieutenant with the Royal Navy who was responsible for charting safe passages through the Whitsundays. Like the other Whitsunday islands, Lindeman had an early history of sheep and goat grazing. Angus and Elizabeth Nicholson took over the grazing lease in 1923 and later opened the first resort. Goats still survive from those early days and you're likely to spot them while you're out around the island bushwalking.

In 1946 the Nicholsons reopened the resort with new accommodation and the area's first swimming pool. After the war the resort was managed by their son, Loch, and his wife, Thora. It remained in the hands of the Nicholson family for 56 years, until it was sold in 1979. Thora Nicholson still lives on the island, in an old timber house behind the new resort. She's a friendly, talkative lady who wanders about the place with a matriarchal air, very much an integral part of the island.

The island is a national park and has 20km of walking trails. There are seven beaches dotted around the island and there are also a number of islands close to Lindeman itself. Seaforth Island, with its fine beaches on both sides of the island, is right in front of the resort and is a popular excursion.

The resort is built on the very steep sides of a small cove, and therefore has a very 'vertical' feel – which makes it somewhat claustrophobic at the lower levels. The golf course, sports facilities and airstrip are all at the top of the hill above the other resort buildings.

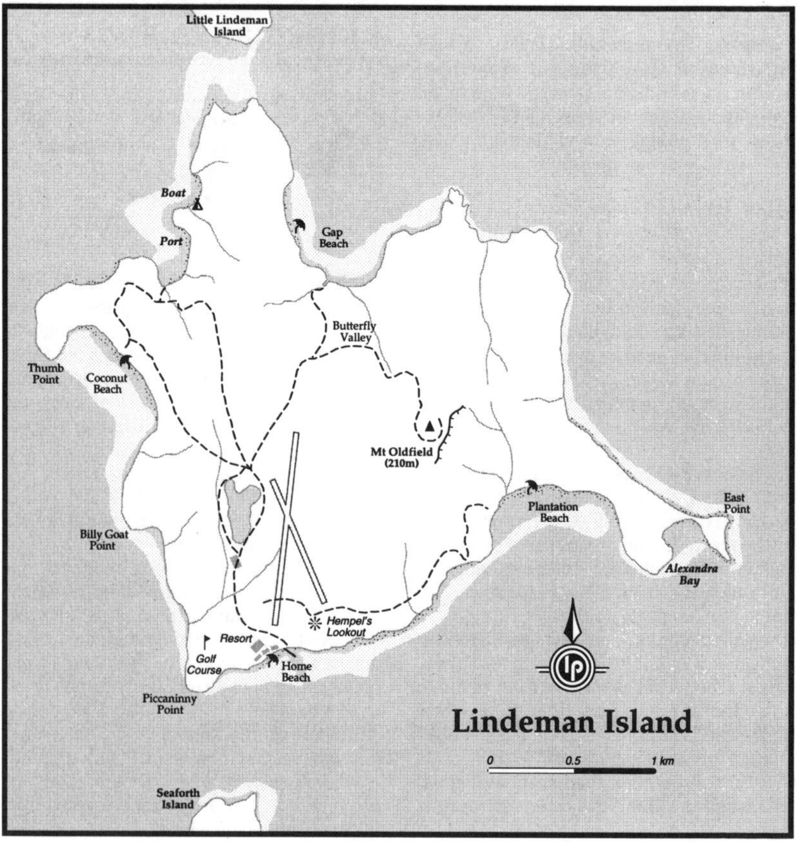

Lindeman Island

0   0.5   1 km

Information

The phone number of the resort is ☎ 4946 9333, the fax number is 4946 9598, and the postal address is Club Med, PMB 1, Mackay Mail Centre, Qld 4741. Bookings can be made within Australia by phoning ☎ 1800 807 973 toll free.

The resort shop sells Club Med clothing and souvenirs and a few of the bare essentials.

The reception desk has EFTPOS facilities and can cash travellers cheques and exchange foreign currency. There is no public phone at the resort, although calls can be made from the rooms.

The Queensland National Parks & Wildlife Service produces a *Lindeman Island* leaflet.

Activities

The daily activities sheet lists the usual array of things to do, although nothing is compulsory or too regimented. You can do everything or nothing. Lindeman has probably the best golf course of the resort islands, and there are also tennis courts, an archery range, a gym, aerobics classes, beach volleyball, pool games, bingo, basketball and water polo. You can even take lessons on the resort's impressive flying trapeze.

Then there are the watersports, including sailing, windsurfing, paddle skis and snorkelling. Scuba dives are available at an extra cost – lessons are given in the pool and dives take place out on the reef.

Like a number of the island resorts, Club Med does its best to take care of the kids. There's the Baby Club (for kids aged one to two years), the Petit Club (two to three years), the Mini Club (four to seven years) and the Kids' Club (eight to 12 years). All run a broad range of daily activities from 9 am to 9 pm.

Diving & Snorkelling Lindeman is not the best island for scuba divers. Nevertheless, there's a diving school on the island and a variety of dive courses are offered. Introductory lessons are given in the pool, some local diving is done around Lindeman Island and longer diving trips are made to other islands in the Whitsunday group.

There are also snorkelling trips out to Hardy Lagoon on the reef every Monday, Wednesday and Friday, costing $165, plus another $80 if you want to go scuba diving.

Cruises & Flights If you feel the need to escape the island for a while, there are a number of day trips organised on a regular basis. These include a sunset cruise to the beautiful Whitehaven Beach ($70), seaplane trips over the reef with snorkelling at Hardy Reef ($255, plus $80 for scuba), or to Whitehaven Beach ($118).

Walks Most of Lindeman Island is a national park and the Queensland Parks and Wildlife *Lindeman Island* leaflet has information on the island's wildlife and where you might find it. Apart from birds, the island is also noted for its many butterflies, particularly the impressive Blue Tiger, which is very common from October to May. It is often seen in shady gullies on hot days.

All walks on the island start from the airstrip and the favourite one is the 4km climb to the top of Mt Oldfield (210m). From near the north end of the airstrip path climbs gently through scrub and forest, passing through Butterfly Valley, before emerging into clearer land around the summit. The path circles right round the peak and to the east there is a sheer cliff face, looking down on the eastern side of the island. From the summit there are superb views of the whole island and across to other islands in the group. To the north you can see the unmistakable shape of Pentecost Island and off to the north-east is Hamilton Island with its airport runway.

Starting off in the same direction from the airstrip you can take the 6km loop that drops down to Coconut Beach and to Boat Port, with the remains of an old pier. A trail branches off the Mt Oldfield path and descends to Gap Beach, on the northern side of the island.

Another trail crosses the airstrip and passes Hempel's Lookout before dropping down to the water's edge, crossing a small gully and continuing on to the long sweep of Plantation Beach. You can cross the headland at the far end of the beach and go down to Princess Alexandra Bay. Watch for the many small stingrays basking on the shallow sandy bottom off Plantation Beach.

Finally, shorter strolls loop around the dam lake sometimes known as Loch Nicholson, after the farmer who established the first resort here. At the end of the golf course there are fine views from Piccaninny Point.

Places to Stay

Camping There is a basic national parks campsite at Boat Port, on the north-west side of the island.

Club Med As with Club Meds around the world, the guests are referred to as GMs *(gentile members)* and the staff as GOs *(gentile organisateurs)*. The GOs are there to help you organise and enjoy your holiday, but not to serve you. Everything here is meant to be very egalitarian and informal.

The resort was totally rebuilt in 1988, so everything is still fairly modern. The main resort complex, with its pool, dining and entertainment areas, is flanked by three-storey accommodation blocks, all looking out over the beach and water. All rooms have their own bathroom, a fan and air-conditioning, telephone, TV and a small refrigerator. Each room is fronted by a small balcony.

The nightly rate here ranges from $199 to $255 per person, depending on the time of year you visit. The rates include all meals and most activities. There are also five-night packages available that include return flights and transfers to the island: eg $1095 to $1425 from Cairns (depending on the time of year), $1345 to $1725 from Sydney, to $1725 to $2275 from Perth.

If you'd like a brief sample of Club Med, one and two night packages are available from Mackay/Airlie Beach, from $265/235 per person for one night and from $420/390 for two nights, including air taxi transfers, meals and activities. You can also do day trips by light plane for $190/140, including lunch.

Places to Eat
All meals, as well as beer, wine and juices are included in the rates. The *Main Restaurant* opens for breakfast, lunch and dinner. Everything is the usual buffet-style, and you sit at tables of seven or eight people so you get a chance to meet other guests – it's all very social. The buffets vary each night, from French, Italian, seafood, Asian, Mexican, to the gala buffet.

The *Top Restaurant* serves very casual lunches. You can eat indoors or by the pool and tennis courts, and have barbecued chicken or steak and salads, fruit etc. The other choice is *Nicholson's*, which is a small and pleasant à la carte restaurant that opens for dinner from 7.30 pm.

Entertainment
Club Med is big on participation when it comes to entertainment. At night the staff transform themselves from hosts into entertainers, and you're just as likely to find yourself up on stage at some time. Every night at 9.30 pm there's a live 'animation' show in the main theatre – comedy sketches, dancing, Madonna concerts and the like. Later in the evening, *Silhouettes* nightclub opens up.

Getting There & Away
Air Much of Lindeman Island is a high plateau and it's topped by a grass airstrip. Island Air Taxis (☎ 4946 9933) flies here from Mackay ($105) and Shute Harbour ($60 one way; $75 day return).

Sea Club Med has its own launch that connects with flights from the airport at Hamilton Island.

Other Islands

Apart from the main resort islands there are a great many other islands in the Whitsundays. The largest of all, Whitsunday Island, is unpopulated apart from campers, visiting yachties and the many day-trippers who come to the magnificent Whitehaven Beach. Other islands range from popular camping get-aways and good anchorages for cruising yachties, to isolated dots on the map that hardly see a visitor from one year to the next.

BORDER ISLAND
To the east of Whitsunday Island there's good snorkelling and diving at the entrance to Cataran Bay on Border Island. It's a good area for camping but there are no facilities and no water. Border Island is a popular destination for many cruise trips.

HASLEWOOD ISLAND
To the east of Whitsunday Island there are good diving possibilities at White Bay on Haslewood Island. Across from Windy Bay is Lupton Island.

HENNING ISLAND

Immediately north of Dent Island and to the south-west of Whitsunday, Henning Island has a fine campsite on Geographer's Beach. There's sheltered camping in the forest behind the beach and good views from the grassy hill to the east, but there's no water available. The anchorage off the beach is poor so you're unlikely to be disturbed by too many day visitors. North Spit also has a camping area, although once again, with no water.

NORTH MOLLE

The narrow Unsafe Passage, which is actually quite safe for most vessels seen in the Whitsundays, separates North Molle from Mid Molle and South Molle islands. It's one of the closer islands to Shute Harbour and has a popular national parks campsite. The coral beach at Hannah Point, at the north of the island, is popular with day visitors.

Places to Stay

There is a small campsite at Cockatoo Beach at the southern end. Seasonal water is available and there are toilets.

PENTECOST ISLAND

The unique shape of Pentecost Island rises almost sheer from the sea between Lindeman and Hamilton islands. It's easily spotted from aircraft approaching or departing Hamilton Island airport. The island was named by Captain Cook and has a 208m cliff face shaped remarkably like an Indian head.

SHUTE HARBOUR ISLANDS

There are several small islands in Shute Harbour, some of which offer good coral for snorkelling.

Shute Island has a small campsite and a sandy beach, but there is no water and no facilities. Repair and Tancred islands are even closer in. Tancred has some camping possibilities but the sites are so close to the activity at Shute Harbour that it hardly seems worth the effort getting out there in the first place.

WHITSUNDAY & CID ISLANDS

The largest of the Whitsunday islands, Whitsunday covers 109 sq km and rises to 438m at Whitsunday Peak. There is no resort development on the island, but Whitehaven Beach on the north-east coast is the longest and finest beach in the Whitsunday Group and it's a popular destination for many cruises.

Right at the northern tip of the island, Whitsunday Wonders is a popular diving spot with excellent snorkelling near the shore.

Whitehaven Beach

The Whitsunday's best known beach stretches for 6km, so there's enough for everybody. Off the southern end of the beach there's good snorkelling around the coral bommies.

Cid Harbour

The story that the US fleet assembled here before the Battle of the Coral Sea is considerably exaggerated, but this deep harbour, sheltered by Cid Island, is a popular spot for day-trip cruises and has several good camping areas. There's a walking track between Dugong Beach and Sawmill Beach.

Sawmill Beach takes its name from the sawmill James Whitnall set up there in 1888. For the next 13 years hoop pine timber from the island was cut there, but today it's the sandy beach, good anchorages and the coral off the southern headland that attract visitors.

Places to Stay

Whitsunday Island has a number of popular camping spots and, because many cruise boats go to Whitsunday, they're easy to get to. The Scrub Hen Beach site at the north-west end of Whitsunday, close to the passage between Whitsunday and Hook islands, is used mainly by organised camping groups.

There are three camping areas along Cid Harbour. Dugong Beach is a large site (40 people) with water, showers, toilets and other facilities, including gas BBQs. There's a good sandy beach and an interesting rainforest area behind it. There's a 1km walking track that leads from Dugong Beach through coastal rainforest to Sawmill Beach, where a creek has water for part of the year. Another campsite here also has good facilities, including showers and toilets.

At the southern end of Cid Harbour is Joe's Beach. This is a good small campsite (10 people) with a fine beach and snorkelling, but no water supply.

NORTHERN ISLANDS

To the north-west of the Whitsunday Group, **Gloucester Island** has a campsite with limited facilities at Bona Bay.

Other small sites can be found on **Armit**, **Saddleback** and **Olden** islands.

SOUTHERN ISLANDS

Neck Bay on **Shaw Island**, close to Lindeman, has a small, undeveloped campsite with no facilities. Western Beach on **South Repulse Island**, immediately south of Cape Conway, is similarly spartan.

Thomas Island is south of Shaw Island. There is good snorkelling off the sandy Sea Eagle Beach to the south-east. There is a larger camping area here with some facilities, although there is no water. Naked Lady Beach to the north-west also has good anchorages.

THE OUTER REEF

Cruise boats operate out to the Great Barrier Reef from the Whitsundays every day. It's a 30 to 60km trip and the modern high-speed catamarans get you out there from Shute Harbour in about two hours. A typical day trip costs around $120, and while you are anchored at the reef there's time for

some snorkelling, a peek beneath the surface in a glass-bottom boat or in the semi-submersible 'submarines' that have become *de rigeur* on Barrier Reef trips, or, if you arrange it in advance, a couple of scuba dives. Lunch is usually included in the price.

Be warned if you're prone to seasickness, as some people find they get very sick indeed on these trips. The catamarans are very fast and on a choppy day they seem to give a lot of people very severe and very high-speed seasickness. It's not uncommon for sufferers who can afford it to charter a seaplane to come out from the mainland to fly them back. If you are likely to suffer from seasickness, it's wise to take some sort of prophylactic medication before you depart.

Bait Reef, Hook-Hardy Reef and Black Reef are the most popular reefs for Whitsunday trips. Furthest to the west, Bait Reef is a small, oval-shaped reef offering some superb diving opportunities. Diving trips from Hayman Island often come here to explore some superb diving locations like the Stepping Stones, Anemoneville, Gary's Lagoon, Manta Ray Drop-off and Gorgonia Hill.

The Hook and Hardy reefs are particularly popular for Whitsunday day trips and there's a regular flotilla of pontoons, glass-bottom boats and semi-submersibles parked out here. Popular diving spots are the Canyons, the Pinnacles (good for snorkelling), the Pontoon (lots of fish come here to be fed by divers and snorkellers), the Beach (also good for snorkelling) and Shark Alley (aptly named). Black Reef, further east, also offers good diving, including a variety of caves and canyons at the Cathedral, and many turtles at the spot known as Turtle Street.

Magnetic Island

Magnetic is one of the most popular reef islands for backpackers because it's so inexpensive and convenient to get to and has such a great selection of cheap places to stay. In general the population is around 2500 but at peak times the number of people on the island can balloon up to 7000. Magnetic Island is also big and varied enough to offer plenty of things to do and see, including some really fine bushwalks.

Only 8km offshore from Townsville (a 20 minute trip on the high-speed catamaran ferries), Magnetic Island is almost a suburb of Townsville and a popular day trip from that city. The island was given its name by Captain Cook, who thought his ship's compass went funny when he sailed by in 1770. Nobody else has thought so since. The island is often rough, rugged and rocky, but it has some fine beaches, lots of bird life, excellent bushwalking tracks, a koala sanctuary and an aquarium. It's dominated by Mt Cook (497m).

There are several small towns along the coast and a variety of accommodation possibilities. Since the island is a real year-round destination it has quite a different atmosphere compared to the purely resort islands along the reef. This is one of the larger islands along the reef and about 70% of it is national park; much of the wildlife is extraordinarily fearless.

Aboriginals certainly lived on the island, which they could easily reach from the mainland, but the first European settlement was established by timber cutters at Nelly Bay in the early 1870s. They left the island not long after and in 1887 Harry Butler and his family settled at Picnic Bay. The Butlers soon started to accommodate visitors from the mainland and thus the Magnetic Island tourist business was born. The Butler story is recounted in *The Real Magnetic* by Jessie Macqueen, another early resident of the island.

The arrival in 1899 of Robert Hayles

MAGNETIC ISLAND

Highlights
- Explore the island: hire a scooter, a horse or go for a walk on one of the many excellent trails

Area:	52 sq km
Type:	continental
High point:	497m

(who built a hotel at Picnic Bay) really put Magnetic on the map as he also started a ferry service with an ex-Sydney Harbour ferry, *The Bee*. The Hayles operation was the main force in Magnetic Island tourism right up to the late 1980s.

Orientation

Magnetic Island is roughly triangular in shape with Picnic Bay, the stop for the ferries from Townsville, at the bottom corner of the triangle. All the development

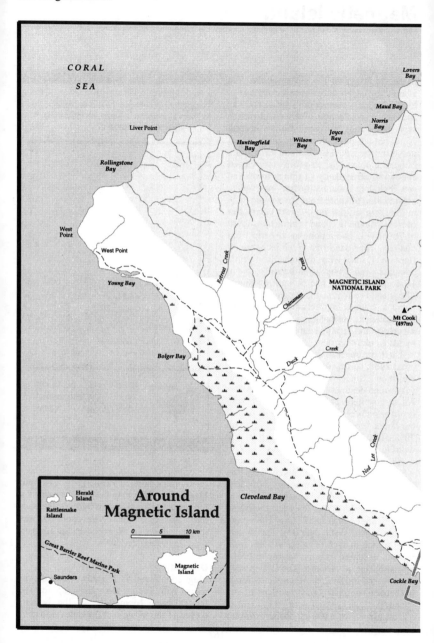

CORAL

SEA

Lovers
Bay

Maud Bay

Norris
Bay

Liver Point

Huntingfield
Bay

Wilson
Bay

Joyce
Bay

Rollingstone
Bay

West
Point

West Point

MAGNETIC ISLAND
NATIONAL PARK

Young Bay

Retreat Creek

Chinaman Creek

Mt Cook
(497m)

Bolger Bay

Creek

Duck

Nel Let Creek

Herald
Island

Around
Magnetic Island

Cleveland Bay

Rattlesnake
Island

0   5   10 km

Great Barrier Reef Marine Park

Magnetic
Island

Saunders

Cockle Bay

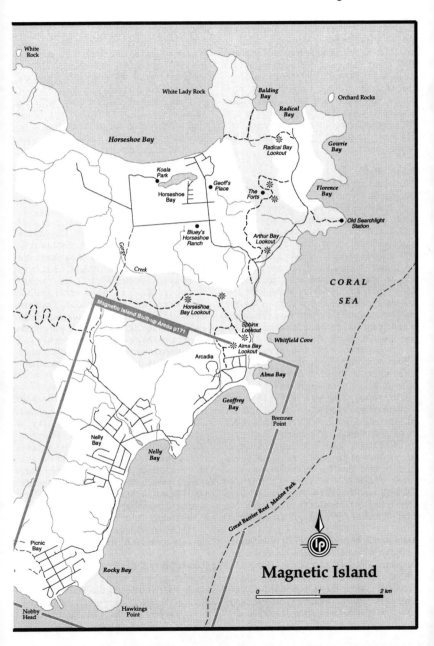

White Rock

White Lady Rock

Balding Bay

Orchard Rocks

Radical Bay

Horseshoe Bay

Radical Bay Lookout

Gowrie Bay

Koala Park

Geoff's Place

The Forts

Florence Bay

Horseshoe Bay

Old Searchlight Station

Bluey's Horseshoe Ranch

Arthur Bay Lookout

Gorge

Creek

CORAL

SEA

Magnetic Island Built-up Areas p171

Horseshoe Bay Lookout

Sphinx Lookout

Whitfield Cove

Alma Bay Lookout

Arcadia

Alma Bay

Geoffrey Bay

Bremner Point

Nelly Bay

Nelly Bay

Great Barrier Reef Marine Park

Picnic Bay

Rocky Bay

Magnetic Island

0   1   2 km

Nobby Head

Hawkings Point

is along the eastern side of the island and there's a road running through a string of small towns from Picnic Bay to Horseshoe Bay along that coast. A rough track runs along the uninteresting west coast but along the north coast it's a walking track only. Picnic Bay is the main town on the island and has shops, bicycle, motorcycle and Moke rental agencies and other amenities, but there are places to stay in each of the small centres.

Information

The Island Travel Centre (☎ 4778 5155), by the jetty in Picnic Bay, has tourist information. It offers a variety of brochures and will book tours, accommodation, rent-a-vehicles and anything else you might require, and can also handle domestic and international travel arrangements. There are loads of brochures churned out by the travel operators on Magnetic Island and you can stock up on them in Townsville at the ferry terminals. Probably the most useful is the free *Magnetic Island Guide* booklet, which has a good map and details of transport and activities, plus plenty of ads.

The Department of Environment has an office (☎ 4778 5378) in Picnic Bay. It has information on the various walks along the island's 22km of walking tracks.

Discovering Magnetic Island, by James G Porter, has information on the island's history, shipwrecks, wildlife, climbing Mt Cook and other fields of interest.

There are no bank branches on Magnetic, but most of the supermarkets and hotels on the island have EFTPOS facilities.

Zoning Geoffrey Bay, Arcadia and Five Beach Bay, on the island's north coast, are Marine Park B and fishing is not permitted.

Dangers & Annoyances Box jellyfish are found in the waters around Magnetic Island between October and April. There is a netted swimming area at Picnic Bay and on weekends Alma Bay is patrolled and the waters netted, but otherwise swimming is not recommended during the danger months.

Picnic Bay

Many travellers stay in Picnic Bay because it's convenient for the ferry, has a good selection of shops and places to eat, and has a number of good places to stay. There's a lookout above the town and just to the west of Picnic Bay is **Cockle Bay**, with the wreck of the *City of Adelaide*. The 1112 ton ship was being towed to Picnic Bay to be used for a breakwater when she ran aground in 1916; she's remained there ever since. Heading east around the coast from Picnic Bay you soon come to Rocky Bay, where a short, steep walk leads down to a beautiful and secluded beach.

Nelly Bay

Next round the coast is Nelly Bay with a good stretch of beach and a reef at low tide. At the far end of the bay there are some pioneer graves but the unsightly remnants of the controversial Magnetic Quay development are also here. Arguments raged for years over whether the planned development, which was to include a marina, hotel and shopping centre, should go ahead. Eventually the developers went broke and disappeared, leaving behind a badly scarred hillside, piles of broken rocks and a half-built marina.

Arcadia

Round the headland from Nelly Bay you come to the pleasant **Geoffrey Bay**, a marine park area that has an interesting 400m low tide walk over the fringing coral reef; a board indicates the start of the trail at the southern end of the beach. Then there's Arcadia with the popular Arcadia Hotel Resort with a swimming pool, which is open to the public, and live entertainment at weekends.

Just round the headland from Arcadia is the very pleasant **Alma Bay beach**.

Radical Bay & the Forts

After Arcadia the road runs back from the coast until you reach the junction to the Radical Bay road. There's a choice of routes here. You can take the road that runs down

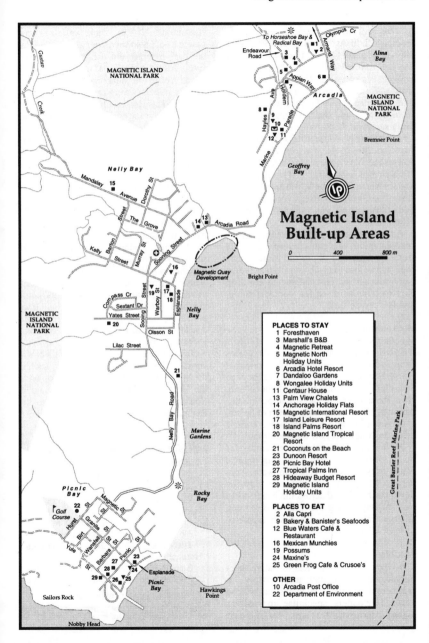

Magnetic Island Built-up Areas

0   400   800 m

PLACES TO STAY
1 Foresthaven
3 Marshall's B&B
4 Magnetic Retreat
5 Magnetic North
   Holiday Units
6 Arcadia Hotel Resort
7 Dandaloo Gardens
8 Wongalee Holiday Units
11 Centaur House
13 Palm View Chalets
14 Anchorage Holiday Flats
15 Magnetic International Resort
17 Island Leisure Resort
18 Island Palms Resort
20 Magnetic Island Tropical
   Resort
21 Coconuts on the Beach
23 Dunoon Resort
26 Picnic Bay Hotel
27 Tropical Palms Inn
28 Hideaway Budget Resort
29 Magnetic Island
   Holiday Units

PLACES TO EAT
2 Alla Capri
9 Bakery & Banister's Seafoods
12 Blue Waters Cafe &
   Restaurant
16 Mexican Munchies
19 Possums
24 Maxine's
25 Green Frog Cafe & Crusoe's

OTHER
10 Arcadia Post Office
22 Department of Environment

to the Radical Bay resort with tracks leading off to **Arthur Bay** and **Florence Bay**, or you can take the track via the forts. On the Radical Bay road there's also a walking track leading off to the old **searchlight station** on a headland between Arthur and Florence bays. There are fine views from up here and the bays are also pleasantly secluded.

Alternatively you can take the walking track to **the forts**, starting right at the Horseshoe Bay-Radical Bay road junction. It's also a pleasant stroll (1.4km each way) and the views from the WWII forts are very fine. The forts comprise a command post and signal station, gun sites and an ammunition store.

As an alternative to backtracking to the road junction you can continue downhill from the forts and rejoin the Radical Bay road just before the bay, and from here you can walk across the headland to **Balding Bay** (a popular place for skinny-dipping) and Horseshoe Bay.

Horseshoe Bay

Whether you continue along the road from the Radical Bay junction or walk across from Radical Bay you eventually end up at Horseshoe Bay, which is the end of the road and literally the other end of the island. Here there are more shops and accommodation possibilities, a long stretch of beach, a mango farm and a koala park, a short drive (or long walk) off the main road.

At the fine beach there are rentals for boats, surfboards and those big plastic water tricycles. You can also walk from here to Maud Bay, round to the west, or down the beach and across the headland to Radical Bay. Along the Radical Bay track another trail branches off down to pretty little Balding Bay.

Wildlife

The island has a great deal of native Australian wildlife. Possums are probably the creatures most often seen by visitors – these noted freeloaders specialise in making nightly courtesy calls at a number of island restaurants. Koalas, rock wallabies and wombats are also seen around the island, as are rock-pythons and dangerous but inactive death adders. The koalas were introduced to the island in the 1920s and the prolific possums were probably also an introduced species.

The bush stone curlew, or southern stone plover, is the bird you will hear, if not see, most often on Magnetic Island. All night long the relatively fearless birds' haunting 'wee-loo' wail can be heard around the island. The island has other birdlife, including noisy sulphur-crested cockatoos and rainbow lorikeets.

Bushwalks

The National Parks produce a walks leaflet for Magnetic Island's excellent bushwalking tracks. You can string several walks together to make an excellent day's outing. Starting from Nelly Bay walk directly inland along Mandalay Ave and follow the signpost to Horseshoe Bay Lookout, from where the trail drops down and around to Arcadia. This walk is about 6km and takes about two hours.

Towards the end of the track there's a choice of routes. Take the longer track via the Sphinx Lookout, which brings you on to the Horseshoe Bay road beyond Arcadia. You've then only got a short walk to the Radical Bay junction from where you can

---

Bushtrack Walks

Nelly Bay to Arcadia	6km	2 hours
Picnic Bay to		
West Point	8km	2½ hours
Horseshoe Bay road to:		
Arthur Bay	2km	30 minutes
Florence Bay	2.5km	1 hour
The Forts	2km	45 minutes
Horseshoe Bay		
Balding Bay	3km	45 minutes
Radical Bay	3km	45 minutes

All times and distances are one way.

walk to the forts and on down to the Radical Bay resort. From here it's up and over to Horseshoe Bay, via Balding Bay if you wish. You've then walked almost the entire length of the island and from Horseshoe Bay you can take the bus back to the other end.

Diving
Magnetic Island Pleasure Divers (☎ 4778 5788), at the Arcadia Resort Hotel, offers a basic five day dive course for $199, or a more comprehensive course for $295. The Townsville based dive operators also offer dives to the reef.

Fishing Trips
Barnacle Bill (☎ 4758 1237) takes up to three people out on fishing expeditions, with all gear and bait supplied. Two hours costs $40, four hours $70. The company also has dinghies for hire on the beach at Horseshoe Bay.

Other Attractions & Activities
There's a Koala Park in a rather barren and desolate setting at Horseshoe Bay, open 9 am to 5 pm daily. It also has a few wombats and wallabies. Admission is overpriced at $7.

Bluey's Horseshoe Ranch (☎ 4778 5109), at Horseshoe Bay, offers a few different horse trail rides, costing $18 an hour, $40 for two hours or $45 for a half-day ride.

Places to Stay
Magnetic Island's great popularity with travellers is due in part to the wide choice of very popular backpackers hostels. You'll find them in Picnic Bay, Nelly Bay, Arcadia and Horseshoe Bay. On top of that there are hotels, resorts and a great many holiday flats. Despite this diversity of accommodation the island can still get booked out at certain times of year so if you're coming during a busy season it's wise to phone ahead and book.

Hostels Most of the backpackers places offer special deals including transport over and back and a certain number of nights accommodation. These can be good value and are easy to check out in Townsville. The Magnetic Island hostel scene is very competitive with hostel minibuses often meeting ferries at Picnic Bay.

Picnic Bay Only a short walk from the Picnic Bay ferry pier, the *Hideaway Budget Resort* (☎ 4778 5110), 32 Picnic St, is a clean, renovated place with a small kitchen, a good pool, a TV room and laundry facilities. A bed in a twin or double room costs $14, or there are self-contained cabins at $45.

Nelly Bay As you round the corner into Nelly Bay, you'll notice the blue-and-white-striped 'camp-o-tel' accommodation (a cross between a cabin and a tent with beds or bunks) at *Coconuts on the Beach* (☎ 1800 065 696). It costs $8 per person to camp in your own tent (no shade), $16 per head in an eight-bed dorm or the camp-o-tels, which get unbearably hot in summer.

The *Magnetic Island Tropical Resort* (☎ 4778 5955), on Yates St just off the main road, is a very good budget resort with a swimming pool, an inexpensive restaurant and a pleasant garden setting. A bed in a four to six-bed timber cabin with attached bath costs $16, or you can rent a whole cabin – they range from $45 to $79 a double, plus $10 for each extra adult. This place is good if you're after somewhere quiet and relaxed.

Arcadia The popular *Centaur House* (☎ 4778 5668), at 27 Marine Pde, is a rambling, old-style hostel opposite the beach. The atmosphere is relaxed and friendly, there's a pleasant garden, and a bed in the downstairs dorms costs $15; double rooms are $35.

Also in Arcadia is *Foresthaven* (☎ 4778 5153) at 11 Cook Rd. This hostel has seen better days and is fairly spartan, although the peaceful bush setting is nice. Accommodation is in old-fashioned but adequate two and three-bed units that have their own kitchen; dorm beds cost $14, twins/doubles cost $34, or there are self-contained rooms from $25 per person. It's a friendly place and the owners speak German and French.

Horseshoe Bay *Geoff's Place* (☎ 4778 5577) is one of the island's most popular places for young travellers, although maintenance and service are suffering these days. There are extensive grounds, and you can camp for $6 per person or share a four or eight-bed A-frame cedar cabin for $14 (eight-bed cabins have their own bathroom). There's a communal kitchen and bar, and basic meals cost around $5. The hostel's courtesy bus shuttles between here and Picnic Bay to meet the ferries.

Hotels & Holiday Flats Magnetic Island has a wide variety of accommodation possibilities apart from the backpackers places but holiday flats predominate. They're indicative of the quiet, family holiday nature of the island and vary from larger commercial operations with a full-time office and daily room service to small operations that you may only find out about by word of mouth.

Most of the holiday flats quote weekly rates although it's always worth asking if you want to stay for a shorter period. Prices vary with the season and with demand – even in the high season you may find bargains if there just happens to be a room vacant. The flats usually have cooking facilities and fridges but check whether you have to supply bedding, towels and the like. Most of the Magnetic Island holiday flats have a swimming pool, BBQs and other facilities. They're essentially like a modern motel, except better equipped, and you're left to fend for yourself more.

Single-bedroom flats are typically in the $200 to $300 per week bracket, two-bedroom flats are in the $250 to $400 range.

Despite the predominance of holiday flats there are also a few conventional hotel/motel places, like the larger Arcadia Hotel and the Magnetic International Resort.

Picnic Bay Right by the pier on The Esplanade is the *Picnic Bay Hotel* (☎ 4778 5166). Motel-style rooms are $50 for twins, all with bathrooms, fan, tea/coffee-making equipment and refrigerators, plus use of a laundry and pool. There are also two-bedroom self-contained units for up to four people from $75.

At 34 Picnic St, right behind the hotel and next door to the Hideaway Budget Resort, is the reasonably new *Tropical Palms Inn* (☎ 4778 5076). Units with an air-con, fans, TV and a kitchenette are $63 for two, and there are self-contained cottages from $325 a week. Round the corner at 16 Yule St the *Magnetic Island Holiday Units* (☎ 4778 5246) has eight one and two-bedroom units accommodating two to five people. The rooms are fully equipped right down to kitchen and laundry facilities, and there's a pool and BBQ. Four-bed rooms cost $55 to $65.

The *Dunoon Resort* (☎ 4778 5161), on the corner of Granite St and The Esplanade, is an older resort that has been refurbished. It has one and two-bedroom units that sleep four to six people, all with a fully equipped kitchen, TV, ceiling fan and air-con. The resort is set in landscaped gardens and has two pools and a guest laundry. Daily costs are from $76 a double, plus $10 for each additional person.

Nelly Bay The *Magnetic International Resort* (☎ 4778 5200) is on Mandalay Ave and is the biggest resort on the island. There are 80 units and 16 suites, all with air-con, fans, telephone, TV, radio, tea/coffee-making equipment and refrigerator. There's a swimming pool, tennis court and laundry facilities. Room costs are from $140 to $170.

Nelly Bay has lots of holiday flats. The *Palm View Chalets* (☎ 4778 5596), 114 Sooning St, are a collection of modern timber chalets in a leafy garden setting. The split-level chalets sleep up to six people and are fully self-contained with a kitchen, bathroom and air-con, and are good value from $75 a double.

The *Anchorage Holiday Flats* (☎ 4778 5596), also on Sooning St, is a reasonably new development of two-bedroom units with kitchen and laundry facilities. The units accommodate from two to six people; there's a swimming pool and BBQs. Nightly costs are from $89. Unfortunately, the view from these units is spoilt by the remnants of the unfinished Magnetic Quay development.

At 13 The Esplanade, the *Island Palms Resort* (☎ 4778 5571) is one of the larger Magnetic Island developments with 12 two-bedroom units, which accommodate two to six people. Everything is supplied and the rooms have air-con, TV, cooking facilities and fridges. There's also a BBQ, swimming pool, spa, half tennis court and laundry facilities. The cost is from $89 a day for the units.

Around the corner at 4 Kelly St is the impressive *Island Leisure Resort* (☎ 4778 5511). It's a modern complex with good facilities, including a pool in a garden setting, floodlit tennis court, gym, games room and guest laundry. All the units have a double bed and three bunks and cost $94 a double.

Arcadia The *Arcadia Hotel Resort* (☎ 4778 5177) has motel-style units with attached bathroom, air-con and fan, TV, telephone, radio, tea/coffee-making equipment and refrigerator. The resort also has a laundry and guest pool, as well as a public swimming pool near the bar and restaurant area. Poolside rooms are $60/70, terrace rooms $70/80.

There are a number of holiday flats along Hayles Ave. Starting from the Alma Bay end of the street, *Magnetic Retreat* (☎ 4778 5357) is on the corner with Rheuben Terrace. There are modern one and two-bedroom units, all fully equipped, a swimming pool and BBQs. Prices range from $50 to $80 for doubles.

The *Magnetic North Holiday Units* (☎ 4778 5647) is at 2 Endeavour Rd, on the corner of Hayles Ave. Once again the two-bedroom units are modern and well equipped and there's a pool and BBQ.

Nightly costs are from $65 for up to six people, and there's a weekly rate of $390. *Dandaloo Gardens* (☎ 4778 5174), 40 Hayles Ave, has eight one-bedroom units that accommodate up to five people. The rooms have attached bathrooms, fan, TV, cooking facilities and fridge, and there is also a BBQ, laundry, swimming pool, plus a playground. Costs are from $60 per unit.

Wongalee Holiday Flats (☎ 4778 5361) is at 17 McCabe Crescent, a little further along Hayles Ave. The old-fashioned two and three-bedroom units accommodate two to six people. As usual there's a BBQ, laundry and swimming pool, and nightly costs are from $55 for two.

There are also two B&Bs in Arcadia. The friendly *Marshall's B&B* (☎ 4778 5112) at 3 Endeavour Rd is a relaxed place with singles/doubles from $35/50. *Beaches B&B* (☎ 4778 5303) is a stylish timber cottage with a pool and separate guest wing. Rooms cost $60 a double.

Places to Eat
Picnic Bay All the Picnic Bay eating possibilities are along the waterfront on The Esplanade. Right in front of the jetty the *Picnic Bay Pub* has a bistro section in the beer garden with counter meals ranging from $6 to $12.

Heading along The Esplanade from the hotel you come to *Crusoe's*, a straightforward little BYO restaurant with evening meals from $10 to $12. It serves breakfast, lunch, dinner and takeaways, including good pies.

Further along, the *Green Frog Cafe* is a nice little lunch-time place with good sandwiches and cakes. Breakfasts and Devonshire teas are also available.

Down at the end of The Esplanade is *Maxine's*, a stylish bar and restaurant and a good place for a drink or a meal. Main courses range from $10 to $17, and the speciality here is oysters.

Nelly Bay *Mexican Munchies* (☎ 4778 5658), at 31 Warboy St in Nelly Bay, runs the Mexican gamut from enchiladas to tacos with mains from $12 to $14, and is open for dinner from 6 pm. Nearby, in the small shopping centre on Sooning St, there's also *Possums* for snacks and takeaways. Also here is a *bakery*, which does a good full breakfast for $5.

Arcadia The *Arcadia Hotel Resort* has a number of dining possibilities including a poolside snack bar. The usual steak, chicken and other counter meals cost around $10 to $14. The more expensive *Gatsby's Restaurant* opens on weekends and has main courses from $15 to $17.

Alla Capri at 5-7 Hayles Ave is just behind the Arcadia Resort. It has pastas from $6.50 to $9 and a pleasant indoor/outdoor eating area with visiting possums to provide entertainment. Other main course dishes cost around $11 to $15, pizzas are $15 for a medium or $18 for a large, and there's house wine. On Tuesday there is an all-you-can-eat pasta night for $7.50. The food is only average but there is lots of it, and it's a pleasant place for a late night drink. It's open Tuesday to Sunday from 6 pm.

There's a small shopping centre on the corner of Hayles Ave and Bright St in Arcadia. Here you'll find the *Blue Waters Cafe & Restaurant*, which looks deceptively like a basic takeaway joint, but actually has some of the best food on the island. The dinner menu has an interesting selection of mains priced from $14 to $17, or a three-course set menu for $15. It's open Tuesday to Saturday, and there's a pleasant courtyard out the back with candlelit tables.

On the Hayles Ave side of the junction, the *Bakehouse* is good for early morning coffee and croissants. Next door is *Banister's Seafoods*, which is basically a fish and chips place with an open dining area outside. It's open from 8 am to 8 pm, the food is excellent and it has a BYO licence so you can bring a bottle of wine or cans of beer from the Arcadia Hotel Resort's bottle shop.

Horseshoe Bay On the waterfront at the bay you can get takeaways or snacks at *The Bounty*, and the general store next door has a small supermarket selling groceries and supplies.

On the other side of The Bounty is *Cotters on the Beach*, a licensed indoor/outdoor restaurant that opens for lunch and dinner. There's a small brunch menu with light meals around $5 to $9, and the dinner menu offers steaks, chicken and seafood dishes from $10 to $17.

Getting There & Away
Two companies operate passenger ferries between Townsville and Magnetic Island.

Sunferries (☎ 4771 3855) operates about 10 services a day between 6.20 am and 7.15 pm from its terminal on Flinders St East. The trip takes about 20 minutes and costs $7/13 one way/return. The only inconvenience is that there is not much car parking in the Flinders St area.

Magnetic Island Ferries (☎ 4772 7122) runs a similar service from its terminal at the breakwater on Sir Leslie Thiess Dve near the casino. The first ferry leaves Townsville daily at 6 am; the last to the island is at 6.15, 7, 10.30 or 11.30 pm, depending on the day of the week. The trip takes about 15 minutes and the return fare is $14 ($11 for students).

You can also buy package deals that include return ferry tickets and accommodation; one-night packages start at $29. Check with the hostels in Townsville for deals.

The Capricorn Barge Company (☎ 4772 5422) runs a vehicular ferry to Arcadia from the south side of Ross Creek four times a day during the week and twice a day on weekends. It's $96 return for a car and up to six passengers, $31 return for a motorbike, and $12 return for walk-on passengers.

Bicycles are carried free on all ferries.

Getting Around
Bus The Magnetic Island Bus Service (☎ 4778 5130) operates up and down the island between Picnic Bay and Horseshoe Bay from 11 to 20 times a day, meeting all ferries and dropping off at all accommoda-

tion places. If you've got a ferry to catch it takes about 45 minutes from Horseshoe Bay to Picnic Bay, and 30 minutes from Arcadia to Picnic Bay. You can get individual tickets ($1.50 to $3.50) or a full-day pass ($9).

Taxi Taxis meet arriving ferries at Picnic Bay. If you've missed one you can phone for a taxi on ☎ 13 1008.

Motorcycle Rental Road Runner (☎ 4778 5222) is at Shop 2, Picnic Bay Arcade on the Picnic Bay waterfront. Scooter hire, including insurance and a crash helmet, costs $19 for a half-day, $25 for a full day (from 9 am to 5 pm) and $30 for 24 hours. No motorcycle licence is required for these small 50cc scooters, just a valid car drivers licence. You certainly don't need anything larger to explore Magnetic with.

Moke & Car Rental Moke Magnetic (☎ 4778 5377), in an arcade of the Picnic Bay Mall, and Holiday Moke Hire (☎ 4778 5703), based in the Jetty Cafe in the Picnic Bay Mall, have Mokes from $33 a day ($30 if you're over 25) plus 30c per kilometre. Both companies also have Suzuki Sierras, Mazda 121s and other vehicles.

Bicycle Magnetic Island is ideal for cycling, and mountain bikes are available for rent at several places, including the Esplanade in Picnic Bay, Foresthaven in Arcadia, and on the waterfront in Horseshoe Bay. Bikes cost $10 for a day, and $6 for half a day.

Hitching You could also hitch around, observing the precautions in the Getting There & Away chapter. Plenty of people do hitch – just start walking, and if you don't get a lift you'll soon end up in the next town anyway.

Around Magnetic Island

There are various trips out from Townsville to outer reefs and to the Palm Islands, north of Magnetic. These trips usually stop at Magnetic on their way out from Townsville. Possibilities include the following.

KELSO REEF
Pure Pleasure Cruises (☎ 1800 079 797) has day trips on its 30m wavepiercer catamaran to Kelso Reef, east of the Palm Island Group. The cost of $130 (children $65) includes lunch and snorkelling gear; scuba dives are an optional extra.

Wreck of the Yongala
The 3664 ton Adelaide Steamship Company vessel *Yongala* sank off Townsville in 1911 during a cyclone. She went down with all 121 of her crew and passengers and for years her disappearance was a mystery.

During WWII the ship's location was discovered and the first diver went down to the *Yongala* in 1947. The 90m-long wreck lies intact in 30m of water, and has become a haven for a huge variety of marine life. It is one of Australia's best dives.

A number of Townsville dive operators run one day and extended trips to the *Yongala*. Day trips cost from $165.

RATTLESNAKE & HERALD ISLANDS
These two adjacent islands north of Magnetic, and Acheron Island further north, are used for RAAF target practice and boats must keep away during this time. Advance warning notices appear in the Townsville *Bulletin*, or ring the RAAF Visits Coordinator on ☎ 4752 1135 for information.

Orpheus & the Palm Islands

Orpheus is one of the islands of the Palm Island Group, south of Hinchinbrook. The group consists of 10 main islands, all but two of which are Aboriginal reservations, which you need permission to visit. Orpheus and Pelorus are the only islands of the Palm Group not part of the reserve. Orpheus is a national park while Pelorus, immediately to its north, is crown land.

Orpheus Island

Area:	14 sq km
Type:	continental
High point:	172m
Max visitors:	72

Orpheus is long (about 11km from end to end), narrow (less than 1km wide) and heavily forested. The island, second largest in the Palm Island Group, is a national park and there is a lot of birdlife, some fine beaches, and some of the best fringing reef to be found on any of the Great Barrier Reef islands. The resort is quiet, secluded and fairly expensive.

Traces of the island's original Aboriginal visitors can still be seen – there is a shell midden near the Marine Research Station. The island was named by Lieutenant GE Richards on the HMS *Paluma* in 1887. He named the island after HMS *Orpheus*, the largest warship in Australia when it was wrecked in 1863 in New Zealand with the loss of 188 lives.

Later, sheep were run on the island and there are traces of stone sheep pens and the remains of an old stone homestead above Pioneer Bay. The wild goats that roam the island are the descendants of animals released here to provide food for possible

shipwreck survivors. It's estimated there are now as many as 4000 goats on the island and controlling their numbers is proving very difficult.

At one time oysters were also gathered here commercially and at Yank's Bay cement pilings mark the position of an old WWII submarine degaussing, or demagnetising, station. This process was intended to stop the submarines from detonating magnetic mines.

Information

The resort phone number is ☎ 4777 7377, the fax number is 4777 7533, and the postal address is Orpheus Island Resort, Private

Mail Bag 15, Townsville, Qld 4810. For reservations phone ☎ 1800 077 167. There is a cardphone at reception for guests. There are no banking facilities but the resort does take credit cards and can cash travellers cheques.

The Department of Environment produces a visitor information leaflet about the island.

Zoning Most of the water around the island is zoned Marine National Park B – 'look but don't touch'. From the top of Hazard Bay to the southern tip is zoned 'A', which allows limited line fishing. Collecting shells or coral is not permitted.

Marine Research Station

At Little Pioneer Bay, north of the resort, the James Cook University Marine Research Station specialises in breeding and raising giant clams and other Barrier Reef clams. Clams raised here are being transplanted to Pacific island reefs where overgathering has wiped them out. The clams grow surprisingly fast and it's hoped that the station will also raise them commercially as a food supply. In the station you can see the clams in the large water tanks (including the 'stud clams' used for breeding), while others are raised out in the shallow waters of the bay. The station manager can tell you where to find the Aboriginal shell midden. Phone ☎ 4777 7336 to inquire about visiting the station.

Activities

The resort has a tennis court, swimming pool, catamarans, windsurfers and a small fleet of outboard-powered dinghies. All this equipment is free to guests.

Although this is a low-key resort where organised activities are not the norm, there is a snorkelling trip each afternoon to some nearby giant clams and coral.

Beaches & Snorkelling Orpheus has some of the finest fringing reef to be found around any island along the reef and also has some very pleasant sandy beaches.

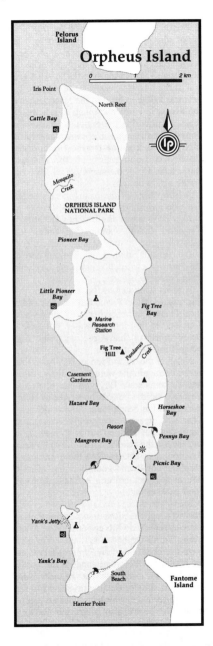

Orpheus Island

Guests at the resort can take out an outboard dinghy and find their own private beach for the day. Turtles are often seen around the island and you may spot schools of dolphins, particularly off the southern end of the island.

Hazard Bay, in front of the resort, is very shallow at low tide and much of it actually dries. At high tide the extreme tidal variations here make it a pleasant place for a swim, but at low tide the most interesting activity is wading through the shallow water looking for the stingrays which bask on the sandy bottom.

A little south of the resort there's better low-tide swimming at Mangrove Bay or at Yank's Bay, where the beaches are attractive and there's some fine coral for snorkelling or diving. At the southern end of the island is South Beach, looking across the narrow channel separating Orpheus from Fantome Island.

A short walk across the island from the resort takes you to Picnic Bay on the eastern side. There's no beach here, just stones and boulders leading into the water, but there's a very pleasant shady tree and some fine snorkelling just offshore.

North of the resort Pioneer Bay has a fine beach but again the water is shallow at low tide. As at Hazard Bay you can often see stingrays on the bottom here. About 100m back from the beach there's the remains of what was clearly once a quite substantial stone cottage. Further out in Pioneer Bay and around the headland from Little Pioneer Bay round to Hazard Bay there are some excellent corals and good bommies. Cattle Bay at the northern end of the island has good snorkelling.

Diving Orpheus' fine fringing reef offer some excellent diving opportunities. Apart from around Orpheus itself there are also good stretches of reef off Fantome Island, to the south, and Pelorus Island, to the north. Local reef dives with the island's dive centre cost $90 for the first dive and $70 for subsequent dives, which includes all equipment. The centre also offers introductory

dives for $90 or a full five day course leading to PADI certification for $499. Trips to the outer Barrier Reef can also be arranged from Orpheus.

Walking There aren't many walks on Orpheus although the open, grassy areas scattered around the island offer fine views if you can get to them. From Orpheus you can see across to the coast, 20km west, and to Curacoa, Fantome and Great Palm islands to the south. A short walk leads from the villas, above the resort, to Pennys Bay and Horseshoe Bay on the eastern side of the island. Orpheus is only a few hundred metres wide at this point. From here you can walk north towards Fig Tree Bay and up to Fig Tree Hill.

Mr Nicholson

Close to the top of Fig Tree Hill you can find the gravestone of a fox terrier named Mr Nicholson, a visitor from a yacht. The dog died in 1966 from, so it is said, the effects of cane toad consumption. The ugly toads are poisonous and can kill whatever eats them. Apart from cane toads Mr Nicholson also liked to chew on shoes – his owners left the last shoe he had been working on by his grave. In the years since then a collection of shoes has grown around the grave, and it's said to be lucky to leave an old shoe here.

A more interesting walk winds through a forested area from the southern end of the Hazard Bay beach across the island to Picnic Bay. This is a popular snorkelling spot and the shady tree behind the beach is a good spot for a picnic.

Although there are no permanently flowing streams on Orpheus, the greener vegetation clearly shows where water flows after rain. At the northern end of Hazard Bay a jumble of rocks tumbling down the hillside marks an impressive, though usually dry, waterfall. The vegetation in the open woodland is typically Moreton Bay ash and acacias, while the rainforest found in the gullies and around sheltered bays includes fig trees. The best patch of rainforest is on the western side of Iris Point, at the northern end of the island. Interestingly, some of the open grassland areas are natural features, and did not appear as a result of human activity on the island.

Orpheus' most visible wildlife is introduced – goats and cane toads have done a fairly comprehensive job of taking the island over. Around the resort at night, bandicoots make a shy appearance and echidnas can also be seen. There is a variety of harmless snakes and small skinks and geckos. The birdlife is prolific and includes herons, pheasants, sunbirds, scrub fowl and some very impressive ospreys.

Places to Stay

Camping Applications to camp on Orpheus Island should be made to the Department of Environment office (☎ 4066 8115) at Cardwell; information is available from the office at the Great Barrier Reef Wonderland in Townsville.

There are bush campsites at Yank's Jetty, South Beach and Little Pioneer Bay. All sites have toilet facilities and a picnic area but there is no regular fresh water supply and a fuel stove should be used. Yank's Bay offers the best low tide swimming and snorkelling.

Resort The resort is low-key but sophisticated – the staff manage to combine black-tie waiters in the evening with first name terms with the guests. The original Orpheus resort dates from the 1940s but in 1981 it was totally rebuilt in a very Mediterranean style by two Italian Australians. The resort has subsequently changed hands but the flavour remains. The prolific bougainvilleas and other tropical flowers add to the atmosphere, and the stylish rooms are a definite cut above the typical square boxes found at so many other Great Barrier Reef resorts.

Along the beach are 15 Studio Units, eight Terrace Suites and two slightly larger bungalows. They're tastefully furnished with a veranda area out the front and air-con and ceiling fans. There's piped music, a fridge and tea/coffee-making equipment, but no telephone or TV in the rooms. The Terrace Suites are slightly smaller than the Studio Units, while the bungalows have a large spa. The Terrace Suites are $525/840 and the Studio Units $625/1012 per night. The bungalows are only available as doubles at $570 per person. Tariffs include all meals and use of all the resort equipment.

Above the main resort, up the hill towards the island's central saddle, are six delightfully designed and furnished two-bedroom villas. Architect Marco Romoli of Florence was responsible for the villas and it was originally intended that they would be sold at something like $350,000 each. This plan somehow went awry and they're now available at $590 per person per night for a minimum of two people, $405 per person for four people.

Places to Eat

Orpheus is an island that prides itself on its food, and with some justification – it is superb. There are no menus; breakfast is anything to order, while lunch is just a matter of making a choice between the couple of options given. Dinner starts with hors d'ouevres at the bar, followed by a long, languorous, five course, candle-lit affair. There's a bar and a well chosen wine list with most wines around $25 to $60, but it goes right up to Bollinger at $160. The open dining area looks right out on the beach and the sunsets can be particularly spectacular.

For between-meal snacks the lounge area has coffee and tea, and a fridge with cold water or juice and usually also has something interesting with which to wreck any diet.

If you're planning on taking a dinghy to find your own island beach for the day, the resort staff will provide you with a picnic hamper for lunch.

Getting There & Away

Orpheus is 80km north of Townsville and about 20km offshore from Lucinda Point, near Ingham. The Great Barrier Reef is only about 20 to 25km east of the island. Hinchinbrook, with its high peaks, is only a little to the north and is very visible from Orpheus.

Air Most resort guests arrive by seaplane and the resort flies guests more or less to order from Townsville or Cairns to Orpheus. The flight costs $145 each way from Townsville, $230 from Cairns. At high tide the amphibious aircraft lands in the bay right in front of the resort and taxis in to the beach right outside the dining room; at low tide it ties up at a pontoon about 4m square bearing a sign announcing it as 'Orpheus Island International Airport', from where guests are ferried by boat to the jetty.

Sea Few guests come to the resort by sea although it is only a little over 20km from Lucinda Point. You can get out to Orpheus from Dungeness, near Lucinda, by water taxi. Count on about $120 per person return – contact the MV *Scuba Doo* (☎ 4777 8220) for details.

Although they have to anchor a long way out from shore, visiting yachties often pause at Hazard Bay in front of the resort, although there is no access to it. There is also good anchorage at Pioneer Bay but care should be taken to anchor well clear of the Marine Research Station's reef research

areas in the bay. Prawn trawlers working this stretch of coast often anchor during the daytime in these bays.

Other Palm Islands

The 10 islands that make up the Palm Island Group are Orpheus and Pelorus, and the Aboriginal islands of Brisk, Curacao, Eclipse, Esk, Falcon, Fantome, Havannah and Great Palm. To visit any of the Aboriginal reserve islands you need permission from the Aboriginal & Islander Affairs office in Townsville.

GREAT PALM ISLAND

The largest island in the Palm Island group, this island was named by Captain Cook who actually stopped and landed there. At that time it was inhabited by an Aboriginal tribe. An Aboriginal mission was established here in 1918 and the population of Casement Bay is about 1300. Great Palm Island has an airstrip.

FANTOME ISLAND

Immediately south of Orpheus Island and separated from it only by a narrow channel, Fantome Island had a leper colony until a fire destroyed all the buildings in 1974 and the inhabitants were shifted to Palm Island. The remains of the buildings are on the low saddle near the northern tip of the island.

Hinchinbrook Island

Hinchinbrook is the largest island off the Queensland coast, a magnificent, mountainous island cloaked in incredibly dense rainforest, soaring to 1121m at the top of Mt Bowen, and separated from the mainland only by the narrow but deep and mangrove-fringed Hinchinbrook Channel. The island stretches 34km north to south, and viewed from the Bruce Highway or the sea it's often difficult to tell that it's actually divided from the coast.

Indeed when the *Endeavour* sailed by in 1770 Captain Cook did not realise he was passing an island. At that time Hinchinbrook may have had a permanent Aboriginal population. Traces of the tidal fish traps constructed by the Bandjin Aboriginal tribe can still be seen near the campsite at Scraggy Point.

The island can be divided into three main areas. In the south, lush tropical rainforest on the mainland side rises to rugged granite peaks that form a backbone to the island. These towering mountains slope down to long sandy beaches and secluded bays on the eastern side. On the north-west peninsula there are lower, older volcanic rocks that slope down to the sandy beach at Hecate Point. The north-east peninsula, ending at Cape Richards, is notable for the 8km-long strip of sand at Ramsay Bay, backed by the extensive mangrove forests of Missionary Bay. Ramsay Bay ends at Cape Sandwich and, round the corner from this cape, the long beaches of South and North Shepherd lead up to Cape Richards.

The whole island is a national park and most of it is untouched wilderness, some of it barely explored, but up at the northern tip at Cape Richards there's a small resort and also a camping area a couple of kilometres south of the cape. Other camping areas are scattered around the national park, particularly at Zoe Bay. The information that follows is divided into two parts: The Resort, which includes the Missionary Bay

HINCHINBROOK ISLAND

Highlights
- Walk the world-renowned Thorsborne Trail
- Take a picnic and go snorkelling on the Brook Islands

Area:	393 sq km
Type:	continental
High point:	1121m
Max visitors:	50

mangrove forests and the walk to Macushla Bay, and the rest of the island.

Information

The Department of Environment has two useful leaflets on Hinchinbrook and the islands to the north. Those planning to walk the coastal track from Ramsay Bay to George Point should get a copy of the *Thorsborne Trail* leaflet.

The *Hinchinbrook to Dunk Island* park

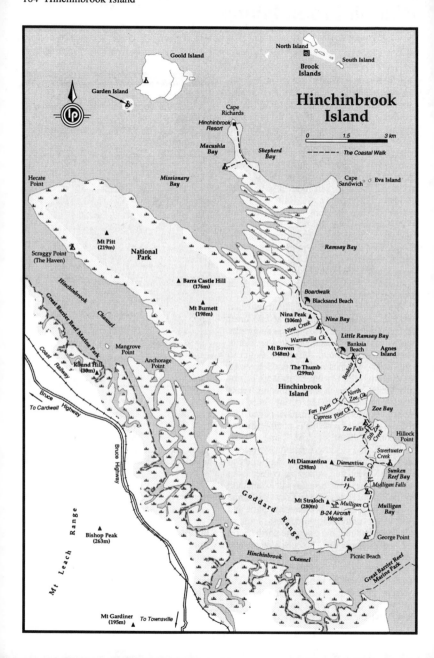

guide is a small brochure full of fascinating information about Hinchinbrook Island, Goold Island, the Brook Islands, the Family Islands and Dunk Island. There's a Department of Environment Reef & Rainforest Centre (☎ 4066 8601) on the Bruce Highway in the centre of Cardwell. The rangers can issue camping permits and advise on Hinchinbrook walks and climbing the mountains.

Hinchinbrook Island, with text by Arthur and Margaret Thorsborne and photos by Cliff and Dawn Frith, is a coffee-table book on Hinchinbrook with some superb photos and an engrossing text revealing a real love for the island.

THE RESORT

The whole of Hinchinbrook is a national park, although the tip of Cape Richards is leased as a resort. From the resort guests can easily walk to Macushla and Shepherd bays.

Information

The resort phone number is ☎ 4066 8585, the fax number is 4066 8742, and the postal address is Hinchinbrook Island Resort, PO Box 3, Cardwell, Qld 4816. Bookings can be made by phoning ☎ 1800 777 021 toll free, direct with the resort or through the airlines or travel agents.

The resort has a small shop and a lending library of books. There are no bank facilities on the island.

Wildlife

Hinchinbrook has plenty of wildlife, but visitors should come prepared for the small six-legged variety in particular. March flies are one pest you'll meet with if you come at the wrong season. They're big ugly monsters, but fortunately they are so slow-moving you should win every encounter. Mosquitoes and sandflies are also waiting to greet you at certain times of year. In summer they can be a serious nuisance so insect repellent and, if you react badly to bites, some sort of treatment are a good idea.

There are other rather more interesting varieties of wildlife to be seen, particularly the very tame, pretty-faced wallabies that appear around the resort mornings and evenings. They've learnt that resort guests are often willing to hand out bits of apple and other goodies, and put on a great act for children. Equally visible are the huge goannas that roam the resort area, scrambling up trees and hissing ominously if you approach too closely. There are lots of tiny lizards and skinks to be seen but the big, spotted grey-black goannas are a fine sight. Other creatures you'll see around the resort include cane toads, echidnas, bush rats and bats.

The short stroll from the resort to Turtle Bay may well reveal why this little inlet gets its name. If you clamber up to the rocks above the bay you may see large turtles popping up in the waters, peering round myopically and then sinking beneath the waves again. Mud skippers, those strange walking fish, can also be seen at this bay.

Bird spotters will have a field day at Hinchinbrook. Birds provide a constant background burble and flit across the scenery continuously. Each of the cabins at the resort is named after a bird found on the island so you might stay in a cabin named Reef Heron or Boobook Owl. Scrub fowl, or megapodes, are one bird whose presence you'll often see signs of. This ground-dwelling bird builds huge mounds of vegetation in which it lays eggs. The heat of the decaying vegetable matter incubates the eggs. You'll often see these impressively large 'bumps' and the birds themselves scampering off into the bush. Over 200 species of birds have been spotted on Hinchinbrook.

Mangroves

Missionary Bay is fringed by an extensive mangrove forest with twisting inlets leading in to it. The Australian Institute of Marine Science has constructed a boardwalk across from one inlet almost to the next one and you can walk the 500m pathway and study this fascinating area. You can approach the boardwalk pontoon jetty in a dinghy borrowed from the resort or on a Reef Explorer tour.

The boardwalk stands a couple of metres above the muddy surface of the swamp and you can see bins, nets and instruments as evidence of numerous experiments being conducted in the mangroves. A constant background burble of noise indicates just how lively the mangroves are. Listen for the loud cracking of the snapping prawns – there's obviously a lot of them in there but, as they're hidden in the mud, you won't see them. More visible are the numerous small mud crabs and the curious mud skippers, small square-faced fish that have adapted to life out of the water and skip across the surface of the mud using their front fins as 'legs'. They'll even climb trees. You may see them peering out of the little volcano-like mudhills they build to live in.

The mangroves, with their twisting and intertwined roots, are surprisingly varied in form. In all, there are 23 species of mangrove and the ability of these plants to live in saltwater creates a unique environment that scientists are now studying closely. Another boardwalk, right at the end of an estuary, leads to the long sand dunes that separate Ramsay Bay and the open sea from the sheltered mangrove forests of Missionary Bay.

Activities

The resort has a pool and canoes, snorkelling gear, surf skis, fishing equipment and so on, but this is not a heavy-activity resort and nightlife means talking to people over dinner or in the bar.

Beaches & Snorkelling Orchid Beach is as fine a sweep of beach as you could ask for, and it's only a few steps from the resort cabins or the swimming pool. Apart from the rocky headlands at each end of the beach there's not much snorkelling potential around the resort, however. The trip across to the Brook Islands, where there is some fine coral and plenty of fish, is the popular snorkelling excursion.

Hinchinbrook is close enough to the mainland for you to be cautious about box jellyfish during the November to March summer season, particularly on the coast side of the island.

Walks There are a number of walks around the resort and further afield into the national park.

Around the Resort From the resort you can take a short stroll from the end of the beach up to the top of the rocky headland at **Cape Richards**. From there you have a fine view across to the misty outline of the Family Islands and Dunk Island, about 30km away. In the other direction there's the idyllic sweep of **Orchid Beach**, the resort beach and as pretty a stretch of sand as you can ask for.

At the other end of Orchid Beach an equally short trail leads to tiny **Turtle Bay**, a rocky little inlet round the headland. Alternatively you can scramble round the headland to the bay.

To Shepherd & Macushla Bays A longer walk leads from the resort to North Shepherd, Macushla and South Shepherd. The trail starts from the cabins and is signposted as a 40 minute walk to North Shepherd Bay, although you can do the 2km stroll much faster. The trail winds through the rainforest, climbing up to a ridge with fine views across to the Brook Islands before dropping precipitously down to the bay. **North Shepherd** is a long stretch of very wide beach with rocky headlands at each end.

It takes a good 20 minutes to walk the 1.3km from one end of the beach to the other and at the far, or southern, end the trail leads off to Macushla Bay, crossing the peninsula to the sheltered beach on the calmer, coast side of the island. Look out for scrub fowl along this 2km stretch of the walk, there seems to be plenty of them around. Skirting around the Kirkville Hills, it only takes about 20 minutes to cross the peninsula to **Macushla Bay**. The beach is not always good for swimming, as it's very flat and muddy at low tide, but it is littered with countless tiny shells. A large camping area with toilets and tables, but not much fresh water, sprawls on either side of the headland. Mangroves start only a short distance north and south of the headlands.

The trail on to **South Shepherd** starts about halfway across the peninsula between North Shepherd and Macushla. It's signposted as a 3½ hour walk but two hours is probably a better estimate for most walkers. Like North Shepherd, there's an endlessly long stretch of beach at South Shepherd.

Places to Stay

The resort was established on the island in 1975, when 15 simple cabins were built. In 1989 it was closed down for major renovations and an additional 15 'treehouses' were built, increasing the capacity to a maximum of 50 people.

The emphasis here is on seclusion and the natural environment – the accommodation is comfortable and stylish without being luxurious. If you're looking for peace and quiet, and easy access to one of Queensland's most spectacular national parks, this may well be the perfect place. They push the fact that the guest population is low and that there are no heavy entertainment schedules – no entertainment director, no competitions and games, no disco. There's no TV or radio and only one phone too for that matter. Missionary Bay is popular with families and couples – the island is big enough and the resort population small enough for you to have as much solitude as you could wish for.

The architect-designed 'treehouses' are individual timber cottages, built into the steep hillside behind Orchid Beach and linked by a series of timber boardwalks. Inside they are lined with several different types of timber, and are comfortably furnished, with full-length windows looking out across the treetops to the sea. There are one and two-bedroom cottages, each with a separate bathroom and lounge area, fans, a fridge and tea/coffee-making facilities.

Seven of the 15 original cabins are still in use. These are also timber-lined, each with a deck out front, a bedroom with a couple of single beds, a bathroom and another bedroom with a double bed and a divan-sofa-whatever, which could fold out to sleep a couple of more people. These older cabins are fairly basic and the furnishings equally straightforward but they're quite comfortable, with ceiling fans in the two rooms. The accommodation is certainly well hidden. From the air or from the sea, even from just standing on the beach, there is hardly any sign of the cabins or cottages.

The restaurant, bar and pool area are quite separate from the accommodation. This area is close to the jetty, a couple of minutes' walk along an unsurfaced road from the cabins, which are scattered up the hillside above the beach. The restaurant is a spacious and pleasant open-sided building and the swimming pool, with a wide decking area around it, is just fine.

Daily costs in the older cabins are $225/430 for a single/double and $95 for children. The newer one-bedroom treehouses cost $315/590, and the two-bedroom treehouses cost $355/640 for a single/double and $120 for children. These rates include all meals and use of most equipment.

Places to Eat

Food at Hinchinbrook is surprisingly good, far better than at some of the large resorts. The restaurant is open-air and pleasant. Breakfast is a serve-yourself buffet with fruit, cereals, juice and tea or coffee, plus there's toast, great croissants and cooked breakfasts for the big eaters. Lunch might be in the restaurant (a choice of two main courses, dessert and tea or coffee), a poolside BBQ or, if you're off on a walk, they'll pack you a sandwich lunch.

At night they'll feed children early while the regular four-course dinner (with a choice of mains) starts at 7.30 pm. Usually, one is seafood and the other a meat dish. The food seems to be consistently imaginative and well prepared, and the ingredients fresh and top quality. A superb resort for eating, Hinchinbrook is like a good small restaurant, whereas big resorts like South Molle or Great! Keppel are like large fast-service pubs.

As with most other resorts shorts and T-shirts are the usual dress standards, although there's often a bit of dressing up at night-time.

Getting There & Away

Launch transfers on the resort boat between Cardwell and Hinchinbrook cost $80 return, or you can also transfer to Cairns or Townsville using launch and limo for $300 return.

OUTSIDE THE RESORT

Although there's plenty to see around the resort and walks lead from the resort to Macushla Bay and North Beach and South Shepherd Bay, that only touches on a small part of the island. The great bulk of the beautiful island is only open to intrepid bushwalkers.

The Thorsborne Trail

The island's best walk is the 30km Thorsborne Trail coastal track from Ramsay Bay to Zoe Bay and on to George Point. This is the finest island walk along the Great Barrier Reef. It can be completed in two hard days, but allowing for at least three nights of camping on the island is a much better idea.

The walk includes long sandy beaches, mountain streams, humid rainforests and magnificent mountain scenery. The trail is ungraded and includes some often challenging creek crossings. The maximum elevation along the trail is 260m, reached between Upper South Zoe Creek and Sweetwater Creek.

Information & Permits

The walking details that follow are southbound from Ramsay Bay to George Point but the walk can be done in either direction. Get a copy of the Department of Environment's *Thorsborne Trail* leaflet.

All walkers on the trail must have Department of Environment permits, and because numbers on the trail are restricted to 40 people at any one time, advance bookings are also advisable. Permit applications and bookings are made through the Reef & Rainforest Centre (☎ 4066 8601) in Cardwell.

Before a permit is issued to them, all potential walkers must view the Department's 15-minute video *Without a Trace*, which gives guidance on minimal impact bushwalking. It is available for viewing at the Reef & Rainforest Centre in Cardwell and at other Department offices in Queensland and various centres interstate. Phone the Cardwell office for details.

Trail Conditions The trail is rough and not always well marked although triangular orange trail markers, rock cairns and coloured tape may be found at some difficult spots.

The trail is recommended for moderately experienced bushwalkers who should be adequately prepared and carry a map, compass and drinking water.

From November to May box jellyfish can be a danger, particularly at George Point, Mulligan Bay and Zoe Bay.

Preparation Walkers intending to do the coastal track should be fit, experienced and well prepared. Water can be a problem, and it is only reliably available year-round at Nina Bay, Little Ramsay Bay, and at the southern end of Zoe Bay. During the dry season, from April to October, water may be very scarce and adequate supplies should be carried. If you find a dry creek or the water is salty it's often possible to find freshwater further upstream. During the wet season from December through March too much water can pose problems at the opposite extreme. The trail may be very slippery, creek crossings can be difficult and you should be prepared for heavy rainfall. In tropical conditions walking in a raincoat or poncho is likely to be very uncomfortable – it's better to carry an umbrella or simply get wet and have dry clothes to change into later.

At any time of the year it can be hot and humid during the daytime but from May to September the nights can be cold enough to require a sleeping bag. A good tent is necessary if there is heavy rain at night.

Insects like mosquitoes, sandflies and march flies can be a nuisance so bring a good insect repellent. As anywhere along the Great Barrier Reef a good sunscreen and a shady hat are also vitally important.

Protecting your food supplies from the native bush rats is another of Hinchinbrook's challenges. These ever-hungry critters will eat anything and can chew their way through just about any type of food container, including metal ones. Rat-proof food boxes are provided at some campsites. Check with the national park rangers for advice on ways of protecting your food. One of the most effective methods is to hang your food container from a length of nylon fishing line strung between two trees.

Open camp fires and cooking fires are not allowed; you must carry your own fuel stove. A hand trowel is also handy for digging toilet holes.

Ramsay Bay to Nina Bay: 4km, 2½ hours You reach the starting point on Ramsay Bay by going up the mangrove estuary from Missionary Bay and walking across the boardwalk. It's about 1km from the boardwalk at the south end of Ramsay Bay to Blacksand Beach. Look for the fossil crabs found along Ramsay Bay; thought to be from 8000 to 10,000 years old, they are a relic of rising seas at the close of the last ice age. Between January and June fresh water can usually be found at the small lagoons behind Blacksand Beach.

The trail starts two-thirds of the way along Blacksand Beach, a little south of the second lagoon, and between three paperbark trees. Initially, it follows a small dry watercourse, but then it turns left off the creek and goes through tall, open forest to the saddle to the east of Nina Peak before descending along a creek flowing south-

east towards Nina Bay. The trail emerges on the mangroves behind the beach, which can be difficult to cross at high tide. The track follows the western side of the mangroves and finally ends at the north end of the beach, where there is a good campsite with pit toilets.

It's an interesting, but steep and tiring, climb up Nina Creek to the pronounced top of Nina Peak. The views from the summit are superb.

Nina Bay to Little Ramsay Bay: 2.5km, 2 hours From the rocks at the south end of Nina Beach you make your way round the headland and over a small cliff, following rock cairns to rocky Boulder Bay. Rock cairns mark the start of a well-defined trail from the headland at the southern end of this bay. The trail goes south-east to the northern end of Little Ramsay Bay. You can find fresh water in the creek that runs into the lagoon behind the beach here, and there's a good campsite with pit toilets on the south bank of the lagoon. Watch out for crocodiles in the lagoon.

Little Ramsay Bay to Banksia Creek: 2km, 1 hour From the rocks at the end of Little Ramsay Bay it's only 50m or so to a very small beach. At the end of this beach the trail continues to a larger sandy beach. The trail bends east and climbs a steep slope before dropping to Banksia Creek. The trail continues upstream on the western side to a waterfall then crosses to the eastern side and climbs a very steep slope to the top of the waterfall. The trail crosses back and forth over the creek and eventually reaches a large waterfall, where water is usually available for much of the year. After August it may be dry until the rains come later in the year.

A short way up the trail from the second beach you can divert off to sandy Banksia Beach.

Banksia Creek to Zoe Bay: 6km, 5 hours From the waterfall the trail leaves the creek and heads south-east over a saddle

Crocodiles

Films like *Crocodile Dundee*, together with the odd tourist ending up as snack food, have combined to make Australia's crocodiles very well known. There are two types of crocodile, but you're very unlikely to meet either of them in the wild along the Great Barrier Reef.

The smaller freshwater crocodile is not dangerous to humans and in any case is found mainly on the Gulf of Carpentaria coast of Queensland, not on the Pacific coast (except in the far north of the Cape York peninsula). As the name indicates, freshwater crocodiles are generally found in fresh water, such as steams, creeks, billabongs and in rivers – although they're also found in the tidal reaches of rivers. They live on insects, fish, frogs, birds, lizards, and sometimes even small mammals.

Saltwater crocodile

The dangerous crocodile is the estuarine, or saltwater, crocodile. Although 'salties' can be found all the way along the Queensland coast north of Rockhampton, it's only in creek and river mouths that you might spot this generally shy creature. Hinchinbrook is the only Great Barrier Reef island where you need to keep a watchful eye out for crocodiles, and even there it's only around the mangrove inlets or crossing Zoe Creek that you need to be careful. Saltwater crocodiles grow to a larger size than the fresh water variety, and can reach up to 6m in length – but 4m is about as big as they usually get. The way to distinguish between the two – should you be in such a need – is by the salties broad snout.

and then follows a dry watercourse through open forest, and into a stretch of rainforest. The trail then runs inland around the Zoe Bay mangroves to North Zoe Creek.

The route runs uphill from the mangroves and crosses North Zoe Creek before turning back down to the coast. Permanent fresh water can usually be found at Fan Palm Creek, while Cypress Pine Creek has a good swimming hole just upstream from the creek crossing. If the water at creek crossings is salty or the creek is actually dry, it's worth heading upstream a few hundred metres, where you should be able to find fresh water. The trail reaches Zoe Bay a little north of South Zoe Creek. There are beach and forest campsites at the southern end of the bay.

Zoe Bay to Diamantina Creek: 6.5km, 4 hours From Zoe Bay the trail follows the western bank of the creek then crosses to the eastern side about 100m before the falls, 1.5km from Zoe Bay. Above the falls the trail crosses back and forth over the creek then follows the western side of the creek through heavy undergrowth to Upper South Zoe Creek.

Leaving South Zoe Creek the trail climbs a spur with good views of Mt Bowen to the saddle separating South Zoe Creek from Sweetwater Creek. At 260m this is the highest elevation of the whole walk. It then crosses the headwaters of Sweetwater Creek, after which it goes down a slope with good views of Sunken Reef Bay to Diamantina Creek. This creek rarely runs dry and can be difficult to cross after heavy rain.

Shortly before Diamantina Creek there is a short side track (30 minutes) to Sunken Reef Bay, which has a campsite behind the fore dunes.

Diamantina Creek to Mulligan Falls: 1km, 30 minutes From the Diamantina Creek crossing the trail climbs a ridge before dropping down to Mulligan Falls, where there is a good campsite, just south of the falls, with a fine swimming hole (below the falls).

Mulligan Falls to George Point: 7.5km, 2½ hours The trail skirts around the mangroves, crosses the creek and comes to Mulligan Bay, where there is another good campsite south of the mouth of Diamantina Creek. Fresh water is available about 300m before you reach the beach.

The trail continues along the bay, crossing Mulligan Creek about two-thirds of the way along. The crossing can be difficult at high tide. The trail continues to the picnic area at George Point, from where you cross to Lucinda.

Places to Stay

Permits for camping should be applied for at least six weeks in advance. Applications for the Macushla Bay and The Haven (Scraggy Point) sites, and for bush-camping, should be made to the Cardwell Reef & Rainforest Centre. The nightly cost is $3.50.

You can walk to the Macushla Bay site from the Cape Richards resort. A maximum of 30 campers can stay here, and there are toilets, tables and gas BBQs but no drinking water. The site at Scraggy Point is on Hinchinbrook Channel, below Mt Pitt. As at Macushla Bay there is a maximum limit of 30 campers and there are toilets, tables and gas BBQs but Scraggy Point also has drinking water available from Pages Creek.

Campsites along the coastal trail are on the south bank of the large lagoon on Little Ramsay Bay and where the track crosses

North Zoe Creek. On Zoe Bay, on the north side of South Zoe Creek, there is a site with toilets and a maximum limit of 15 campers. Further south there are sites at Sunken Reef Bay, Mulligan Falls, Mulligan Bay and George Point.

Getting There & Away

Cardwell, the main access point for the resort and the northern end of the island, is 192km south of Cairns and 157km north of Townsville. It's relatively easy to arrange drop-offs and pick-ups for the coastal walk, the Cardwell-Ramsay Bay and Lucinda-George Point boat operators work together to drop-off and collect walkers at each end.

Hinchinbrook Island Ferries (☎ 1800 682 702), 131 Bruce Highway, has a ferry departing daily at 9 am and returning around 4.30 pm (return fare $69). This service operates daily from June through November, and three times a week from December through May. If you want to walk the Thorsborne Trail the one-way cost is $45 with Hinchinbrook Island Ferries. You also need to arrange your southern boat pick-up with Hinchinbrook Wilderness Safaris (☎ 4777 8307). The cost is also $45, which includes transport back to Cardwell.

Hinchinbrook Island Ferries also do various day trips to the island. For example, you could spend a day at the resort and have lunch there or, alternatively, they will drop you at the resort and you can then walk from there to North Shepherd beach and across to Macushla. At Macushla the boat will meet you again and take you up through the mangroves on Missionary Bay to the Ramsay Bay boardwalk. You'll have time to walk down to Blacksand Beach and even beyond (towards Nina Bay), on the first part of the Hinchinbrook coastal walk. The trip up through the mangroves to Ramsay Bay depends on the tides so you may find that sometimes it has to be done in reverse. The cost is $66.

Access to other points on the island is not so easy. There are no safe anchorages on the eastern side, although boats can get in to Zoe Bay when conditions are favourable.

Islands near Hinchinbrook

Two national park island groups lie immediately north of Hinchinbrook: Goold Island, immediately north of Hinchinbrook, and the small Brook Islands group to the north-east. Further north are the Family Islands, also mainly national parks, and then the larger Dunk Island.

GOOLD ISLAND

Only 4.5km north-west of Cape Richards and 17km north-east of Cardwell the whole 8.3 sq km island is a national park. The granite island is covered in eucalyptus forest with smaller patches of rainforest in the gullies. The noisy call of sulphur-crested cockatoos rings across the island, and turtles and dugong are often seen feeding on the seagrass beds that spread across the shallow waters south and west of Goold.

Just south of Goold Island is tiny Garden Island, with a recreation reserve controlled by the local council. Unlike the national park restrictions, which apply to Goold, there are no restrictions on camping here and the island has a good sandy beach but, as usual, no fresh water is available.

Places to Stay

The campsite on the western beach has toilets, tables and fireplaces but the creek at the northern end of the beach usually dries up between August and December so it is necessary to bring water. A permit from the Cardwell Reef & Rainforest Centre is necessary and there is a limit of 50 campers.

Getting There & Away

The Cardwell-Hinchinbrook boat operator can drop campers at Goold Island on request.

BROOK ISLANDS

The four small islands of the Brook group are covered in dense vegetation and lie about 8km north-east of Cape Richards. South Island has a Commonwealth lighthouse but the other three islands – Middle Island, Tween Island and North Island – are all national park and only cover an area of 0.9 sq km. There are regular charter boats operating to these islands from Cardwell and the Hinchinbrook Resort. The fringing reef around the three northern islands offers fine snorkelling and North Island's beach is a good picnic spot. However, there are no facilities and camping is not permitted.

The islands are a nesting place for a huge colony of Torresian imperial-pigeons. Up to 30,000 of these black and white birds arrive here from Papua New Guinea in September to breed, departing with their offspring in February. The male and female birds take turns to incubate the eggs, while the bird enjoying a day off flies to the mainland, where it feeds on rainforest fruits.

The summer months also find black-naped terns breeding on the islands. During these months visits to the islands are not permitted.

MICHAEL AW

MICHAEL AW

TONY WHEELER

Top: Magnetic Island
Middle: Pool at a Magnetic Island resort
Bottom: Radical Bay, Magnetic Island

Top Left: Yankee Bay, Orpheus Island
Top Right: The south of Hinchinbrook Island is dominated by lush rainforest
Middle: Mangroves encroaching into Missionary Bay, Hinchinbrook Island
Bottom Left: Crossing South Zoe Creek on Hinchinbrook's Thorsborne Trail
Bottom Right: Looking across Wina Bay towards Nina Peak, Hinchinbrook Island

TONY WHEELER

TONY WHEELER

HUGH FINLAY

QUEENSLAND TOURIST AND TRAVEL CORPORATION

Top Left: EJ Banfield's grave, Dunk Island's famous beachcomber
Top Right: Wheeler Island, near Bedarra Island
Middle: Handicrafts from the artists' colony on Dunk Island
Bottom: Dunk Island jetty

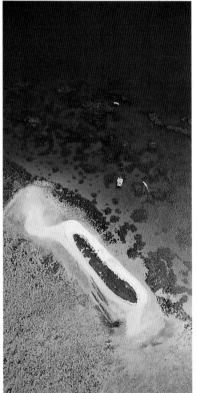

Left: Fitzroy Island
Top Right: Green Island
Bottom Right: Michaelmas Cay is a national park and popular rendezvous for outer reef trips

Dunk, Bedarra & the Family Islands

The Family Islands group consists of Dunk Island and the seven smaller islands to the south. They lie off the coast of Tully, about 30km north-east of Cardwell. Dunk Island is about three-quarters national park; Wheeler, Coombe, Smith, Bowden and Hudson islands are also national parks; while Timana (Thorpe) and Bedarra (Richards) islands are privately owned. Dunk has a large resort, Bedarra has a very small and very exclusive (read: expensive) resort, and camping is permitted on Dunk and several of the other national park islands.

Dunk, the largest island of the group, is sometimes referred to as 'The Father' – Bedarra is 'The Mother', Wheeler and Coombe are the 'The Twins', and Smith, Bowden and Hudson make up the 'The Triplets'. The name 'Family' was given to them by Cook when he sailed through the group on 8 June 1770. He sailed between The Twins and The Triplets and passed to the east (seaward) side of Dunk, which was the only individual island he named. Lord Montague Dunk was at that time the First Lord of the Admiralty, and Cook made very certain of keeping important personages and possible patrons firmly on side. (Lord Dunk was also the Earl of Sandwich and a very keen gambler. He is credited with inventing the 'sandwich' in order not to waste important gambling time by stopping for a meal.)

Cook's journal comments that 'we saw on one of the nearest Islands a Number of Natives collected together, who seemed to look very attentively upon the Ship; they were quite naked, and of a very Dark Colour, with short hair'.

Although the Aborigines have now completely gone from the Family Islands, EJ Banfield, Dunk Island's famous reclusive 'Beachcomber', made sure the Aboriginal names to all the islands of the group have been recorded:

Aboriginal Name	European Name
Coonanglebah	Dunk
Timana	Thorpe
Bedarra	Richards
Toolghar	Wheeler
Coomboo	Coombe
Kurrumbah	Smith
Budjoo	Bowden
Coolah	Hudson

The Family Islands were given their European names by Lieutenant GE Richards when he came here on his survey ship HMS *Paluma* in 1886. The officers, engineer and ship's surgeon each had an island named after them; double-barrelled Lieutenant

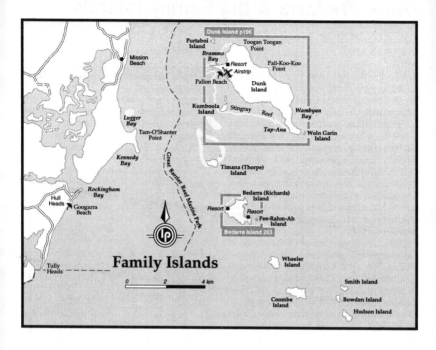

Family Islands

0   2   4 km

Bowden-Smith actually got two islands. The close linguistic relationship between Coomboo and Coombe suggests that Richards may well have been aware of the Aboriginal place names. Timana and Bedarra are the only islands of the group still generally referred to by their Aboriginal names – although it is thought that Banfield erred in his transcription of Bedarra, and that it should really be Biagurra. This island has also been known as Allason Island, after Captain Henry Allason, an early but brief European occupant.

The name 'Family' seems neatly appropriate for the group, with all the island sharing one clear family characteristic – each island ends in its north-west corner with a fine sandspit (on Dunk this is the location for the resort and centre of the island's activity), the result of the prevailing winds and currents through the group.

Climate

The Family Islands are cloaked in heavy rainforest, which is hardly surprising since they lie off the wettest area in Australia. Either Innisfail or Tully usually records the highest annual rainfall in Australia, generally around 3700mm. The temperatures in this tropical region are fairly even year-round, averaging around 25 to 30°C in the warmer October to April months, and dropping to 20 to 25°C in the cooler months from May to September.

Rain, however, has a much more decisive effect on determining when it's best to visit these islands. The wet season starts in December when the average rainfall is around 150 to 200mm, but in January, February and March the average figure is 400mm or more, peaking in March before dropping dramatically in April. Although you can have dry, sunny days during the wet season, it often rains every day – and, if you are unlucky, it can rain all day every day. Those who come to these islands expecting tropical sunshine in the wet season can go home very unhappy.

Further Reading

More has been written about the Family Islands, and particularly about Dunk Island, than any other island on the Great Barrier Reef. This is largely due to the activities of EJ Banfield, Dunk Island's famous 'Beachcomber', who lived there from 1897 to 1923. During that time, he wrote *The Confessions of a Beachcomber* (1908), *My Tropic Isle* (1911), *Tropic Days* (1918) and *Last Leaves from Dunk Island* (1925), which was published after his death. These books, with their detailed and sympathetic observations of the island's natural history, were immensely popular when first published and remain of great interest today. The *Confessions*, his first and most popular book, has been regularly reissued and reprinted until the present.

Equally interesting is Michael Noonan's biography of Banfield, *A Different Drummer*. This publication is also available in paperback. This is an extremely readable account of Banfield's family's move to Australia during the Victorian gold rush, his later career as a journalist, and his life on the island.

There have been various other books that dip into his writings. James Porter's *Beachcomber's Paradise* is an attractive coffee-table book that includes photographs of birds, plants, fish and other reef features, accompanied by Banfield's descriptions.

Even without Banfield's books, Dunk and the other Family Islands have been unusually well described. *Discovering the Family Islands*, by James G Porter, is a small book on Dunk Island and the other islands of the group. It has chapters on the islands' natural history, plants and wildlife, and Aboriginal history. He also covers their European discovery, the prolonged stay of EJ Banfield, and the islands' colourful collection of post-Banfield beachcombers, settlers, owners, artists and resort operators.

The other writer who has had some interesting things to say about Dunk is the poet Mark O'Connor, who spent some time at the Dunk resort from 1976 to 1977, working as its gardener. He wrote the Dunk Island chapter in *The Book of Australian Islands*, and his poem *The Sunhunters* (published in *The New Oxford Book of Australian Verse*) is about the island's rich rainforest. More amusingly, *Planting the Dunk Botanic Gardens* is a lengthy poem about the trials and tribulations of working as a resort gardener. It provides some interesting insights into resort management, the passing tourists and tropical lotus eating. It is included in O'Connor's anthology *The Fiesta of Men*.

Finally, the Queensland Department of Environment's publication *Hinchinbrook to Dunk Island National Parks*, a Park Guide leaflet, has a great deal of interesting information about the island and its natural history.

Dunk Island

Area:	10 sq km
Type:	continental
High point:	271m
Max visitors:	360

Dunk is a lush rainforest island with steep hills and some fine walks – 13km of walking trails wind across the island. Over 7 sq km of the 10 sq km island is set aside as a national park and the island is noted for its dense vegetation, prolific birdlife (nearly 150 species have been spotted here) and many butterflies. Some people say that it's the most attractive of the Barrier Reef islands. The climb to the top of Mt Kootaloo (271m) offers superb views over the other islands of the Family group and south towards the jagged peaks of Hinchinbrook Island.

Dunk Island has also had one of the most interesting histories of any of the Barrier Reef islands. It was named by Captain Cook and at one time had an Aboriginal population which named many of the island's features. The island is, however, inextricably linked with the period from 1897 to 1923 when EJ Banfield lived here and wrote *The Confessions of a Beachcomber* and his other books about the island and its natural history.

After his death in 1923, his wife, Bertha, stayed on the island with Essie McDonough, their faithful housekeeper, for another year and returned several more times before her death in 1933. Her ashes were buried with the Beachcomber in his grave just above the resort.

The Banfields' part of the island was the taken over by their friend, Townsville businessman Spenser Hopkins, and in 1934 their bungalow became the main building in a small resort. A year later, Hopkins sold most of the Banfield part of Dunk, keeping only the small section where the artists' colony is today.

The Original Beachcomber

'If a man does not keep pace with his companions, perhaps it is because he hears a different drummer. Let him step to the music which he hears.'

HD Thoreau

Born in England in 1852, EJ Banfield came to Australia when he was only two years old, during the Victorian gold rush. His father found his fortune not on the goldfields, but as the publisher of the *Ararat Advertiser*, a Victorian country-town newspaper that continues to this day. Eventually, Banfield moved north to Townsville where he worked as a journalist on the *Townsville Daily Bulletin*. He eventually became the paper's editor, but eventually overwork and ill health forced him to seek an alternative lifestyle.

His doctor had warned that he had only months to live if he continued working, and in 1897 with his wife, Bertha, he set up camp on Dunk Island, determined to follow the lead of the US writer Walden Thoreau in leading a life close to nature. For the following 26 years, until his death from appendicitis in 1923, he lived on Dunk continuously with only a handful of brief departures, the longest of which was in 1901 when he returned to his paper in Townsville for nine months. During those years on Dunk the Banfields lived a basically self-sufficient life, running a small farm and supplementing their income by the regular 'Rural Homilies' column he wrote for his Townsville paper and from the proceeds from his books about life on Dunk Island.

The books proved an instant inspiration to a host of other would-be Robinson Crusoes, none of whom lasted, but, more importantly, have been a continuing delight to the many people interested in this wonderful area's fascinating natural history. *The Confessions of a Beachcomber*, Banfield's first and most popular book, has been almost continuously in print since its original publication.

Banfield was worried that with his death his beloved island would inevitably be spoilt, but he would probably be delighted to find that despite the resort, most of Dunk today has changed remarkably little from his early description.

During WWII the RAAF set up a radar station on top of Mt Kootaloo that played a part in the Battle of the Coral Sea, the turning point in the Pacific war. The rusty remains of the radar equipment can still be seen.

Various changes of ownership followed the war until 1978 when TAA took over sole control of the resort. TAA was later renamed Australian Airlines, and was then taken over by Qantas Airlines. In 1998 Qantas sold the resort to P&O Resorts.

The Resort

At peak capacity Dunk accommodates 360 people, but despite this it manages to avoid being a real mass-market resort like South Molle or Great Keppel. The food is better here, the activities somewhat lower key, and things are done with a little more taste and style. Perhaps it's a throwback to the island's interesting history, but poor Banfield's name is exploited shamelessly – you could imagine the Beachcomber turning in his grave only a couple of hundred metres away, at the thought of rock 'n' roll night or island night at the Beachcomber restaurant.

Flora & Fauna

The Beachcomber's long and enlightened study of his island has focused a great deal of interest on the natural wonders of Dunk, and his writing forms a wonderful basis for a closer study of the island. Like the Aborigines, for whom Banfield had so much respect, he was a keen observer of nature and his books provide anecdotes, lists, observations and insights into the island's luxuriant vegetation, numerous birds, and other natural features. That Banfield was such a keen observer despite having lost one eye simply makes you respect the man all the more.

Dunk's rainforest vegetation is a direct result of its heavy rainfall. The towns on the nearby mainland annually tot up the highest rainfall figures in Australia, and although Dunk doesn't quite reach that level of dampness, it's definitely in the same league. When it rains in these parts it really rains. The result may be disheartening at times for holiday-makers chasing the sun, but for the vegetation it's terrific.

The island harbours a rich variety of birds, in which Banfield was keenly interested. The scrub fowl, or megapode, is one of the most interesting of the Family Island birds. The megapode hen, which is a little smaller than a domestic chicken, lays an enormous egg that it covers in a huge mound of decaying vegetation. The heat generated by the rotting leaves and other vegetable matter incubates the egg. The mounds can be several metres across and a couple of metres high – so large that they're easily mistaken for some natural feature.

You will often hear the scrub fowl's loud cackle and may glimpse them scampering away as you approach.

The yellow-breasted sunbird is a complete contrast – 'sired by a sunbeam, born of a flower, gaiety its badge,' wrote an obviously entranced Banfield. The brilliant yellow little bird hovers like a hummingbird while dipping its long curved bill into flowers. A great many other birds can be heard in the rainforest or seen flitting among the trees in the resort.

The animal life on Dunk is as sparse as the birds are prolific. Despite the proximity of the mainland, Dunk has no wallabies, no possums, no large mammals at all, apart from introduced species like feral pigs. There are echidnas (spiny anteaters), bats, some rats – including Banfield's own eponymous rat, the fruit-eating *Uromys banfieldi* – and plenty of lizards, but that's about it in the non-avian department.

Dunk does, however, have another aerial wonder – the wonderful butterflies seen all over the island, including Australia's two protected insects, the Cairns birdwing and the Ulysses. The Ulysses has become the symbol of the island, and although some people fear that they are not as prolific as during the Beachcomber's days, if you're observant you should be able to spot some of these large and spectacular butterflies.

The Ulysses is a big butterfly with a wingspan claimed to often exceed 10cm. The Ulysses' wings are edged with black and coloured deep, brilliant blue, like 'a flake of sky'. Apart from its size and bright colouring the Ulysses is also remarkable for its speed. No gently fluttering creature, it zooms across the sky like a bird of prey.

Information

The resort phone number is ☎ 4068 8199 and the fax number is 4068 8528. Reservations can be made through P&O Resorts on ☎ 13 2469.

There are a couple of pay phones (cards only) near the reception area, and EFTPOS facilities are also available.

There's a small shop in the upper level of

the main resort building with the usual island selection of toiletries, clothes, magazines, postcards and the usual. There is usually a good selection of Dunk books, including *The Confessions of a Beachcomber*.

Day-trippers are actively encouraged at Dunk, but there are certain sections of the resort, such as the main Cascades swimming pool, which are reserved for house guests only.

Banfield & the Gardens Unfortunately, very little trace remains of Banfield's time on the island. For a time during the 1930s, his house was used as the basis of the small resort. As the resort grew, the original structure was lost in extensions, renovations and rebuilds and in time it disappeared completely (probably some time in the 1940s). Similarly, his carefully tended gardens have also disappeared, although the overgrown area around his grave was once the homestead garden and keen botanists could probably find traces of the tropical fruit trees he spent so much time and energy growing. The stately avenue of palm trees that led up to his cottage remains, now leading from the resort up to the staff quarters. And, of course, the modern resort farm (non-working) is a direct descendant of the small farm Banfield once tended.

At one time, the resort gardener tried to follow Banfield's earlier aim to grow a wide variety of tropical fruit trees. Although that vision appears to have gone by the way, the resort's gardens are lush, colourful, carefully tended and a real delight. There's a weekly walking tour of the gardens and the garden staff are always happy to talk about their work.

Artists' Colony The Family Islands seem to attract artists: Noel Wood spent many years on Bedarra, and Deanna Conti is a long-term resident on Timana. Dunk's artist is Bruce Arthur, a former Olympic wrestler, who has lived on Dunk Island since the early 1970s, weaving large tapestries. He leases an area of land beyond the resort together with a number of other artists who form a small artists' colony. The colony welcomes visitors on Monday and Friday from 10 am to 3 pm when they charge you $4 and give you a brief introduction to the island and their activities, and an opportunity to purchase their work, which includes pottery, ceramics, jewellery and Bruce Arthur's tapestries.

Activities
The resort has the usual range of resort activities including squash and tennis courts, a small golf course, two swimming pools (one for house guests only) and a variety of indoor activities. More unusual activities include tandem skydiving ($275), horse riding ($35), archery and a clay-target shooting range.

Watersports equipment includes windsurfers, catamarans and paddle skis (all free to guests). You can also hire outboard dinghies ($80 a day), or go waterskiing ($20) and parasailing ($50). Visitors to the island who are not staying at the resort can still use some of the resort's equipment.

Dunk is a family resort and children are taken good care of. A children's meal time is organised between 5.30 and 6 pm. The Kids Club, free for children aged from three to 14 years, operates from 8.30 to 11.30 am and 4.30 to 8.30 pm. Activities on offer include fish feeding, face painting and bushwalks. Babysitting costs $10 an hour ($15 per hour after midnight).

Beaches Dunk has some fine beaches, although at low tide the water is often far too shallow to be enjoyable. There's no great snorkelling around Dunk either.

The main beaches include north-facing **Brammo Bay**, the sweep of sand right in front of the resort. At the Spit the beach turns the corner and becomes **Pallon Beach**, an equally long and fine stretch of sand facing south-west. At low tide you can wade across to nearby **Kumboola Island**. **Purtaboi Island**, directly north of Brammo Bay, is off limits when birds are nesting there.

Only a short stroll from the resort is

Muggy Muggy Beach, pleasantly quiet and secluded. Finally, you can walk an hour or so south to the long stretch of **Coconut Beach**. There are other smaller beaches, like **Naturist's Beach**, which you can reach by rock hopping even further south.

Dunk is very close to the mainland and although the dreaded box jellyfish have apparently not been spotted around the island, it's conceivable that they could get this far out from the coast during the November to March danger period. The resort gives guests information sheets about them, and there are large containers of vinegar kept by the beaches just in case. If jellyfish were present, the beaches least likely to have them would be north-facing Brammo Bay and Muggy Muggy Beach.

Walks Dunk has 13km of walking tracks and you can walk around almost all of the island in one 10km circuit, which is one of the most interesting and enjoyable walks to be found on any of the Barrier Reef islands.

The walk runs most of the length of the island and includes the 271m summit of Mt Kootaloo, the highest point on the island. Although the walk can be made in either direction, it's probably best to walk it clockwise as you can then follow the steep climb to the peak and the long descent along the ridge that forms the island's backbone with a pleasant pause and swim at Coconut Bay.

The walk takes about three hours but, with a picnic break on the beach, that can easily be extended to an all-day stroll. If you're a guest at the resort, they'll pack you a picnic lunch to take on your walk.

Starting from the northern edge of the resort, the walk first heads for Banfields' grave, but just before it there's the turn-off to Muggy Muggy Beach. For a short time the walk proceeds alongside a deep gully – Dunk's heavy rainfall means the many streams run noisily for most of the year. The trail then crosses the gully by a picturesque swing bridge and then starts to climb the hillside. Occasionally, there are views out over Brammo Bay and the resort,

but most of the time you walk in deep shade from the dense rainforest. During the January to March wet season it can be extremely humid and you can work up a prodigious sweat – by the time you reach the top of the peak your clothes will be soaking.

Eventually, you reach a signposted junction where the trail meets the circuit track around the top of Mt Kootaloo. From here you can continue directly to Palm Valley, but the longer and more interesting way is to follow the Mt Kootaloo sign to the left. This takes you right around the peak to the turn-off up to the actual summit, before continuing on to Palm Valley. In front of you here is Kumboola Island, Thorpe Island and Bedarra Island; Battleship Rock is the bare rock rising just east of Bedarra, and Goold and Hinchinbrook are far in the background.

The short spur leads off from here to the summit, topped by the rusting, crumpled remains of a WWII radar installation. The timber lookout platform at the summit was constructed commando-style by the Australian Army in late 1993. The trail actually continues beyond that point for a short distance before fading out.

Backtracking down to the circuit track you then turn right and descend steeply to a junction signposted back to the resort and on, again, to Palm Valley. If you head back towards the resort you soon reach the earlier junction where you started the circuit of the peak. The straightforward Resort-Mt Kootaloo round trip takes about two hours.

Continuing on the longer walk you follow the ridge line towards Palm Valley, dropping down to a saddle then climbing up again, passing an easily missed turn-off back to the resort via the farm area, and eventually reaching the Coconut Beach Lookout. You may not be able to see the beach unless the vegetation has been cut back recently. From here the trail descends slowly, following a stream bordered by palms in the aptly named Palm Valley. Eventually, the trail reaches the coast and immediately doubles back towards the resort, running only a few metres away from the beach.

As with other Dunk beaches, the water can be very shallow if the tide is low, but this is still a pleasant place for a break. At the resort end of the beach there's a picnic table. From here you will have to head back onto the trail, because the shore is fringed with mangrove swamps beyond the rocky headland. The trail climbs round the headland, passes the entrance to the artists' colony and crosses a swiftly flowing little stream before running along the edge of the farm back to the resort. At the airstrip you can either walk along the roadway on the inland side, or cross to the beach and walk down to the sandspit point along Pallon Beach.

This one walk covers almost all the available walking track on the island. The other alternatives are to take the shortcut down from the ridge track through the farm to the resort, or to rock hop along the coast from Coconut Beach south to Staff Beach and Naturist's Beach. The coastal track from the resort round to the pleasantly secluded Muggy Muggy Beach is only about a kilometre in length.

Cruises The high-speed catamaran MV *Quick Cat* makes daily trips to Beaver Cay on the Great Barrier Reef. Departures are at 11.30 am, returning at 4.30 pm, and the cost of $117 includes lunch. It takes about 50 minutes to get out to the reef, where you can snorkel, observe the reef through a glass-bottom boat or from a semi-submersible, or certified divers can get in a couple of dives ($50/80 for one/two dives).

Day cruises around the Family Islands on the *Neptunius* cost $79; there's also a sunset cruise for $39. Fishing enthusiasts can get out on the *Reef Affair III* for the day ($160). The *Lawrence Kavanagh* also does a daily cruise around the islands, departing every day at 1.45 pm and costing $22.

Scenic flights over the Family Islands can also be arranged, with a 30 minute low-level flight typically costing $50 per person (minimum of four people).

Places to Stay

Camping Like a number of other islands, Dunk is a resort island where you can also camp. Most of the island is national park, and camping is permitted at the campsite right across from the jetty on the sandspit at the north-west end of the island. The site is nothing flash, but campers have access to the resort's day-use area. It has toilets, tables and BBQs, and showers and drinking water are available. There is a maximum limit of 30 campers and a maximum stay of three days. Bookings are handled by the resort reception.

The Resort The resort's 141 rooms are of four types and costs (for one or two people) are:

Banfield Units	$340
Garden Cabanas	$410
Beachfront Units	$480
Bayview Villas	$520

The tariff is room-only but includes most activities – generally it's the powered activities that cost extra. Children aged three to 14 years are charged at $30. Two/three meal packages are $57/75 ($30/38 for children) per person per day.

The Banfield Units and Garden Cabana rooms are mostly set back from the beachfront, while the Beachfront Units and Bayview Villas face the water, and the villas also have impressive views out over Brammo Bay. All rooms have attached bathroom, air-conditioning and ceiling fans, a patio or veranda, telephone, TV with in-house videos, tea/coffee-making facilities, and a refrigerator.

The Banfield Units are fairly straightforward. Garden Cabanas are in groups of four, have cathedral ceilings, a double and one or two single beds, and shady verandas. The larger Beachfront Units have a double and a single bed, and there are some interconnecting rooms. The top of the range Bayview Villas are more modern. Although smallish, they are bright and airy with a double and a divan bed, and so are really not suitable for families. The Beachfront Units and Bayview Villas have hip baths as well as showers. There are laundry blocks with washing machines and dryers. Although the rooms are basically straightforward boxes, they're quite comfortable and the lush Dunk greenery certainly helps to hide them.

Places to Eat

Dunk's dining possibilities should keep most people happy. There's always the risk at larger resorts of the food becoming an exercise in tropical island pub food.

Meal times in the main *Beachcomber* restaurant when the resort is busy can involve feeding 350-plus guests, but fortunately, they seem to cope with aplomb. Breakfast is the usual buffet-style one but there's plenty of fresh fruit, a wide choice of cereals and hot food from food warmers as well. Lunch is also usually a buffet-style affair. Dinner is served from a menu with a choice of starters ($8 to $14), main courses ($23) and dessert. It's good food, pleasantly served and backed up by a solid, if not inspired wine list with a variety of wines from around $20 to $40. In the Beachcomber you're likely to find the usual (for Barrier Reef resorts) shortage of tables for two – if you want a romantic tête-à-tête or simply don't feel like making new acquaintances, it's wise to book a table.

Outsiders can also eat in the Beachcomber restaurant if they buy a resort pass for $10, or a $25 pass that includes lunch.

EJ's on the Deck is a casual, open-air lunch-time cafe, with an interesting menu. Inevitable focaccias ($10) are supplemented by dishes such as laksa ($10) and gulf prawn wontons ($15).

Dunk also has its smaller, more formal *Cascades* restaurant, by the Cascades swimming pool away from the main resort building. There's an à la carte menu, but with more inspired and exotic choices – lobster, buffalo, duck, even crocodile – and the food is excellent. Entrées range from $12 to $18, mains from $25 to $30. Cascades is not open every night, so check first.

Campers or day visitors to the island (or resort guests who can't last from one meal to the next) can also find food at the *Tavern by the Jetty*, where there's typical fast-food featuring, among other staples, burgers ($4), and fish and chips and salad ($10).

Getting There & Away

Air Dunk has an airstrip and there are regular flights to and from Cairns (40 minutes, $134) and Townsville (45 minutes, $135). Dunk is also the arrival point for guests flying in bound for Bedarra Island.

Sea Dowd's Water Taxis (☎ 4768 8310) has seven daily services from Wongaling Beach to Dunk, and back. The fare is $22 return. Surprisingly, there is no jetty at Wongaling and the water taxi doesn't use the jetty at Dunk, so at either end passengers will have to get their feet wet.

There are also several cruise companies based at the Clump Point jetty, just north of Mission Beach. Day trips to the island with the *Quick Cat* (☎ 4068 7289) cost $22, or you can do a day trip out to the reef, which offers snorkelling and a ride in a glass-bottomed boat, for $122.

The MV *Lawrence Kavanagh* (☎ 4068 7211) does Dunk Island trips from $18, and for another $22 you can also join its 1½ hour cruise around Bedarra. Lunch is available for $8.

Bedarra Island

Area:	1 sq km
Type:	continental
High point:	107m
Max visitors:	32

Bedarra Island is 6km south of Dunk and about 5km offshore. The island is shown as Richards Island on marine charts but not on general maps.

Like Dunk, Bedarra is a rainforest island with natural springs. It is a rocky, hilly island cloaked in rainforest and fringed with some fine, sandy beaches, a short stretch of mangroves and a wildly tumbled collections of giant boulders. Off to the south-east end is tiny Pee-Rahm-Ah Island, also known as Battleship Rock.

Bedarra, like the other islands of the Family group, has a history of Aboriginal habitation and it has subsequently had an interesting and varied European history. The publication of Banfield's *The Confessions of a Beachcomber* (see the Dunk Island section) flushed numerous other would-be beachcombers out of the woodwork, including Captain Henry Allason, who came over from England in 1913, sought Banfield's advice on a suitable island, and purchased the whole of Bedarra from the Queensland Land Department for £20. They threw in Timana Island as well.

Allason set up home near the sandspit and soon became locally famous for setting out on long distance swims from one island to another. Unfortunately for the captain, his spell of island lotus-eating was a short one. Only a year later WWI erupted in Europe, and he was called up and was later gassed in France during one of the notorious episodes of chemical warfare. Although he survived, he spent the rest of his life convalescing in Nice in the south of France.

Allason's £20 investment proved to be a sound one, however, as he sold the island during the 1920s to Ivan Menzies for £500. Menzies' plan to turn the island into a home for underprivileged English boys came to nothing, and in 1934 he sold the island to a group known as the Harris syndicate. The Harris group also failed to make anything of their island ownership, although in 1936 they did sell a corner of the island to the Australian artist Noel Wood. He built a

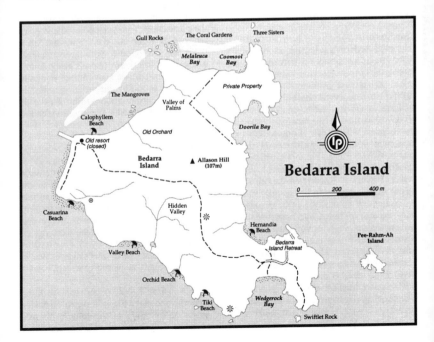

home on the peninsula between Doorila and Coomool Bay and only moved in 1993.

The rest of the island went back and forth between various parties until in 1940 the Englishman Dick Greatrix and the Frenchman Pierre Huret bought the whole thing and established the gardens of the Hideaway Resort at the sandspit end of the island. Meanwhile, John Busst, another artist, leased the south-east corner of the island and his homestead eventually became the Plantation Resort, now Bedarra Island Retreat.

In 1947 Greatrix and Huret sold out to the Bussts and in subsequent years more owners came and went before TAA (later Australian Airlines, now part of Qantas) bought the northern part, including the Hideaway Resort (currently closed), in 1980, and the southern part, including the Plantation Resort, in 1981. The two resorts were owned and managed by Qantas until early 1998 when they were bought by P&O Resorts, the current owner.

The Resort

Although Bedarra's resort has a long history with guests first staying here during the 1940s, the current resort is a late 1980s creation. It has just 16 individual villas, so full-house usually means only 32 guests. Bedarra Island Retreat is small and exclusive; so exclusive in fact that intrusive day-trippers – and pesky Lonely Planet researchers – are not welcome. (For this reason we were not able to visit the island for this latest update.) A second similar resort (Hideaway Resort) on the other side of the island appears to be closed.

Exclusivity comes at a price. Bedarra is very expensive, but it interprets the words 'all-inclusive' in a novel way. At other resorts the tariff may include all your meals and non-powered equipment like windsurfers and catamarans, with some letting you use powered equipment as well, but at Bedarra absolutely everything is included. The bar, for example, doesn't have a barman. If you feel like a bottle of French champagne, you just stroll over to the cooler and help yourself – and some legendary tales of Moet & Chandon consumption have leaked out. If you want to take an outboard dinghy to find your own private beach, that's included too. The staff will pack you up a picnic (complete with the French champagne if you wish), and off you go.

Information

The phone number for the resorts is ☎ 4068 8233, the fax number is 4068 8215, and the address is Bedarra Bay Resort, Bedarra Island, via Townsville, Qld 4810. Reservations can be made through P&O Resorts on ☎ 13 2469.

There's a small 'shop' in the resort with essentials such as suntan lotion, toiletries, cigarettes, postcards and the like. You help yourself and note what you've taken to be charged to your account.

Activities

Bedarra is not a heavy-activity resort, but the catamarans, windsurfers, paddle skis are all waiting right out the front; and since there are few people, you rarely have to queue up to use them. There's also a tennis court and, of course, a swimming pool and spa. There is a TV and video recorder in each room, although on rainy days you might wish they had a few more videos as well.

Beaches Bedarra has some great beaches – Wedgerock and Hernandia, on each side of the Bedarra Island Retreat, are particularly fine. Doorila Bay, directly facing Hernandia and the resort, was commended by Banfield as the prettiest spot in the Family Islands, but is private property. There are several other small beaches around the western side of the island, accessible by dinghy. Nearby Wheeler Island has a fine sandspit beach, and it's unlikely to be too crowded.

Walks There's only one real walk on Bedarra, and that's the 1.5km stroll from the resort on one side to the jetty at the old resort on the other. The walk through dense rainforest takes from half an hour to 45 minutes and is rated by the resorts as 'strenuous', which it probably is for some of their elderly guests. It can also be rather slippery if there has been heavy rain.

Starting from the Bedarra Island Retreat end the trail commences only a few steps beyond the dining room terrace and almost immediately climbs steeply upwards, eventually reaching the resort's water tank and then continuing up to a lookout with a survey marker on a large rock beside the track. Through the trees you can see down over Hernandia Beach and the resort, but this is the only view you glimpse on the whole walk. The entire rest of the way you are in dense, lush rainforest – which doesn't mean there isn't plenty to see and hear. There are flowers, creepers, ferns, the twittering of birds, the towering mounds of megapode nests and, if you're lucky, an occasional glimpse of the bird itself.

From the lookout the trail undulates gently, passing a short distance to the south of Allason Hill (107m), the highest point on the island. The trail then drops gently down to the other side.

A shorter alternative walk starts from just behind the Bedarra Island Retreat tennis court and winds up to Swiftlet Rock overlooking Battleship Rock, Wheeler Island and The Triplets. It's a fine view across these other islands, but you're asked not to climb on the rocks since this is one of the few nesting places of the grey swiftlet.

Cruises The resort will transfer you over to Dunk Island to join Barrier Reef cruises or helicopter flights, and the fishing charter boat *Reef Affair III* and local island cruise boat *Neptunius* will also operate from Bedarra. The general cost is POA, but the resort often organises parties of 6 to 8 for the fishing trips or 10 to 15 people for the local island cruises.

Places to Stay

Both resorts were rebuilt by Byron Bay architect Christine Vadasz. Bedarra Island Retreat was reopened after its total rebuild in 1986 and from the bay in front of the resort the 16 villas are virtually completely hidden in the rainforest. Each villa has a two level room with a sleeping area above and a living area below (a few steps lower in some, under a mezzanine level in others). Out the front there's a veranda where you can laze, getting glimpses of the sea and the rocky island coast. The rooms are very pleasant indeed, luxurious enough but maintaining an island feeling. At Bedarra you know you're on an island, not in some faceless five-star resort.

Bedarra Island Retreat actually has two bays: the main resort building and most of the villas overlook Hernandia Beach, and a couple more villas look out on to Wedgerock Beach on the other side of the peninsula. The two bays are only minutes' walk apart so you can easily switch beaches as the sun, the wind or the mood dictate. They're both very fine beaches – Bedarra is blessed with some of the nicest beaches to be found on the Barrier Reef islands.

Daily costs at Bedarra are $1000/1290 for one/two people. As noted above, that is very 'all-inclusive' – it's rather like being a guest at the home of a very rich friend.

Places to Eat

The Bedarra Retreat's small size and high costs are reflected in the food – they can afford to cater for personal whims, and if you want to indulge yourself, they'll go out of their way to help you. If your idea of tropical island eating is oysters and lobster for every meal, I'm sure they'd lay them on for you. So the menu on offer need only be a starting point, although most visitors will find it quite interesting enough.

Breakfast is the usual combination of serve-yourself juices, fruit and cereals followed by toast, croissants, muffins or a full cooked breakfast if you wish. Lunch is served from a menu with interesting light dishes like a cold champagne and fruit soup or an avocado and lime soup, followed by a spicy Thai salad or more conventional meat or fish dishes. Of course, many guests take an outboard dinghy and picnic off to find their own beach, or cross over to the other resort to see how the other half lives.

Dinner is usually preceded by drinks and hors d'oeuvres in the help yourself bar, and the resort's small guest list makes it a pleasantly social occasion. You can also scan the dinner menu at this point and decide what wine to take down from the shelf. Again, there's an interesting and imaginative menu.

Getting There & Away
Bedarra is reached from Dunk, a 20 minute boat ride away. The Bedarra boat connects with Dunk flights or the water taxis between the mainland and Dunk.

Other Family Islands

The five small national park islands of the Family group are Wheeler, Coombe, Smith, Bowden and Hudson islands. They cover a total of 1.2 sq km and their tangled vegetation is strongly influenced by the prevailing winds.

The windswept south-eastern side of the islands is covered in a tangle of casuarinas, wattles and eucalypts, while the sheltered northern side has grander and more stately stands of figs, palms, milky pine, satin ash and other rainforest species.

The prevailing winds and seas have also formed sand spits on the island's north-west sides, which provide convenient sheltered landing areas for boats.

Between Bedarra and Dunk lies the privately owned Timana Island, where Deanna Conti, an artist and wool-tapestry weaver, has lived for many years. There are also a couple of smaller national park islands just off Dunk. Tiny Purtaboi lies just to the north-west; incoming or outgoing flights generally pass over it. Kumboola and Mung-Um-Gnackum islands, mere dots on the map, are just to the south-west.

Places to Stay
With a permit from the Department of Environment at Cardwell, you can camp on Wheeler and Coombe islands. There are tables at the campsites, but no toilet facilities. Only Wheeler has fresh water, and then only during the cooler months. The maximum number of campers is limited to 20 on Wheeler Island, and 10 on Coombe Island.

Getting There & Away
Charter boats operate to these island from Clump Point jetty at Mission Beach, or from Cardwell. There are also boat ramps at Hull River and Tully River.

Islands off Cairns

Cairns is the biggest tourist centre along the Great Barrier Reef, and there is a constant stream of vessels heading out to the islands and reefs off the coast. Cairns has two popular islands close by: Fitzroy and Green islands, both of which attract lots of day-trippers (too many, some think) and some overnighters too. The resorts on both of these islands are operated by the cruise company Great Adventures, which in turn is owned by the Japanese corporation Daikyo.

Just up the coast off Port Douglas are the Low Isles, which are popular cays for day tripping, although nowhere near as commercialised as Green Island. South of Cairns, the Frankland Islands group is a cluster of undeveloped national park islands. You can do day trips to these islands, or camp overnight – or longer.

There are also numerous reefs, popular targets for the hordes of scuba divers who head out from Cairns. Tiny Michaelmas Cay, with its huge population of seabirds, is one of the most popular destinations.

Getting There & Away

There is an armada of tourist operators out of Cairns. Great Adventures, which operates the resorts at Fitzroy and Green islands and owns a fleet of high-speed catamarans, is the biggest name, with numerous services and cruises operating to the two islands and to the other reefs and cays. Sunlover is another big operator, while there are also literally dozens of smaller operators offering a huge range of possibilities, including transport to the islands, reef trips, sailing cruises and overnight diving expeditions.

If you want something faster, helicopters go out to the reef as well. Contact Helijet (☎ 1800 630 755) for details. Northern Air Adventures (☎ 4035 9156) has joy flights over the reef and islands; a 30 minute flight ($50) takes you out over Green Island and Arlington and Upton reefs, while a 60 minute flight ($90) also includes Batt Reef.

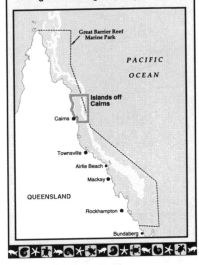

ISLANDS OFF CAIRNS

Highlights
- Take in the tour of the Reefarm research facility on Fitzroy Island
- Book a cruise to the outer Barrier Reef and go snorkelling or diving

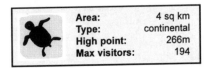

Fitzroy Island

Area:	4 sq km
Type:	continental
High point:	266m
Max visitors:	194

Six kilometres off the coast and 26km south-east of Cairns, Fitzroy Island has been developed as a resort since 1981. The lighthouse on the island and other activities, though, date from far earlier.

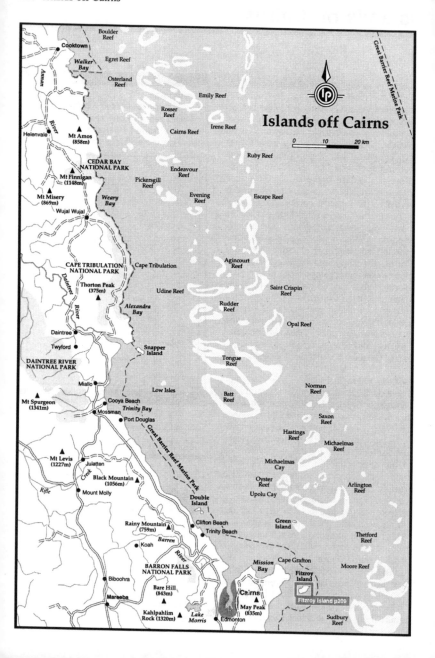

Islands off Cairns

Fitzroy is a larger continental island with beaches that are covered in coral, so they are not ideal for swimming and sunbathing. There's good coral for snorkelling only 50m off the beach in the resort area. The island also has its own dive school.

The island was named by Captain Cook after the Duke of Grafton, a noted politician of the era who had a reputation for putting more effort into wine, women and horse racing than government. Phillip King stopped at Fitzroy in 1819 and his good report on the anchorage, fresh water and supplies of timber made Welcome Bay (where the resort is now located) a popular shelter for passing ships.

In 1877 the island was made a quarantine station for Chinese immigrants bound for the north Queensland goldfields. New arrivals were supposed to stay there for 16 days to ensure that they were free of smallpox, and there were soon 3000 of them squeezed onto the island. Inevitably, the miserable conditions led to a violent dispute with the colonial authorities and the island still has a number of Chinese graves from that period. Fitzroy Island also had a bêches-de-mer industry for a time.

Information

The resort phone number is ☎ 4051 9588, and the fax number is 4052 1335. For reservations contact Great Adventures (☎ 1800 079 080; greatadventures@internetnorth .com.au).

There is also a resort shop selling the usual variety of souvenirs, clothing and beach gear. There are pay phones in the resort, and reception has EFTPOS facilities.

Reefarm

Located just beyond the island's campsite, Reefarm is a giant-clam breeding centre and pearl-oyster hatchery. Here research is being conducted to commercially breed the giant reef clams whose numbers have been severely reduced by Asian poachers, where the adductor muscle has a reputation as an aphrodisiac. After initially raising the clams in tanks, they are transplanted to the reef just off the island.

A half-hour educational program that explains the work being done here is held every day at 10 and 10.45 am and 1 pm. Admission (which helps support the important work being done here) costs $8 for adults and $4 for children.

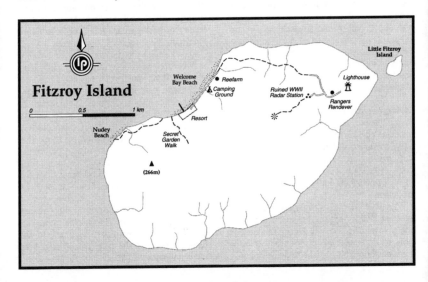

Wildlife

Fitzroy Island has a large variety of birdlife, butterflies, iguanas, as well as its own token kangaroo.

Activities

The resort has a variety of watersports equipment for hire, including catamarans ($19 an hour), windsurfers ($11 an hour), paddle skis ($7.50 an hour) and canoes ($8.50 an hour).

There's a swimming pool in the resort area, but it's used by both day-trippers and resort guests and tends to be rather crowded, especially on weekends.

Otherwise, this is a resort where you make your own amusements.

Beaches & Snorkelling Fitzroy's beaches are not ideal for lazy sunbathing and dabbling in ankle-deep water.

The **Welcome Bay** beach in front of the resort is made up of broken coral, so it's not very comfortable for lying on. It also shelves off very steeply from the shore so you're out of your depth within a few paces. On the other hand, there is some good coral for snorkelling only a few strokes out from the shore at both ends of the main resort beach.

A short walk round from the resort area to the south-west brings you to **Nudey Beach**. The sand here is much more conducive to lazy days in the sun and it's reputed to be a good place to collect an all over suntan – hence the name.

Diving Fitzroy can be a good place to do a diving course, safe from the day-to-day distractions of Cairns, with good diving water right offshore and the Great Barrier Reef itself not far out. The Great Diving Adventures dive shop offers a PADI course for $360, or $495 including gear and accommodation.

The dive shop also hires out snorkelling gear for $10 a day, diving gear for $55 for one dive or $75 for two. And it is also possible to do a special introductory dive off the island for $60.

Walks Fitzroy has several good walks through the island's lush and often surprisingly dense rainforest, or up the boulder-strewn slopes to the peak.

Secret Garden Walk Starting from behind the Rainforest Restaurant, a 20 minute stroll follows a damp valley running inland with dense rainforest vegetation embellished with ferns and creepers. The walk ends at a picturesque jumble of boulders topped by ferns.

Lighthouse & Peak A pleasant walk takes you to the lighthouse at the north-east end of the island and on to it's high point.

The walk starts past the bunkrooms and campsite and first of all passes the giant-clam breeding centre. It is through shady rainforest for the first part, but enters open bushland higher up. Bring a hat and water.

The lighthouse walk runs up an often very steep paved vehicle track, with glimpses of Green Island to the north. A lighthouse was originally established here in 1943, rebuilt in 1959, and again in 1973. The most recent rebuild has left an extremely inelegant structure, seemingly designed by the Australian government's 'public-toilet' architectural team. It's no longer staffed, and has been replaced by an automatic beacon on Little Fitzroy Island. There is a national parks ranger's residence just before the old lighthouse – definitely not a hardship posting!

Retrace your steps down from the lighthouse and another paved vehicle track branches off east and climbs up to the site of a now demolished WWII radar station. From here it is a real walking track that climbs steadily up the ridge line to the 266m peak, which is Fitzroy's high point. There are good views northward from the huge boulders that are strewn around the top. Green Island is clearly visible.

From the peak it's a matter of retracing your steps back to the resort, although an alternative trail from the peak back to the resort, closed at the time of writing, may have reopened.

Places to Stay

Although Fitzroy is to a large extent a day trip island (fast catamarans shuttle out regularly from Cairns with the mainland only a stone's throw away), there is also a variety of accommodation and the island is one of the few along the Great Barrier Reef with real possibilities for travellers on a very tight budget.

Overnight possibilities at Fitzroy come in three categories – villas, bunkrooms and the campsite.

Camping The shady campsite is owned by the local council but administered by the Queensland Department of Environment. Permits must be obtained in advance from the Department of Environment office in Cairns.

It's next to the resort and just a stone's throw from the beach, and costs $3.50 per person.

There are several electric BBQs and cold showers, and campers have access to most of the resort's facilities.

Beach House Bungalows Cairns is the backpackers' capital of the Queensland coast, so it's only right that there should be backpackers' accommodation on an island near Cairns.

Fitzroy's *Beach House Bungalows* are typical bunkrooms for four people; straightforward rooms with just two-bunk units and a locker for each bed. Toilets and showers are shared and there's a kitchen and dining area, plus plenty of fridge space.

Nightly costs are $28 for a bed or $112 if you take a whole room for four. Costs include bed linen (towels can be hired) but they are room-only. Meals are available at the day visitors' area, the resort restaurant or you can fix your own food – bring supplies with you from Cairns.

Villas Strung along the waterfront there are just eight of the villa units, straightforward but comfortable and quite attractive little units. They comprise a veranda out the front, a bedroom with double bed, separated by the bathroom and the fridge and tea/coffee-making area from a second mini-bedroom with a bunk-bed unit.

The units cost $240/340 a single/double and $79 for each child (four to 14). These costs include breakfast and dinner at the Rainforest Resturant; you fend for yourself at lunch time.

Places to Eat

In the main part of the resort, by the swimming pool, there are a couple of open-air eating possibilities. The kiosk is open from 8.30 am to 4.30 pm and does straightforward snacks and light meals of the fish and chips, reheated pizzas, pies, pasties and sandwiches variety. It's a bit downmarket and regularly resonates to the sounds of the staff calling out 'Number 45, your meal is now ready'.

At lunch time the *Flare Grill* here does pub food like steak and chips, fish and salad and so on. This is where you eat when you're on a day trip that includes lunch as part of the package. There's also the *Mango Bar*, which is open from 10 am until late for drinks.

Villa residents have breakfast and dinner at the *Rainforest Restaurant*, which is included in their room costs. The restaurant is also open to other island visitors and the food here is surprisingly good. A three course set menu is $17.50.

Getting There & Away

Great Adventures (☎ 1800 079 080), which operates the resorts at both Fitzroy and Green islands, has a variety of excursions to Fitzroy. A return trip to Fitzroy Island costs $30 for transport only, or $46 for a half-day trip (10.30 am to 3.30 pm) with lunch and snorkelling gear thrown in. The trip takes about 45 minutes each way. You can get picked up from your accommodation in Cairns for an extra $5.

Sunlover Cruises (☎ 1800 810 512) has day trips to the outer reef (Moore Reef), with a one hour stop at Fitzroy Island ($130). Transport only to Fitzroy Island costs $30 return.

Green Island

Area:	0.13 sq km
Type:	coral cay
High point:	3m
Max visitors:	90

Offshore from Cairns, 27km to the north-east, Green Island is a true coral cay. The island is only 660m long by 260m wide and rises only a few metres above sea level. The huge platform of coral debris that surrounds the island, and is indeed the island itself, is gradually being pushed north-westward by the prevailing currents. Green Island is by far the most accessible of the Barrier Reef's true coral cays.

The island and its surrounding reef are all national park.

It was named by Captain Cook, but not for its forest cover – Green was the chief astronomer on the *Endeavour*. In the 1870s, at the peak of the bêche-de-mer boom, the island was squabbled over by gatherers of that oriental delicacy, and most of the island's trees were cut down for fires to boil the bêche-de-mer.

Local eccentric George 'Yorkey' Lawson later settled on the island, which he claimed was haunted by victims of the bêche-de-mer battles. In the 1890s he started to develop the island as a picnic spot for Cairns residents and in 1937, already suffering from over-use, the island was made into a national park. In 1974 the surrounding reef area was declared a marine park.

Green Island is an extremely popular day trip from Cairns, and is visited by over 200,000 people a year. It's actually a really beautiful island, and if you take a 10 minute stroll down from where you arrive to the other end of the island you can forget that the tourist clutter is even there.

The beach, right around the island, is beautiful, the water fine, the fish still reasonably prolific, although the coral is not as extensive as it used to be, partly due to that reef scourge the crown-of-thorns starfish.

The island's vegetation makes an interesting contrast to the cays further south. Here it is denser, rainforest-style vegetation, unlike the pisonia dominated cover of the southern cays.

The small resort reopened in 1994 after a $55 million rebuild.

Information

The resort phone number is ☎ 4031 3300 or ☎ 1800 673 366 toll-free, the fax number is 4052 1511, and the postal address is Green Island Resort, PO Box 898, Cairns, Qld 4870.

There's also a clothing boutique and a resort shop, selling T-shirts, souvenirs, sunscreen, hats, film, books and magazines. There are pay phones in the day visitors' area, beside the Lite Bites ice-cream bar.

Despite the large number of day-trippers, the resort is big enough not to feel crowded and yet not so big that it feels impersonal. House guests are also well screened from the day-trippers, who are only on the island between 9.15 am and 4.30 pm.

The island is far enough from the coast for the waters to be box-jellyfish free all year round.

Marineland Melanesia

Green Island's most interesting attraction is Marineland Melanesia, which has been on the island for more than 20 years. This museum, gallery and aquarium houses an eclectic private collection of Melanesian art and artefacts, plus a wide variety of fish and corals in aquarium tanks, and larger creatures like turtles and stingrays in pools or enclosures. It's also home to some of the largest crocodiles in captivity. Admission costs $7 for adults and $3 for children.

Other Attractions

At the end of the pier is the now rather ancient and decidedly less than state-of-the-art underwater observatory, where lots of fish can be seen around the windows 5m below sea level.

The observatory was built in 1954, and it's not really worth the $3 admission to see the unimpressive collection of coral, although there are plenty of colourful fish. If you are a house guest or come to Green Island on one of the day trips (rather than the transport only trips), admission to these wonders is included.

Activities

The time you get on the island on a typical day trip is quite enough to have a wander around it, go for a swim, and see as many of the attractions as you need to. It takes about 15 minutes to walk right around the island.

The resort has a section for day visitors with a very pleasant swimming pool surrounded by banana lounges and umbrellas, a bar and several eateries.

The dive shop rents out snorkelling gear for $10 a day and operates guided snorkelling tours for $15 ($25 including gear hire). You can do an introductory dive off the island for $85, and certified divers can hire a full set of gear with one tank for $50.

Glass-bottom boats ($8) and semi-submersibles ($12) operate short trips from the pier.

On the beach there are beach lounges and umbrellas, although these cost $5 each! Watersports include canoes ($10 per hour), surf skis ($10), parasailing ($75) and sailboards ($20).

Places to Stay

The very stylish two-storey accommodation units have been built right in and among the trees, and so are very unintrusive. The lush vegetation also gives a lot of privacy – from the day-tripper area you'd hardly even know that there was any more to the resort, even though it is all in a very small area.

There are two levels of accommodation: 36 Island Rooms and 10 Reef Suites. All rooms are beautifully and comfortably furnished, featuring lots of timber and polished floors. Facilities include air-conditioning, fan, TV, phone, fridge, balcony or veranda,

and an en-suite with separate shower and bathtub. Most of the rooms look out on a wall of tropical vegetation, while some look over the resort pool area. All guests have access to laundry facilities complete with washers, dryers and irons.

The Island Rooms have either a king-size bed or two double beds, and cots and roll-away beds are also available. There are also a few interconnecting rooms suitable for families. The split-level Reef Suites are slightly larger than the Island Rooms, and have a king-size bed and a separate changing room.

The room rates are $500 for the Island Rooms, $600 for the Reef Suites. Children under 15 stay free of charge, unless an extra bed is needed, in which case there is a charge of $60. These rates include use of watersports equipment and most activities.

Places to Eat

The day visitors' area has several eating options. At the *Canopy Grill* the choices range from fish and chips for $11.50 down to pies or chips ($3.50), and you eat at the open-air tables beside the pool. There's also *Reflections*, a pool-side cocktail bar, and the *Lite Bites* ice-cream bar.

The more formal *Emeralds Restaurant* is open to both day-trippers and house guests, and has a timber-decked outdoor section in addition to an interior section, which is reserved for house guests' use at lunch time. Breakfast is outdoors and is the usual buffet; it is finished by the time the first day-trippers arrive. Lunch consists of snacks and salads (from $12 to $15), and mainly seafood main courses (from $17).

In the evening the house guests can have a three or five course set menu ($45 or $75 respectively) or order à la carte. There's a tempting variety of dishes available, with seafood featuring heavily. Entrees range from laksa to crab salad, and cost $12 to $15. A choice of about 10 main courses, ranging from $22 to $30, includes at least one vegetarian dish and other interesting options such as pan-fried stingray or coral trout. Desserts are in the $7.50 to $10 range.

The wine list features a wide selection of mostly Australian wines in the $30 to $50 range, but goes right up to Hill of Grace at $210 and the obligatory Dom Perignon at $200 a pop.

Getting There & Away
Green Island is 27km north-east of Cairns, about halfway to the outer reef. Great Adventures (☎ toll-free 1800 079 080) is the main operator to Green Island and will take you out and back for $50 by fast catamaran. The return trip plus the various island activities will cost you $65, or $90 with lunch. Finally, you can go further afield, for $125 you can have three hours on Green Island, plus a visit to Michaelmas Cay.

There are other operators to Green Island. The *Big Cat* (☎ 4051 0444) does a return trip in 80 minutes for $42, which includes either snorkelling or a glass-bottom boat trip; another $8 gets you a BBQ lunch.

Other Islands

You can conveniently visit a number of islands from Cairns on day trips. South of Fitzroy are the Frankland Islands; Michaelmas Cay is a popular day trip north of Green Island; and the Low Islands are an enormously popular day trip from Port Douglas.

Because the reef is closer to the mainland at this point, Cairns has become a popular jumping-off point for lots of diving trips heading out to the reefs.

Diving Trips
There are numerous boats operating Cairns, offering day trips, or longer ones. Popular day trip targets out of Cairns include Moore Reef beyond Fitzroy Island, Norman Reef to the north of Green Island, or the Agincourt Reefs, reached from Port Douglas. The Cod Hole, a dive site on the outer reef off Lizard Island noted for its huge potato cod (or grouper), is a particular attraction.

A typical trip would be four days and three nights aboard the *Taka II*, costing from $600 including equipment, 11 dives and all meals.

Four days and three nights on *Rum Runner* (☎ 4042 7430), which heads 240km offshore to Holmes Reef in the Coral Sea, costs $910, including 11 dives, meals and equipment. Four days to the Cod Hole and Bougainville Reef is also $910. Standby rates of around $600 are available if space permits and you book less than five days in advance.

FRANKLAND ISLANDS
The Frankland Islands are a group of relatively untouched national park islands south of Fitzroy Island and about 12km off the coast. They were named by Captain Cook after Admiral Sir Thomas Frankland. The islands consist of High Island to the north and four smaller islands – Normanby, Mabel, Round and Russell islands – to the south.

They're continental islands with good beaches and some fine snorkelling. On the day trips from Cairns the island time is usually spent on Normanby Island while divers go to Round Island.

Places to Stay
Camping drop-offs can be arranged on High or Russell islands, but there are no facilities on either island so you must come totally equipped. Usually campers go to Russell Island; High Island drop-offs are only made at peak periods (like Christmas) when Russell is full.

A maximum of 15 campers are allowed on each island. Permits are available from the Department of Environment office in Cairns.

Getting There & Away
There's an $89 day trip to the islands operated by Frankland Islands Cruise & Dive (☎ 4031 6300 or 1800 079 039).

You're taken by bus from Cairns to Deeral on the Mulgrave River from where you go out through the mangroves to the islands. A BBQ lunch is included in the cost of $125.

Certified divers pay another $50 for one dive, while the camping drop-off cost is $140 return from Cairns.

MICHAELMAS CAY

North of Green Island and 40km from Cairns, tiny Michaelmas Cay is a national park and a popular rendezvous point for trips out to the Barrier Reef.

The island is still in an early stage of cay development, just a stretch of sand topped by low, scrubby vegetation. Behind the island a narrow strip of reef stretches for 10km providing good snorkelling and diving.

Visitors to the cay are kept strictly to one area of beach; you're not allowed to walk elsewhere on the island or into the vegetated area.

The cay is home to thousands of seabirds – in the summer peak nesting season 30,000 or more cram onto it. At least 14 different species of seabirds have been sighted here and six are known to breed here. Noddies, sooty terns, crested terns and lesser crested terns are the most numerous nesting birds.

The sooty terns lay a single egg in a simple 'nest', which is really just a depression in the sand. Both parents incubate the egg and care for the chick. When it's about a week old the parents leave it to its own devices during the day and the sooty tern chicks soon form wandering groups known as crèches. At least once a day the parents return to the island, call their chick out of the create and feed it by regurgitation. It takes about 70 days from hatching before the sooty tern chicks can fly and they then spend three to six years wandering the world before returning to breed, often in their own original colony.

South of Michaelmas is **Upolu Cay**, a small cay to which some day trip operators go.

Getting There & Away

Great Adventures have a $125 day trip, which includes three hours on Green Island

en route to Michaelmas Cay, plus a smorgasbord lunch.

The huge sailing catamaran *Ocean Spirit I* (☎ 4031 2920) also operates daily trips to the cay which cost $139 including lunch, snorkelling equipment and semi-submersible trips. The smaller *Ocean Spirit II* does day trips to Upolu Cay for $94.

HASTINGS, NORMAN & MOORE REEFS

North of Michaelmas Cay, Hastings and Norman reefs are a popular destination for day trips from Cairns to the reef. Sunlover Cruises offers a $132 day trip to Moore Reef, east of Fitzroy Island. A number of other operators also do day trips to these reefs.

LOW ISLES

Offshore from Port Douglas, this extremely popular destination for day-trippers has two islands. The Low Isles were named by Captain Cook in 1770, and in 1928 they were the site for CM Yonge's Great Barrier Reef Expedition. This detailed study took a year to complete and greatly advanced modern understanding of coral reefs.

Low Island is a fine little coral cay topped by an incredibly well kept old lighthouse dating from 1878. On the other side of the reef, **Woody Island** is an extensive area of the reef that has been claimed by mangroves. These mangrove islands become increasingly common if you continue north from here towards Torres Strait.

A trip out to the Low Isles from Port Douglas gives you a day of snorkelling, viewing from a glass-bottom boat, general lazing around, and the obligatory smorgasbord lunch.

Getting There & Away

Quicksilver (☎ 4099 5500) is the biggest operator to the Low Isles. Its 300 passenger luxury sailing catamaran *Wavedancer* takes about an hour to get to the island and the day trip costs $89 (from Cairns or Port Douglas), including lunch, snorkelling gear and a glass-bottom boat ride. Introductory dives can be done for another $75. Departures are from Marina Mirage in Port Douglas. If you'd rather go on a smaller, more personalised trip, there are plenty of options, including *Sailaway III* (☎ 4099 5599), *Willow* and *Shaolin*. Costs on these smaller boats range from $85 to $100.

In peak seasons, all the Low Isles trips are heavily booked, so plan ahead.

SNAPPER ISLAND

This continental island is close to the mainland, just off Cape Kimberley and the mouth of the Daintree River. It's a national park and has some good fringing reef for snorkelling.

Camping is allowed on the island with a permit from the Cairns office of the Department of Environment.

Cook's Cannons

North of Low Island towards Cooktown is Endeavour Reef, where Captain Cook's barque *Endeavour* ran disastrously aground on the night of 11 June 1770. (See the following Lizard Island to Cape York chapter for more information on the crew's miraculous escape.) In the desperate struggle to free the ship from the reef, six cannons were pushed overboard along with a great deal of other heavy material – according to Cook's log, they threw overboard '40 or 40 Tun weight'.

This legacy of Cook's expedition remained where it lay (despite a couple of unsuccessful attempts) until Vince Vlasoff with his Cairns charter boat *Tropic Seas* began his ultimately successful search for the cannons in 1960. A chance meeting with US oil expert Virgil Kauffman introduced the technology needed to locate the coral-encrusted objects. Kauffman raised $45,000 and organised sponsorship from the United States Academy of Natural Sciences, and early in 1969 the first cannon was located, using a magnetometer. During the course of that year, all six were recovered, along with fragments of the gun carriages, and large amounts of stone and iron ballast. The cannons were sent for conservation to the Defence Science Laboratories in Melbourne.

Two years later, the *Endeavour*'s anchor was also recovered and weighed in at the Cairns game fishing wharf at 966kg.

Since the *Endeavour* sailed, of course, under the British flag, the guns technically remained the property of the British Government, but it relinquished these rights to the Australian Government. In return, one of the cannons was presented to the British National Maritime Museum in Greenwich. Of the remaining five, one went to the Academy of Natural Sciences in Philadelphia, in acknowledgement of the funding; one was presented to New Zealand and is now housed in the National Museum in Wellington; and one was given to the New South Wales Govern-

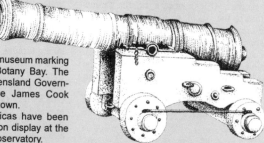

ment to be displayed in the museum marking Cook's landing place on Botany Bay. The last, presented to the Queensland Government, can be seen in the James Cook Historical Museum in Cooktown.

In addition, several replicas have been made, and one of these is on display at the Green Island underwater observatory.

AGINCOURT REEFS

Directly east of Cape Tribulation, on the outer edge of the Great Barrier Reef, the Agincourt Reefs offer some of the best diving in the region. It's the only outer ribbon reef reached in a day trip from the mainland.

Quicksilver in Port Douglas operates daily trips to the reef in its wave-piercer catamarans. The cost is $130 from Port Douglas or Cairns and includes lunch, snorkelling equipment, an underwater observatory and semi-submersible trips. For certified scuba divers, two dives cost an additional $90.

If you'd rather go in a smaller group, there are quite a few smaller boats, including *Wavelength*, *Poseidon* and MV *Freestyle*, which offer similar but much more personalised snorkelling and diving trips, starting at about $90.

HOPE ISLANDS

North of Cedar Bay and south of Cooktown, the two tiny Hope Islands are on reefs separated by a deep channel. The western island is mainly mangrove, but the eastern one has a good encircling beach and in suitable winds there's a reasonably secure deep anchorage on its north-west side that is popular with yachties.

You can camp on the eastern island with a permit from the Cairns office of the Department of Environment.

Lizard Island to Cape York

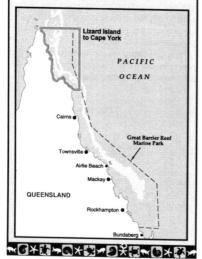

On the face of it, the area from Lizard Island to Cape York is the most undeveloped region of the Great Barrier Reef. There is only one resort, on Lizard Island, despite the fact that the reef itself is closer to shore here than anywhere else, and there are dozens of islands and reefs. The reef is also at its most pristine, and devoid of the hordes of day-tripping tourists and cruise boats you can see off Cairns, for example. The isolation of the area is one of the reasons Lizard Island is so popular.

However, in spite of all this it is far from idyllic. Most of the islands this far north are barren and windswept, and few provide safe anchorages for yachts. And with no pubs or restaurants between Lizard Island and Thursday Island, the area does not lend itself to independent travellers. It is, though, still possible to explore the region.

Lizard Island

Area:	21 sq km
Type:	continental
High point:	368m
Max visitors:	80

The furthest north of the Barrier Reef resort islands, Lizard Island was named by Joseph Banks after Captain Cook spent a day here, trying to find a way out through the Barrier Reef to open sea. The islands of the Lizard group are the only high continental islands close to the outer Barrier Reef. The island has superb beaches (23 of them), great for swimming or snorkelling.

Lizard is one of the more expensive resorts and what you're paying for is not glossy sophistication – here your money buys you isolation and a location only 15km from the outer edge of the reef. Furthermore the reef here is virtually untouched, as close to nature as you'll find. Naturally the diving is superb. The island has been a national park since 1939 and the other islands in the Lizard group were added to the national park in 1987. The resort was opened in 1972 and is operated by Qantas Airlines. The research station opened in 1975.

History
Cook's Visit After an already eventful voyage up the east coast of Australia, Cook had not sighted the Great Barrier Reef but he was not entirely oblivious to it – their sailing instincts told them something was

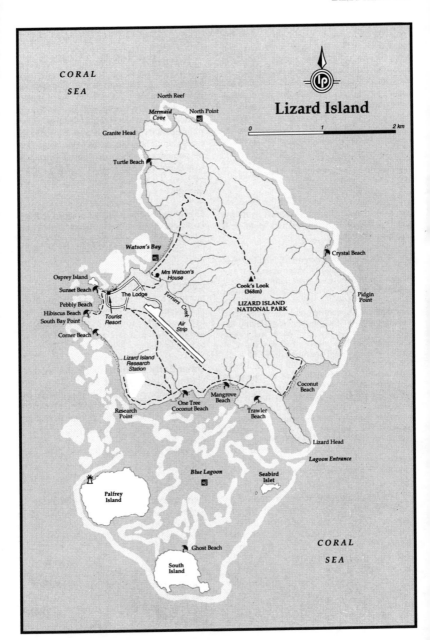

CORAL
SEA

North Reef
Mermaid Cove North Point

Granite Head

Turtle Beach

Lizard Island

0   1   2 km

Watson's Bay

Crystal Beach

Osprey Island
Sunset Beach
Pebbly Beach
Hibiscus Beach
South Bay Point

Mrs Watson's House

The Lodge

Cook's Look
(368m)

Pidgin Point

LIZARD ISLAND
NATIONAL PARK

Corner Beach

Tourist
Resort

Air
Strip

Ferriers Creek

Lizard Island
Research
Station

Coconut
Beach

Research
Point

One Tree
Coconut Beach

Mangrove
Beach

Trawler
Beach

Lizard Head

Lagoon Entrance

Blue Lagoon

Seabird
Islet

Palfrey
Island

CORAL

SEA

Ghost Beach

South
Island

out there from the unusual calmness of the sea and the frequent minor reefs they met with. He and his crew had sailed close to the coastline from Botany Bay, but as the *Endeavour* pressed further north it entered the funnel of the reef, and Cook's tribulations were about to begin. He wrote in his log:

… we have sail'd above 360 Leagues [*more than 1700km*] by the Lead without ever having a Leadsman out of the Chains, when the ship was under sail; a Circumstance that perhaps never happened to any ship before …

On the night of 11 June 1770 the *Endeavour* sailed past the Low Isles, off modern-day Port Douglas. Cook named them, and wrote in his log:

My intention was to stretch off all Night as well to avoid the danger we saw ahead as to see if any Islands lay in the Offing, especially as we were now begun to draw near the Lat. of those discover'd by Quiros [*modern-day Vanuatu*], which some Geographers, for what reason I know not, have thought proper to Tack to this land. Having the advantage of a fine breeze of wind, and a clear Moon light Night in standing off from 6 until 9 o'clock, we deepened our Water from 14 to 21 fathoms, when all at once we fell into 12, 10 and eight fathoms. At this time I had everybody at their Stations to put about and come to an Anchor; but in this I was not so fortunate, for meeting again with Deep Water, I thought there would be no danger in standing on. Before 10 o'clock we had 20 and 21 fathoms, and Continued in that depth until a few minutes before 11, when we had 17, and before the Man at the Lead could heave another cast, the Ship Struck and stuck fast … upon the SE Edge of a reef of Coral rocks …

By heaving numerous items, including an anchor and six cannons overboard, the *Endeavour* was eventually freed from the reef that bears its name. A sail was hauled under the hull in an attempt to plug the gaping hole and then a miraculous drop in the breeze enabled them to limp up the Endeavour River to the site of modern-day Cooktown. Here the barque was careened on the banks of the river and repaired. It was during this enforced interlude that

Cook's party first saw that remarkable animal, the kangaroo.

Two months later the patched up *Endeavour* ventured out from Cooktown and set sail north. The presence of the reef was now very evident to Cook, as here it is very near the coast. Cook and Joseph Banks landed on Lizard Island in the ship's pinnace to try and find a way out from the reef. Banks later suggested that the island be named after the many large lizards he saw there. The two men climbed to the top of Cook's Look and from here Cook observed:

To my Mortification I discover'd a Reef of Rocks laying about two or three Leagues [*10 or 15km*] without the Island, extending in a line NW and SE, farther than I could see, on which the Sea broke very high.

Cook climbed the peak again the next morning to scan the horizon for some break in the reef, but the crew, which he had sent out in a pinnace to search for a passage, had already located a safe route out of the reef to deeper water.

Other Early Visitors Aborigines had been visiting Lizard Island long before Cook made his famous visit. Shell middens, left when they feasted on shellfish, can be found at various points around the island, and care should be taken not to disturb them.

Cook's comments on the island attracted other European visitors in subsequent years, and many wrote of their feelings as they climbed Cook's Look in the footsteps of their famous predecessor. Commander JL Stokes wrote of his visit to the island in HMS *Beagle* in 1839, while Joseph Jukes, the naturalist on HMS *Fly*, kept a chronicle describing his visit in 1843. Both their accounts were lyrical in their description of the beauty of the surrounding scenery, but Thomas Huxley, naturalist on HMS *Rattlesnake* (and father of the novelist Aldous Huxley), had a tougher climb to the top of the island:

The natural beauty of the scene was heightened by the recollection that one stood on ground rendered classical by the footsteps of the great Cook, who from this height sought some exit from the dangers which had so nearly put an end to him and his glory. I say 'was heightened' Truth requires that I should substitute 'ought to have been heightened', for in fact, the sun had been pouring on my back all the way up and my feelings more nearly approached sickness than sublimity when I reached the top.

Domestic Tragedy During Cook's visit Banks had noticed that 'the Indians had been here in their poor embarkations' and later observers also noted that Aborigines had visited the island, visits that were to lead to a domestic tragedy.

In 1881 Mary Beatrice Watson and her husband had built a small brick and stone cottage on the island in order to collect bêches-de-mer, a noted Chinese delicacy. Robert Watson left the island with his partner John Fuller to search for new fishing grounds, leaving Mary Watson with her baby, Ferrier, and their two Chinese servants, Ah Sam and Ah Leong.

In her brief, curiously dispassionate diary (which was found in the abandoned house, and another journal with her body), she noted the arrival of a party of Aborigines and the events that led to her death:

29 September Blowing strong SE breeze, although not as hard as yesterday. No eggs. Ah Leong killed by the blacks over at the farm. Ah Sam found his hat, which is the only proof.

1 October Natives (four) speared Ah Sam; four places in the right side, and three on the shoulder. Got three spears from the natives. Saw ten men altogether.

(This part of her diary was found in the abandoned house and a subsequent diary with her body.)

At this point, Mary Watson made the decision to leave the island and with some supplies, the baby and her wounded houseboy. She paddled away in an iron tank used for boiling the bêches-de-mer. For at least 10 days they moved from sandbank to island to reef to mangrove swamp, narrowly missing passing steamers or signalling unsuccessfully to them until all eventually died of thirst. Her last diary entry was made on 11 October.

Not until late January in the next year were the bodies found on one of the Howick islands. It was subsequently named Watson Island. They were still in their iron tank, which in the ensuing months had, ironically, half filled with rainwater.

Today, visitors to Townsville can see the iron tank in the North Queensland branch of the Queensland Museum, at the Great Barrier Reef Wonderland where the superb Great Barrier Reef Aquarium also is.

Her two diaries are in Brisbane in the Oxley Memorial Library, while in Cooktown you can see her tombstone with the inscription:

Five fearful days beneath
the scorching glare
her babe she nursed.
God knows the pangs that
woman had to bear.
Whose last sad entry showed
a mother's care.
Then – 'near dead with thirst'.

The tumble-down walls of the old house can still be seen on Lizard Island, but near the top of Cook's Look there are also traces of stones marking an Aboriginal ceremonial area – it's possible that Mary Watson's unhappy end may have come because she and her group had unwittingly strayed into a sacred area.

Information
The resort's phone number is ☎ 060 3999, the fax number is 4060 3991, and the postal address is Lizard Island, PMB 40, Cairns, Qld 4870.

There's a pay phone at the research station that campers and yachties can use.

Books The Department of Environment puts out a *Lizard Island Group* information leaflet and the resort has a number of useful leaflets for their guests with information on birds, plants and fishing. *Lizard Island – Some of its History,* by Allan McInnes, is an interesting small book with extracts from the journals of James Cook and Joseph Banks, Mary Watson's diary and other interesting writings relating to the island. It's also supplied to guests at the resort.

Zoning The waters immediately around Lizard Island are all zoned as Marine National Park, where shell and coral collecting and spear fishing are not permitted.

Around the northern part of the island it's Zone A, which permits limited line fishing but not commercial fishing.

The southern part, including all of Blue Lagoon and the waters around Palfrey and South islands and Seabird Islet, as well as Watson's Bay and Turtle Beach north of the resort, are all Zone B where all fishing is prohibited.

Research Station

In 1974 the Australian Museum in Sydney founded the privately funded Lizard Island Research Station, which pursues projects as diverse as investigating marine organisms for cancer research, the deaths of giant clams, coral reproductive processes, seabird ecology, the life patterns of reef fish during their larval stage, and many other subjects. Funding has come from many companies in Australia and overseas, as well as from private donations.

Tours of the station are conducted at 9.30 am each Monday and Friday for guests at the resort and other island visitors, such as yachties or campers.

The station can accommodate up to 24 visiting scientists and, although preference is normally given to marine researchers, high school and university groups are also accommodated from time to time.

Information on the station or its accommodation possibilities can be obtained from The Co-Directors, Lizard Island Research Station (☎ 4060 3977), PMB 37, Cairns, Qld 4871.

Other Islands

There are four other smaller islands in the Lizard group. **Osprey Island**, with its nesting birds, is right in front of the resort and can be waded to. Around the edge of Blue Lagoon, south of the main island, are **Seabird Islet**, **South Island** and **Palfrey Island**, with its automatic lighthouse.

Activities

The resort has the usual sporting facilities including a floodlit tennis court and swimming pool. All watersports equipment, including windsurfers, catamarans, outboard dinghies and waterskiing are included in the daily tariff. There are also double paddle skis with panels for coral viewing, and glass-bottomed boat trips.

Boating trips do cost extra (see below) and these are offered every day, either for fishing or diving and snorkelling.

Diving Lizard Island offers some of the best diving along the Great Barrier Reef. In fact, there's so much of it you're really spoiled for choice.

There are good dives right off the island, particularly along the eastern side or on the southern side of South Island and at the western end of Blue Lagoon. With the outer barrier reef so close it's hard to resist the temptation of heading a little further afield, particularly to what is probably Australia's best known dive, the Cod Hole.

Despite the proximity of the dive sites, diving at Lizard certainly isn't cheap – spectacular yes, economical no. A diving day trip to the inner reef costs $110, to the outer reef $150. A day's hire of regulator, buoyancy compensator, wetsuit and two tanks of air will set you back another $65, so for a day's diving on the outer reef you're looking at $215.

Inner Reef Dives Immediately north of Lizard Island is a series of shoals – Underwood, Stewart and Petricola shoals – plus Bank's Bank, where a sand cay has formed on the shoal. There are wonderful coral formations and a great variety of reef and pelagic (open sea) fish. The diving off Bank's Bank is particularly good.

South-east of Lizard there's good diving at Kevin's Reef and superb coral for diving or snorkelling off the northern side of North Direction Island. Rocky Islet, further south, also has good diving and snorkelling.

Outer Reef Dives It's only 18 to 20km from Lizard Island to the edge of the outer reef, where the ribbon reefs are cut by a number of openings. They include the historic Cook's Passage, where the great navigator made his escape to the outer ocean.

On Hick's Reef, at the northern end, the Top of Hicks dive can be a fine-drift dive along One & a Half Mile Opening. Outside the reef, Don's Wall is a drop-off where you may find patrolling reef sharks. Remora Point, on the outer corner of Day Reef, has very clear water and a wide variety of fish.

Day Reef is separated from Carter Reef, a research reef where no diving is permitted, by Cook's Passage. There are numerous dives around Yonge Reef, popular because of its proximity to Lizard Island. These include Half Mile Opening, where there is also good snorkelling. Jackson's Wall is on the outer edge of the reef, while other inner reef dives include Bubble's Bommie, the Three Sisters and Hook Point.

Further south is No Name Reef, with Carroll's Corner on the outer edge. The Fish Markets and Dynamite Passage are on the narrow pass between No Name and Detached reefs.

Separating Detached Reef from the long Ribbon Reef Number 10 is Cormorant Pass, with the famous Cod Hole. It's a favourite destination for dive trips out of Cairns and dive boats from Lizard Island usually come here every second day. Its fame is well earned as a group of six to 10 huge potato cod live here and have become very familiar with the pleasures of being fed by visiting divers. The larger ones are up to 2m in length and will bump up against you or allow themselves to be stroked as they swim around looking for a handout. Friend-ly moray eels and a host of other fish also appear for their regular feeds. This dive can be equally good for snorkellers as the potato cod come virtually to the surface and the dive only goes down to about 10m.

Round the corner from the Cod Hole is Shark Alley, where you can see some other interesting large fish!

Outside Ribbon Reef, Syd's Place and Second Corner are vertical wall dives for the more experienced diver.

Fishing Lizard Island is famed for its fishing as well as its diving, particularly heavy-tackle fishing. The annual heavy-tackle competition over Halloween night (31 October) is a big attraction; the season runs from September to December.

The Marlin Centre, at the north end of the resort bay, caters for the many game fishing boats that use Lizard as a base at the height of the season. Its bar is renowned for extremely tall fishing tales.

The MV *Coocoran* is the resort's main fishing boat. During the marlin fishing season it costs $1595 to charter the boat for the day for up to four people.

At other times, you can go light-tackle trolling (for mackerel or trevally) or bottom fishing (for red emperor or coral trout) – a day trip costs from $745 to $1100 for up to four people.

Of course, you can easily arrange your own fishing trip – all it needs is a dinghy and a line. The resort has an interesting *Fishing Guide* leaflet for its guests.

Beaches & Snorkelling Lizard Island has the finest beaches of any of the Barrier Reef islands. Some islands have no beaches to speak of, or have been forced to create artificial beaches by bringing in sand, or have such severe tidal changes that their beaches are unswimmable at low tide.

Lizard, in contrast, has superb beach after superb beach. There are long stretches of sand or perfect picture-book little bays, all of them lapped by glass-clear water with magnificent coral. If you're a keen snorkeller, Lizard is superb.

There's good snorkelling right in front of the resort, particularly along the north-east edge of Osprey Island. Immediately south of the resort are three picture-postcard beaches – Sunset Beach, Pebbly Beach and Hibiscus Beach. They each offer great swimming, coral and snorkelling, and despite their proximity to the resort (only a couple of minutes' walk away) they feel like they're light years away.

One Tree Coconut Beach, Mangrove Beach, Trawler Beach and Coconut Beach are all at the south-eastern end of Lizard Island and there is good snorkelling from the latter two.

Watson's Bay, to the north of the resort, is a wonderful stretch of sand with great snorkelling at both ends and a clam field in the middle. Other beaches round the northern end of the island are easily reached by dinghy, and at Turtle Beach, Mermaid Cove or Crystal Beach you can really feel you've escaped from civilisation. They all offer good snorkelling.

At several good snorkelling places around the Blue Lagoon or North Point there are marine park mooring buoys where you can tie up your dinghy without damaging the coral by anchoring. The coral around the north-east side of the island has numerous caves in the reef edge.

Walks There are several good walks on Lizard Island, but don't set off without sun protection, including a hat and a good sunscreen. Take a water bottle as well – Lizard is hot and dry.

The Watson House & Watson's Bay It's only a short walk from the resort to the remains of the Watson house by Watson's Bay. The trail from the resort climbs up over Chinaman's Ridge, which separates the resort from Watson's Bay. There are fine views over the bay where yachts can often be seen at anchor.

A stream emerges from a mangrove swamp into the bay at its southern end and the trail follows a boardwalk through the swamp, with a neat little bridge arching over the stream. Two stout walls are all that remains standing from the Watson house, but it's easy to trace the outlines of the foundations of what must have been a surprisingly large residence.

From here you walk along the beach to its northern end, where there's excellent snorkelling both on the fringing reef around the northern headland and the isolated heads slightly further out from shore. Apart from the usual selection of colourful fish the coral also has a phenomenal number of clams including many giant ones, some alive, others just empty shells. There's also coral at the southern end of the bay, out from Chinaman's Ridge, and a superb clam garden in the middle of the bay.

The small campsite at the north end of the bay is also a popular BBQ spot for visiting boats. There's at least one large goanna that has learnt to pop up here at lunch time and grab whatever handouts are going.

Cook's Look The climb to the top of Cook's Look is undoubtedly the most popular walk on the island. The trail starts from the northern end of the beach, near the campsite. You can easily walk here from the resort, passing the Watson house on the way.

From the extreme end of the beach the start of the trail to Cook's Look is clearly signposted and the trail, although it can be steep and a bit of a clamber at times, is easy to follow all the way with regular white or blue painted arrows.

The trail starts off heading north then curves round and heads steadily south to the top, dipping down slightly into a saddle before making the final push to the top. The words 'Not Far Now', painted on a rock, urges you on over the last few hundred metres.

There are breathtaking views over Watson's Bay as you ascend. The top is marked with a cairn bearing one of those 'X km to places A, B, C' plates. There are great views out towards the outer reef from this point.

Watson's Bay, Lizard Island, was named after one of the island's earliest European occupants, Mary Watson, who was driven from the island by Aboriginals, who killed her Chinese servants, and later perished with her son, Ferrier, in a water tank they used as a boat.

PHOTOS BY HUGH FINLAY

Top & Middle Left: Thursday Island township
Middle Right: Grave markers of Japanese pearl divers in the cemetery, Thursday Island
Bottom: A number of rusting guns still remain at Thursday Island's old Green Hill Fort

On a clear day you can clearly see the opening in the reef where Cook made his escape, but in actual fact the reef here offers a number of passages. It's a popular outing for yachties cruising the Great Barrier Reef to exit through one of these passages – perhaps Cook's Passage – just to say they've sailed outside the reef, then to come back in to the reef's protected waters through another passage.

The stroll to the top can take anything from half an hour if you run most of the way to 1½ hours at a very leisurely pace, 45 minutes is probably a good walk. It's worth imagining Cook making his weary trudge to the top, 'with a mixture of hope and fear proportioned to the importance of our business and the uncertainty of the event'. Under the cairn there's a plastic box with a book inside where you can write your name and any comments worthy of your own historic moment at the top.

In *Cruising the Coral Coast*, Alan Lucas writes that a few hundred metres down the north side of the slope are some Aboriginal rock formations that may have had some bearing on the fate of Mary Watson. These were only discovered in 1972 during the filming of *At Home on the Lizard*.

Movie trivia buffs may be interested to know one of the first-timer film makers involved in this project was a Dr George Miller, who was so inspired by this first attempt at film making that he packed-in medicine and went on to become one of Australia's most financially (if not critically) successful movie makers with the Mel Gibson *Mad Max* series. Aboriginal ruins buffs may have less success finding the formation – there are an awful lot of jumbled rocks down the north side of the slope and just which ones might be a real formation is hard to tell.

The resort regularly organises excursions to Cook's Look with a refreshment at the top, followed by breakfast on return to the resort.

Other Walks There are several other interesting walks around the island and the dry,

rocky and grassy ground cover makes it pretty easy to walk almost anywhere.

From the resort a trail leads down the side of the airstrip then continues directly from the end of the airstrip to Mangrove Beach and Trawler Beach, both on Blue Lagoon.

A trail climbs up the side of the steep Lizard Head ridge and drops equally steeply down to Coconut Beach. Some real rock scrambling is necessary, but Lizard Head offers superb views.

Another trail from the resort starts near the airstrip and leads to One Tree Coconut Beach, from where you can rock hop around the headland to Mangrove Beach. If you stick to the trail rather than turning off to One Tree Coconut Beach, it continues round to the Lizard Island Research Station. From the station you can continue around the bay and rock hop round the series of headlands and idyllic little bays back to the resort.

For those interested in the island's vegetation, the resort has a *Plants Guide* report.

Wildlife Lizard's most famous wildlife are, of course, the huge lizards that Cook and Banks commented on. The island has 11 species of lizards but it's the large sand goannas, often up to a metre in length, which are most interesting. They can often be seen around the resort on the front lawn. When young goannas are hatching out you will see many new holes dug by them in the sandy road between the resort and the research station.

Other examples of wildlife include five species of snakes, none of them seen with any frequency, and a small colony of bats, which may be seen winging their way over the resort soon after sunset.

Birds More than 40 species of birds have been recorded on the island, and a dozen or so actually nest there.

Resident birds include the beautiful little sunbirds with their long, hanging nests, which they even build inside the airstrip terminal.

Bar-shouldered doves, crested terns, Caspian terns and a variety of other terns, oystercatchers and the large sea eagles are other resident species.

Seabird Islet in the Blue Lagoon is a popular nesting site for terns and visitors should keep away from the islet during the summer months.

The resort has a list of the birds that might be seen.

Cane Toads Cane toads *(Bufo marinus)*, the ecological disaster of Queensland, first gained a toehold on Lizard Island in late 1987. Thought to have come over with plantings for a landscaping project at the resort they were first spotted near the resort's swimming pool, and later some dead goannas, which were probably poisoned after they ate cane toads, were also found.

Fortunately, the story is much happier here than on the mainland where, since their introduction in 1947, cane toads have subsequently spread all over Queensland and even moved into New South Wales and the Northern Territory.

On Lizard Island, 10 adult toads were caught almost immediately, and four more were caught when tape recordings of mating toad noises were played to the randy creatures.

Today, you may spot some pretty little green frogs around the resort, but, hopefully, the hideous cane toads are gone.

Places to Stay

Camping Camping permits for Lizard Island must be obtained from the Department of Environment office in Cairns.

There's a small campsite ($3.50 a night) at the north end of the Watson's Bay beach. The site has toilets, BBQs, tables and benches, and fresh water is available from a pump about 250m from the site, near the top of the mangrove swamp that extends in from the south end of the bay.

Although campers are extremely unlikely to be welcomed with open arms at the resort, the island's history, walks, fine beaches, excellent snorkelling and the research station make this an interesting island to stay on – if you can get here.

No food is available from the resort or the research station, so campers must be totally self-sufficient. There is also no garbage collection either – you must take it all out when you leave.

The Resort Lizard Island's accommodation is comfortable, modern and first class but in no way spectacular. 'Straightforward' is the only way to describe the resort's design – there are no prizes for the architecture.

The rooms have air-conditioning and ceiling fans, fridges, tea/coffee-making facilities, bathrobes and toiletries, ISD and direct-dial telephones, but no TV or radio. Coming to Lizard is supposed to be an escape from the real world.

There are 30 double rooms at $860/1040 per night, and two larger suites with a separate lounge and living area at $1000/1280 per night. These rates include all meals, activities, and general equipment use.

Elevated on Sunset Ridge are eight villas that were completed in 1995. These feature high ceilings, polished wooden floors and louver doors. The cost is $625 per person.

Food

Lizard has an excellent reputation for its cuisine. The main dining area is an open-air sundeck with a great view across the lawns to the sea.

You can have a buffet-style or à la carte breakfast. A typical lunch menu will offer a choice between a cold soup and an entree, three main courses (one of which is seafood), and two desserts. Of course, if you'd prefer something simple like oysters kilpatrick and a salad, that can be arranged too.

The dinner menu is more extensive, offering a hot soup, several starters, three main courses and ice cream, sorbet and/or a cheese platter. The wine list features predominantly Australian wines ranging in price from around $25 to $50.

If you want to get away from it all for the

day you can request a picnic hamper to take away in a dinghy.

Getting There & Away

It's a long way to Lizard Island, 240km from Cairns, and this distance adds to the resort's isolation and its expense.

Air Almost all guests at the resort arrive by air. Sunstate Airlines has daily flights from Cairns and the hour-long flight by Twin Otter costs $388 return.

Aussie Airways (☎ 4053 3980) has a day trip from Cairns to Lizard Island depending on demand, which costs $290 per person, including lunch and snorkelling gear.

Sea There is no regular shipping or ferry service to Lizard Island.

The *Reef Endeavour*, operated by Captain Cook Cruises (☎ 1800 221 080), does a four night cruise from Cairns to Lizard Island and back, leaving Cairns every Monday at 2 pm. The ship calls in at Fitzroy Island on day one, Cooktown on day two, before continuing onto Lizard Island where you spend two days snorkelling, diving, walking or just lazing around.

Fares range from $1010 per person in a three-berth cabin, to $1460 per person in a deluxe twin stateroom, which includes all meals, entertainment and activities.

Alternatively, the Cairns to Thursday Island cruise ship, the *Kangaroo Explorer* (☎ 4032 4000), spends a day at Lizard on its way north and south.

A four day trip from Cairns costs from $1134 in a four-berth lower-deck cabin to $1659 for an upper deck double, including airfare back to Cairns. To do the full seven day trip to or from Thursday Island costs between $1753 and $2628.

Lizard Island is one of the most popular anchorages on the Great Barrier Reef, and it's certainly the last really good anchorage before you get to Thursday Island. Yachties usually anchor in sheltered Watson's Bay or in the Blue Lagoon. Intrepid madmen even come over to Lizard Island from the main-

land in outboard powered 'tinnies' (small fishing dinghies) – it's about 30km from Cape Flattery. The red carpet is not, however, rolled out for yachties by the resort.

The difficulty and expense of getting to Lizard Island puts off campers, although a few do manage it. An interesting way of making a camping trip to the island would be to take one of the cruise boats up and continue on to Thursday Island on the same boat a week later, or fly out and back to Cairns. Fortunately, you do not have to bring fresh water to Lizard, but you'll need to bring your own stove or solid fuel for the BBQs, as all timber on the island, including driftwood, is protected. If you are flying in, you can't carry liquid fuel or gas in your luggage – charcoal is the only option.

Around Lizard Island

There are a number of continental islands and small cays dotted around Lizard Island and south towards Cooktown.

Camping is permitted on a number of the islands with a Department of Environment permit. The sites are all very basic and the permit costs $3.50 a night.

ROCKY ISLET

Immediately south of Lizard Island is Rocky Islet, wooded and with good beaches, and two adjoining islets, one covered in scrub, one bare rock. Day trips are sometimes made to the islets from Lizard Island and there is good snorkelling and diving there.

During last century these islets played a part in the Queensland 'blackbirding' business – naive Pacific islanders were collected by unscrupulous labour recruiters to work on the North Queensland sugarcane fields or in the gold mines in conditions of near slavery.

Rocky Islet was a slavers' haven, where the hapless islanders were transferred from

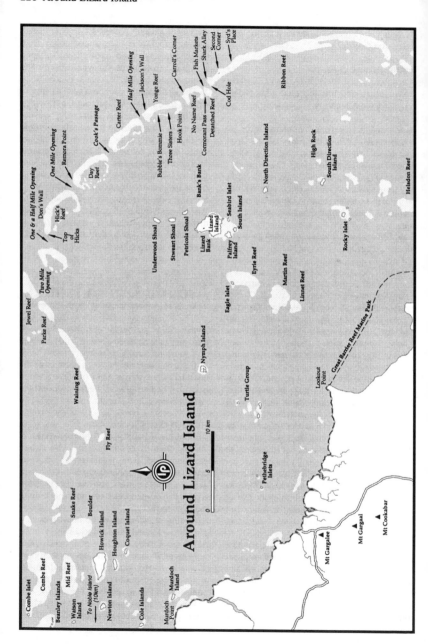

Around Lizard Island

the ocean-going ships to await collection by ships from the mainland. Even after the practice had been banned, recruiters continued to smuggle labourers ashore by this means.

Camping is permitted on the north side of the main island from April through September.

SOUTH DIRECTION ISLAND

Just north of Rocky Islet this island is scrub covered, but without beaches. Yachts sometimes anchor here, although it's not easy to get inside the reef.

NORTH DIRECTION ISLAND

This prominent island is another popular destination for day trips from Lizard Island.

There's a good beach and sand spit and some fine coral for divers or snorkellers. Aboriginal rock paintings can be seen on the island.

EAGLE ISLET

Cook passed Eagle Islet and his log notes that his less than ecologically minded men killed the young eagles found in a nest. Fortunately, the islet is still noted for its three eagle nests.

From December to March it harbours a huge number of seabirds, particularly nesting sooty terns and white-crested terns.

The small cay sits at the northern end of the large Eyrie Reef. It's only about 8km from Lizard and is a popular destination for day trips from the resort.

NYMPH ISLAND & THE TURTLE GROUP

About 25km west of Lizard Island is Nymph Island, another good picnic spot with good snorkelling around the reef. Crocodiles have even been reported in the island's inner lagoon. It's a good island for walking and camping is permitted from April through September.

Slightly south-west of Nymph Island are the small sand cays of the Turtle group. Camping is permitted on three of the islands.

THREE ISLANDS & TWO ISLANDS

Seasonal camping is permitted on both these island groups. Three Islands are about 40km north-west of Cooktown, while Two Islands are 10km further north again.

A Prolonged Visit to the Reef

Lizard Island visitors flying to or from Cairns may spot a rusting ship, high and dry on Emily Reef, about 40km south-east of Cooktown. It's the MV *Debut*, sister ship to the ill-fated Greenpeace *Rainbow Warrior*, and she's been stuck there since 1987. Her captain and owner lived on board for several years after she was first grounded. The *Debut*'s owner had been kicking around the Pacific for over 10 years, scraping a living as best he could, until one day he ran out of money and fuel and drifted into Australian waters. Lent fuel by the Australian navy the *Debut* limped into Cairns and tied up, unable to raise the cash for fuel or port charges.

Finally, when the owner's visa expired and Australian immigration officials were closing in, the *Debut* again put to sea but, before a role in a proposed *Rainbow Warrior* film could be settled, the ship ran aground (some say it was deliberately done) in its current resting place. For some time there was dispute between the owner and the government as to what would next happen to the vessel, but the issue has now faded and, as the wreck poses no environmental hazard, it seems the *Debut* will rust away on the reef.

Lizard Island to Cape York

The tourist stretch of the reef ends abruptly at Lizard Island, but there are still plenty of interesting islands north of Lizard.

Cape York Peninsula

Thursday Island
Hammond Island
Wednesday Island
Friday Island
Horn Island
Mt Adolphus Island
Cape York
Prince of Wales Island
Albany Island
Possession Island
Somerset Ruins
Mottee Heads
Somerset
Bamaga
Turtle Head Island
Jacky Jacky Airfield
Jardine River National Park

Gulf Of Carpentaria

Pandora's Passage

Raine Island

Great Detached Reef

Shelburne Bay
Sunday Islet
Charles Hardy Group
Cape Grenville
Yule Detached Reef
Haggerstone Island

Temple Bay
Farmer Islet

Wenlock

Iron Range National Park
Portland Roads
Cape Weymouth
Restoration Island
Lockhart River
Cape Direction
Night Island

River

Welpa

CORAL SEA

Providential Channel

Bligh's Passage

Great

Mungkan Kaanju National Park (Archer Bend Section)
Archer River Roadhouse
Cape Sidmouth
Morris Islet

Archer River

Mungkan Kaanju National Park (Rokeby Section)

Kendall River

Barrier

Coen

Flinders Group
Bathurst Bay
Pipon Island
Cape Melville

Holyroyd River

Princess Charlotte Bay

Howick Group

Cape Melville National Park

Reef

Edward River

Great

Howick Island
Lizard Island
Lookout Point

Musgrave

Lakefield National Park

Normanby River

Starke National Park

Mitchell & Alice Rivers National Park

Dividing

Peninsula Dev Road

Kowanyama

Alice River

Laura

Cooktown

Mitchell

Lakeland

Cape Tribulation

River

Range

Daintree

Staaten River

Mossman
Port Douglas

Staaten River National Park

Burke Development Road

Cairns

Mareeba

Gilbert River

Karumba

Bullepinga National Park

Normanton

Ravenshoe

Innisfail

These, though, are generally not so attractive; the south-east trades blow for most of the year, so the islands are often windswept and barren. Also safe anchorages are not easy to find – Lizard Island is the last really good anchorage on the way north.

Getting There & Away
Even without your own yacht, visiting the islands north from Lizard to Torres Strait is certainly possible.

The *Kangaroo Explorer* does a variety of cruises between Cairns and Cape York, including four and seven day return cruises, and seven day one way cruises with a return flight. Launched in 1990, the ship is a 25m cruising catamaran with 15 twin cabins, each air-conditioned and with its own bathroom.

Fares for the seven day cruises range from $2068 per person for a twin cabin on the lower deck, to $2628 for a cabin on the main or upper deck. Prices include all meals and activities.

Phone ☎ 4032 4000 or fax 4032 4050, or write to PO Box 7110, Cairns, Qld 4870 for details.

ALONG THE INNER PASSAGE
Despite the relative density of islands along the route north, making landfall on them is often far from easy. Lizard Island is the last really secure island anchorage, so which islands you visit on a cruise to Thursday Island depends on the prevailing weather conditions. It's a busy route with a steady flow of cruising yachts, prawn trawlers, container ships to and from Asia, and bulk carriers shuttling between Gladstone, south down the coast, and the Weipa mine on the west side of Cape York in the Gulf of Carpentaria.

The coastal route is fairly tight – along this stretch the reef presses close to the coast so there's little option but to zigzag and find your own route. Until a safe 'inner passage' was plotted, sailing along the coast was usually done outside the reef, with the considerable associated problem of finding

a safe passage back into the sheltered inner reef waters when need be.

HOWICK ISLANDS
About 50km north-west of Lizard Island is the Howick Group, where Mary Watson's ill-fated escape from Lizard Island came to its dismal end.

Howick Island, the main island in the group, is a continental island with several prominent hills. Off to the west stretches a large reef flat that has been totally filled in by mangroves.

Just to the north-east of Howick is **Snake Reef**, an oval-shaped reef, not snake-like at all. While yachties and shallow-draught boats sail west of Howick towards the coast, deep-draught vessels have to take a tight dog-leg between Howick Island and Snake Reef, a route known as Snake Gully.

Watson Island is to the north-west of Howick, a low-lying, anonymous little mangrove island. It was here that Mary Watson, her baby and their Chinese servant Ah Sam died.

Noble Island, nearer to the mainland to the west, has a prominent mountainous peak rising to 122m. A brief gold rush took place here after surveyors unearthed a nugget purely by chance.

FLINDERS GROUP
The Flinders Group in Bathurst Bay has two larger islands, **Flinders** and **Stanley** and a number of smaller islands. Flinders Island is said to have some Aboriginal cave paintings.

This area was swept by cyclone Mahina in March 1899 causing great damage. Many ships had sheltered in the bay – one lighthouse ship, two pearling mother ships and 50 pearling luggers were sunk, with 300 divers in all losing their lives. It is said that the seas were so high that dolphins were dumped on the top of 12m-high cliffs on Flinders Island. There is a cyclone monument on **Cape Melville**.

Today, you'll see numerous prawn trawlers anchored around the islands, especially in Owen Channel, during the daytime.

Prawn trawling being a nocturnal activity, the crews sleep during the day.

MORRIS ISLET

About halfway between Cape Melville and **Cape Direction** is tiny Morris Islet, a small sand cay on a huge reef. At low tide a long sandbar runs north-east from the tip of the island for nearly 2km.

The cay is covered in low scrub, most of it needle-sharp kapok plants, but towards the southern end is a single palm tree and under the palm tree is a so-called diver's grave, possibly the result of a pearl or trochus shell diver meeting his death at sea on an old lugger. Floats, shells and other bits and pieces decorate this lonely grave.

NIGHT ISLAND

Like a number of other mangrove islands along this stretch of the coast Night Island is a tiny cay surrounded by the mangroves that have spread to cover almost all the reef. The Low Isles, off Port Douglas further south, are rather similar.

Night Island is a major nesting site for the Torres Strait pigeons, which fly back to the island from the mainland every night. The island is only 5km off the mainland and the bêches-de-mer gatherer Robert Watson was heading here when he left his family on Lizard Island.

BLIGH'S PASSAGE & RESTORATION ISLAND

About 250km north of Lizard Island is Bligh's Passage, or Entrance. In 1789 William Bligh, having suffered the mutiny on his ship the *Bounty*, found his way through the reef here.

The mutiny had taken place in the Tongan islands. Bligh and the crew who remained faithful sailed 6000km in a small 23 foot (7m) open boat, eventually reaching safety at Kupang, on the island of Timor, then in the Dutch East Indies.

This remarkable voyage lasted 41 days and, despite having to contend with everything from violent weather to unfriendly indigenous people in Fiji, Bligh still found time to chart his route with such accuracy that aspects of modern maps are still based on his work.

Bligh made landfall at Restoration Island, just off Cape Weymouth and immediately south of Portland Roads, where today you will often see a group of prawn trawlers anchored. He named the island both after the fact that he and his men could 'restore' themselves after their long and difficult journey, and because it was the anniversary of the Restoration of Charles II to the English throne in 1660.

PROVIDENTIAL CHANNEL

Not far north from Bligh's Passage is Providential Channel, where Cook, recently a relieved escapee from the Great Barrier Reef, made his way back inside it. Having sailed out near Lizard Island, the unhappy captain found that things were no better outside the reef. The prevailing winds and currents were pushing him back onto the reef and, when the wind died completely, he found himself simply drifting towards the reef in water too deep for dropping anchor:

… we both sounded now and several times in the night but had no ground with 140 fathoms of line. A little after 4 o'clock the roaring of the Surf was plainly heard and at day break the vast foaming breakers were too plainly to be seen not a Mile from us towards which we found the Ship was carried by the waves surprisingly fast. We had at this time not an air of wind and the depth of water was unfathomable so that there was not a possibility of Anchoring, in this distressed situation we had nothing but Providence and the small Assistance our boats could give us to trust to …

Despite launching the *Endeavour*'s yawl and longboat in an attempt to tow the ship, they still drifted closer and closer to the reef. By 6 am the *Endeavour* was less than 100m off the reef and the water depth was still over 120 fathoms! The ship's pinnace, which had been under repair, was also in the water this time, but as Cook wrote:

At this critical juncture when all our endeavours seem'd too little a small air of wind sprung up, but so small that at any other time in a Calm we should not have observed it, with this and the assistance of our boats we could observe the Ship to move off from the Reef in a slanting direction ...

Eventually, the *Endeavour* was carried clear, and the aptly-named Providential Channel enabled them to duck back within the shelter of the reef:

... where we anchor'd in 19 fathoms a Corally & Shelly bottom happy once more to encounter those shoals which but two days ago our utmost wishes were crowned by getting clear of, such are the Vicissitudes attending this kind of service and must always attend an unknown Navigation.

CAPE WEYMOUTH TO CAPE GRENVILLE

North of Cape Weymouth in Temple Bay on one part of the extensive **Piper Reef** are two small islets, Farmer and Fisher. There's a good beach, some coral and swimming on **Farmer Islet** and from here you can walk right out to the lighthouse at the tip of the reef at low tide. The shipping channel passing by here is the narrowest along the Queensland coast.

Privately owned **Haggerstone Island** is just off Cape Grenville. The high, rounded hump of this continental island dips down to what looks to be a delightful sandy bay where two houses stand among the numerous palm trees. It's hard to think of a more remote hideaway.

Just north of Cape Grenville there are more Bligh connections at Sunday Islet. Here the unfortunate captain nearly faced another mutiny when one of his crew challenged him. Bligh tossed the man a sword and suggested that they sort the matter out there and then. His opponent promptly backed down.

Near the islands of the Sir Charles Hardy group off Cape Grenville, the 313 ton barque *Charles Eaton* struck a reef in 1834. The crew and passengers escaped on a boat and two rafts and were taken aboard a large indigenous canoe. The canoe then sailed to

a nearby island where all the hapless survivors were slaughtered, except for two boys who lived with the tribe on Murray Island for two years until they were retrieved by the ship *Isabella*. This incident prompted the construction of a beacon on Raine Island.

RAINE ISLAND

Directly east of Cape Grenville and only about 35km south of Pandora's Entrance, this 30 hectare coral cay is, despite its minute size, of great interest for both its wildlife and its history. The island measures less than 1km long by less than 500m wide and is completely treeless. Its highest point is only 6m above sea level and high tides and cyclonic storms can wash waves right over the island. The island is on the outer edge of the reef, and close by the sea bottom drops over 600m.

It would seem to be a very inhospitable place, but for some reason, this little island attracts immense populations of turtles and birds. Raine is a major breeding ground for

Moulter (Pandora) Cay

Originally named Pandora Cay, it was renamed in 1984 to Moulter Cay to commemorate the humane deed of William Moulter, the bosun's mate on the *Pandora*. When the *Pandora* struck the Great Barrier Reef, Captain Edwards refused to release the 14 captured *Bounty* mutineers imprisoned on the quarterdeck in 'Pandora's Box'. As the ship was sinking, the master-at-arms unlocked the door and then contrived to 'drop' the keys to the irons inside the box. Moulter pulled the long bar through the prisoners' irons and assisted several prisoners over the side; however, four didn't make it. Of the 10 who survived this ordeal (and the remainder of the journey back to England), six were found guilty of mutiny and sentenced to be hung, but only three were.

the green turtle, which comes here between November and February. Green turtles are found as far afield as the Caribbean and Borneo, but today the Great Barrier Reef is their main habitat and Raine Island is their most important nesting ground.

At times, the turtles arrive here in unbelievable numbers. An 'invasion' took place in 1974 and again in 1984, when it was estimated that 50,000 to 100,000 female turtles arrived to lay their eggs here and at nearby Moulter (Pandora) Cay. Observers counted over 10,000 turtles on the island at one time. Studies have been made of the migratory patterns of turtles from the island. The poor green turtle is the most popular

turtle species for human consumption and many are captured around the eastern islands of Indonesia and shipped to Bali where they are an important delicacy.

Turtles, however, are not the only form of wildlife that finds Raine Island's meagre attractions irresistible. Various species of seabirds also nest on the island, some of them finding turtle eggs and newly hatched turtles a useful addition to their diet. It has been estimated that over 100,000 common and black noddies and sooty terns congregate on the island at one time and observers once counted 17,000 common noddy nests on the island. Other seabirds visit this remote and tiny island – in some cases this

HMS PANDORA

The *Bounty* mutiny is probably one of the best known stories from the annals of maritime history. However, few people realise to what lengths the British Admiralty went to avenge itself.

In 1791 a 24 gun frigate, HMS *Pandora*, was sent into the South Pacific; its commander, Captain Edward Edwards, was charged with a policeman's mission to capture the mutineers and bring them to justice. The voyage began successfully and 14 mutineers were captured in Tahiti, but Edwards was forced to abandon his mission of finding Fletcher Christian and the rest of the mutineers after losing his ship in far northern Great Barrier Reef waters, north of Raine Island.

The unfortunate mutineers had been kept on deck in appalling conditions in a 3m-long cell dubbed 'Pandora's Box'. As the *Pandora* started to sink, Edwards repeatedly refused to allow the prisoners to be released, but the master-at-arms unlocked the box and contrived to drop the keys to the irons into the box. Most of the prisoners scrambled free, but four, weighed down by their manacles, were lost with the ship along with 31 of the crew.

Once off the ship, Edwards was scarcely less cruel to the mutineers. He permitted them only extremely limited water and did not even allow them to shelter from the fierce sun as they huddled on a sand cay. Eventually, using the ship's boats, the survivors made their way to Kupang, following the route traced out by Bligh.

is the only place in Australian waters where certain species have been sighted.

The island, which is thought to be only a few thousand years old, has also had an interesting human history. It was named after Thomas Raine, captain of the convict transport ship HMS *Surry*, which he sailed to China from Australia in 1815, charting parts of the reef en route. Nearby, Pandora's Entrance had claimed its most famous victim in 1791 but numerous other sailing vessels, trying to enter the reef, went down near Raine Island, and in 1844 it was decided to build a stone beacon on the island to warn seafarers.

HMS *Fly*, which had done so much survey work along the reef, brought a convict party that erected a 15m-high tower. It was noted that the unfortunate convicts suffered not only from the heat, lack of water and lack of shade, but also from the lice that infested the island. A particularly annoying tick still lurks on the island today to irritate visiting scientific parties.

The tower, restored in the 1980s, was unlit because it was intended only to be a landmark visible in daylight. When it was built, the only light on the whole east coast of Australia was at the entrance to Sydney Harbour. As the inner route through the Great Barrier Reef became more popular, the old outer route was soon abandoned and

---

Even here, Edwards' pitiless character was to bring disaster to others. William and Mary Bryant had earlier escaped from Sydney together with their baby son and young daughter and seven other convicts. In a feat of seamanship scarcely less amazing than Bligh's they rowed and sailed their open boat the full length of the east coast, rounded Cape York and crossed open sea to Timor, where they claimed to be shipwreck survivors. To their great misfortune Edwards' party arrived two weeks later and clapped the escaped convicts back in irons and shipped them off to Batavia (modern-day Jakarta). There the luckless William Bryant and his son died, and Edwards even refused his wife permission to visit her dying husband in hospital until overruled by the angry expatriate Dutch community.

Tales of Edwards' single-minded cruelty were to pursue him the rest of his life, but back in England Mary Bryant was befriended by the author and lawyer James Boswell (remembered chiefly for his *Life of Samuel Johnson*), who eventually secured her release and personally provided her with an annual allowance of £10, a not inconsiderable sum in those days.

The full story of the *Pandora's* fateful journey can be read in *Pandora's Last Voyage* by Geoffrey Rawson.

The *Pandora* is one of Australia's most important historic shipwreck sites, not only because of its association with the famous (or infamous) mutiny. Archaeological excavation in recent years has established that the wreck is in very good condition and contains an exceptionally well-preserved collection of artefacts reflecting day-to-day life on board a British naval frigate in the late 18th century.

An archaeological team from the Queensland Museum has recovered a diverse assemblage of artefacts, including a very impressive collection of Polynesian objects collected by the *Pandora*'s crew in the South Pacific. Intended for the private collections of 18th century 'scientific gentlemen' in the UK and Europe (many of which eventually became the first collections of Pacific ethnography in major European museums), these Polynesian objects are now public museum pieces.

More information on the Queensland Museum's Pandora Project is available from their website (Qmuseum.qld.gov.au/culture/pandorawelcome.html).

Peter Gesner

the tower eventually became redundant. Prominent though it was, numerous ships continued to founder around the island – 13 known and a number of unknown vessels went down between 1850 and 1860. Today, few ships enter Australian waters at this point, but in 1985 the *Kanai* managed to wreck itself on the reef here.

In the 1870s bêches-de-mer were harvested on Raine Island for shipment to China, and a little later the island was first exploited for its considerable guano deposits. It's thought that tens of thousands of tons of guano were removed. The guano miners' jetty and houses were dismantled when mining stopped in 1892. The grave of Annie Eliza Ellis, the wife of a guano miner who died in 1891, is a lonely reminder of that period.

PANDORA'S ENTRANCE

In 1789, two years after Bligh came through the reef at Bligh's Passage, the *Bounty* saga played out another chapter 200km further north when the HMS *Pandora* sank at what is now known as Pandora's Entrance.

ALBANY PASSAGE

Curiously, Albany Island, just south-east of Cape York, was once proposed as a major trading port, the 'Singapore of Australia'. A settlement named Somerset was established on the mainland side of Albany Passage. It was eventually abandoned in favour of Thursday Island and little trace remains of its historic past. There is a small cultured pearl project across the very narrow strait on Albany Island.

MT ADOLPHUS ISLAND

North-east of Cape York is Mt Adolphus Island, just south of which is Quetta Rock. Despite a number of surveys over several years, the shoal had been completely missed until the steamship *Quetta* rammed into it in 1890. The ship, with 290 passengers and crew, sank within three minutes, with the loss of 133 lives.

CAPE YORK

Eborac and York islands stand just north of Cape York, the extreme northern tip of mainland Australia. There's a cairn to show that you are as far north as you can go.

POSSESSION ISLAND

To the west of the top of Cape York and south of Horn Island is Possession Island, where Captain Cook officially took possession of all of the east coast of Australia. There's a monument on the north-west side of the island.

Thursday Island & the Torres Strait

The Torres Strait contains a scattering of islands that run like stepping stones from the tip of Cape York to the south coast of Papua New Guinea.

The islands are territorially part of Australia, although some of them are only a few kilometres from Papua New Guinea.

The population of the islands is about 9000 and the people are Melanesians, racially related to the peoples of Papua New Guinea.

History

The islands of the strait would seem on paper to have been an obvious conduit for early migration to Australia, but in actual fact there seems to have been remarkably little movement across the strait. The dramatic differences between the social development evident in Papua New Guinea and that of the Aborigines of Australia is of great scientific interest.

Agriculture and or animal husbandry are two of the fundamental stages in human development, but although these skills were known in Papua New Guinea about 4000 years ago, they never crossed the strait to Australia. Gardening did spread to the eastern and central islands and to some of the western islands, but it never got as far south as the islands close to the tip of Cape York. Why this important development only made it partway across Torres Strait is an intriguing question.

By the 15th century, vessels from Makassar (in modern-day Indonesia) and from China were regular visitors to the Arafura Sea in search of bêches-de-mer, and a century later the Portuguese had made their way to the Spice Islands (Moluccas or Maluku), while the Spanish had established themselves in the Philippines. In 1606 European eyes were first set on the Torres Strait from both east and west, but quite independently and with neither party aware of the other.

THURSDAY ISLAND

Highlights
- Travel to Thursday Island on the *Gulf Express* cargo boat
- Explore the cemetery, and try to attend a tombstone unveiling

Area:	3.25 sq km
Type:	continental
High point:	104m
Max visitors:	104

The Dutch explorer Willem Jansz sighted the west coast of Cape York from his ship, the *Duyfken*. He led a party ashore and could have claimed the honour of being the first European to set foot on Australia, except that he thought he was still in Papua New Guinea. Jansz continued east into the strait, but currents and winds prevented him from crossing through into the Pacific. He continued to believe he was simply sailing in a bay, never realising that the land he had

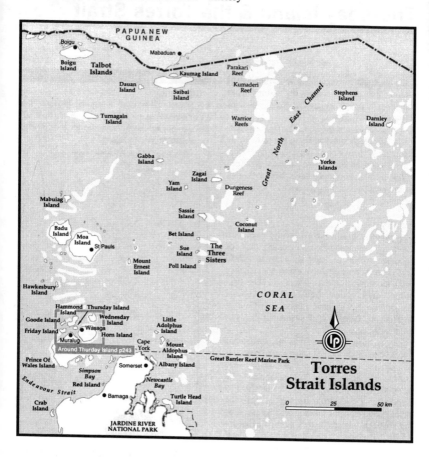

set foot on was not Papua New Guinea, but a separate continent.

Meanwhile, Spanish explorer Luiz Váez de Torres was approaching the strait from the eastern side in the *San Pedrico*. He had set out from Peru in company with another ship to search for *Terra Australis Incognita*, the Unknown South Land, and along the way to do as much Christian proselytising as he could manage. The party stumbled first upon the New Hebrides (Vanuatu) and thought they had found the mysterious land of the south.

The two boats were then separated and while Pedro Fernandez de Quiros, the expedition leader, sailed back to Mexico, Torres continued east and would have reached the Australian east coast, or more likely, foundered on the Great Barrier Reef, had he not given up the search only 200km outside the reef.

He turned north to sail for the Philippines, but by this time he was already too far west to round the eastern end of Papua New Guinea and the same winds and currents that prevented Jansz from sailing east through the strait swept Torres through from the opposite direction. He landed on several of the islands and eventually inched his way through to the Arafura Sea and then looped around Papua New Guinea to reach the Philippines.

The Spanish, however, did not reveal Torres' historic discovery, and for the next two centuries the strait separating Papua New Guinea from Australia remained a rumour until James Cook eventually confirmed its existence in 1770. After his involuntary halt at Cooktown to repair his damaged vessel, Cook continued north and then, like Torres, was carried through the straits. He paused long enough at Possession Island to claim the whole east coast of Australia for King George III.

William Bligh, after the *Bounty* mutiny, passed through in 1789 and named Wednesday Island as he went by. The *Pandora* survivors (see the Lizard Island to Cape York chapter) came through the strait in 1791, but made no additions to the charts.

In 1802 Matthew Flinders, during his epic circumnavigation of Australia, made the most systematic survey yet of the islands and channels of the strait and also named the waters after Torres, although remarkably little about the Spaniard's expedition was known even at this time.

By the mid-1800s the strait had become a major sailing route, but the tricky waters led to frequent shipwrecks (with often disastrous results). If the unfortunate passengers and crew survived the actual wreck, they still had to face islanders who had often been terrorised by unscrupulous seamen, who naturally offered little mercy when the tables were turned.

A settlement was established at Somerset, opposite Albany Island, in 1864 to police the strait. At that time, bêches-de-mer were the main economic attraction but in 1869 the first shipment of mother-of-pearl shell from the straits was unloaded in Sydney and a rush for the valuable shells started soon after.

The easily reached pearl shells were soon exhausted and primitive diving suits came into use so that shells could be gathered from greater depths. A motley international crew of pearl divers descended upon the strait's islands and fortunes were soon won and lost, murders committed, lives lost and general mayhem ensued.

In 1872 Captain John Moresby from HMS *Basilisk* reported that 'anarchy and savagery' were the order of the day. The station at Somerset was proving to be a distinctly bad idea, and in 1877 the settlement was shifted to Thursday Island.

Christianity, in the form of the London Missionary Society, arrived in the islands in 1871 when a mission station was set up on Darnley Island, in the east of the strait. The missionaries had great success and Christianity still plays a strong role in the life of the islands.

By the end of last century, things were not going well for the Torres Strait Islanders, and a number of the tribal groups had been all but wiped out. The Kauralgal people had been depleted by struggles with the British colonists, while the Badulgal people had managed to pretty much wipe out the Moa.

Thursday Island had become a prosperous centre, however, and gold was found on Horn and Hammond islands. The pearl shell industry also continued to grow and, at its peak, 1600 people worked on the pearling fleets out of Thursday Island, Albany, Somerset and other ports. The pearling fleets used many skilled Japanese divers as well as islanders and a variety of other nationalities.

The Torres Strait was uncomfortably close to the bitter fighting in Papua New Guinea during WWII, although, remarkably, Thursday Island was never attacked. Some historians attribute this to the fact that there were many Japanese divers living on the island, and many more buried in the cemetery there.

The development of plastics after the war dealt a death blow to the pearl shell industry. Mother-of-pearl was extensively used for making buttons, but these were soon all made of plastic, with the result that the pearling industry simply disappeared. Farming artificial pearls brought a little employment to the region, but the choice remained largely one of either returning to a traditional lifestyle or emigrating to the big cities of Queensland. There are now large Islander communities in Cairns, Townsville, Mackay and Brisbane.

Geography

The islands of Torres Strait are of three types, with 17 islands in all being inhabited.

At the western end of the straits the main Torres Strait islands are flooded mountain tops, a final northern fling of Australia's Great Dividing Range. During the last ice age, sea levels were much lower and Australia and Papua New Guinea were joined by dry land. Rising sea levels cut this land bridge about 7000 to 8000 years ago, but even today the straits are very shallow – in some shipping lanes the minimum depths are as little as 10m.

The shallow water, narrow straits and often ferocious tidal currents make the straits a difficult place for navigation.

The inhabited islands in this western group are the tight cluster around Thursday Island (known locally as Waiben) close to Cape York, including Prince of Wales (Muralag), Horn (Nurapai) and Hammond (Keriri) islands. A little further north, Moa (Banks Island), Badu (Mulgrave Island) and Mabuiag (Jervis Island) are also inhabited. Three other inhabited islands – Boigu, Dauan and Saibai – are very close to the Papua New Guinea coast.

Interestingly, Thursday Island, the administrative and population centre of the islands, was uninhabited prior to the European arrival. Its indigenous name, Waiben, meaning 'no water', may provide the reason for this.

The second group of islands in the straits is a scattering of coral cays on the reefs to the east of the main islands. Inhabited islands here are Sue, Yam, Coconut (Paremar) and Yorke (Massid) islands.

Finally, there is a group of volcanic islands, cloaked in luxuriant vegetation, to

the extreme east of the straits. Of this group, Mer (Murray Island), Darnley (Erub) and Stephens (Ugar) are populated.

THURSDAY ISLAND (WAIBEN)

'TI' (tee-i), as it is usually known, is the best known of the Torres Strait islands. It's only 39km from the tip of Cape York.

Thursday Island was once a major pearling centre and pearlers' cemeteries tell the hard tale of what a dangerous occupation this was. Some pearls are still produced here, from seeded 'culture farms'.

Although Thursday Island has lost its former importance as a stopping point for vessels, it's still a popular pause for passing yachties. It's an interesting and easy-going little place with a tropical torpor reminiscent of many Pacific islands, although the island itself is somewhat dry and unprepossessing.

History

Nearby Wednesday Island was certainly named by Captain William Bligh during his *Bounty* misadventures, but how Thursday Island got its name is less clear. Various explanations have been advanced, but the most likely one is that it was named by Captain Owen Stanley during a surveying voyage on HMS *Rattlesnake* in 1848. Curiously, he appears to have named Thursday and Friday islands in reverse order, but some tidy-minded individual later switched them around so that Wednesday, Thursday and Friday fell neatly in order from east to west.

Thursday Island's busy European history started with the establishment of a settlement in 1877. The opening of the Suez Canal had made the northern route around Australia a far more economic proposition than the old route around the south of the continent. The new passage was shorter and the advent of steam ships meant the old problem of prevailing winds was no longer a factor. The reefs certainly were a problem, however, and numerous ships went down around Cape York, including the *Quetta*, which sank on an uncharted reef in 1890

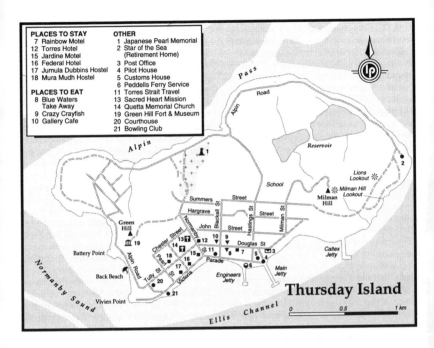

PLACES TO STAY
7 Rainbow Motel
12 Torres Hotel
15 Jardine Motel
16 Federal Hotel
17 Jumula Dubbins Hostel
18 Mura Mudh Hostel

PLACES TO EAT
8 Blue Waters
   Take Away
9 Crazy Crayfish
10 Gallery Cafe

OTHER
1 Japanese Pearl Memorial
2 Star of the Sea
   (Retirement Home)
3 Post Office
4 Pilot House
5 Customs House
6 Peddells Ferry Service
11 Torres Strait Travel
13 Sacred Heart Mission
14 Quetta Memorial Church
19 Green Hill Fort & Museum
20 Courthouse
21 Bowling Club

Thursday Island

with the loss of 133 lives. Thursday Island soon became an important port for the pilots who guided ships through the perilous reef waters.

At the same time, the pearling boom continued, particularly from 1885, when restrictions on using the island as a pearling base were relaxed. At that time the population was only a few hundred, but within 10 years it had increased to over 2000. The first Japanese divers, who were to be the mainstay of the diving force, arrived in the straits in 1883 and there were soon thousands of men working on the pearl luggers. TI was a very cosmopolitan place with Torres Strait Islanders, Europeans, Japanese, Melanesians, Aborigines, Polynesians, Malays, Micronesians, Chinese and many other nationalities adding to the mix.

Pearl diving with the primitive equipment of the time was desperately unsafe and over 1000 divers, a very large proportion of

them Japanese, lost their lives. The Thursday Island cemetery has the tombstones of about 500 divers.

In this cut-throat economic struggle the poor Torres Strait Islanders were completely forgotten and were actually banned from living on Thursday Island until after WWII. Part of the paternalistic mood of the times, the authorities believed that allowing the islanders to live on TI would expose them to alcohol and other forms of European exploitation.

The pearling business continued until first the Great Depression, then WWII, and, finally, the invention of plastics made pearl buttons (the main use of mother-of-pearl) redundant. There was a brief resurgence in the pearl business when artificial pearls were cultivated in the 1960s, again an activity where the Japanese led the way, but the enterprise failed, and today frozen seafood is the islands' economic mainstay.

At the time of Papua New Guinea's independence in 1975 there was some dispute over where the national boundary should be drawn and whether some of the islands should go to PNG, but they ended up remaining Australian territory.

Piloting The operation of a pilot service was a prime reason for the establishment of the settlement at Thursday Island and today the Queensland Coast & Torres Strait Pilot Service is more important than ever. The service was established in 1884 and over 100 million tonnes of shipping are piloted each year.

Somewhat surprisingly perhaps, the main shipping route runs inside the Great Barrier Reef close to the coast. All vessels over 70m long or carrying hazardous cargo must be piloted.

Pearl Shells Despite the popular image, pearls were not what the Torres Strait pearl divers sought. The pearl shell itself was the thing of value – actual pearls were just an occasional lucky bonus.

Pearl shell (or mother-of-pearl) was used for buckles, jewellery, inlays, cutlery handles and, most importantly, for buttons. The gold-lip and silver-lip pearl shells of the Torres Strait are the most valuable pearl shells found, although the silver is actually worth more than the gold. Pearl shells are graded from AA ('chicken') shells, then through A to E.

Although it is uncertain when pearl diving started, the first big shipment of pearl shells was taken down to Sydney in 1869. Diving suits and hand operated air pumps started to be used in 1874 and, by the late 1870s, over 100 vessels were operating in the Torres Strait. By 1913 there were over 1000 people working on the pearling boats, almost half of them Japanese.

The old pearl luggers have disappeared with the decline in the industry. Originally, they were indeed luggers – carrying two masts with a jib and two lug sails. The later diving boats were ketch-rigged, but the name 'lugger' remained.

The Thursday Island cemetery speaks clearly of the dangers of pearl diving – there are more than 700 Japanese buried here, many of whom were divers.

Information
Old TI, by MJ O'Riley and IB Wallace, is a readable little sketchbook of interesting places on the island. You should be able to find it on sale in TI or in Walkers Bookshop in Cairns. The *Torres News* is a weekly newspaper that labels itself 'the voice of the islands'.

Thursday Island has a post office, shops and a healthy selection of pubs for those in need of a cold beer. The post office has a Commonwealth Bank agency and, diagonally opposite, there's a National Australia branch (no ATM). A number of town businesses have EFTPOS facilities, including the bottle shop at the Grand Hotel.

There are good views from the top of Milman Hill, beside the two huge wind turbines. These were recently installed at a cost of around $3 million and reportedly generate only 5% of the island's power.

Quetta Memorial Church
The Quetta Memorial Church was opened in 1893 as a memorial to the British Indian Steamship *Quetta*, which went down near Thursday Island in 1890 with the loss of 133 lives. The church has a number of relics from the disaster including the ship's bell and riding light, a porthole, and a life buoy. There is also a *Quetta* stained-glass window and various other connections with the ship. (See the Mt Adolphus Island section of the Lizard Island to Cape York chapter for more details about the wreck.)

The pews with swinging seat-backs were retrieved from the wreck of the *Volga*, and the church's font is a memorial to James Chalmers, a missionary who was killed on Goaribari Island in Papua New Guinea in 1901.

Other Interesting Buildings
At the south-west end of the island the old **Court House** predates the establishment of

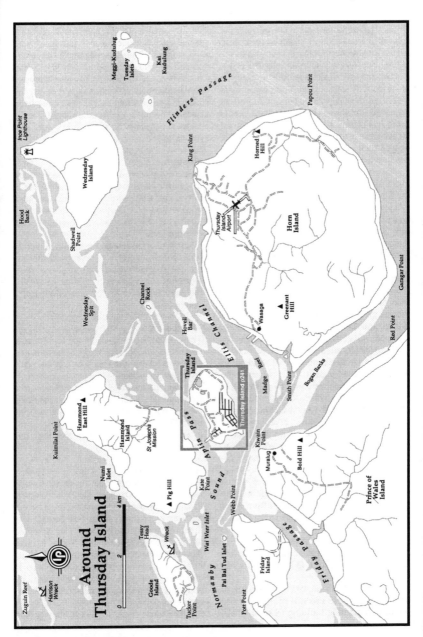

Around
Thursday Island

TI as the administrative centre for the islands. It was built in 1876 and is still used by the local government.

Right in front of the main jetty the original **Customs House** was built on this site in 1889. The present building dates from 1939, but the original building can still be seen on John Street. Adjacent to the Quetta Memorial Church, the Catholic **Sacred Heart Church** was built in 1885 and is the only TI church that remains unchanged from its original construction.

The island's historical ethnic diversity is also evident in a couple of the old stores in the main street – Ah Boo and See Hop.

The magnificent old **Metropole Hotel** was burnt down during WWII and the fine old **Grand Hotel** burnt down in 1993, leaving the **Federal**, with its wooden veranda, the only original waterfront pub.

Cemetery

The Thursday Island cemetery, on the north side of the island, has many picturesque graves of Okinawan and other Japanese divers, and the Japanese Pearl Memorial to the many divers who worked here. The Islanders' graves are also very interesting.

You may notice a number of headstones wrapped in black plastic. This is part of the 'Tombstone Opening', or unveiling ceremony, which takes place exactly one year after the death of the person. These interesting ceremonies are usually 'open invitation', so it should be no problem to attend if there's one happening while you're there (they're pretty frequent), but be sensitive and discreet.

The downside of the ceremonies is that accommodation at the TI hostels can be booked out by people coming in from other islands to attend a ceremony.

Green Hill Fort

Thursday Island's strategic importance led, in 1891, to the decision to build the fort on Green Hill.

It was abandoned in 1939, but a number of the rusting guns are still in position and the only remaining building (a small shed)

is now used as the base of the local State Emergency Service.

Curiously, Thursday Island was never attacked by the Japanese during WWII. Local legends relate that it was because a mysterious Japanese princess was buried on the island, but in actual fact it may have been because the Japanese forces thought that the many Japanese pearl shell divers were still on the island.

Museums

There is an interesting, small, underground museum in a former ammunition bunker at Green Hill Fort, with local history displays and photographs. It's only open on Saturday afternoons, or on request for groups. Admission is $2.

Over on Horn Island, the Gateway Torres Strait Resort operates a museum. It consists mainly of hundreds of well-displayed photographs, many of them relating to WWII, but there are also a few other exhibits. Entry is free.

Wongai Trees

The wongai, a tree native to the Torres Strait islands, is said to have magical powers and anyone who eats the tree's fruit is bound to return to the islands.

A very famous wongai tree once stood in front of the Federal Hotel, on Victoria Parade, but it was blown down by a cyclone in 1977.

There's a stand of them on the shore just to the east of Rebel Jetty.

Places to Stay

Thursday Island The modern *Jumula Dubbins Hostel* (☎ 4069 2122), on Victoria Parade, has basic rooms costing $19 per person, twin share, with full board. The meals are pretty basic and dinner is served at the inconvenient time of 5 pm. It is an Aboriginal hostel catering primarily to visitors from the outer islands coming in to TI and is often full. Other travellers are welcome when space permits, but bookings are necessary.

The *Mura Mudh Hostel* (☎ 4069 2050),

around the corner on Douglas St, is very similar and only a couple of dollars more expensive.

The old *Federal Hotel* (☎ 4069 1569) has air-conditioned motel rooms with attached bathrooms at $55/75 for singles/doubles, and hotel rooms for $45/65. At the *Torres Hotel* (☎ 4069 1141) accommodation costs $40/50 for singles/doubles.

The *Rainbow Motel* (☎ 4069 2460), easily missed on the main street opposite the shire building, has comfortable air-conditioned rooms for $60/90. There's limited car parking, but as most visitors arrive by plane or boat, this is not usually a problem.

The *Jardine Motel* (☎ 4069 2555 or 1800 650 447) has a pool, bar and restaurant, and air-conditioned motel rooms cost $130/160 for singles/doubles.

Horn Island At Wasaga on Horn Island, just a short ferry ride across the bay, there are a few options. The *Gateway Torres Strait Resort* (☎ 4069 2222), one block back from the jetty, has rooms and a separate camping area with cabins (weekly rates only). The motel-type rooms have a fan, TV and limited cooking facilities, and cost $109/135, including a full breakfast.

A 10 minute walk away, and right on the beach, is their new *Elikiam Holiday Park*. Small rooms in well fitted out transportable cabins cost $161 per week for two people. The rooms are cramped, with fridge, limited cooking facilities, and a ridiculously huge TV bolted to the wall. There are also deluxe cabins with en suite ($259 weekly), and two-bedroom cabins for $357. All cabins have air-conditioning, which take $5 cards available from the kiosk here. Camping is also available.

The *Wongai Hotel Motel* (☎ 4069 1683) has just four rooms in a separate new building out the back, and these cost $55, although they are pretty much permanently occupied.

Places to Eat

There's a number of snack/takeaway joints on the main street. The best is the *Burger Bar*, at the rear of the Rainbow Motel, but it is only open at lunch time. The *Blue Waters Take Away* and the *Crazy Crayfish* are others on the main street.

Offering something a bit different is the *Gallery Cafe,* on the corner of Douglas and Blackall Sts. Here you can while away a pleasant hour or so on the veranda of an old timber home and choose from the interesting (but limited) menu. There are also paintings and craft works to look at while you wait.

The *Federal Hotel* is a bit rough around the edges but is the better of the two pub options (the rebuilt Grand being the other). Meals (lunch and dinner) can be eaten in the beer garden, and cost between $9 and $14.

The *Somerset Restaurant* at the Jardine Motel specialises in seafood and beef dishes and is TI's top eating spot. À la carte dishes cost $20 to $25, the buffet is $20, and the Wednesday night seafood buffet is $26.

Entertainment

There's not a lot to do in the evenings here other than go to the pub.

The *Bowling Club* (!) has a disco on Friday nights, and the *Federal Hotel* has bands most Thursdays.

Getting There & Away

Air The TI Airport is actually on neighbouring Horn Island. Sunstate (Qantas) Airlines has regular flights between Cairns and Thursday Island. The flight takes 2 hours and the one-way fare is $254. You complete check-in for outgoing flights at the Sunstate office at Torres Strait Travel (☎ 4069 1264), on the corner of Victoria Parade and Blackall St. The airfare includes a shuttle across the harbour between Horn and TI.

A number of smaller airlines operate flights and charter services around the islands of the Torres Strait, and to Cape York. These include Northern Air Services (☎ 4069 2777), Coral Sea Airlines (☎ 4069 1500) and Uzu Air (☎ 4069 2377). Coral Sea Airlines flies to Bamaga (among other places) for $80.

Sea The Torres Strait's south-east trade wind is the strongest and longest lasting trade wind in the world. Combine this with numerous reefs and islands, plus fickle tides and currents, and it's easy to see why this is frequently not an easy area to sail through.

The cheapest and most interesting way to travel between TI and Cairns is on the weekly *Gulf Express*, a cargo boat that makes the trip at the very relaxed rate of 11 knots. It hugs the coast for the bulk of the way and although there's not much to do, there's plenty to look at – the trip through the narrow Albany Passage just off the tip is probably the highlight – and the relaxed pace is the perfect introduction to life on TI.

The boat is operated by Jardine Shipping (☎ 4035 1299). It takes about 40 hours and costs $240/400 one way/return, including meals and accommodation in a four-berth, air-conditioned cabin. There's accommodation for eight passengers, and bookings should be made a few weeks in advance, although it's rarely full.

Vehicles can also be transported, which might be handy if you have driven from Cairns to the tip of Cape York and can't face driving back. The fare is $600 from TI to Cairns ($750 in the opposite direction) and this includes barge transport between Horn Island (TI's port) and Seisia (Bamaga) on the mainland.

The *Kangaroo Explorer* operates a regular Cairns-Thursday Island-Cairns service, but this is more of a cruise than simple 'Point A to Point B' transport. (See the Lizard Island to Cape York chapter for more details.)

There are regular ferry services between Seisia and Thursday Island. Phone Peddells Ferry Services (☎ 4069 1551) on TI for details. From November to May they have morning and afternoon runs on Monday, Wednesday and Friday, and from June to October they have two runs every day (except Sunday).

The fare is $60 same-day return or $35 one way. In the tourist season there are also connections between Pajinka Wilderness Lodge (Red Island Point) and TI ($40 one way). These are basically day trips, leaving Pajinka in the morning and returning from TI in the afternoon.

Intrepid travellers have, in the past, continued on from the Torres Strait Islands to Papua New Guinea by finding a fishing boat across the straits to Daru, from where you can fly or take a ship to Port Moresby. These days you will probably run into severe visa problems if you try this, as the Papua New Guinean officials frown on this unconventional entry method.

Getting Around

NETS (☎ 4069 2132) operates a regular ferry service (daily, except Sunday) between Thursday Island and the airport on Horn Island. The ferries run roughly hourly between 6.30 am and 5 pm, the trip takes about 15 minutes and costs $4.50 one way.

Around TI there are plenty of taxis, and Peddells also run bus tours on demand ($14 including the museum), usually when a day trip group comes across from Pajinka.

TI is small enough to walk around quite easily in a couple of hours.

Index

LONELY PLANET PHRASEBOOKS

Building bridges,
Breaking barriers,
Beyond babble-on

Listen for the gems

Speak your own words

Ask your own
questions

Master of
your
own
image

- handy pocket-sized books
- easy to understand Pronunciation chapter
- clear and comprehensive Grammar chapter
- romanisation alongside script to allow ease of pronunciation
- script throughout so users can point to phrases
- extensive vocabulary sections, words and phrases for every situation
- full of cultural information and tips for the traveller

'...vital for a real DIY spirit and attitude in language learning' – Backpacker

'the phrasebooks have good cultural backgrounders and offer solid advice for challenging situations in remote locations' – San Francisco Examiner

'...they are unbeatable for their coverage of the world's more obscure languages' – The Geographical Magazine

---

Arabic (Egyptian)
Arabic (Moroccan)
Australia
  Australian English, Aboriginal and
  Torres Strait languages
Baltic States
  Estonian, Latvian, Lithuanian
Bengali
Brazilian
Burmese
Cantonese
Central Asia
Central Europe
  Czech, French, German, Hungarian,
  Italian and Slovak
Eastern Europe
  Bulgarian, Czech, Hungarian, Polish,
  Romanian and Slovak
Ethiopian (Amharic)
Fijian
French
German
Greek

Hindi/Urdu
Indonesian
Italian
Japanese
Korean
Lao
Latin American Spanish
Malay
Mandarin
Mediterranean Europe
  Albanian, Croatian, Greek,
  Italian, Macedonian, Maltese,
  Serbian and Slovene
Mongolian
Nepali
Papua New Guinea
Pilipino (Tagalog)
Quechua
Russian
Scandinavian Europe
  Danish, Finnish, Icelandic, Norwegian
  and Swedish

South-East Asia
  Burmese, Indonesian, Khmer, Lao,
  Malay, Tagalog (Pilipino), Thai and
  Vietnamese
Spanish (Castilian)
  Basque, Catalan and Galician
Sri Lanka
Swahili
Thai
Thai Hill Tribes
Tibetan
Turkish
Ukrainian
USA
  US English, Vernacular,
  Native American languages and
  Hawaiian
Vietnamese
Western Europe
  Basque, Catalan, Dutch, French,
  German, Irish, Italian, Portuguese,
  Scottish Gaelic, Spanish (Castilian)
  and Welsh

LONELY PLANET JOURNEYS

JOURNEYS is a unique collection of travel writing – published by the company that understands travel better than anyone else. It is a series for anyone who has ever experienced – or dreamed of – the magical moment when they encountered a strange culture or saw a place for the first time. They are tales to read while you're planning a trip, while you're on the road or while you're in an armchair, in front of a fire.

JOURNEYS books catch the spirit of a place, illuminate a culture, recount a crazy adventure, or introduce a fascinating way of life. They always entertain, and always enrich the experience of travel.

ISLANDS IN THE CLOUDS
Travels in the Highlands of New Guinea
Isabella Tree

Isabella Tree's remarkable journey takes us to the heart of the remote and beautiful Highlands of Papua New Guinea and Irian Jaya – one of the most extraordinary and dangerous regions on earth. Funny and tragic by turns, *Islands in the Clouds* is her moving story of the Highland people and the changes transforming their world.

Isabella Tree, who lives in England, has worked as a freelance journalist on a variety of newspapers and magazines, including a stint as senior travel correspondent for the *Evening Standard*. A fellow of the Royal Geographical Society, she has also written a biography of the Victorian ornithologist John Gould.

'One of the most accomplished travel writers to appear on the horizon for many years . . . the dialogue is brilliant' – Eric Newby

---

SEAN & DAVID'S LONG DRIVE
Sean Condon

Sean Condon is young, urban and a connoisseur of hair wax. He can't drive, and he doesn't really travel well. So when Sean and his friend David set out to explore Australia in a 1966 Ford Falcon, the result is a decidedly offbeat look at life on the road. Over 14,000 death-defying kilometres, our heroes check out the re-runs on tv, get fabulously drunk, listen to Neil Young cassettes and wonder why they ever left home.

Sean Condon lives in Melbourne. He played drums in several mediocre bands until he found his way into advertising and an above-average band called Boilersuit. *Sean & David's Long Drive* is his first book.

'Funny, pithy, kitsch and surreal . . . This book will do for Australia what Chernobyl did for Kiev, but hey you'll laugh as the stereotypes go boom'
– Time Out

LONELY PLANET TRAVEL ATLASES

Lonely Planet has long been famous for the number and quality of its guidebook maps. Now we've gone one step further and produced a handy companion series: Lonely Planet travel atlases – maps of a country produced in book form.

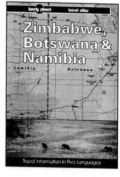

Unlike other maps, which look good but lead travellers astray, our travel atlases have been researched on the road by Lonely Planet's experienced team of writers. All details are carefully checked to ensure the atlas corresponds with the equivalent Lonely Planet guidebook.

The handy atlas format means no holes, wrinkles, torn sections or constant folding and unfolding. These atlases can survive long periods on the road, unlike cumbersome fold-out maps. The comprehensive index ensures easy reference.

- full-colour throughout
- maps researched and checked by Lonely Planet authors
- place names correspond with Lonely Planet guidebooks
  – no confusing spelling differences
- legend and travelling information in English, French, German, Japanese and Spanish
- size: 230 x 160 mm

Available now:
Chile & Easter Island • Egypt • India & Bangladesh • Israel & the Palestinian Territories •Jordan, Syria & Lebanon • Kenya • Laos • Portugal • South Africa, Lesotho & Swaziland • Thailand • Turkey • Vietnam • Zimbabwe, Botswana & Namibia

LONELY PLANET TV SERIES & VIDEOS

Lonely Planet travel guides have been brought to life on television screens around the world. Like our guides, the programmes are based on the joy of independent travel, and look honestly at some of the most exciting, picturesque and frustrating places in the world. Each show is presented by one of three travellers from Australia, England or the USA and combines an innovative mixture of video, Super-8 film, atmospheric soundscapes and original music.

Videos of each episode – containing additional footage not shown on television – are available from good book and video shops, but the availability of individual videos varies with regional screening schedules.

Video destinations include: Alaska • American Rockies • Australia – The South-East • Baja California & the Copper Canyon • Brazil • Central Asia • Chile & Easter Island • Corsica, Sicily & Sardinia – The Mediterranean Islands • East Africa (Tanzania & Zanzibar) • Ecuador & the Galapagos Islands • Greenland & Iceland • Indonesia • Israel & the Sinai Desert • Jamaica • Japan • La Ruta Maya • Morocco • New York • North India • Pacific Islands (Fiji, Solomon Islands & Vanuatu) • South India • South West China • Turkey • Vietnam • West Africa • Zimbabwe, Botswana & Namibia

The Lonely Planet TV series is produced by:
Pilot Productions
The Old Studio
18 Middle Row
London W10 5AT UK

For video availability and ordering information contact your nearest Lonely Planet office.

Music from the TV series is available on CD & cassette.

PLANET TALK

Lonely Planet's FREE quarterly newsletter

We love hearing from you and think you'd like to hear from us.

When...is the right time to see reindeer in Finland?
Where...can you hear the best palm-wine music in Ghana?
How...do you get from Asunción to Areguá by steam train?
What...is the best way to see India?

For the answer to these and many other questions read PLANET TALK.

Every issue is packed with up-to-date travel news and advice including:

- a letter from Lonely Planet co-founders Tony and Maureen Wheeler
- go behind the scenes on the road with a Lonely Planet author
- feature article on an important and topical travel issue
- a selection of recent letters from travellers
- details on forthcoming Lonely Planet promotions
- complete list of Lonely Planet products

To join our mailing list contact any Lonely Planet office.

Also available: Lonely Planet T-shirts. 100% heavyweight cotton.

LONELY PLANET ONLINE

Get the latest travel information before you leave or while you're on the road

Whether you've just begun planning your next trip, or you're chasing down specific info on currency regulations or visa requirements, check out Lonely Planet Online for up-to-the minute travel information.

As well as travel profiles of your favourite destinations (including maps and photos), you'll find current reports from our researchers and other travellers, updates on health and visas, travel advisories, and discussion of the ecological and political issues you need to be aware of as you travel.

There's also an online travellers' forum where you can share your experience of life on the road, meet travel companions and ask other travellers for their recommendations and advice. We also have plenty of links to other online sites useful to independent travellers.

And of course we have a complete and up-to-date list of all Lonely Planet travel products including guides, phrasebooks, atlases, Journeys and videos and a simple online ordering facility if you can't find the book you want elsewhere.

www.lonelyplanet.com
or
AOL keyword: lp

LONELY PLANET PRODUCTS

Lonely Planet is known worldwide for publishing practical, reliable and no-nonsense travel information in our guides and on our web site. The Lonely Planet list covers just about every accessible part of the world. Currently there are nine series: *travel guides, shoestring guides, walking guides, city guides, phrasebooks, audio packs, travel atlases, Journeys – a unique collection of travel writing and Pisces Books - diving and snorkeling guides.*

EUROPE

Amsterdam • Austria • Baltic States phrasebook • Berlin • Britain • Canary Islands• Central Europe on a shoestring • Central Europe phrasebook • Czech & Slovak Republics • Denmark • Dublin • Eastern Europe on a shoestring • Eastern Europe phrasebook • Estonia, Latvia & Lithuania • Finland • France • French phrasebook • Germany • German phrasebook • Greece • Greek phrasebook • Hungary • Iceland, Greenland & the Faroe Islands • Ireland • Italian phrasebook • Italy • Lisbon • London • Mediterranean Europe on a shoestring • Mediterranean Europe phrasebook • Paris • Poland • Portugal • Portugal travel atlas • Prague • Romania & Moldova • Russia, Ukraine & Belarus • Russian phrasebook • Scandinavian & Baltic Europe on a shoestring • Scandinavian Europe phrasebook • Slovenia • Spain • Spanish phrasebook • St Petersburg • Switzerland •Trekking in Spain • Ukrainian phrasebook • Vienna • Walking in Britain • Walking in Italy • Walking in Switzerland • Western Europe on a shoestring • Western Europe phrasebook

Travel Literature: The Olive Grove: Travels in Greece

NORTH AMERICA

Alaska • Backpacking in Alaska • Baja California • California & Nevada • Canada • Chicago • Deep South• Florida • Hawaii • Honolulu • Los Angeles • Mexico • Mexico City • Miami • New England • New Orleans • New York City • New York, New Jersey & Pennsylvania • Pacific Northwest USA • Rocky Mountain States • San Francisco • Southwest USA • USA phrasebook • Washington, DC & the Capital Region

Travel Literature: Drive thru America

CENTRAL AMERICA & THE CARIBBEAN

•Bahamas and Turks & Caicos •Bermuda •Central America on a shoestring • Costa Rica • Cuba •Eastern Caribbean •Guatemala, Belize & Yucatán: La Ruta Maya • Jamaica

SOUTH AMERICA

Argentina, Uruguay & Paraguay • Bolivia • Brazil • Brazilian phrasebook • Buenos Aires • Chile & Easter Island • Chile & Easter Island travel atlas • Colombia Ecuador & the Galápagos Islands • Latin American Spanish phrasebook • Peru • Quechua phrasebook • Rio de Janeiro • South America on a shoestring • Trekking in the Patagonian Andes • Venezuela

Travel Literature: Full Circle: A South American Journey

ISLANDS OF THE INDIAN OCEAN

Madagascar & Comoros • Maldives• Mauritius, Réunion & Seychelles

AFRICA

Africa - the South • Africa on a shoestring • Arabic (Moroccan) phrasebook • Cairo • Cape Town • Central Africa • East Africa • Egypt • Egypt travel atlas• Ethiopian (Amharic) phrasebook • Kenya • Kenya travel atlas • Malawi, Mozambique & Zambia • Morocco • North Africa • South Africa, Lesotho & Swaziland • South Africa, Lesotho & Swaziland travel atlas • Swahili phrasebook • Tunisia • Trekking in East Africa • West Africa • Zimbabwe, Botswana & Namibia • Zimbabwe, Botswana & Namibia travel atlas

Travel Literature: The Rainbird: A Central African Journey • Songs to an African Sunset: A Zimbabwean Story